Seven Medieval Kings

SEVEN
MEDIEVAL
KINGS

Joseph Dahmus

BARNES
&NOBLE
BOOKS
NEW YORK

This edition published by Barnes & Noble, Inc.,
by arrangement with Doubleday & Co.,
a division of Bantam Doubleday Dell.

1994 Barnes & Noble Books

ISBN 1-56619-629-9

Printed and bound in the United States of America

M 9 8 7 6 5 4 3 2 1

"It is quite evident that the Sacred Scriptures frequently express by means of this number [seven] whatever they desire to be understood as continuous and perpetual." Cassiodorus, *An Introduction to Divine and Human Readings*, II, Preface.

"No one may rightly take precedence over [the king] since no one is favored with so many and so great blessings. . . . Wherefore he is not to be called a layman, for he is the anointed of the Lord, by grace a God, the highest ruler, the father, master, defender, and instructor of holy church, lord over his brothers and deserving of adoration from all men since he is the most distinguished and highest bishop." *York Tractates* (ca. 1100).

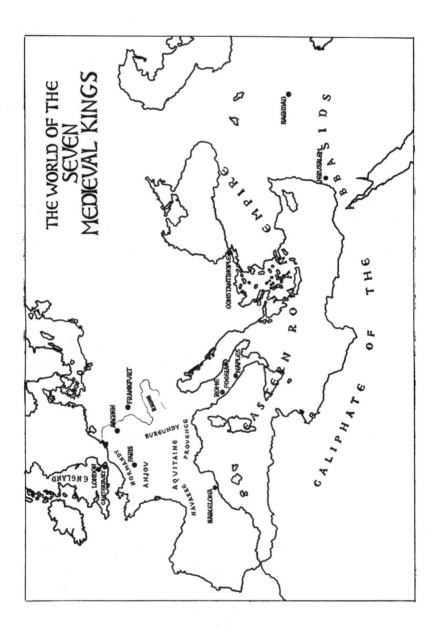

A Prefatory Note

Seven Medieval Kings does not fall into the category of historical novels, nor should it be confused with the products of ambitious writers who attempt to entertain the reading public with biographies of eminent generals from Joshua to Eisenhower. Within the limits of time and linguistic competency, the author has observed the canons of historical writing. He has not violated the reader's confidence by filling in gaps with romantic speculation, nor has he attempted to make these kings appear more important and interesting than they were. In the case of six kings, he has consulted the best secondary literature as well as some primary sources. Since he knows no Arabic, he contented himself in the preparation of Harun al-Rashid's life with recent monographic literature and translations from Arabic sources.

These seven kings may not have been the most able and influential in the Middle Ages, although the majority of them can pass muster on their own merits. One or the other king may find himself in this distinguished company because of chronological necessity. For the author intends the biographies to span the period of the Middle Ages, from the decline of Rome until the close of the fifteenth century. For this reason, the background material which appears with each biography serves two purposes: first, to illuminate the setting for the particular king himself; second, to provide the reader a general acquaintance with the history of the Middle Ages.

Contents

Seven Medieval Kings

Justinian

What kind of a man was Justinian, heir of the Roman Caesars and ruler of the Byzantine empire? Procopius provides the most detailed description. "He was neither very tall nor short, but of a medium height, yet not thin, rather inclined to be stout. His face was round and not uncomely, for his complexion remained ruddy even after two days of fasting." From the coins that bear Justinian's image and the well-known mosaic in the nave of San Apollinare in Ravenna, the emperor appears to have had a straight nose and a high forehead. His coins reveal a full, round, smooth-shaven face, a slight smile, and perhaps a not ungenerous disposition. The mosaic is the image of an older man, a diplomat, and serious thinker. This image may have been what Justinian asked the artist to portray. All evidence supports the view that he was strong and vigorous. The fact that he lived to be eighty-three and for almost fifty years (counting the reign of his uncle) directed the administrative machinery of his great empire suggests he enjoyed excellent health. Possibly most influential in shaping his philosophy of empire was the fact that he was a Latin, not a Greek, and that his homeland (roughly present-day Yugoslavia) had suffered a long, tragic history of barbarian invasions.

Justinian's character is more difficult to describe. He was without question a man of unusual talents. Had he not become emperor, he would surely have attained eminence in some other career. Men referred to him as "the man who never sleeps," and while the same praise has been paid to others, in Justinian's case all evidence points to the essential accuracy of the tradition. He was temperate if not abstemious in his tastes, and was probably a faithful husband. Although Procopius appears to have racked his brain for the most vile allegations he could possibly make of the emperor, he referred only once, and almost in passing, to his "sensual vices." Under the circumstances, one may conclude that his reference is a fabrication.

Lenten regulations Justinian observed beyond what the Church demanded. During the long penitential season he shunned wine and lived on wild herbs. He was affable and showed himself approachable to all who came to see him, nor was he ever provoked with those "who did not behave or speak properly in his presence." He has been accused of a want of resolution, of giving ear to flatterers and informers, and of having devoted more attention than prudent to details he should have left to others. Yet the evidence critics introduce to substantiate these weaknesses of characer is not convincing. Particularly successful was Justinian in finding able men to do his work, "and we are compelled to admire the intelligence of the Emperor," wrote Procopius, "in being able to choose the most suitable of mankind to carry out the noblest of his works."

THEODORA

Of all the people Justinian selected to assist him in bearing the burden of imperial administration, none proved more valuable nor so loyal as his wife Theodora. Procopius' lurid description of her "past" has made her one of the best-known women in history. How much of this past was hers, how much Procopius' malicious pen, no one will ever know. That she appears to have lived a life of marital fidelity after her marriage to Justinian would seem to cast doubt on the truthfulness of Procopius' charges. Had she been the nymphomaniac he paints her, marriage could scarcely have worked the transformation it did. Her father was an animal keeper at the Hippodrome, and it is true that she appeared on the stage when no virtuous girl graced that profession. Her physical beauty must have been exceptional although not extraordinary. From Procopius' description, we can imagine a small pale brunette with dark piercing eyes. She "was fair of face and had a graceful figure, but was short of stature and lacked color, having a rather sallow complexion, although her eyes were brilliant and piercing." Procopius is especially wroth at Justinian for having married one whom he calls "the common refuse of all mankind" when "he might have chosen the best born, the best educated, the most modest and virtuously nurtured virgin in all the Roman Empire, with outstanding bosom. . . ."

For twenty-one years, until her death from cancer in 548, Theodora lived with Justinian as his faithful spouse and adviser. Only negative evidence remains as to their relations as husband and wife: there is no

gossip of strife, unfaithfulness, or incompatibility. That Justinian remained a widower after Theodora's death may be significant. Theodora
occupied a magnificent palace Justinian had built for her and which
he appears to have respected inviolably as her own. It is said she sheltered scores of Monophysites there to shield them from his persecution.
For in religious matters she and Justinian did not agree. She approached the question of Christ's nature through the eyes of an East-
erner. To her there was something essentially base about matter, and
for that reason, it would have been impossible, in her opinion, for
Christ to have assumed a human, physical nature. Despite the emperor's efforts to enforce orthodoxy, therefore, her sympathies remained
with the Monophysites.

Yet their disagreement over the issue of Monophysitism may have
been deliberately staged in order to neutralize the criticism of the
court. Procopius insists that Justinian and Theodora "did nothing without the other. For a long time they appeared to all to be at variance
both in their characters and in their actions; but afterwards this disagreement was seen to have been purposely arranged between them, in
order that their subjects might not come to an agreement and rise
against them, but might all be divided in their opinion." That they
did work together we have on the testimony of both husband and wife.
On one occasion when Justinian promulgated a law eliminating corruption in the appointment of provincial governors, he announced: "We
have taken as partner in our decision our most pious consort given to
us by God." Theodora, for her part, gave the impression that Justinian
always sought her counsel. In a letter to an intermediary she hoped
would be able to persuade the king of Persia to make peace, she wrote:
"I promise you, in that case, the fullest recompense on the part of my
husband, who never does anything without my advice."

Justinian's gifts had already made Theodora wealthy when he married her, and during his reign he continued his munificence. Some of
this money she expended on luxury, in which respect she was quite
unlike her husband. It is probable that the greater portion of her
wealth she spent for the purpose of providing the two services the subjects of monarchs traditionally expect: first, beneficence to the poor,
and second, pomp and magnificence. Theodora had a warm heart and
lavished large sums on hospitals, orphanages, and other charities. She
showed particular interest in the lot of fallen women and sponsored
legislation facilitating their rehabilitation and curbing the white-slave

trade. Across the Bosporus she converted a palace into a nunnery which she called "Repentance" where prostitutes could find a home.

Her name and fame are always linked with the Nika riot that took place in Constantinople in 532 and which almost ended Justinian's career before it had scarcely begun. The riot began at the Hippodrome under quite ordinary circumstances, for it was not uncommon for the rival factions, the Greens and the Blues, who supported different charioteers, to vent their respectively high and low spirits after a race, in violence. Justinian appears to have been a Blue as a young man, but once emperor he sought to curb the tumultuousness of these parties. It happened on the occasion of one of these riots that several people lost their lives, whereupon the government ordered those guilty of the crime to be executed. Two of the men who were to be hanged miraculously escaped when the rope broke or slipped, whereupon both the Blues and Greens took up the cry that the two men, one a Blue, the other a Green, be pardoned. When Justinian refused to intervene, the two factions joined hands against the government and with the cry *nika,* meaning "conquer," began to pillage and burn. They first insisted that the emperor dismiss several unpopular ministers, one of these, Tribonian, another, John the Cappadocian. Yet when Justinian acceded to these demands, the rioting continued. It is believed that aristocratic elements hostile to Justinian were now directing the rioting and would accept nothing less than his overthrow. The palace guards might have saved the situation, but they refused to take a stand. The situation finally grew so critical that Belisarius and others who had taken refuge in the palace urged Justinian to flee. This the emperor was about to attempt when Theodora remonstrated. They might flee if they wished she declared, but she would remain. "For a man born into this light, not to die, is impossible. But for one that hath been an emperor to become an exile, is not to be endured. For let me never come to be without this purple robe, nor live that day in which they that speak to me call me not their Lady and Mistress. If Sir, you have a mind to escape, this is not a hard matter. We have much money, there is the sea, and yonder are ships. But consider whether you may not have cause most willingly to exchange your safety for death after you have saved yourself. For me, I like the old saying that royalty is a good burial-shroud."

Theodora's firmness aroused new determination in the group. Justinian dispatched Belisarius to the Hippodrome with a thousand of his retainers; to Narses, a trusted eunuch, he gave money to buy off the leaders of the revolt and sow discord among the rioters. Between the two men, the throne was saved, although some 30,000 people are said to have been killed by Belisarius and his troops in the Hippodrome. For the balance of his reign Justinian had no more trouble from the Blues and Greens.

THE REIGN OF JUSTIN

Justinian's origins were as lowly as Theodora's. The name given him in baptism was Peter; that by which he is known he derived from his uncle Justin who adopted him and brought him to Constantinople. Both Justinian's father and his uncle were peasants, born and reared in Thrace, near the modern Serbian town of Skoplye. Nothing is known of his father except his name, Sabbatius, which was probably a pure Thracian name. His uncle was among those youths who found the harsh life of a peasant intolerable because of the depredations of the Goths from across the Danube. He threw a bag of biscuits over his shoulder and, with two other young men, made his way to the great city on the Bosporus. Some years later Justinian may have been thinking of his own uncle when he complained: "We have found that while the provinces are generally becoming depopulated, our great city is troubled with the problem of a mounting population swelled by different kinds of men and above all by farmers who have abandoned their homes and their fields."

The three youths "were all men of very fine physique," a fact that enabled them to find places in the new imperial guard that the emperor Leo I was organizing. Justin proved himself an able and loyal soldier and rose in time to command the corps he had joined as a youth. In the state of uncertainty that attended the death of the childless Anastasius in 518, Justin's position as commander of the imperial guard enabled him to play a decisive role. After a number of candidates had been proposed and rejected, the palace officials, senators, and army prevailed upon the reluctant Justin, probably with the help of Justinian's manipulations, to accept the crown. It is not entirely certain whether Justin's reluctance was genuine or feigned. Procopius, the historian of the age, is certain that it was an unwise choice, for Justin was "already an old man with one foot in the grave, so utterly ignorant of letters, that one may say he did not know one letter from another."

Justin's rise from peasant station to rule history's greatest empire was unusual, though not miraculous. A half-dozen emperors, including Diocletian and Constantine, had accomplished that feat before him. In each instance, the means these men employed had been the army, which they had joined as youths and where they had demonstrated their capabilities. Because the army had been making and unmaking emperors since the close of the second century, it was not extraordinary that men like Diocletian and Constantine should have been pushed to the top, for they were men of superior talents. Justin's rise was purely circumstantial.

Whether competent men, as in the case of Diocletian and Constantine, or less gifted soldiers such as Justin emerged as emperors, it augured poorly for Rome's future that the army should decide who would rule. This problem of imperial succession had actually vexed Rome since Octavian's victory at the battle of Actium in 31 B.C. had enabled him to establish autocratic rule. During the first century of imperial rule Rome had tried succession by inheritance, the customary principle of succession followed in an autocracy, but few emperors had sons. For the greater part of the second century, a system of imperial adoption had been employed, with each aging emperor adopting a mature and experienced administrator, usually a general, to succeed him. This system had worked admirably, and no country in history can boast so eminent a succession of distinguished rulers as second-century Rome when Nerva, Trajan, Hadrian, Antoninus Pius, and Marcus Aurelius followed each other to the throne. Still succession by adoption worked only because none of these men had a son, that is, none save Marcus Aurelius. When his depraved son Commodus succeeded in A.D. 180, the glorious century of the Good Emperors ended abruptly and a hundred years of near-anarchy ensued.

A wrestling companion strangled Commodus after a disreputable rule of twelve years, whereupon first the praetorian guard, then the army stepped in to claim the right to determine the succession. Simple military rule would not have produced tragic consequences for the Roman empire here in the third century had there existed but one army and had that been under one unified command. Instead there were several powerful corps stationed in different parts of the empire, each bent on having its own general become emperor. The reason each corps insisted upon naming its emperor reveals how seriously military morale had fallen since the days of the Republic. Then the Roman

army had been composed of Roman citizens, of men who had a love
for their country and a real stake in its survival. By the third century
A.D. the Roman army remained Roman only in name. Because military
service had grown uninviting, citizens shunned it, with the result that
the majority of the soldiers were now non-Romans, men who had
been recruited from the border provinces, men who looked upon service
in the army, not as years during which they would help protect the
empire, rather as an opportunity for advancing their own fortunes. The
empire would serve them, not they the empire, and to this end their
own generals would best listen to their demands. The consequence
was civil war among the different "Roman" armies and all its attendant
evils during much of the third century.

There were, of course, factors other than Rome's failure to solve the
problem of imperial succession, the barbarization of the army, and
civil wars, that brought the empire to its knees in the third century.
The more significant of these were depopulation, the decline of industry and trade, and the impoverishment of the curial and peasant
classes as a result of inflation and heavy taxation. A growing manpower
shortage left fewer landowners to pay higher taxes, and forced the
government into greater dependence upon Germans, not only to maintain the frontiers but even to raise crops.

The less apparent factors in Rome's decline have provoked deep
thought among a score of eminent scholars. Edward Gibbon attributed
the misfortune in his *The Decline and Fall of the Roman Empire,*
the most famous of all literary obituaries, to the very magnitude of
the empire. He saw "the decline of Rome as the natural and inevitable
effect of immoderate greatness. Prosperity ripened the principle of decay;
the causes of destruction multiplied with the extent of conquest, and,
as soon as time or accident had removed the artificial supports, the
stupendous fabric yielded to the pressure of its own weight. The story
of its ruin is simple and obvious; and, instead of inquiring why the
Roman empire was destroyed, we should rather be surprised that it
had subsisted so long."

As a contributing factor Gibbon accused Christianity of introducing
a philosophy of life and a set of values wholly incompatible with those
of pagan Rome. Since Christianity won out, the empire was doomed.
This subjective judgment has drawn considerable fire, more than the
less dramatic charge of other scholars that the superiority of Roman
culture was no longer sufficiently marked and attractive as to assimilate

the masses who came into the empire in the second and third centuries. These people chose rather to retain their native mores and values, in effect to remain non-Roman. Because of this attitude, indifference greeted the emperor Caracalla's edict of A.D. 212 in which he granted citizenship to all freemen. Two centuries earlier men had accepted twenty-five years of hard service in the auxiliary branch of the army in order to gain that boon.

These altered values, together with the wars and destruction of the third century, produced by A.D. 300 a Roman world substantially different from that of Cicero and Vergil. Officially it remained the Roman empire, and into its aging arteries Diocletian forced enough new blood by means of a series of reform measures that it was vouchsafed another century of life. That a new era had begun, nevertheless, was made clear by two events. One was Diocletian's decision to move his capital to the eastern Mediterranean, to Nicomedia, and to share his rule with a western Augustus. The other event was Constantine's edict that granted Christians toleration. The pagan Roman empire was shortly to become Christian.

Almost immediately the attention of the empire was turned outside its frontiers, to the Germans along the northern frontier and to the Persians to the east. Defense of the empire was now the principal concern of the emperors, not the well-being of its citizens to which the Good Emperors of the second century had devoted their attention. For while the empire had been growing old and decrepit, the Germanic tribes to the north had waxed strong and numerous. How critical was the issue of defense is demonstrated by the location of the four capitals in the empire from which the two co-emperors and their two imperial assistants, called Caesars, ruled the empire. They were located at Trier and Milan in the west, at Sirmium near the Danube, and at Constantinople in the east.

The critical year in the history of the later empire was A.D. 375 when the powerful Visigothic nation asked and received permission from the Roman emperor Valens to cross the Danube. What had impelled the Visigoths to make this request was their anxiety to escape the rush of the oncoming Huns who had already overwhelmed their eastern cousins, the Ostrogoths. Valens had no choice but to permit the Visigoths into the empire, a fact they proved in 378 at Adrianople when they slew him and destroyed his army. Theodosius, the successor of Valens, was able to pacify these Germans, but after his death their king, Alaric, took his people westward to Italy where they sacked Rome in 410. Shortly after Alaric's brother-in-law led them to southern France and Spain where they carved out of century-old Roman territory a Visigothic kingdom for themselves. What the Visigoths did, other Germanic tribes repeated during the next fifty years. By the end of the fifth century the entire western half of the ancient Roman empire had fallen to German rule: to Angles and Saxons in Britain; to Vandals in Africa; to Visigoths in Spain and southern France; to Franks and Burgundians in the rest of Gaul; and to Ostrogoths in Italy. Only in the Balkans, Egypt, and the provinces along the eastern littoral of the Mediterranean did Roman rule continue. This was the empire over which Justin, the uncle of Justinian, reigned.

Historians have given the name "Byzantine empire" to this truncated empire of Justin. The longer term Eastern Roman Empire lacks an adjectival form. A better reason for preferring "Byzantine" is the fact that this eastern half of the empire was hardly more than Roman in name. Even though Justinian considered himself a Latin and wanted above all else to restore the Roman empire, he had to admit that his world in the East was not Latin. For that reason he had his laws promulgated in Greek. The word Byzantine derives its origin from the name of the Greek village upon whose site Constantine erected the city that bore his name for sixteen hundred years. The strategic qualities of the site, incidentally, proved of utmost importance in the survival of this Eastern empire. Since the city stood on a finger of land almost surrounded by water, so long as Constantinople commanded these waters, the city remained impregnable. Other factors in the survival of Byzantium must be mentioned: the enormous wealth of the east, its great cities, its thousand-year-old economy, and Constantinople's seven-mile-long bay that attracted cargoes from all over the known world.

Justin ruled from 518 until 527. Procopius says he only reigned, which may be correct, although when Procopius wrote of men he knew, he was apt to let his emotions guide his pen. "Justin," he declared, "was not strong enough to do his subjects either good or harm; he was utterly simple, a very poor speaker, and a complete boor. Justinian was his sister's son, who, when quite a young man, practically governed the state." How early the uncle must have brought Justinian to the capital, there is no way of knowing. It may have been in Justinian's late teens, for when his uncle succeeded to the crown he was thirty-six years of age and already well educated. His name, in fact, was proposed for the succession even before that of his uncle in 518 when Anastasius died, so highly did the court regard him.

Since Justinian took a deep interest in theological matters throughout his life, historians assume he had a major part in the most important achievement of Justin's reign, which was the re-establishment of communion with the pope. For a period of thirty-five years this communion had been interrupted. Justin's predecessors, Zeno and Anastasius, had adopted a conciliatory policy toward Monophysitism, a policy Rome had condemned as favoring heresy. Because these emperors refused to terminate that policy, virtual schism had prevailed between Constantinople and the papacy during their reigns.

The doctrinal issue that had estranged the eastern and western halves of Christendom was the Christological question concerning the two natures of Christ. Many of the early heresies sprang from this issue, and the first five ecumenical councils had all pondered the problem. If Christ had two natures, a divine and a human, how were these related, how did each nature function, and what was their relative importance? Most Christians believed that Christ had two natures, that is, all except the Monophysites. In the anxiety of this latter group to defend Christ's unitary nature from the Nestorians who were proposing an absolute separation of the two natures, they eventually found themselves denying him a human nature. Much was written and spoken during these early centuries regarding the problem of Christ's nature and almost as much since, while some scholars still maintain the last word has not been said. If theologians continue to argue today when the issue no longer arouses the tremendous popular passions it did from the fourth to the seventh centuries, it is small wonder that emperors like Justin and Justinian were at their wits' end seeking a solution.

Two months after Justin's accession, the emperor asked Pope Hormisdas to send an embassy to Constantinople to discuss reunion. When the papal legates arrived they brought with them a formula which the pope directed the patriarch of Constantinople and the bishops of the empire to accept if they wished to re-establish communion with Rome. This formula simply affirmed the primacy of the bishop of Rome and proclaimed the judgment of the apostolic see in matters concerning doctrine. Though this was not wholly what the emperor had wanted, the patriarch and those bishops present in Constantinople accepted the formula on Maundy Thursday in March 519.

The high expectations of the pope that the emperor would immediately implement the agreement and force it upon the Eastern patriarchs proved premature. Justin and Justinian were undoubtedly sincere in their acceptance of the formula, but their motive in seeking reunion with Rome had been chiefly political. A theological rapprochement, they hoped, would prepare the way for the eventual political reunion of Byzantium and Italy. Yet if in effecting a reunion with the West, their concessions to Rome would cost them the adherence of Egypt, they would be no closer to imperial unity than before. They were willing to enforce acceptance of the formula in Syria and Palestine, and even in Asia Minor where imperial authority could compel its acceptance. In Egypt, however, they felt constrained to permit the Monophysites to practice without molestation the particular kind of Christianity they preferred, since Egypt was rich and powerful. Even the Edict of Heretics that Justin and Justinian issued as co-emperors in 527, which deprived heretics of their possessions "so that they might languish in misery," did not extend to Egypt, nor for that matter to Arians among the Goths who, as *foederati* (allies), were needed for the defense of the frontiers.

There was also grave danger of antagonizing Theodoric, the aged king of the Ostrogothic kingdom of Italy. Theodoric was the most powerful of the Germanic kings of the West and he ruled an extensive domain which included Italy, Sicily, and the Dalmatian coast. Until these last years Constantinople always considered him a loyal king and a devoted friend of Roman culture. He had never assumed the title of king of Italy, nor had he stamped coins with his own image. While other Germanic chieftains had shown indifference if not hostility to things Roman, he had expended considerable money and effort in an endeavor to preserve the material and cultural greatness of Rome. Still Theodoric was an Arian, and the conciliatory gestures between pope and emperor caused him uneasiness. Was this doctrinal reconciliation to be the first step looking toward the re-establishment of imperial control in Italy? Theodoric's own succession was in doubt. He was in his seventies, yet had only a widowed daughter Amalasuntha and her ten-year-old son to offer his Gothic people who had never been known to accept female rulers or regents. Furthermore, the system of marriage alliances he had so carefully arranged with his Germanic neighbors was crumbling. Consequently, because Theodoric was apt to be in a suspicious and sensitive mood, Justin and his nephew had to move with caution.

The reunion with Rome dominates the political history of Justin's short reign. A few other matters deserve comment. Justin inaugurated an extensive building program aimed at bolstering the frontier defenses of the empire. He also erected a great church in Constantinople dedicated to Sts. Peter and Paul. This was the first church built in the East that honored these founders of the Western church. Its appearance reflects the new orientation of religious policy. The construction of both church and fortifications suggests the influence of Justinian. Surely the nephew's hand is seen in the promulgation of an edict "On Marriage" which permitted actresses to marry and lead normal lives, after relinquishing "their evil and dishonest condition." Until this law was enacted, Justinian could not have married Theodora. As Procopius writes: "Since it was forbidden by the most ancient laws of the state that anyone of the senatorial order should marry a courtesan, he prevailed upon the emperor to repeal the existing law and introduce a new one, whereby he was allowed to live with Theodora as his legitimate wife." His uncle had been willing for him to marry Theodora, but not the empress Euphemia, Justin's devoted wife. She would have no such person as Theodora in her family, although she was herself of lowly stock and had been Justin's slave and concubine before he married her. But she had never been an "actress"!

Justin fell ill in the spring of 527 when an old leg wound became ulcerated, and in April he co-opted Justinian, then forty-five years old, as his colleague. He died on August 1 at the age of seventy-five (or seventy-seven), when Justinian succeeded without incident.

THE WARS OF JUSTINIAN

The history of warfare burdens most of the years of Justinian's long reign. The greater part of this fighting was Justinian's own choice, although he made the usual mistake ambitious men make of vastly underestimating the cost his projects would amount to in years, manpower, and resources. His wars were concentrated in three areas for the most part: in the east, that is, in Syria, Armenia, and Mesopotamia, against the armies of the formidable Persian empire; along the Danube where a half-dozen German and Hunnic tribes were conducting raids; in the west where he hoped to recover the provinces his predecessors had lost to the Germans. In two of these areas, in the east and along the Danube, fighting was forced upon Justinian. He would have preferred peace to have prevailed there, although he might have purchased a truce with Persia had he been willing to make a dangerous surrender of territory, and even have accomplished the same in the Balkans by scattering gold lavishly and indiscriminately among the semi-barbarous tribes that were pressing into that area. Where Justinian elected to wage war was in the west, in Italy and Africa, since he felt it his sacred responsibility as emperor to recover those provinces.

Justinian's predecessors had made little effort during the century or so preceding his day to drive the Germans and other intruders from Roman soil. Several of these emperors had, of course, accepted the fiction that the West was still theirs, and that the German chieftains in Italy, Gaul, and Spain were simply their representatives, consuls, and patricians. When the opportunity arose, as it did under Zeno, they might encourage one chieftain (Theodoric) to go west in order to destroy another (Odoacer) in the hope that the new ruler would be more respectful of imperial authority. To Justinian such a timid policy was intolerable. He could not permit semi-civilized Germans to dominate lands that hundreds of years of enlightened Roman rule had sanctified. To him these Germans were only slightly better than the brutish Goths who had periodically ravaged the homeland of his youth. God wanted them destroyed and he was willing to make himself God's agent. "God," he declared, "has appointed us to subdue the Vandals, Alans, and Moors . . . and we are confident that the Lord will grant us the Empire which the Romans of old extended to the bounds of two oceans, and which they lost through indolence." If energy and ambition were sufficient to win back these lost provinces, Justinian was the man for the job.

For his purpose Justinian had the best soldiers of the period. These were mounted archers, called cataphracts (meaning clothed in mail), the product of Gothic, Hunnic, and Persian influences. Procopius provides this description of these horsemen: "Now our archers . . . go into the field cuirassed and with greaves that come up as high as their knees. They have in addition a quiver of arrows on their right side and a sword on their left; and some of them have a javelin also fastened about them, and a kind of short buckler, as it were, but without any handle, made fast to their shoulders, which serves to defend their head and neck. They are also excellent riders, and though their horses run never so fast, they can shoot with ease either way and annoy their enemies, either pursuing them or flying. Besides, they draw their bow-string toward their forehead, up to the right ear, which gives such force to the arrow, that where it lights it kills, no shield nor corselet being able to resist its force."

Cavalry made up the bulk of Justinian's army. Some of these had been recruited by trusted officers who received permission to enlist troops in their own personal service. The name *bucellarii* was attached to these troops, from the *bucella* or biscuit which was their principal fare. The emperor took them and their officers into the imperial service and maintained them as part of the army. The most dependable part of the army consisted of troops recruited from both barbarian and Roman subjects in areas such as southern Asia Minor. These were organized as Roman troops under Roman officers. Finally, there were thousands of barbarians, often Huns, their number steadily increasing, who were given land or subsidies in return for service under their native chiefs. These were the least dependable of all.

Justinian was fortunate in having the services of two of the ablest generals whose feats are recorded in the annals of warfare. They were Belisarius and Narses, both masters of strategy and students of military science and both thoroughly loyal. Had it not been for two circumstances, these generals would have won many more battles for Justinian than they did and that in far less time. One was the insatiable demand for troops created by three active fronts and aggravated by a significant population drop following the Great Plague of 541–43. The second circumstance was Justinian's reluctance to entrust a sufficient number of troops to any one general that would have enabled him to win a war in short order. We can appreciate the emperor's quandary. Not only was the loyalty of the Hunnic allies always an uncertain factor, that of the imperial officers with their *bucellarii* was little better. Presented the prospect of rich rewards, they might have no hesitation in repudiating the emperor in favor of a pretender. It is said that Belisarius had some 7000 retainers of his own whom he could count on. If Justinian had entrusted Belisarius with the supreme military command in the West, he might have won the war in a few short years, but at the cost of his imperial crown. It was Justinian's misfortune that he did not give Belisarius his complete trust, for this general's loyalty, like that of Narses, was unquestioned.

The Danube frontier was the least costly to Justinian in terms of manpower, although the areas of Thrace and Macedonia suffered grievously from repeated enemy tribes' raids that carried, on occasion, even to the suburbs of Constantinople. What often served the emperor as effectively as troops in dealing with these semi-civilized tribes was money with which he bought off their rapacious chieftains or bribed them to fight one another. Two of his ablest generals on this front were Chilbudius, a Slav, and Mundus, a Gepid, who among others joined the Romans in order to advance their fortunes. A less expensive maneuver was that of inviting chieftains to send their sons to Constantinople where they would grow up and be showered with gifts and honors on the one hand and impressed with the might and magnificence of Byzantium on the other. Even missionaries were recruited to aid in pacifying the area, on the principle that a Gepid or Bulgar was apt to be less dangerous once he was baptized.

Three different races were represented by these restless peoples along the Danube. On the middle Danube were located the German Lombards, Heruls, and Gepids, while along the lower reaches of the river were Slavs and various Hunnic tribes. All were among the most destructive groups ever to invade the empire. Procopius called the Gepids "the worst people in the world," although the barbarity of the Kotrigurs, a Hunnic tribe, would have been difficult to match. Agathias, a contemporary writer, gives this description of the atrocities they committed in 558, before the very walls of Constantinople. "Since no one offered them any opposition or drove them back, they ravaged the country and pillaged it savagely, capturing immense booty and a very large number of captives. Among these were many well-born women of chaste life whom they carried off most cruelly and forced to undergo the worst of all evils, that of serving the unbounded lust of these barbarians. Some other women who from youth had renounced children and husbands and the pleasures, cares, and occupations of this life and had joined some isolated religious community, they dragged from their holy cloisters and shamefully violated. Many other women who were married and happened to be pregnant, when their time came, brought forth on the march, nor were they permitted either to hide their delivery and their throes nor to embrace or swaddle their infants, but were dragged along nevertheless. . . . The wretched infants they left behind on the road to be eaten by dogs and birds of prey." In desperation Justinian called the aged Belisarius from retirement, who managed, more by means of ingenuity than troops, to drive the barbarians off.

For a number of years before serious warfare had erupted along the Danube frontier, heavy fighting had been in progress in Syria with the Persians. Hostility between Persia and Rome was centuries old. Back in

53 B.C. Crassus had been slain by the Persians, and in 44 B.C. Julius Caesar was about to lead an army against them when he was assassinated. At that time the Parthians had ruled the country. Now it was the Sassanid Persians, but only the dynasty had changed, not the threat that country could pose to Byzantine control of the area. For in the absence of natural frontiers such as the Danube to hold them in, these Persians were constantly making raids to the west against the cities of Syria and Asia Minor, searching for loot and slaves or for tribute from Constantinople in return for remaining quiet. An equally persistent source of friction between Byzantium and Persia existed in northern Armenia where both empires claimed possession of Lazica, a small Christian state. Its occupation by the Persians would provide them direct access to the Black Sea and an open road to Constantinople. The Romans could use Lazica to bypass the Persian monopoly of the silk trade with China and also to strengthen their position among the dangerous tribes of the area. Friction even developed over a matter in which both Persia and Constantinople generally co-operated. That was the responsibility for blocking the Caucasus passes to the Hunnic tribes to the north.

In 532 Justinian negotiated the "Endless Peace" with the young Persian monarch Chosroes, and for the moment there was peace between the two empires. This Persian king Chosroes was the ablest and most aggressive of the Sassanid monarchs. His ruthlessness has suggested comparison with the fierce Assyrian emperors of antiquity, although he has also been likened to Alexander the Great because of the manner in which he brought to fruition reforms inaugurated by his father. Though he devoted most of his attention to the army and to expansion, he appears to have had a genuine interest in learning. It is said he studied many books of philosophy and religion in order to learn which were true and wise, and that he came to revere above all others the writings of the Christians.

What proved to be of as much value to Justinian during the thirty years of warfare with Persia as the generalship of Belisarius and Narses and the gold he used to purchase Hunnic allies, was the system of fortifications he had constructed. Justinian never led his troops. Yet his appreciation of the crucial importance of fortresses in the fighting in western Asia demonstrated a knowledge of military science of which a professional general might have been proud. In the semi-arid Levant, where water and food were scarce and where battles were fought over fortresses, a well-provisioned, stoutly-built fortress could hold off an enemy indefinitely.

In 539 Chosroes broke the "Endless Peace." The successes of Justinian's armies in Italy (of these later) may have alarmed him, if they did not fill him with envy. He overran Syria and captured Antioch, the largest city of western Asia, and left it in smoldering ruins, after enslaving its huge population and carrying off all the gold and silver he could find, including that from the case enclosing the relic of the true cross. Edessa he could not take nor the formidable fortress of Daras just west of the Upper Tigris. From Daras the fighting shifted to the north, to Lazica, where it continued on for another ten years. When peace finally came in 562 Byzantium remained in possession of this small country, but Justinian agreed to pay over 30,000 gold pieces annually in return for which Persia assumed the defense of the Caucasus passes. The demand for 210,000 gold pieces to cover the payments for the first seven years Justinian accepted and met on the spot. The wealth of Byzantium was truly enormous.

The heavy burden of the Persian war affected—it did not halt—the war in the West which was already in progress. This was the emperor's great design, the recovery of the West. He prudently began with the Vandal kingdom in North Africa, the weakest of the Germanic states. Even this undertaking appeared foolhardy to his advisers. Procopius says he did so "against the advice of all men, who shrank in terror from the enterprise, and only [was he] led on and assisted by God. . . ." Several circumstances made the Vandal kingdom weak: the small size of its population, a handful in a sea of Afro-Romans; their Arian faith; the harsh rule of the king. Justinian was not without a pretext in attacking the country. The former king, Hilderic, who had been deposed in 530, had been his friend and ally. When the new king Gelimer refused to step down, hostilities got under way. Despite Vandal weaknesses, the undertaking remained a perilous one, first, because of the war in the East against Persia, second, because of the Vandal fleet which was superior to Justinian's. The mistakes of Gelimer lost him what advantages he had. His fleet was off in Sardinian waters to put down a revolt when Belisarius landed, while a good part of his army was in Tripolitana suppressing an uprising there. Gelimer also bungled in the defense of Carthage, and his capital fell without much difficulty. All Belisarius and his cataphracts needed were two engagements in which to destroy the considerably larger Vandal armies. Gelimer surrendered and was taken to Constantinople to grace a triumph commemorating the recovery of the Vandal kingdom. Then he retired to an estate the emperor had given him. One of Justinian's finest virtues was the clemency he showed fallen enemies, even conspirators.

Justinian's forces occupied Sardinia, Corsica, and the Balearic Islands without opposition, but the Berbers in the interior, to the south and west of Carthage, were a different matter. These wild tribes had a long history of wearing down powerful conquerors who had attempted to subjugate them. (They still do this today.) In their mountain retreats, without cities or wealth to lose but with a fierce love for freedom that enables them to subsist at a level more civilized people would exchange for bondage, they have rarely accepted subjugation or remained long in that condition. Fourteen years of fighting persuaded them to accept a measure of Byzantine rule. No attempt was made to conquer Mauretania (western Algeria and northern Morocco).

Long before the Vandals and Berbers had submitted to Roman rule, Justinian had opened his campaign for the conquest of Italy. Here both the ecclesiastical and political situations invited intervention. The schism with the pope had been healed and Justinian could count on the sympathy of the hierarchy. And Theodoric, the great king of the Ostrogoths, had died in 526. Only a daughter, Amalasuntha, remained and, as regent for her ten-year-old son Athalaric, had become Justinian's ally. When the son died in 534, Amalasuntha married her cousin Theobad in the hope of preserving her throne which the pro-Gothic faction wanted to take from her. Theobad was the leader of this group. In no time at all he had Amalasuntha in prison and, when she appealed to Justinian, had her strangled. Justinian could now attack Italy and its ruler Theobad in order to avenge the death of his ally Amalasuntha.

One Roman army invaded Dalmatia, while Belisarius took another of some 7500 men to Sicily. The Sicilians, who had no love for the Goths, welcomed his coming. From Sicily he crossed to Italy and before Naples ran into his first resistance. It required a siege of three weeks before the city capitulated. Rome offered no resistance. The Goths realized the city could not be defended, that in its present condition it was more a trap than an asset, and so withdrew without giving battle. Belisarius realized this too, so no sooner had he marched into the city than he began immediate work on its defenses. The Goths attacked as he suspected, and for over a year they lay encamped about the city. In order to cut off the water supply and force the city's surrender by that method, they destroyed the city's aqueducts where they entered the walls. This move actually caused the city little grief, but the fact that these aqueducts were never repaired meant an end to the century-old tradition of luxurious bathing and baths for which pagan Rome had long been famous.

The disruption of Rome's water supply proved unimportant, and between the strategy of Belisarius and the confidence of his troops in his masterly leadership, victories came easy for the Romans in these first stages of the war. Belisarius attributed his victories to the superior weapons of his troops. When asked on one occasion why he felt so confident of victory, he explained "that when he first began to fight with them, he studied the differences between the two armies for the purpose of ascertaining how he might adapt his method of fighting in order to neutralize the inferiority of his numbers. He found the difference to be that almost all the Romans and their Hunnic allies were horse-archers, a mode of fighting not practised by the Goths, whose horsemen carried only lances and swords, while their archers fought on foot and went into battle covered with their cavalry. Their horsemen, as a consequence, had no protection except in hand to hand fighting, and could be easily shot at and ruined by an enemy's missiles, their infantry meantime not being able to make attacks of their own on the horsemen."

Belisarius might have gone on to win the war in a short time had it not been for—of all ironies—the appearance of a supporting army from Byzantium under the command of Narses. Historians believe Justinian ordered this army to Italy less to assist Belisarius than to keep an eye on him and prevent his conquering Italy singlehandedly and then proclaiming himself emperor. Justinian's suspicions almost cost him the war. Because of the divided command and friction between the two generals, Byzantine armies suffered several reverses, the most tragic being the capture and razing of Milan, the massacre of its 300,000 male inhabitants and the enslaving of its women. This disaster convinced Justinian of his mistake and he recalled Narses. Shortly after, in 540, Belisarius captured Ravenna and announced the end of the war.

No sooner had Belisarius and most of his army returned to Constantinople than the Goths regrouped under the leadership of one of the most admirable leaders the early German tribes produced. This was Totila, a man who resembled Belisarius in his sense of honor, in the consideration he showed his captured foes, and in his anxiety to reduce the horrors of war for the civilian population. What fed this Gothic revolt was the misrule of the imperial officials, and what gave Totila his first victories was again Justinian's policy of entrusting the campaign to more than one general. When the emperor learned that Rome was under siege (544), he belatedly sent over Belisarius, but furnished him with a wholly inadequate army. The general wrote back to the emperor to complain: "We are come into Italy wanting men, horses, arms, and money. . . . To raise contributions in Italy is not possible since the enemy controls the country, and being in arrears in paying the soldiers has deprived me of my authority and I cannot command them. The majority of those who served your Majesty have deserted to the enemy. . . . No general can succeed without men. Above all things it is, therefore, urgent that you send me my own armed retainers and a large host of Huns and other barbarians, and you must also send me money."

Belisarius asked in vain, and in 546 Rome fell again to Totila. Only five hundred inhabitants remained of the civilian population; the others had fled or died. This time Totila decided to destroy the city since he could not hold it, but a plea from Belisarius dissuaded him. Procopius quotes Belisarius' letter to Totila: "It has been the work of wise and civilized men of old to construct beautiful buildings, and none except barbarous men who are not ashamed to leave posterity proof of their barbarism have destroyed such cities. Of all the cities under the sun, Rome is admitted to be the greatest and most famous. She is not the work of one man's genius, nor has she attained to this beauty and magnificence in a short time. Many emperors and excellent men, many long years and much wealth have been responsible in bringing materials and skilled artisans from all countries, so that little by little the city has risen as you now see it. They have filled it with monuments of all their virtues. Wherefore the violence done to this city is an injury committed against all mankind, since such a deed serves to take from our progenitors memorials of their worth and from posterity the right to enjoy such beautiful works. Know then, that one of two things must happen, either you will be vanquished by the emperor or you will prevail. Should you be victorious and order the destruction of Rome, you will be ruining, Great Sir, not another's city but your own. If you rather preserve the city, you will be rich in owning the most precious possession in the world. Should you be vanquished after having preserved the city, you will have merited a conqueror's abundant thanks. On the other hand, if you destroy it, you will have forfeited all right to mercy. And remember that your reputation in the judgment of the world waits upon your action."

Totila spared the city but he destroyed the gates and demolished sections of the walls before withdrawing. The walls Belisarius hastily repaired when he marched back in, although he had not replaced the gates before Totila turned about and again laid siege to the city. Though the Goths failed in this attempt, Belisarius appears to have had no stomach for continuing a war with so few troops under his command, so he asked to be recalled. Justinian replaced him with Narses whom he sent over with a powerful army of 30,000 men, most of whom were Lombard mercenaries. Totila was no match for Narses and was killed in a decisive battle in Umbria (about fifty miles north of Rome). Narses then took Rome for the fifth time, after which he defeated what was left of the Gothic army and permitted the defeated fragments to leave Italy unmolested. By 562 the area north of the Po had been conquered, although only after Narses had slaughtered a huge army of Franks that 'had marched into the valley in search of plunder. Only five men of an army of 80,000 are said to have escaped.

One other land figured in Justinian's effort to reconquer the western half of the empire. That was Spain. Little is known of the campaign in that distant country. It seems the Byzantine fleet brought in an army in 554 in order to support the cause of a pretender to the Visigothic throne. The army managed to occupy several cities along the southern coast including Córdoba and Cartagena, but that was the extent of Byzantine penetration.

No other campaign was undertaken after the conquest of Italy. Had Justinian been a vigorous young man when this was completed (562) and not a tired old man of eighty, he would unquestionably have continued on. And after the manner Narses had slaughtered a large Frankish army in northern Italy, no one could have convinced him that he could not conquer Gaul (France).

But the question traditionally asked is not whether Justinian would have continued on had he been a young man. The usual question concerns rather the wisdom of his ever having attempted to do what he did accomplish. Historians say no, his undertaking was unwise. True, he made the Mediterranean a Roman lake again, but only for a few years. Lombards began spilling through the Alpine passes into northern Italy shortly after his death, and soon most of the Italian countryside was in their possession. Within a century of the emperor's death all his costly conquests had been lost except for Sicily and scattered holdings in Italy. While these Byzantine outposts proved of considerable cultural and economic value to the West until the eleventh century when the last of them was lost, one would hardly dare place them in balance against the appalling cost of Justinian's western campaigns. These wars seriously strained the empire's resources and so embittered the Monophysitic populations of Syria and Egypt because of the heavy taxation they entailed, that these people offered Islamic armies little resistance when these appeared early the next century. There was also the tremendous cultural injury Justinian's wars had done to the West. Large cities like Milan almost disappeared. Rome fell to hostile armies five times; she never recovered her position as the leading city of the West. No longer could Italy and North Africa be considered important depositories of classical culture. Not enough of that culture remained.

Yet are not historians being harsh with Justinian? Could not the emperor protest that he had no notion the conquest of Italy would prove so costly? Once undertaken, however, could he have turned his back? And what if it had been Narses, not Belisarius, to whom he had initially entrusted the task of conquering Italy? Since Narses was a eunuch and could never have hoped to unseat him, he might have placed complete faith in his loyalty. It is possible that Belisarius' enemies poisoned Justinian's mind against his great general and led him to follow a policy that crippled his efforts in Italy. Furthermore, had the successors of Justinian been competent and ambitious men, emperors as dedicated to the preservation of Rome as Justinian had been, would these territories have been lost? And who could have suspected that out of such a dusty, God-forsaken corner of the world as Mecca, a mighty force would shortly emerge that would engulf the Persian empire and a good part of the Byzantine as well? Perhaps it is only just to close the books on Justinian's reign when he died. In all probability he left sufficient wealth and manpower to maintain the empire he had won.

CODIFICATION OF ROMAN LAW

"The vain titles of the victories of Justinian are crumbled into dust; but the name of the legislator is inscribed on a fair and everlasting monument." It is Justinian's codification of Roman law, not his reconquest of Italy nor the building of Hagia Sophia, that entitle the emperor to his great place in history. Today millions of people of Western Europe and the world over where Western civilization has penetrated continue to abide by laws and legal concepts that were Roman in origin but, without the work of Justinian, would have long since been forgotten.

The rule of law is Rome's principal contribution to the development of Western civilization. No people in history placed such faith in their laws as did the Romans, nor paid such reverence to the jurists who nourished the evolution of her legal principles. The origins of Roman law were themselves no more promising than those of most other peoples —a set of customs handed down by the gods to a selfish class of patricians who hoped to use them to preserve their own dominant place in society. They were also harsh laws. Among those recorded in 451 B.C. in the Twelve Tables, when a defiant plebs forced the writing down of the laws, were provisions of capital punishment for bribery, slander, and theft. Yet harsh though they were, the people hallowed these laws as the guardians of their rights, they had their children memorize them in the schools, and they added to this modest beginning other laws in the course of time which they forced from the reluctant patricians. So was born Rome's devotion to law.

This kind of law the world would not have greatly missed, even though the practical-minded Romans as a people adopted an unusually pragmatic approach in their development of a legal code. What worked for them and was reasonable, they concluded must be right. However, this law of the early Republic remained too "Roman" to have ever recommended its adoption to non-Roman peoples. Several factors or circumstances operated to broaden its concepts and to replace its peculiar Roman character with one that was universal. One was the work of the urban praetor who served as judge in civil suits. At the beginning of his term he would publish an edict setting forth the manner in which he would interpret certain laws and apply certain legal principles during his year of office. These edicts might vary only slightly from year to year, but over a period of generations their divergence could be significant, thereby providing Roman law the quality of flexibility that enabled it to grow. More significant in its broadening influence upon this native Roman law was the contribution of the foreign praetor whose responsibility extended to strangers in the city and to disputes involving citizens and non-citizens. Given Roman respect for reason, it was only natural that the legal philosophy this praetor applied would be based upon reason and would generally represent a rational compromise between legal principles which Romans and non-Romans considered reasonable. This kind of law came to be known as the *ius gentium* or the law of nations.

While Roman law was undergoing this revolutionary development within the tribunals of the empire, there were men called *iuris prudentes* and *iuris consulti,* specialists in the interpretation of law, who were expressing opinions and writing treatises on various aspects of Roman law. These men, several of them notably influenced by the humanitarian philosophy of Stoicism, proposed greater application of the principles of equity, that is, of that essential justice which supersedes the formal barriers of man-made laws and rests upon a philosophic conception of a natural law binding upon all men. So cogently did these jurists write and so great was Roman reverence for the legal profession, that their views gradually found acceptance into the body of Roman law, occasionally even by fiat of a Roman emperor like Hadrian. During the second and third centuries, when the distinction between citizen and non-citizen gradually disappeared, there emerged finally from the combining of the *ius gentium* and the humanized Roman law one universal law that was wonderfully suited for use throughout the Roman world. This law in turn, because it was the product of centuries-long adjustment among the laws of different nations and the influences of some of the world's most learned jurists, became by reason of the work of Justinian, the universal law of a good part of the Western world.

During the hundreds of years that Roman law was growing, it acquired a vast and unwieldy mass of legislation and legal literature which periodic codifications might have sloughed off had these been carried out. Julius Caesar recognized the critical need for a thoroughgoing reform, but his plans were cut short by his death. Laws going back to the Twelve Tables were still considered valid in his day, and opinions handed down centuries before were still being respected as binding to a nation to whose essential conservatism customs and precedents had a powerful appeal. *Moribus antiquis stat res romana.* The Roman state rests upon ancient custom. Included in the tremendous mass to which Roman law had grown by A.D. 500 were regulations the small agrarian Roman state in Italy had adopted, edicts a pagan imperial autocracy had proclaimed, together with those the Christian emperors from Constantine's day had promulgated. "In the space of ten centuries," Gibbon points out, "the infinite variety of laws and legal opinions had filled many thousand volumes, which no fortune could purchase and no capacity could digest." Unless an urgently needed reduction of this accumulation of a thousand years had been carried out and obsolete and contradictory laws eliminated, Roman law would inevitably have followed the path into oblivion already taken by Roman religion.

Justinian had been emperor no more than a few months when he announced what was to be his most enduring work, the codification of Roman law. For this task he appointed a commission of ten expert jurists, headed by the eminent pagan lawyer Tribonian. As their first task he assigned them the job of assembling those imperial edicts they judged still applicable. The group decided to ignore all edicts made prior to the reign of Hadrian, which was a prudent decision, not only because older edicts could hardly have been other than obsolete, but because Rome's most advanced legislation dates from the time of this emperor. After a year of diligent effort, the commission produced in 529 a volume known officially as the *Codex constitutionum* or Book of Constitutions. This contained 4652 enactments which were organized after the twelvefold division of the original Twelve Tables.

The commission's second task was that of selecting from the voluminous writings of a score of distinguished jurists those opinions and interpretations that they considered most valuable. Here again the group decided not to go beyond the jurists of the second century, the greatest century in the history of Roman jurisprudence. Of a galaxy of jurists whose writings they examined, the commission drew principally upon those of Julian and Gaius who wrote under the Antonines, and of Papinian, Ulpian, and Paulus who were active in the early third century. Their selection, known as the Digest or *Pandects,* required four years to complete and represented in final form a reduction to 150,000 lines legal literature of some three million.

A month before the appearance of the Digest (533), the commission published a short work of fifty pages entitled the Institutes. The purpose of this manual was to provide students an introduction to the study of Roman law. It was based for the most part on the earlier work of Gaius, although it incorporated changes recommended by the passage of three hundred years. Justinian proclaimed these three works, the *Codex,* Digest, and Institutes, to be the law of the empire and the official matter to be studied in the imperial law schools. A fourth work that the emperor planned but never completed was to consist of enactments made to supplement or modify those in the *Codex.* A group of private jurists prepared such a compilation shortly after Justinian's death. This work bears the name of Novels (new laws). It includes

154 enactments, most of these expressed in Greek, which had become the official language in Constantinople.

These four works made up what is called the *Corpus juris civilis.* Though itself a codification, it constitutes a massive work and runs some 2000 closely printed pages in a modern edition. The Novels, the fourth part, is least important. Its laws are those of Justinian's reign and hold interest principally for historians. The unique value of the *Corpus* rests upon the first two parts, particularly upon the Digest. Here is expressed not the wisdom of one generation but that which a highly civilized nation accumulated over a period of many centuries. For this reason the Digest has been acclaimed the most important law book ever produced. Its contents are not actual laws that age with time and grow obsolescent. It is composed rather of legal concepts that, having met the test of time, know no time and are ageless.

The *Corpus juris civilis* provides the basis for the law of most European countries, although its influence upon English law, while substantial, has been only indirect. It makes its influence felt particularly in the realm of property. The Roman who was conservative by nature had a deep reverence for private property, a reverence shared by his jurists. Their learned disquisitions on the subject had the effect of establishing this conservative attitude as objectively valid and not just the prejudiced judgment of a propertied class. For this reason the influence of Roman law in the area of property has been doubly persuasive, and those civilizations that have adhered to Roman law have tended to preserve this same conservative attitude toward property.

A brief glance at the contents of the Novels will reveal what particular problems were the concern of the legislators during Justinian's reign. The civil service, the Church, and the family as holders and transmitters of property command most attention. A number of laws had for their objective the elimination of corruption in the government about which there was constant complaint. One law required high officials to remain in the provinces they had served for fifty days after the expiration of their term of office in order to facilitate their prosecution for malfeasance. Another law required officials to punish the actual perpetrators of serious crimes without making a profit from arresting a succession of innocent people and then, after failing to hold any individual culpable, fining the community in which the crime was committed. Another law required litigants to swear that they had not made gifts to the judges in order to secure their favor.

Legislation concerning religion occupied considerable space. Churches in Africa belonging to Arians and pagans were ordered turned over to Catholics. Priests were to be tried by their bishops except in cases of serious crimes, when they were first to be unfrocked and then tried by the civil courts. Judges were not to require bishops to appear in court to present testimony, but must themselves visit these prelates to receive their evidence. The clergy were forbidden to take part in games, to attend the theater, or frequent taverns. Married deacons might be ordained, but an unmarried priest who took a wife was to be expelled from the Church. Property given to bishops and other ecclesiastical dignitaries in their official capacity as churchmen was to be spent on ransoming captives and assisting the poor, and was not to be transferred to their relatives. Heretics were not permitted to build churches, nor Jews to erect synagogues.

Civil laws enacted during Justinian's reign did not always conform with ecclesiastical regulations in matters concerning marriage. A marriage could be dissolved, for example, if one party was impotent or had been in prison for five years. A marriage between a free man and a slave was not to be considered a marriage. A man could divorce his wife if she attended the theater, if she absented herself at night without his permission, or if she laid violent hands on him. Several laws revealed an attempt to ameliorate punishments which had become traditional. A criminal was not to have both hands or feet cut off, but only one hand or one foot. Even in the case of theft, the thief was not to be deprived of any limb nor be put to death. Moneylenders were declared to have no further claim against a debtor after they had received twice the amount loaned.

The influence of the Church and perhaps Justinian's own convictions are seen in the enactment of stringent laws against immorality. Owners of shows were prohibited from requiring women to take an oath to continue in that profession. Blasphemy was forbidden "since it is owing to offenses of this kind that famines, earthquakes, and pestilences occur." Homosexuals were warned to abandon their evil ways for a similar reason, that is, the danger that the same fate might befall Constantinople as Sodom and Gomorrah had suffered. If a man who had been imprisoned for adultery managed to escape and then repeated his offense, he was to be tortured and executed. The woman was to be chastised and immured for life in a nunnery. On the other hand, no woman was to be imprisoned as a result of any financial suit. If she were convicted of a serious crime, she was to be placed, not in a prison, but in a nunnery where her chastity would not be in danger.

The laws compiled in the Novels reveal no basic trend that would set Justinian's reign off from those of his immediate Christian predecessors like Theodosius II. More rigorous prosecution of Monophysites and pagans was provided, but this is what might be expected. While Justinian's interest in enforcing doctrinal uniformity may arouse criticism in the ecumenically minded modern world, his repeated insistence to his legal advisers that conditions change and laws must be modified to conform to such change, strikes a sympathetic chord. So does his implied confession concerning the fallibility of his efforts. And before the modern critic deals too severely with this sixth-century emperor, he should remember that the penal code of eighteenth-century England was no more humane or tolerant.

THE RELIGIOUS POLICY OF JUSTINIAN

The age of Justinian was an age of violent religious controversy. Religion and creed were as explosive issues then as they came to be again in the sixteenth century in central Europe. The general explanation was similar, namely, the conviction of many people that their religious views were those which God approved, while the conflicting views their neighbors held were an abomination to the Lord. What helped produce this sensitivity over religious belief and practice in Justinian's day was the remarkable concern the people of the eastern Mediterranean had for these matters. The complaint Gregory of Nyssa voiced about the people of Constantinople in the fourth century remained just as true of the sixth. "This city," he lamented, "is full of mechanics and slaves who are all of them profound theologians and preach in the shops and the streets. If you want a man to change a piece of silver, he tells you in what way the Son differs from the Father; if you ask him the price of a loaf of bread, you are told by way of reply that the Son is inferior to the Father; and if you inquire whether the bath is ready, the answer is that the Son was made of nothing."

Gravely aggravating this sensitivity were physical and racial differences. That religious differences often followed lines of linguistic and national demarcation made these differences doubly irreconcilable. In this heightened religious atmosphere, not love of neighbor but intolerance marked the conduct of many Christians, who instead of quietly worshiping

God or helping the poor, engaged in bitter discussion over theological questions so fine as to tax the minds of learned theologians. When the people of Alexandria learned of the decision of the Council of Chalcedon in 451 condemning Monophysitism, they butchered the Roman garrison to a man; when they learned of the death of the anti-Monophysite emperor in 457, they tore their patriarch to pieces on Good Friday in his own church.

When Justinian became emperor the number of major warring Christian groups had dwindled to two, the one known historically as the Catholic or orthodox, the other as the Monophysite. Arianism lingered on in scattered places particularly in the western part of the empire, but was without influence in Constantinople. The Nestorians who had been powerful in the early fifth century had since been driven from the empire and had taken refuge in considerable numbers in Persia. The absence of these once influential sects might be expected to have contributed to religious tranquillity, but that was not the case. The cleavage between the orthodox and Monophysites was simply the more bitter. What further aggravated the situation was the fact that the Monophysite bishops of Syria and Egypt controlled not only religious but political policy as well. Not the imperial governor, but the patriarch of Alexandria, was the real ruler of Egypt.

Byzantine emperors usually shared the concern of their subjects over doctrinal orthodoxy although not so singlemindedly as to forget that they had a crown to preserve and that political expediency might on occasion recommend making concessions to heretical groups. Even Justinian, for all his strong religious convictions, pursued a somewhat ambivalent policy toward Monophysitism, at least in Egypt where it was so strongly entrenched. Harsh, relentless persecution there might have caused a revolt and cost him his throne. There was also his wife Theodora to be considered. Her sympathy for the views of the Monophysites limited Justinian's ability to deal too harshly with the group. On the other hand, Justinian probably possessed beyond most of his fellow emperors the conviction that God demanded of him the establishment of uniform orthodoxy throughout the empire. Therefore, where other emperors sought to establish religious uniformity as a means of providing them a more stable throne, Justinian sought that objective in order to please God. "We believe," he affirmed, "that the first and highest blessing for all mankind is the confession of the true and pure faith of the Christians, to the end that it may be established in all matters, and that all the most holy priests of the whole world may join together in unity and with one voice preach the orthodox confession of the Christian faith and quash every plea that heretics may devise."

That Justinian should dictate church policy was traditional. The pagan emperor of Rome had claimed authority over his subjects in all matters, including religion, and that view had prevailed after Constantine's conversion. When Ambrose the saintly bishop of Milan protested that in spiritual matters the emperor must bow to the Church, he was affirming a revolutionary doctrine only the pious Theodosius could accept. It would require more than Ambrose's single victory to destroy a tradition. Justinian, the "uncrowned theologian," was the elect of God, emperor and priest, the vicar of God on earth, the defender of the faith, the one man to whom all Christians, including the pope, owed a double allegiance, one obedience as their ruler in civil affairs, another as their lord in spiritual matters. Justinian's aim was to unite Church and State into a single organism of which he was the head, in effect, to establish a state church and a church state. He legislated on religious matters, on the conduct of monks, on adultery and divorce, on the election of bishops, even on doctrinal questions. He was both emperor and pope and one of the Byzantine emperors to whose religious policy the word "caesaropapism" may be applied.

When Justinian became emperor he continued the religious policy his uncle had inaugurated probably under his inspiration, that is, union with Rome and suppression of Monophysitism. This religious stand, as noted, aroused deep resentment in Syria and Egypt. It also displeased and disturbed Theodora, who finally persuaded her husband that it might be dangerous to antagonize so many of his subjects. What Justinian needed was some concession from Rome on the question of Christ's nature which the Monophysite bishops of the eastern Mediterranean could accept. An opportunity to secure such a concession seemed to present itself in 536 when Pope Agapitus died. But Goths were in control of Rome at the time and used their influence to secure the election of Silverius who they expected would be adamant on the question. The Goths favored a religious policy that would cause friction between Rome and Constantinople. Shortly after Silverius' election, Rome fell into the hands of Justinian's army, whereupon Pope Silverius was seized, deposed, and exiled to the island of Palmaria where he is believed to have died of hunger. The new pope was Vigilius, who had accompanied

Agapitus to Constantinople as his secretary and there had made a good impression on Theodora. Justinian summoned Vigilius to Constantinople where he hoped Byzantine theologians and imperial pressure might induce him to accept a compromise on the question of Monophysitism. In this he was partially successful. The harassed pope finally persuaded Justinian to summon a general council and have this group decide the issue. This council, the Fifth Ecumenical, convened at Constantinople in 553. After much debate the assembled bishops agreed to condemn certain doctrines suggestive of Nestorianism to which the Monophysite bishops had voiced bitter objection. Pope Vigilius who had managed to escape Constantinople for the greater freedom of Chalcedon confirmed the council's condemnation of these doctrines and left for Rome but died on the way. While his action eased the religious situation in the eastern part of the empire, it precipitated a schism in the West. Even in the East, the Monophysites were not happy.

There was no problem to which Justinian gave greater consideration than the religious question, yet his failure here was almost complete. Its worst consequences would appear after his death when the Mohammedan invaders would find Monophysite Syria and Egypt offering them little resistance. Even Justinian appears to have accepted a form of Monophysitism in his last years. Only his death prevented the persecution of the orthodox patriarchs of the East.

The emperor had more success suppressing other heresies, although the measures he employed strike the modern reader as harsh. Relapsed heretics and Manichaeans he executed. Heretics and pagans were barred from the schools and civil service and their property might be confiscated. Yet the enforcement of these measures fluctuated with the mood of the emperor. If the person was not guilty of any overt act which caused scandal, he was normally not molested. Tribonian and John the Cappadocian were pagans, yet managed to hold high posts in the government. Justinian did suppress what has been called the university of Athens, actually a center of Neo-Platonism where a few undistinguished pagan philosophers were attempting to continue the traditions of the Platonic Academy.

History holds Justinian's religious policy to have been both intolerant and a failure. That judgment should be tempered by two observations: first, that a greater man than Justinian would probably have found a goal of religious peace based upon tolerance as elusive as the goal of doctrinal uniformity based upon intolerance; second, that Justinian was motivated by the conviction that he was doing God's will. Much may be excused a man who, despite a plethora of other problems, "is accustomed to sit without guards far into the night, in the company of old priests, deep in the study of the holy books of the Christians."

BUILDINGS

Justinian's most imposing physical work still stands proud and un-ruffled in Turkish Istanbul, the magnificent church of Hagia Sophia. With all his other distinctions, Justinian was also a great builder. Procopius devotes an entire volume to a description of the extensive building program he carried on throughout the empire. In his passion for construction the emperor was continuing a distinctly Roman tradition. The Romans loved to build. The ruins of their baths, aqueducts, bridges, temples, theaters, and fortifications lie scattered over the ancient Mediterranean world, from Gibraltar to Palmyra, and from northern England to Timgad. If this building passion subsided after the activity of Hadrian's reign, it received new life when Constantine proclaimed peace for the Christians. Then churches began to spring up all over the Christian Mediterranean, several of them, notably St. John Lateran in Rome, the gift of Constantine himself. Still if Procopius is truthful, no monarch in history erected so many churches as did Justinian. After commenting on Hagia Sophia and other churches near by, Procopius writes: "As for all the other churches which this Emperor raised in honor of Christ, they are so many in number and so great in size that it is impossible to describe them in detail, for no power of words nor one's whole life would suffice to collect and to recite the list of their several names."

Procopius devotes the greater part of his *Buildings* to a description of the fortifications Justinian erected or repaired about the perimeter of the empire: eighty fortresses along the Danube, one hundred and fifty in Africa, and many more in Thrace, Asia Minor, and Syria. Places of exceptional strategic importance received elaborate fortifications, such as Thermopylae which continued to control the road down into Greece as it had back in the days of Themistocles and Xerxes. The fortifications along the frontier were ordinarily arranged in two lines of defense: fortified towns and a chain of smaller forts forming the outer line, an inner line consisting of larger towns and stronger garrisons where the inhabitants might take refuge in case of attack. The construction of these fortifications consumed an enormous amount of labor and time, for it was not simply the citadel that must be built, but adequate provision made at the same time for granaries and cisterns to provide food and water against extended sieges.

Procopius describes Justinian's repair of the fortifications about Hemerium, a city near the Euphrates. Here "finding the walls built in some parts carelessly and dangerously, and in some parts formed only of mud, while the place was deficient in water-supply and consequently despicable as a fortification, he razed them to the ground, and at once carefully rebuilt them of courses of the hardest stone, making the wall much wider and higher than before. He also constructed reservoirs for water in all parts of the works, all of which he filled with rain-water, and placing a garrison there, he rendered the place as powerful and secure as we now see it. Indeed, if one were carefully to consider this, and to inspect all the other good works of the Emperor Justinian, one would say it was for this alone that he had received the crown, by the manifest favor of God, who watches over the Roman people."

These fortifications provide disturbing evidence of the urgent need of defense against dangerous enemies that ringed the empire on all sides. Five centuries earlier a few garrisons sufficed to hold a far longer frontier. During this half millennium not only had the empire weakened, but the frontier tribes had grown more powerful. Still the fact that the empire could erect such an extensive and formidable array of fortifications reveals that considerable vigor and resources remained in the empire. Had Justinian's successors inherited his same ambition and energy, these fortifications might have withstood the enemy indefinitely.

Justinian did not limit his building program to fortifications for the protection of his subjects and to churches in which they might worship. Their convenience he did not overlook nor even their pleasure. For the inhabitants of an ancient spa on the Black Sea he ordered fortifications thrown up "to enable them to take the cure in safety." Under Justinian many cities received their first satisfactory supply of water. For one city he provided "a magnificent aqueduct and furnished the inhabitants beyond their expectation with enough water not only to drink, but also to wash in, and to use for all the other luxuries of life, as they were now supplied with water in abundance." Among other construction were harbor works, a granary depot on the Dardanelles, a huge cistern for Constantinople, market places, fountains, streets, baths, shops, bridges, theaters, sewers, and almshouses. Was all this building actually completed, and was all of it Justinian's doing? Procopius says it was.

What remains the greatest physical tribute to Justinian's genius is the church of Hagia Sophia (Santa or Sancta Sophia) or Holy Wisdom. The former church called "Sophia" by the people of Constantinople had been a casualty of the Nika riot. Its destruction, Procopius believes, was a blessing God had permitted, "knowing how great the beauty of this church would be when restored." The planning of the new church Justinian entrusted to Anthemius of Tralles, "by far the most celebrated architect, not only of his own but of all former times," and to Isidore of Miletus. On the erection of the church Justinian spared no expense, so that it "consequently presented a most glorious spectacle, extraordinary to those who behold it, and altogether incredible to those who are told of it. In height it rises to the very heavens, and overtops the neighboring buildings like a ship anchored among them: it rises above the rest of the city, which it adorns, while it forms a part of it, and it is one of its beauties that being a part of the city, and growing out of it, it stands so high above it, that from it the whole city can be beheld as from a watch-tower. Its length and breadth are so judiciously arranged that it appears to be both long and wide without being disproportioned. It is distinguished by indescribable beauty, for it excels both in its size and in the harmony of its proportion, having no part excessive and none deficient; being more magnificent than ordinary buildings, and much more elegant than those which are out of proportion. It is singularly full of light and sunshine; and you would declare that the place is not lighted by the sun from without, but that the rays are produced within itself, such an abundance of light is poured into the church."

Procopius lavishes most of his encomia on the interior, which is proper, since that is the important part of the building. The first view of the church from the bay is impressive, although a closer view at the exterior is apt to be disappointing. Its great mass is indeed startling, and ten thousand men are said to have crawled about its scaffolding for five years. Still the only purpose the exterior serves is to provide an interior in which men and women can worship, and sacrifices have been made on the exterior, both architecturally and aesthetically, to accomplish this. Yet these sacrifices have been worth their price, since the interior, in the judgment of Procopius, is a true house of prayer. "Whoever enters there to worship perceives at once that it is not by any human strength or skill, but by the favor of God that this work has been perfected; his mind rises sublime to commune with God, feeling that He cannot be far off, but must especially love to dwell in the place which He has chosen. . . ."

The tremendous dome that dominates Hagia Sophia is unique for several reasons: its intrinsic beauty; its extraordinary height above the floor, approximately one hundred eighty feet; the row of windows at its bases, whose apertures create in the bright sunlight a seemingly continuous band of light upon which the dome appears to float; the architectural engineering required to sustain its enormous weight and thrust. This feat is accomplished by means of four huge pendentives, one at each corner of the rectangular base, which curve upward and inward to form together a round plane upon which the dome rests. Multicolored marbles and brilliant mosaics pick up and diffuse the bright sunlight and create an atmosphere of jeweled iridescence. Some day, after more years of repair and reconstruction spent on undoing earthquake damage, centuries of neglect, and the church's conversion by the Ottoman Turks into a mosque, the interior again will resemble that which evoked such extravagant praise from Procopius.

THE GOVERNMENT OF JUSTINIAN

The Roman state of Justinian was historically the successor of that of the Roman Republic, although the relationship was hardly apparent to any but Romans. Rome was no longer pagan, and the Roman gods who had sired and protected the early Republic were now a despised legend. The Roman legions who had won Africa, Gaul, and the East were also only a legend. The army of Justinian was composed principally of horsemen who could not speak Latin, nor Greek for that matter. Not for four hundred years had Rome produced a poet who deserved to have his name mentioned in the same breath with Vergil or Horace. In order to embellish his arch of triumph, Constantine was obliged to pilfer sculptures from earlier structures. No less wide was the gap that yawned between the government of the Republic and that of Justinian, even though both called their governments Roman.

The senate that had controlled the policy of the early Republic had succumbed even before the battle of Actium. Augustus kept it alive in order to provide his autocracy a republican façade. His successors grew progressively less concerned about disguising their power, and tyrants like Domitian and Septimius Severus made little pretense of being anything but the dictators they were. Diocletian introduced a naked despotism although he softened its harshness with the ceremonials and trappings of the Hellenistic and Persian courts of the East. The emperor now ruled by the grace of the goddess Roma, later of the Christian God, although he might secure his selection by a human agency. He was sole ruler, autocrator, responsible only to God, the supreme authority in all spheres of government, legislative, executive, judicial, and military. Because he was the spokesman of God and his representative, men prostrated themselves in his presence and begged favors on their knees.

Purple became the imperial color and only those persons might wear it who had the emperor's permission. Precious appointments of gold and silver, rich mosaics, tapestries, and rugs graced the house of the semi-divine emperor and his court. Ceremonials were fashioned after those of Eastern potentates in order to enhance the sublimity of the Presence. A host of officials with high sounding titles—*illustris, spectabilis, clarrissimus*—and regiments of guards, each with its own brilliant uniforms, created an atmosphere worthy of the ruler who was more god than man.

The principal officials who advised the emperor included the two praetorian prefects, one of the East (Thrace, Egypt, Asia), the other of Illyricum (Dacia, Macedonia, Greece), the prefect of the city, the quaestor of the offices who headed the privy council, and the master of offices who supervised the palace secretariat, the secret service, and the state armories. There were vicars in charge of the dioceses and governors who administered the provinces, although all officials might report directly to the imperial court and receive instructions from the emperor. The result was apt to foster confusion and irresponsibility and an ever growing concentration of officials and authority at Constantinople. The huge bureaucracy that inevitably developed, even though well trained by ancient standards, was under constant attack for its corruption, its slowness, and its insensitivity to the demands of the citizenry.

The man who might best represent Byzantine bureaucracy at its best, and its worst, was John the Cappadocian, whom Justinian raised to the rank of praetorian prefect of the East. John covered his lack of education with his enormous energy and Machiavellian shrewdness, and Justinian kept him for his ability to raise money. Regrettably the emperor did not scrutinize the methods John employed, which were unscrupulous and ruthless. Of the moneys he collected with the help of force and torture, he kept some to finance his debaucheries. Yet he worked hard to please the emperor, introduced various economies in the government, and co-operated with Justinian in effecting reforms even in his own fiscal department. Theodora hated John and accused him to the emperor of dishonesty and tyranny, but the emperor would not dismiss him. Only for a short time was he out of the court, when Justinian bent to the demands of the mob during the Nika crisis. Within a year he was back, and for eight more years pursued policies which earned him the execration of the masses and Procopius' indictment as "the worst scoundrel in the world." His somewhat childish ambition to become emperor brought about his downfall. He was tricked into implicating himself in a fictitious plot to overthrow the emperor, and even though there was no question of his guilt, Justinian did not have him executed. He simply made him a deacon. After this, if John still had a future, it would be in the Church.

That Justinian placed such enormous responsibilities in the hands of so unscrupulous and tyrannical an administrator as John the Cappadocian was not the result of his indifference to good government. A sweeping reform of the bureaucracy was out of the question, had he dreamed of that possibility. But he did give earnest thought to increasing its efficiency and its sensitivity to the needs of his subjects. In an effort to reduce corruption, he delegated to bishops the responsibility of checking the conduct of provincial governors. The latter he held responsible for the activities of the tax collectors. He reduced the number of civil servants, abolished the sale of offices, and raised salaries. Among his reforms of the judiciary were laws aimed at expediting justice and at placing it within easier reach of the poorer classes. He combined the codification of the law with a reform of the law schools, which was a reform of great importance to his government since these law schools had for their purpose, not so much the education of trained men to handle the civil disputes of the citizenry, but rather that of civil servants to administer their responsibilities with efficiency and justice. So he instructed the imperial lawyers "to regard the population paternally, to protect them against injustice, to take no bribes, and to show themselves equitable in their judgments."

Despite the bitterness some of his policies and the harsh policies of his officials engendered, Justinian died a natural death. The few minor plots against his life were inconsequential. One problem to which he might have given more thought was that of his succession. He had no sons, only nephews and cousins. His failure to nominate a successor has been attributed to his fear less the heir apparent seek to anticipate his succession, also to his inability to choose between two Justins, one his nephew, the other his cousin (once removed). Theodora favored the first Justin, his nephew, and arranged to have him marry her niece Sophia. When Justinian died on 14 November 565, this nephew Justin succeeded without opposition.

Harun al-Rashid

Harun al-Rashid was the fifth of the Abbasid caliphs. His great-uncle Abu al-Abbas had overthrown the once powerful Umayyad dynasty that had ruled mighty Islam for almost a hundred years, and in A.D. 750 replaced it with his own more illustrious Abbasid dynasty. A Westerner living in Paris at the time, if he heard of the revolution, would have been little concerned. To the followers of the Prophet, however, the effects would prove significant. The upheaval would mean the shifting of the religious and political center of the empire from Damascus in Syria to Baghdad in Iraq, where Persian influence would replace the Arabic as the dominant force. With this change would shortly come a gradual easing of the moral injunctions of the Koran concerning drink, music, and art. More ominous for the future of Islam would be the progressive loosening of the ties of empire and a weakening of Islamic solidarity that were destined to continue until the dissolution of the empire. The Abbasid caliphate would usher in, on the other hand, the most brilliant cultural age the Western world had witnessed since the brightest days of ancient Greece and Rome.

This cultural splendor is what the ordinary reader remembers about the Abbasids, and when he recalls this brilliance the name of Harun al-Rashid immediately comes to mind. Harun was not the most powerful of the Abbasid caliphs; that distinction probably belongs to his grandfather al-Mansur. Some scholars might even question the tradition of singling out Harun's reign as representing the apogee of Abbasid culture inasmuch as Baghdad probably harbored a larger galaxy of scholars and artists during the reign of his son al-Mamun. Yet where only students of Islamic history know of al-Mansur and al-Mamun, every reader of the Arabian Nights stirs at the mention of Harun al-Rashid since many of the amusing episodes in those exciting tales presumably took place in the Baghdad of his day. Harun may himself have been a partner in one or the other of these escapades.

Harun al-Rashid was born in 763, the second son of al-Mahdi (775–85) by his favorite wife al-Khaysuran. Al-Mahdi's father was the caliph al-Mansur (754–75) mentioned above, who was the brother of Abu al-Abbas, the founder of the Abbasid dynasty. The young and beautiful al-Khaysuran had been brought to al-Mahdi's harem as a Berber slave, but when the boy Harun was twelve years old al-Mahdi gave the woman her freedom and married her. That al-Khaysuran was but a concubine when she bore Harun did not disqualify him from consideration for the succession, although first in line was his older brother al-Hadi. As the boys grew up, both al-Mahdi and al-Khaysuran came to have a greater attachment for Harun and even sought to persuade al-Hadi to surrender his prior claim to the throne.

Little is known of Harun's youth apart from the fact that his upbringing was entrusted to Yahya ibn Barmak. The selection of Yahya for this important responsibility was not unexpected since the long faithful service of the family of the Barmakids to the dynasty had gained them the esteem and confidence of the preceding Abbasid caliphs. The Barmakid family hailed from the city of Balkh in northern Afghanistan where Yahya's grandfather had served as high priest (*barmak*) in the Buddhist monastery located there. Yahya's father Khalid had been one of the earliest supporters of the Abbasid cause, and Abu al-Abbas upon his accession had assigned him such broad powers that one chronicler refers to Khalid as a vizier (chief minister). So close had the families become that the wife of the caliph nursed Khalid's daughter, his wife giving her breast in turn to the daughter of the caliph. Khalid continued to fill important posts during the reigns of al-Mansur and al-Mahdi, although there were occasional intervals when he was out of favor.

In 778 Yahya, the son of Khalid, became Harun's tutor and secretary and accompanied the young man on his first military campaign. The most successful of these campaigns was that of 782 when al-Mahdi sent Harun on an expedition against the Byzantine empire in order to avenge a recent defeat. Some 50,000 Greeks fell in the fighting, and so gratified was al-Mahdi over Harun's victory that he bestowed upon him the title of al-Rashid, meaning "the upright" or "the follower of the right path," appointed him governor of the western provinces, and named him his second in succession to the throne. Harun's success and growing popularity prompted his father to apply new pressure on the elder son al-Hadi to waive his right of succession. Upon al-Hadi's refusal to do so, al-Mahdi marched against him with his army, but died before he reached him.

Rumor had it that he had eaten a poisoned pear one of his slave girls had prepared for another of his concubines.

This was the most critical moment in Harun's life. His brother al-Hadi was caliph, and if the past history of the caliphate provided any lessons it was that the lives of close relatives who might threaten the throne were apt to be snuffed out. The temptation must have been great for Harun to take over command of his father's army and march against his brother, as his friends warned him to do, in order to forestall what they insisted would be his inevitable death. His father's troops were also demanding that he do this. His tutor Yahya counseled otherwise. He urged Harun rather to send al-Hadi the imperial seal and scepter, which Harun did, while he himself raised funds to pay off the mutinous soldiers.

For the moment al-Hadi appeared content. He did not molest Harun, although he shunted his mother al-Khaysuran off to the women's quarters and warned his courtiers to stay away from her. Then in a few months al-Hadi's conduct took an ominous turn. He announced to his court that he planned to set aside Harun's right of succession in favor of his son Djafar. All his counselors and high officials endorsed his proposal with the exception of Yahya, who objected strenuously and was slapped into prison for his obstinacy. On the advice of Yahya, Harun took himself off to the desert, ostensibly on a hunting trip, in order to be out of the way. Events were rapidly coming to a head. On the night that Yahya was to have been executed on al-Hadi's orders, he himself unexpectedly died, that is, unexpectedly to all but his mother and her accomplices. For it appears reasonably certain that his mother, al-Khaysuran, embittered over her seclusion and fearful for Harun's life, had persuaded a number of al-Hadi's slave girls to smother him in his pillows. Harun succeeded without incident.

Harun, just twenty-five, inaugurated what tradition records as one of the most brilliant reigns in the history of kings. What kind of a man was Harun? Was he the charming and princely caliph of the Arabian Nights whose enormous power was matched only by his fabulous wealth and whose harem was filled with girls as numerous as the stars and more ravishingly beautiful than the moon? Part of this picture is true. Contemporary poets and chroniclers extolled Harun's might and munificence, and while no contemporary writer has left an exact number of the female population of his harem, it may have numbered a thousand. The court historians speak of his nocturnal revelries when, despite Koranic prohibitions, wine flowed freely to lighten the hearts of the dancers and the bowstrings of the musicians. The Arabian Nights introduce Djafar, the son of Yahya his adviser, as Harun's favorite companion in these revels, and the probable truth of these stories is borne out by more prosaic sources. That Harun even disguised himself on occasion and roamed the streets and bazaars of Baghdad after nightfall is also true. One may assume that it was not only the novelty of this kind of adventure that prompted the caliph to make such nocturnal expeditions, but more sober motives as well, such as the hope of picking up information about the views of his subjects or the plans of his enemies. Incidentally, if Harun never slept as the saying went, it was revelry, not study or work as in the case of Justinian, that kept him awake.

Ibn Khaldun, the most distinguished of Islamic historians, provides a rare view of Harun as something other than a caliph, a general, or devotee of pleasure. In his discourse on education he introduces as one of the best methods of instruction the directions Harun gave the tutor of his son al-Amin. The tutor was to keep his charge well in hand and school him in the virtue of obedience; to teach him to read the Koran and instruct him in the Sunnah; to teach him history, the art of composing verse, and of speaking well in public. Among his responsibilities was that of teaching the boy rules of good breeding; in fact, he must be training the boy in something useful at all times, never permitting his instruction to become so onerous as to repel his pupil, yet never so lenient as to breed in him a love of leisure. If his charge responded well to gentle instruction, so much the better, otherwise he was to use firmness and even harshness.

Among his people Harun had the reputation of being a devout Moslem. Five times daily he prayed, as the Prophet had prescribed; in fact, contemporary writers say he spent some three or four hours each day in the recitation of his prayers and in the performance of one hundred prostrations. The extent of his almsgiving was equally impressive. He is said to have dispensed 1000 silver dirhams (more than $200) every day among the poor of Baghdad, not to speak of his benefactions elsewhere. Ten times he led the great pilgrimage from Baghdad to the holy city of Mecca, and on each occasion took with him hundreds of indigent pilgrims who could never have made the trip otherwise. During those years when he failed to go on the pilgrimage—Ibn Khaldun says he fought the infidel during these off years—he assisted hundreds of priests and theologians to make the journey.

This pilgrimage was no easy trip. It involved riding some twelve hundred miles on the back of a camel through the blistering heat of wind-swept deserts. Earlier caliphs including Harun's father had attempted to reduce the hardships of the journey by setting up inns, improving the trails, and building reservoirs, and to this same end Harun also expended considerable effort. His principal undertaking was the construction of a large aqueduct to bring water into Mecca which he named after his favorite wife Zubaydah. Harun also receives credit for having introduced the practice of each year providing a new covering of costly material for the Kaaba in Mecca. The Kaaba was the holiest spot in the Islamic world. In pre-Islamic centuries it housed the many idols that helped attract thousands of pilgrims to Mecca each spring during the sacred period of truce. Mohammed destroyed these images when he occupied Mecca in 630, but the Kaaba itself he retained, as well as the sacred black stone imbedded in one of its four walls which, according to tradition, God had given to Abraham.

Despite Harun's manifold acts of piety, certain writers remained skeptical of the sincerity of his faith. They point to the seven wives he had, three beyond the four the Koran permitted, the graven images of birds, beasts, and men in the palace, and the wine and music that enlivened the nightly revels in which the caliph participated. All these practices had drawn the Prophet's denunciation. However, Ibn Khaldun comes to Harun's defense. He insists that Harun never became drunk from wine since the drink that he imbibed was but the juice of dates, raisins, or grapes—nabidh it was called, prepared by soaking these fruits in water and allowing the juice to ferment slightly. According to Ibn Khaldun, one school of Moslem jurisprudence had declared such drink permissible, and for this reason he has only contempt for those men who would malign Harun on this score. Those writers who speak of the caliph's winebibbing and his getting drunk in the company of boon companions, he says, are only to be despised since Harun faithfully fulfilled the requirements of religion and justice incumbent upon caliphs.

Modern historians do not share the loyal Ibn Khaldun's convictions concerning the sobriety of Harun. Some doubt also lingers in their minds about the caliph's observance of the harsh fasting required during the month of Ramadan, partly because no mention is made of this by contemporaries who do commend Harun for his praying, his almsgiving, and his pilgrimages. During Ramadan all sensual gratification was proscribed during the daylight hours; in the words of the Prophet from the moment "the white thread becometh distinct to you from the black thread" until nightfall. This was a truly severe fast. Not only was the good Moslem required to eschew all food during those long hours, but drink as well, in fact any kind of satisfaction, whatever its nature, that might gratify the senses. Scrupulous Moslems even refused to swallow saliva. In view of the liberty Harun took with other moral injunctions of the Koran and his preoccupation for so many years with the pleasures of the harem, it is not easy to conceive of his having observed this rigorous regimen during the daylight hours for an entire month. Still Harun must have considered the preservation of orthodoxy a most sacred duty, for when he heard that a "liberal" theologian was maintaining the Koran had been created, he threatened to kill him in a way he had never yet killed any man.

In some quarters the caliph's generous alms have also failed to pass inspection. His critics affirm they came from a treasury kept brimful with harsh taxes wrung from the impoverished masses. Under the cir-cumstances, such largess involved no sacrifice. That Harun left a larger treasury than any caliph in history tends to bear out this fact. He may have distributed alms from political motives, that is, to gain popular support for his regime. One also hears the charge that Harun prayed customarily in the presence of his subjects, that his devotions were aimed more at edifying them than at pleasing Allah. That the poets and other sycophants about the palace magnified Harun's virtues is what one would expect, nor would these writers leave any doubt in the minds of their audience or readers concerning the caliph's sincerity. Yet it is safest to let Allah judge what motivation inspired Harun's piety. Suffice it for the modern statistically minded world to know that if one added up the number of hours the caliph spent during the twenty-three years of his reign at prayer or on his pilgrimages, they would total a full three years!

Harun was rapacious. He could not have been otherwise and have amassed the enormous sums he expended on alms, on extravagant living, and on wars, and still have left a well-filled treasury when he died. Apart from heavy imposts with which he permitted his governors to oppress his people, he was not above seizing the properties of wealthy men which he coveted. He had the governor of Khurasan brought to Baghdad on a camel, without saddle or protection against the blazing sun. The governor's only offense was his great wealth which the caliph wanted. When al-Mansur's nephew died, he promptly seized his huge fortune even though closer relatives than himself had better claims to it. Harun on occasion mixed treachery with his rapacity. In 792 when returning from the pilgrimage he learned that an Alid leader, Yahya Abdullah, had raised the banner of revolt in Deilem. Harun sent a large army under al-Fadl, the governor of Persia, against him, but al-Fadl needed nothing but diplomacy and rich gifts to convince the rebel to submit. If the caliph would grant him a safe conduct, Yahya Abdullah would be pleased to come to Baghdad to discuss his grievance. Harun gave the rebel his solemn promise of safety and confirmed it with an official letter. Then after feting the rebel for a few days, he pretended to find a flaw in the safe conduct, had him thrown into jail, and confiscated his property.

Harun was guilty of acts of cruelty, even savagery. Perhaps his greatest cruelty was that of permitting his governors to fleece his subjects just so long as they handed over his share. Single acts of savagery mar the greater part of his reign. Particularly vicious was his last act. He ordered the innocent brother of a rebellious chieftain in Khurasan seized, called in a butcher, and then had him cut off the joints of his fingers and toes, then hands and feet, one by one, until the poor man expired. Harun witnessed this barbarity from his deathbed.

THE BARMAKIDS

The act of Harun which most dramatically reveals Harun's cruelty was his treatment of the Barmakids, of Yahya and his two sons al-Fadl and Djafar. Harun inherited Yahya from his father. Yahya had served him first as tutor, then counselor, and no caliph had ever had so loyal and prudent an adviser. Had it not been for Yahya's counsel, Harun might never have become caliph. This much Harun himself admitted. "My dear father," he told Yahya upon his accession, "it is through the blessings and the good fortune which attend you and through your excellent management that I am now seated on this throne; so, I confide to you the direction of affairs." With that Harun handed to Yahya his signet ring and made him his vizier. The title "father" with which Harun addressed Yahya expressed more than the filial respect he owed the older man. Yahya's son al-Fadl was Harun's foster brother. He had been suckled by Harun's mother while Yahya's wife in turn had nursed Harun. So close were the two families.

Actually Yahya served Harun as much as father as he did as vizier.

In the judgment of Ibn Khallikan, the greatest biographer in Islamic history, Yahya was "perfect in talent, judgment, and noble qualities." Ibn Khallikan records a number of incidents that illustrate the wisdom of Yahya and his paternal interest in the development of Harun's character as caliph. One day Harun and Yahya were out riding when a man stopped before them and announced, "My mule is dead." Whereupon Harun turned to one of his attendants and directed, "Let five hundred dirhams (about $50) be given him." Yahya must have made a sign of disapproval when he heard Harun give the order, for when the man had ridden off, Harun turned to him and asked, "Father, you made me a sign about something and I do not understand what it meant." Yahya replied: "The mention of so small a sum as that should never proceed from your lips. A person of your rank should say: five thousand or ten thousand." This struck Harun as a preposterous sum to give for a single mule, so he asked Yahya, "And when a demand such as that is made to me, what shall I answer?" To which Yahya answered, "You must then say simply, 'Buy him a mule.' "

Ibn Khaldun has this story to tell of Yahya's wisdom. Harun was once minded to demolish the great palace of Chosroes in Ctesiphon, but Yahya discouraged him, pointing out that to leave such an impressive structure stand would provide future generations constant proof of the might of his forefathers who had been able to subjugate a people capable of erecting so immense a building. Despite this most commendable advice Harun proceeded to have the building razed, only to learn to his chagrin that the building defied pickaxe, fire, and other methods his workmen applied. Whereupon fearful of the humiliation that would be his now for having failed to bring down this proud monument of a non-Arab people, he again came to Yahya for advice. This time Yahya urged him to continue his efforts to raze the building at all costs, for otherwise men would tell of the Commander of the Faithful, the ruler of the Arabs, who was unable to tear down something that non-Arabs had built. We are told that the damaged but proud monument continued to remind Harun of his mistake as long as he lived.

For seventeen years Yahya and his sons al-Fadl and Djafar administered the affairs of the Abbasid empire. As personal representative of the caliph, the father Yahya exercised what amounted to unlimited authority. Already before Harun's accession, Yahya had governed the western provinces of the empire in his name. When Harun succeeded as caliph he entrusted him forthwith with the general supervision of the government throughout the empire and bestowed upon him the office of vizier. After a few years Yahya took his sons into the administration, and so much did these three men dominate the government that some historians have identified the years from 786 until 803 as "the reign of the Barmakids." What precise powers Harun delegated to Yahya are not described other than the general responsibility "to right wrongs" in the name of the caliph, a statement that must have authorized Yahya to do what he wished. In any event he appears to have made appointments to all the higher positions in the empire as well as to many lower posts, so that the caliph's officials, as Harun was heard on occasion to complain, were actually Yahya's. Even the office of the seal that Harun had initially not entrusted to Yahya he soon surrendered to him. The signet seal that Harun had given Yahya upon his accession remained in the possession of the Barmakids until the disgrace of the family.

As his sons grew in age and maturity, the aging Yahya handed over to them more and more of the responsibilities of government. To al-Fadl, the older and more serious of the two sons, he entrusted first the governorship of the western province of Iran where he put down a revolt, then the larger province of Khurasan. This extensive province enjoyed unusual importance because of its warlike people and its location which controlled the roads to the eastern and northwestern reaches of the empire. Al-Fadl not only pacified the country but recruited a large native army, part of which he sent to Baghdad, perhaps to impress the caliph with his loyalty and efficiency. When Yahya, the father, retired to Mecca in 797, al-Fadl appears to have assumed his duties as vizier.

Meantime the other son, Djafar, had remained at Baghdad where he became the caliph's constant companion in both his serious moments as well as his revelries. Of him Ibn Khallikan writes: "In the high rank which he attained and the great power he wielded, in loftiness of spirit and in the esteem and favor shown him by the caliph, he stood without a rival. His disposition was generous, his looks encouraging, his demeanor kind; but his liberality and munificence, the richness and the prodigality of his donations, are too well known to require mention."

Djafar must have been a most talented young man although it is not easy to distinguish between fact and flattery in the encomia heaped upon him by the court panegyrists. Though al-Fadl was the more industrious of the two, Djafar was the more learned. Quite extraordinary was his eloquence and his command of language, while so superb was his hand in the recording of documents that to him has been traced the popular fame of the Barmakids as the founders of "the people of the pen." Djafar's legal acumen and erudition were also unusual, as were his powers of introspection. It is entirely possible that these qualities appealed as much to Harun as Djafar's willingness to join him in merrymaking. Ibn Khallikan offers the following story to demonstrate Djafar's astuteness. One day when he was with Harun he noticed how depressed the caliph appeared to be, so he asked him what troubled him. In answer Harun told him how a Jewish astrologer had just warned him that he would not live out the year. Djafar went out to look for the astrologer and when he found him he asked, "You say that the caliph is to die within the space of so many days?" "Yes," answered the Jew. "And how long are you yourself to live?" asked Djafar. "So many years," replied the other, mentioning a good large number. Djafar then returned to Harun and gave him the following advice. "Put him to death," he told Harun, "and you will be thus assured that he is equally mistaken respecting the length of your life as that of his own." Ibn Khallikan concludes his account of this incident with these words: "This advice was followed by the caliph, who then thanked Djafar for having relieved his sadness. The Jew's body was exposed on a gibbet."

For a few years Djafar took an active part in the business of government. He held the governorship of the western provinces for a time, although he appointed a deputy in his stead and remained at court. When a revolt broke out in Syria, he personally undertook its suppression, and for a few years served as governor of Khurasan. Indicative of the great trust Harun placed in Djafar was his appointment as governor of the palace bodyguard and director of the post office which invested in him control over communications and espionage, as well as the offices of the mint. Djafar's name appeared on coins struck in the year 792. Harun gave even more convincing proof of his confidence in the Barmakids when he entrusted the education of his two sons, al-Amin and al-Mamun, to al-Fadl and Djafar. Had the precedent of Harun's reign been respected, these two sons, once caliphs, would in turn have made their tutors their viziers, and the rule of the Barmakids would have continued on for at least another generation.

While this did not happen, for seventeen years the Barmakids, with Harun's blessing, continued to manage all the affairs of the empire. There appeared no reason to suppose anything would happen that might endanger their position. Djafar remained high in the caliph's favor, although his father and brother did not always approve his conduct. Al-Fadl criticized his brother for his luxurious ways; Yahya suspected his son's relations with the caliph exceeded what was proper. Djafar turned ever more to a life of pleasure. Across the Tigris, on the east bank, he erected the most magnificent palace of its day. Its complex of houses, gardens, fountains, and promenades rivaled that of Harun and came to be preferred to the caliph's own as the haunt of poets, artists, and hangers-on. In fact Djafar was warned to pretend that he had built it for al-Mamun in order to stave off Harun's envy. As years passed, the Barmakids became almost as much the subject of panegyrists for their affluence and munificence as the caliph himself. Their name, *barmaki*, retains in the modern Arab-speaking world the meaning of generous.

Then of a sudden, as though the angry jinni of Aladdin's lamp had done the deed, the Barmakids were gone. On the night of 28-29 January in the year 803, upon Harun's return from the pilgrimage to Mecca, he issued orders for the beheading of Djafar and the imprisonment of Yahya and al-Fadl. That same night Djafar was executed, his severed head was exposed on one of the principal bridges of Baghdad, while the two halves of his dismembered body were placed on the two other bridges spanning the Tigris. For three years the citizens of Baghdad passed by these grisly remains as they blackened in the sun, no doubt the more sensitive of them pondering as they went the fickleness of fortune that could in an instant bring so eminent a family down to degradation and destruction. At the end of three years Harun gave orders that what remained of Djafar be burned as ordinary refuse. Yahya spent the remaining two years of his life in prison and died at the age of seventy. Al-Fadl died the year following his father. The huge Barmakid fortune Harun kept for himself; the magnificent palace Djafar had built he gave to his favorite son al-Mamun.

Nowhere in history is there a record of a family that possessed such enormous wealth and power as the Barmakids which fell so suddenly and so unexpectedly. Precisely what precipitated the family's disgrace, no one but the caliph himself knew, and he kept the reason for his action to himself. Once when he was asked why he had ordered the execution of Djafar and the imprisonment of the other two Barmakids, he is supposed to have replied: "If this silken coat knew the reason, I would tear it into a thousand pieces," presumably to keep the matter a permanent secret. If it was a matter Harun did not wish to discuss, his reluctance to do so must have risen from remorse over what he had done. The Barmakids may have outlived their usefulness, their position and wealth may have threatened his throne, still the manner in which he had requited their long faithful service, that of Yahya in particular, was the act of a capricious tyrant.

Because Harun's contemporaries were at a loss how to explain the abrupt fall of the Barmakids, they invented a number of stories which later chroniclers introduced into their accounts for want of anything more credible. The most romantic explanation turns about the figure of Harun's favorite sister, Abbasah. Little is known of Abbasah apart from this tale other than that she had three husbands, each of whom predeceased her. This made her an unusual woman and, as might be expected, the butt of witty tongues. The most popular poet of the time, Abu Nuwas, composed a humorous satire about Abbasah wherein he proposed to the caliph that, if he had someone whom he wanted out of the way, the simplest recourse would be to have him marry his sister.

Al-Tabari, a reasonably reliable annalist, incorporates the story of Abbasah and Djafar into his chronicle of the reign, although he does not affirm that it provides the true story of what had happened. Like Herodotus, al-Tabari saw nothing amiss about entertaining his readers with anecdotes they would enjoy even though these might not be true. According to al-Tabari there was nothing Harun enjoyed so much as to be in the company of Djafar and his own sister Abbasah. Islamic conventions being what they were, such company would be difficult for him to arrange since Djafar could not have access to the women's quarters. So Harun decided to have Djafar marry Abbasah. They were to marry but only officially. It would have been demeaning to the caliph and his sister were she to become the mother of a son by a man not of royal blood. So the caliph had them marry but with the strict understanding that they were never to meet except when he was present.

This odd arrangement should make the reader suspicious, but the tale grows even more bizarre. We are told that the much-married Abbasah became so infatuated with her "husband" Djafar that she contrived, through the mother of Djafar, to sleep with him without his recognizing who she was. It happened in this way. Djafar's mother was in the habit of bringing her son a beautiful virgin every Thursday night, with whom he would sleep after first taking some *nabidh*. The mother sympathized with Abbasah's plight and one night, after Djafar had perhaps taken more *nabidh* than was good for him, she brought in the blushing bride to her unsuspecting husband, the result being that before Djafar quite realized what had been going on he found himself the father of a child by the caliph's sister. Father and mother hurried the child off to Mecca, and all might have been well had not Abbasah provoked one of the concubines in the harem by chastising her. The aggrieved girl out of spite spilled the story to Harun. Harun kept the matter to himself until he made his pilgrimage to Mecca, when he hunted up the child and could not help being struck by the resemblance between it and its parents, Djafar and Abbasah. It was then that he issued orders for Djafar's execution.

This romantic tale contains several weaknesses. Historians who lived before al-Tabari and would have known about the incident, do not refer to it, neither does the sharp-tongued Abu Nuwas include Djafar's name when listing Abbasah's three husbands. Furthermore, at the time this episode is supposed to have taken place, Abbasah was forty or more years old, old enough to have known better than to trifle with Harun's strict injunctions, even if not too old for this kind of romance. Ibn Khaldun dismisses the story as palpably untrue, for how could a descendant of such distinguished ancestors, among them the Prophet's own uncle Abbas, have done so sordid a thing! Abbasah was born to royal power, Ibn Khaldun pointed out, a blood relative of Abbas and of the Prophet himself, therefore, of one who had received direct revelations from the angels. She had also lived in an earlier age when the people of Islam were still uncorrupted by luxury and vice. If such a one, Ibn Khaldun asks, could have stooped to sin, where then can one look for chastity? Ibn Khaldun is to be commended for his loyalty.

If one accepts the view that Harun was given to fits of passion, when he would act with brutal haste, then his sudden decision to eliminate the Barmakids becomes explicable. That he executed Djafar and for three years exposed his dismembered body to ridicule suggests the possibility that some act of Djafar's had turned his fondness for the young man into venom, wherefore he ordered his execution. Since Harun could not slay the son without removing Yahya and al-Fadl from power, he had them imprisoned. There they would remain unmolested so long as the friends of the Barmakids caused no trouble; otherwise what had happened to Djafar would be their fate as well.

In sifting through the events of the years immediately preceding the fall of the Barmakids, scholars have uncovered several incidents that tend to rule out the possibility that a single act caused Harun to act so precipitately. The caliph's action may at best have been simply the abrupt carrying out of a step he had long been contemplating. It is not unreasonable to suppose that, as the years passed, he grew increasingly uncomfortable over the contrast between his own self-indulgent, sterile existence and the purposeful careers of the Barmakids who were doing his work and shouldering his responsibilities. In his twenties the pleasures of the harem, the plaudits of the masses over his triumphant progresses about the country, his pilgrimages, and his campaigns, may have satisfied him, together with the flattery of the sycophants at court. In his late thirties he may have recalled the warning counsel his father had given him against frittering his life away in sensual gratification. Before it was too late he, Harun, would put an end to his empty existence. He would be a true caliph as his father, his grandfather, and his great-uncle had been before him.

During the rule of the Barmakids Harun did not entirely ignore the affairs of state, even though he had turned their direction over to Yahya. It even appears that he did not always agree with his "father"; that Yahya's ability to rule so long was in no small measure due to the vizier's shrewdness in knowing when to bend to the caliph's often unspoken wishes. In 796 he had yielded to Harun's will and removed al-Fadl as governor of Khurasan. What Yahya was helpless to prevent was the steady rise in the caliph's favor of one Fadl ibn Rabi whom he appointed *hajib* or doorkeeper and replaced a Barmakid in so doing. That the new official joined others in poisoning the mind of the caliph against the Barmakids may be assumed. Ibn Khallikan tells how the enemies of the family kept filling Harun's ear with stories of their mistakes and misdeeds, and that it was on the occasion when a paper was put into Harun's hand describing the power of Djafar and the magnificence of his palace, greater even than those of the caliph, that Harun had decided on their liquidation.

One act of Djafar's that must have rankled in Harun's breast concerned a certain Yahya ibn Agd Allah. The latter had rebelled against the caliph, had been defeated and captured, then turned over to Djafar for safekeeping. The prisoner's cleverness proved more than a match for his captor's wit. He told Djafar that he was a relative of the Prophet, and he reminded Djafar that one day he must appear before Allah to be judged, when it would be such a comfort to have the Prophet on one's side rather than hostile. Whereupon Djafar released his prisoner without asking Harun's permission. When the caliph learned of this and pressed Djafar about the matter, the latter first denied releasing the man, then finally admitted it. Ibn Khallikan declares this was the final incident that led Harun to decide on the destruction of the Barmakids.

In 799, four years before the fall of the family, Harun removed al-Fadl from his powerful position as virtual vizier. The reason usually advanced to explain this move is Harun's disapproval of al-Fadl's pro-Alid policy (of Ali and his followers later). At the same time Harun deprived al-Fadl of all his other offices as well and left him only his appointment as tutor of his son al-Amin. It is clear, therefore, that some years before Harun's fatal move in 803, the Barmakids had not only surrendered a large portion of their power but that their ability to retain what they still held was in jeopardy.

One reads of charges of impiety against the Barmakids, but they can be discounted. No greater credence need be given the charge that what antagonized Harun above all else was the patronage that the Barmakids had showered upon Iranian poets and artists as opposed to Syrian and Arab. Perhaps the wise observation of one Said ibn Salim on the fall of the Barmakids provides all the explanation that is necessary. "Of a truth," he said, "they committed nothing to warrant al-Rashid's conduct toward them; but the day of their prosperity and power had been long, and that which continues long becomes irksome. There were persons and those among the best of men, who were fatigued with the length of the caliph Omar's reign, although the like of it was never seen for justice, security, wealth, and victories; they also bore with impatience the sway of Othman; and both were murdered. Besides, al-Rashid saw that generosity had become their habitude; that the public were loud in their praise, and that men's hopes were fixed on them and not on him. Less than this suffices to excite the jealousy of princes; and so al-Rashid conceived ill-will against them, wreaked his vengeance on them, and tried to find out faults with which he might reproach them."

Ibn Khaldun attributed the fall of the Barmakids to their immense power and to their retention of tax revenues which they used to finance their munificence and expenditures. When Harun wanted even a small sum of money, he could not get it, so writes Ibn Khaldun. Still this is scarcely reasonable, for one rule the older Yahya at least must have appreciated was that of keeping Harun happy at all costs. More credible is Ibn Khaldun's statement that the Barmakids were filling all offices with their own children. All twenty-five of the highest posts in the palace were held by members of the family. It is easy to understand why men looked to them for advancement rather than to the caliph. Their munificence matched that of the caliph and gained them as many friends, which was doubly dangerous conduct since it angered the jealous caliph already suspicious of where they were getting the money to finance their largess. Gradually other men who were envious of the Barmakids found a receptive caliph to listen to their insinuations that the Barmakids were using the caliph's favor to grow strong and popular. Even poets composed verses aimed at arousing the caliph's anger, one such poem referring to the important person who never seemed to act on his own. And so finally reaching a point where he could suffer no more rivalry, Harun ordered the Barmakids destroyed. Ibn Khaldun ends his account of their fall with the pious observation: "God is our refuge from men's desire for power and from misfortune."

Harun may have regretted his destruction of the Barmakids. Some time after the incident he is supposed to have declared: "There were people who impelled us to punish our ablest and most faithful advisers, and they made us believe that they themselves were capable of replacing them; but when we did what they wanted, they were not of the least use to us." Al-Mamun, Harun's son, had kind words for the family. "Yahya . . . and his sons had none to equal them in ability," he declared, "in elegance of language, in liberality and in bravery."

MILITARY HISTORY OF HARUN'S REIGN

The brilliance of Harun al-Rashid's reign owes little to his military exploits. This is no criticism of the caliph. The empire of Islam had long reached the limits set by nature, which were the semi-arid and generally flat lands to the south and east of the Mediterranean. Conquest westward was out of the question since a powerful and hostile caliphate lay entrenched in Spain. Mountains and the enormous distances from Baghdad discouraged any extension of the empire to the east. The Prophet himself had laid the foundation of the immense empire of Islam. Its origins reach back to Mohammed's sojourn in Medina when he forced Christian and Jewish groups in the neighborhood to accept his rule. His next move, after his triumphant occupation of Mecca in 630, was to negotiate treaties with those tribes of Arabia who recognized Mecca as their holy city and regularly visited it on pilgrimage. These tribes appear to have accepted Mohammed's suzerainty without much hesitation, promised not to attack other members of the growing Islamic family, and agreed to pay the *zakah,* a kind of poor tax. With more distant tribes the Prophet negotiated treaties of friendship.

Mohammed's unexpected death in 632 proved near fatal to Islam's budding empire as many Bedouin tribes withdrew their allegiance. In keeping with Arab tradition, the treaties they had negotiated were between their chiefs and Mohammed, not between states of which the primitive Arab had no concept. Therefore, when one of the partners to such an agreement died, so did the agreement. The Prophet's successor, Abu Bakr, had to devote the two years of his caliphate to the so-called *riddah* wars, that is, wars aimed at recovering control over the tribes that had seceded. The general who deserves most credit for winning back these tribes and then extending Islam's control over the entire peninsula was Khalid. His successes in Arabia whetted his army's appetite for more conquests and he moved northward into Syria. In 634 his troops sacked Damascus and two years later destroyed a powerful Byzantine army at Yarmuk. This victory opened the way to the occupation of Syria and Palestine, including the city of Jerusalem. In 637 Khalid destroyed a large Persian army at Kadesiya, captured Ctesiphon, the Persian capital, and overran Iraq. Shortly after the once formidable Persian empire passed into history, while the badly shaken Byzantine empire pulled back its frontiers to Asia Minor and held on desperately to the mountain ranges that guarded that country. Too late did Byzantium and Persia realize that centuries of exhausting warfare against one another would leave them easy prey to semi-civilized hordes out of a part of the world they had hardly known existed. Still it was not only Byzantine and Persian exhaustion that opened the way to Islamic conquerors. Had these two empires not taxed their peoples to a point of rebellion and had they not forced them to accept religious practices and beliefs they did not want, they would not have found the masses in the lands overrun by Khalid so willing to exchange masters.

After Syria the Arabs pressed on into Egypt which fell with comparative ease, so hated was Byzantine rule. Possession of Alexandria led to the construction of a Moslem fleet, after which Cyprus and Crete and then Constantinople itself came under attack. The massive siege of 716-17 came within a whisker of taking the city, although of the attacking Moslem fleet that took part in this engagement it is said that only five of the 1800 ships involved survived the battle and the storms that followed. Not until the fifteenth century did Islam ever again attempt a naval attack on the great city, and only once until that century did a land army catch a glimpse of Constantinople, and that was under Harun. Meantime Arab power had rolled westward over Cyrenaica and Tripoli into Spain in 711, under command of Tariq who gave his name to Gibraltar, and spilled through the Pyrenees and surged northward into France until stopped by Charles Martel and his Franks at Tours in 732.

Even less resistance did Moslem power encounter in its march eastward through Persia until shortly after 643 when it reached the frontiers of India. Within a hundred years of the death of the Prophet, a new and gigantic empire had come into existence, one that stretched from the Atlantic to the Indus and from Turkestan to the Sudan. Mighty indeed was the arm of Allah.

Before the stupendous achievement of several of the caliphs who preceded Harun the military annals of his reign appear undistinguished. Harun's introduction to war came as a youth in 779 when he accompanied his father al-Mahdi on a raid into Asia Minor against Byzantine power. Upon the urging of Harun's tutor, Yahya, al-Mahdi permitted the young man to lead an expedition of his own, a mission he performed so successfully that his father entrusted him with official command of the western provinces. Fighting continued spasmodically for several years until 782 when Harun took a large army, perhaps as many as 100,000 men, all the way to the Bosporus near Chrysopolis just across from Constantinople. So heavy were the losses he inflicted upon the Byzantine armies that the empress Irene, acting regent at the time, sued for peace and agreed to a heavy annual tribute and to bear the expenses of Harun and his army's march back to Baghdad. It was on this occasion that the proud father al-Mahdi bestowed upon his son the title "al-Rashid" and designated him next in succession after his older brother al-Hadi.

Harun's experience as a young man convinced him of the importance of maintaining a strong line of defense against Byzantium. Once he became caliph he created a new military office whose principal duty was to maintain a powerful system of fortresses to guard Islamic territories in Syria and Asia Minor. Harun placed a Turkish general in charge of the operation with headquarters at Tarsus, whence he directed the construction of the necessary fortifications. In 790 Harun's admirals made successful raids on Crete and Cyprus. Six years later the caliph himself led an army into Asia Minor, and although suffering several setbacks, won victories at Ephesus and Ancyra. Then learning of the palace struggle in Constantinople between Constantine VI and his mother Irene, he pressed forward toward the city without meeting much opposition. What facilitated his progress was the treasonable conduct of Irene, if one may believe the charge, that she bribed the imperial troops to give ground to Harun in order to discredit her son. Harun could not exploit his opportunity since Turks and Khazars elected to invade Armenia just at this critical juncture. Though the generals Harun sent north were able to drive the invaders out of Armenia, the caliph decided against remaining in Anatolia for the winter. He negotiated a new treaty with the momentarily triumphant Irene which provided for a four-year truce and a still heavier tribute.

Irene was able to hold on until 802, when Nicephorus I banished her to the island of Lesbos, repudiated her treaty with Harun, and reopened hostilities. Al-Tabari gives a short but colorful account of what next transpired. "And in this year [803] the Romans broke the peace made between his predecessor and the Moslems, and refused what their previous king had undertaken to pay. . . . And it is recorded that when Nicephoros became king and the Romans were confirmed in allegiance to him, he wrote to al-Rashid: 'The queen [Irene] considered you as a rook and herself as a pawn. That pusillanimous female submitted to pay a tribute, the double of which she ought to have exacted from the barbarians. Restore therefore the fruits of your injustice, or abide the determination of the sword.' And when al-Rashid read the letter, his wrath was roused so much that no one could look at him, much less speak to him; and his household withdrew, fearing to increase it by any speech or action on their part; and the wazir was in doubt whether to give him advice or to leave him to his own deliberations without him. And he called for an inkpot and wrote on the back of the letter: 'In the name of the most merciful God, Harun al-Rashid, commander of the faithful, to Nicephorus, the Roman dog. I have read your letter, O thou son of an unbelieving mother. Thou shalt not hear, thou shalt behold my reply. Salaam.' "

Whereupon Harun marched against Nicephorus and forced him to ask for terms which involved a still heavier tribute than that Irene had been forced to accept. Some time later Nicephorus, whose reign consisted principally of blunders and calamities, attacked again when Harun was off on a pilgrimage. Even though winter had set in, Harun marched into Asia Minor with a huge army of 135,000 men, inflicted heavy losses on the Byzantine armies, and captured Heraclea and Tyana

(806). All Nicephorus could do was ask for terms. This time Harun was not satisfied with simply a heavier tribute. As a mark of personal humiliation he obliged Nicephorus and his family to pay a capitation tax as though they were no better than his subjects. In subsequent fighting, however, Nicephorus was not always the defeated party, so that despite extensive campaigning, Harun did not achieve any permanent success against Byzantium. (In 811 when Nicephorus was killed in battle with the Bulgars, the Bulgar leader Krum had his skull encased in gold. Later when Byzantine envoys came to visit him, he made them drink toasts of friendship from the grizzly cup.)

Harun might have been more successful against Byzantium had it not been for revolts that broke out intermittently during the greater part of his reign. The task of maintaining control of so far-flung an empire as Islam's required the constant attention of a strong military ruler which Harun was not. He was fortunate in suffering no greater losses than he did. These losses consisted of two provinces in Africa. The first serious revolt was that which erupted in Deilem to which reference has been made. Al-Fadl marched against the leader of that rebellion with an army of 50,000 men and managed to effect his submission, not by force of arms, rather through negotiation and a promise of a safe conduct to Baghdad. Though Harun's violation of the safe conduct left a blot on his career, it did end the revolt.

Less successful was Harun's handling of a revolt that broke out in Tunis. The leader was one Idris who had fled to Tunis from Arabia when an Alid revolt there had misfired. Idris was one of the few leaders who escaped the vengeance of Harun's brother al-Hadi who put down that uprising. When Harun succeeded after al-Hadi's death, he proceeded with plans to invade Tunis, but Yahya discouraged him. The disturbed condition of the empire, he advised him, made a campaign in so distant a province a hazardous undertaking. It was decided that poison would do the job more cheaply and just as effectively. Harun and Yahya were correct as far as Idris was concerned, but when he died of poisoning, his son took over command. Harun decided against further measures and in time came to accept the permanent loss of the province. This was the first area to join the caliphate of Cordova in repudiating the rule of the Abbasids.

The next part of the empire to witness a revolt was Nasilin on the Upper Tigris. A local chieftain by name Walid ibn Tarif organized a revolt and ravaged the neighboring provinces of Armenia, Azerbaijan, and northern Mesopotamia. The first two armies Harun sent against the rebels suffered defeat, whereupon he dispatched Yezid whom he considered his ablest general. It seems that Yezid went about his assignment halfheartedly until he received a warning message from Harun, when he organized a massive attack and destroyed the rebels. So grateful was Harun for the assistance he was convinced Allah had given him, that he performed both the Lesser and Greater Pilgrimage and visited the holy stations on foot.

In 796 revolt broke out in the province of Mosul on the Upper Tigris. Since this was just north of Baghdad, Harun took the field in person and had no great difficulty in capturing the capital Mosul. He demolished its walls and only with difficulty was dissuaded from razing the city itself. The governor of the province he had executed for his negligence in permitting the revolt to take place. The following year a revolt broke out among the Berbers in distant Kairawan just south of Tunis. Harun realized the gravity of a revolt in a province so distant from Baghdad, adjacent as it was to rebellious Tunis, and peopled by tribesmen as fiercely independent as the Arabs. For these Berbers, like the ancient Arabs, were nomadic and depended upon their horses and the desert to protect them from would-be conquerors. To defeat them was not difficult, but to conquer them was well nigh impossible. Despite some successes by Harthama, Harun's general, permanent success was out of the question. In the end Harun was forced to accept the province's autonomy. Even this easy limitation on their freedom, involving little more than the payment of the alms tax, the Berbers found oppressive after a few years, and a second province was lost to the empire of Harun.

The most serious revolt of Harun's reign erupted in 806 in the important province of Khurasan which lay southeast of the Caspian. The leader of the revolt was Rafi ibn Laith who succeeded in inducing Samarkand and the tribes of Transoxiana to join him. In the administration of these outlying provinces the caliph had been particularly negligent in checking the rapaciousness of his governors. Most notorious was Ali ibn Isa, the governor of Khurasan, against whose tyranny the people had sent repeated complaints to Harun. Harun had indeed investigated Ali and had visited him in person, but he had permitted himself to be deceived and confirmed him in his office. Now as a first step to putting down the revolt, he sent his general Harthama who arrested Ali, proclaimed himself governor instead, and promised the people honest and just rule for the future. Some of the people accepted Harthama's assurances; most of them did not, and the revolt raged for several years without much promise of success for the government. Finally in 809 Harun, though in poor health, determined to lead an army into the area. On the march his condition steadily deteriorated and when he reached Tus he took to his bed. There he died on 24 March 809 at the age of forty-five. He was buried at Tus. The cause of his death may have been cancer, knowledge of which he had been able to keep from his people.

According to al-Tabari, Harun had sent to the king of Hindustan for his famous physician Manka, once he realized the seriousness of his condition, and as a result of this physician's ministrations, the caliph's health had momentarily improved. Then when he reached Tus, it worsened again but Manka and Harun's private physician, Jibril, could not agree on the proper medicine. Jibril got his way but a mistake was made—exactly what kind of a mistake Tabari does not say—and Harun, aware of his critical condition, gave orders to have Jibril executed on the spot. Jibril managed to persuade the caliph to wait until the following day with the execution: if he had not improved by morning the caliph could do with him as he wished. Manka smiled at these words, for both he and Jibril knew that Harun would not live through the night. This time the physicians had diagnosed correctly.

The armies of Harun were in the main equipped and organized after the manner of those of Byzantium. The most formidable element was the cavalry which wore helmets and breastplates and carried long lances and battleaxes. It is a curious fact that troops of the area have continued to use, to the present day, the plain, rounded saddles which Harun's soldiers used a thousand years ago. A second group of troops consisted of archers and a third of infantry which carried spears, swords, and shields. An important service the latter branch provided was that of leading the attack on fortifications. Somewhat paralleling the Greek fire that the Byzantine navy had used against Moslem ships to thwart an attack on Constantinople in 675 was the naphtha that a group of "naphtha-throwers" hurled at the enemy. A company of such specialists was attached to each corps of archers. They wore fireproof suits to protect themselves from the incendiaries they threw. Heavy artillery included catapults, mangonels, and battering rams. These were transported on the backs of camels, as were also litters and equipment intended for the care of the wounded. Harun is credited with having introduced both the naphtha-throwers and the hospital units.

The armies of Harun also adopted the same system of organization as used by Byzantium. Every ten men were commanded by an officer called an *arif*, every fifty men by a *khalifah*, every hundred by a *qa'id*. A general (*amir*) commanded a group of ten battalions or a corps of 10,000 men. It was rare for corps of this size to be maintained except in wartime, although large armies could be raised within short notice because of the practice of many chieftains of having groups of warriors always ready for raiding. Volunteers might also be recruited from among the townspeople and peasants. All army personnel were relatively well paid, which helps explain the amazing loyalty of Islamic armies. What made the Moslems formidable enemies were their numbers, their mobility, and their high morale. So long as the army continued successful, it was almost irresistible. Once slowed or defeated, however, there was ever present the danger that groups would pull out since for many of them loot had been their principal objective for fighting. Since the era of easy and spectacular victories was long past before Harun's day, Byzantine armies had less difficulty holding their own during his reign than during the earlier years of Islamic history.

EARLY HISTORY OF THE CALIPHATE

The expansion of Islam following the death of Mohammed appears all the more phenomenal in view of the bitter internal struggle that frequently raged over the office of caliph (deputy or successor). Mohammed had made no provision for a successor, neither did he leave a son. Still even had he sired a son, that may have done little good since Mohammed's position had been unique. He was Allah's Prophet. No one else, not even a son, could have claimed that distinction. Fortunately for the success of the new faith, the leaders of Mecca had little difficulty agreeing on the aged Abu Bakr, the Prophet's father-in-law, who had on occasion led in prayer when Mohammed was absent. When Abu Bakr died two years later (634), Umar succeeded, the man who had probably been already exercising actual authority. Umar's reign witnessed the period of greatest expansion. After a reign of ten years he was murdered by a Persian slave (644), when he was succeeded by Uthman. Now serious dissension appeared since Uthman was a member of the Meccan aristocracy which had earlier opposed the Prophet.

The enemies of Uthman also charged him with cowardice and with filling all the higher posts in the administration with members of his own group. He was cut down in 656 after a rule of twelve years, and Mohammed's first cousin and son-in-law, Ali, succeeded. Ali had married Fatima, the only child of the Prophet who had outlived him. Despite Ali's association with the family of Mohammed, his rule proved unacceptable to many who had ambitions of their own. When he replaced Muawiyah, governor of Syria and a nephew of the murdered Uthman, civil war broke out, and only ended in 661 with his own murder and the emergence of Muawiyah as caliph.

Muawiyah founded what is known as the Umayyad dynasty, the most powerful in Islamic history. He moved the capital from Medina to the more centrally located city of Damascus which was better suited to serve as the administrative heart of an increasingly polyglot empire. In fact, during the rule of this dynasty Islam gradually lost its character as a theocracy and assumed instead most of the features of a traditional state. During the hundred years this family ruled Islam, dissatisfaction with the regime was never absent and tended to increase as time went on. There were the tribes of southern Arabia who resented their exclusion from the government and, of course, there was the continuing opposition of the followers of the murdered Ali. The greatest danger to the Umayyads came from a new dissident group, known as the *mawali* or non-Arab Moslems. They paid higher taxes than Arab Moslems, they were not permitted to marry Arab women, and they received less pay when serving in the army and a smaller share of the booty. There was finally the Abbasid faction that championed the claims to the caliphate of the line of Abbas, an uncle of the Prophet. What united these groups was their common dislike of the Arab aristocracy that dominated the empire's economy, its administration, and its religion. Black was the color of the Abbasids, and in 746 black flags of rebellion began to fly in Khurasan. From there the revolt moved westward until in August 750 the last Umayyad caliph was captured and killed, and Abu al-Abbas, the Bloodshedder (*saffah*) as he referred to himself, inaugurated the brilliant dynasty of the Abbasids. He was the great-uncle of Harun.

To make certain that there would be no restoration of Umayyad rule, Abu al-Abbas directed an intensive search for all remaining members of the family. Eighty of them had already been murdered during a banquet to which they had been invited. The chronicler tells how after the slaughter leather sheets were spread over their mangled bodies, while the Abbasid hosts continued on with their feasting, quite undisturbed by the last groans of the dying. Agents were sent about the empire to ferret out any possible survivor. Even the bodies of the long-dead Umayyad caliphs did not escape the purge. The body of one of them was given eighty lashes before being consigned to the flames. The only important member to escape was Abd al-Rahman, among whose spectacular exploits in effecting his escape was that of swimming the Euphrates to evade his pursuers. He eventually made his way to Spain where he set up an independent caliphate with Cordova as its capital.

THE GOVERNMENT OF HARUN'S EMPIRE

The change in dynasty from Umayyad to Abbasid did not greatly alter the character of the Islamic government. At its head stood the caliph who in theory still possessed the fullness of power of the Prophet over all lower officers and over the succession. Since he might have a large number of sons, some by his wives, others by concubines, the principle of succession through the eldest son was not traditional. The caliph might select a younger son or even a brother, should he deem him more competent or suitable than his firstborn. It is curious that the Abbasid caliphs in this respect faced a situation the reverse of that of the Roman emperors. These usually had not even a single son to designate as successor, while the caliphs had a superfluity from whom to choose, but the consequence in both cases was apt to be confusion. In the case of Islam, it was not unusual for a group of rebellious men to encourage the ambitions of a disgruntled son. Harun designated his oldest son al-Amin, the son of Zubaydah, as his successor, and his younger son al-Mamun whom he actually preferred, as next in line. But in designating al-Mamun also to be permanent governor of Khurasan, Harun practically invited the outbreak of civil war and the assassination of al-Amin that followed in 813. Al-Mamun designated as his successor, not his son whom the army wanted, but his brother. In the long history of the Abbasid caliphate which covered the reigns of twenty-four caliphs, in only six instances did a son succeed his father.

The highest official under the caliph was the vizier to whom the caliph might delegate the exercise of complete civil authority. The office was of Persian origin. Its appearance reflected the great increase in Persian influence that accompanied the emergence of the Abbasids and the transfer of the capital of the empire to Baghdad. The principle of entrusting such enormous authority into the hands of one official such as the vizier was unwise. It could only have worked well under the supervision of an able caliph who, rather than assume the burdens of administration himself, chose to rule through an official whose acts he kept under close scrutiny. For the temptation would be great to leave a trusted and efficient vizier pretty much to himself, as Harun had done in the case of Yahya for so many years. Had Yahya been less faithful, he might have given ear to enemies of the caliph and have quite easily effected his overthrow. What deterred viziers less loyal than Yahya from attempting such coups was the belief on the part of the masses that only the caliph and his family had the sacred blood of the Prophet in their veins, and the consequent fear of potential usurpers that the people would accept nothing less. What the vizier could do, and generally did soon after the middle of the ninth century, was to force the caliph to be content with the symbols of power and with his harem, while he himself assumed actual control of the empire. And since he could appoint all governors, judges, and generals, there was nothing to prevent his passing on his office to his son and establishing his own dynasty of viziers.

The principal ruling body of Islam was the council of state which was composed of the heads of the different departments. Harun would have been correct in considering the most important department that of finance or taxes. Revenue came in from a variety of sources. Moslems paid the *zakah,* a tax on wealth whether this consisted of arable land, stock, gold and silver, or whatever were considered productive assets. The money collected from these believers was in turn expended on other believers, that is, on the poor, on orphans, on slaves, and on the ransoming of captives. Other sources of revenue included tribute from foreign states, truce money, poll taxes from non-Moslem subjects, land taxes, and tithes upon merchandise brought into the empire by non-Moslems. Of these taxes the land tax was by far the most lucrative since Islam was essentially an agricultural state. As primitive as was the Islamic fiscal administration it would have been imprudent to depend upon more sophisticated taxes. The land tax was also the most oppressive, its exploitation a scandal on the record of the Abbasids. It was the misuse of this tax that enabled Harun to live in so grand a style, to wage expensive campaigns, and still to leave the huge sum of nine hundred million dirhams in his treasury when he died.

Besides a chancery office which had responsibilities similar to those of western states, there was the audit or accounts office, a board of officials appointed to inspect grievances, a police department, and a postal department. The inspection board reviewed complaints brought against agents employed in the executive and administrative departments of the government. Harun presided with some regularity in public audience to hear such complaints. The chief of police in Baghdad also served as commander of the royal bodyguard. His jurisdiction extended beyond the maintenance of the law to the investigation of trade practices, the payment of debts, and the punishment of the infractions of moral injunctions prescribed by the Koran. By modern standards the police of Baghdad were well paid. This was, of course, only prudent on the part of the caliph, since his own position depended in large measure on the loyalty and efficiency of these men.

The services of the postal department were intended principally for the government, although private individuals might avail themselves of these services for a sizable fee. Harun extended the facilities of the department to cover the entire empire, with hundreds of relays following well-established routes. Where water was sufficient, the ordinary conveyors were boats and mules; over the vast stretches of desert, the ubiquitous camel. Somewhat later pigeons were also recruited as carriers of information. A subsidiary service which the postal department furnished private individuals at no cost included information about the conditions of roads, the location of relay stations, and distances to various points within the empire. Not only did pilgrims find such information valuable, but travelers, explorers, and merchants as well.

What became an especially important function of the imperial post during the reigns of the first Abbasids, including Harun, was that of supplying the caliph information concerning conditions or individuals that might threaten the peace of the empire. This may actually have become the major role of the postal service as the danger of revolts increased, which it did under Harun. The title of the director of the post expresses the dual nature of his responsibilities. He was called the controller of the post and of the intelligence service. Local agents reported anything they found disturbing to the provincial postmaster, who in turn furnished the central office with information he considered significant. Harun's grandfather al-Mansur recruited merchants, peddlers, and travelers for the service, and this policy Harun continued. His son al-Mamun is said to have employed some 1700 aged women.

The Abbasids preserved in the main the division of the empire as had obtained under the Umayyads. There were some two dozen provinces which were administered by governors called *amirs,* whence the Anglicized emir. Because of the vast differences of race, nationality, even religion that existed among the peoples in the immense Islamic empire, and the tremendous distances separating outlying provinces from Baghdad, the tendency toward provincial autonomy was almost inevitable. The policy of the caliphs, and this included Harun, of leaving those governors virtually undisturbed who delivered their quota of taxes and who maintained law and order, contributed to the growth of that autonomy. The vizier appointed the provincial governors and they held office at his pleasure, subject always to the prior authority of the caliph so long as the latter retained that authority. For all the glory that is associated with the Abbasid caliphate, provincial administration did not approach in efficiency and justice that which was the glory of Rome during the first and second centuries A.D., nor did it meet the standard of that which prevailed in Byzantium.

At no place did the Islamic state provide greater evidence of its theocratic character than in the administration of justice. This was entrusted to the priestly community, with individual theologians acting as judges (*qadi*) in the provinces and as chief judges (*qadi al-quday*) in Baghdad. The first justice to receive this last title was the distinguished jurist Abu Yusuf whom Harun inherited from his father. The law that these theologians administered was the law of the Prophet, and this sufficed for the Islamic community. Like the ancient Hebrews, the Moslems recognized no separate system of civil law. For this reason the adjudication of civil disputes among non-Moslems was left to the jurisdiction of their own ecclesiastical authorities. There existed two general classes of judges, one group having final and absolute authority, the other enjoying only limited authority. The principal non-judicial responsibilities of the *qadi* of the first class included the guardianship of orphans, minors, and the feeble-minded, the administration of pious foundations, and the duty of presiding at congregational prayers on Friday.

ABBASID SOCIETY

The most notable change ushered in with the victory of the Abbasids was that affecting the ruling aristocracy of Islam. Umayyad rule had rested upon Arab leadership. The Abbasids swept this away and with it the old tribal system upon which it had rested. Nowhere was the cosmopolitan character of the new regime more evident than in the families and harems of the caliphs. The mothers of all the Umayyad caliphs but one had been Arabs, and she was a Persian princess. On the other hand, only three of the two-dozen Abbasid caliphs had free mothers. Al-Mansur's mother was a Berber slave, Harun's mother was also a slave (origin unknown), and his favorite wife Zubaydah, the mother of al-Amin, was a Persian slave. A new aristocracy gradually took form headed by the family of the caliph, his friends and favorites, with its racial or national character constantly broadened by the recruitment of new members from the bureaucracy and merchant class, and from the acceptance of the harem's offspring, whatever its origin. In only one area did the Abbasid caliphs adopt a purist policy; that was in their treatment of the members of the Hashimite tribe, the tribe from which both the Prophet and Abbas were sprung. They all received regular stipends from the treasury which enabled them to live in affluence. Still intermarriage among members of the aristocracy, regardless of racial or national strain, had the blessing of the caliph, and within a short time Persian and Turkish elements took the place of eminence that the old Arab aristocracy had held since the time of Mohammed.

At the bottom of the social ladder, except for slaves, were the non-Moslem peasants who worked the land, and casual workers who eked out an existence in the cities. Because Moslems generally avoided agricultural work as below their dignity, that occupation fell even lower in repute. Occasional Jews and Christians did rise to important posts in the bureaucracy, although this was not common. They could be found in some number in the medical profession, and it is curious that although Western Europe considered the Arab physician the best in his profession, Harun himself had a Christian doctor. In order to prevent the mingling of the faithful with the non-believers, Harun required Hebrews and Christians to wear distinctive garb, and he also forbade them to occupy buildings that might provide them a view endangering the privacy of neighboring Moslems. Once when he suffered defeat at the hands of the Byzantine army, he ordered all Christian churches in Baghdad demolished.

During the reign of Harun the slave trade continued to flourish throughout the Islamic world, although there was no longer the vast number of slaves that had glutted the markets during the peak days of expansion in the seventh century. Color was no bar to a slave's desirability, and white, black, and brown boys and girls, men and women, were readily available in the slave marts that could be found almost everywhere. Youths of both sexes brought the highest prices, while premium prices could be demanded for beautiful girls who were skilled entertainers. It was not uncommon for entrepreneurs to purchase young attractive girls and train them as singers, musicians, and dancers, when they would put them back on the market.

The practice of polygamy and concubinage tended to reduce the position of women even among the upper classes. A significant trend that had become visible already during Harun's reign was toward greater seclusion for women and their segregation from the other sex. This applied principally to women of the wealthier classes. The tradition, too, of the large harem guarded by eunuchs also dates from the Abbasids.

What influence the wives of the Abbasid caliphs enjoyed with their husbands remains moot, at least among feminists. The probability is, however, great that al-Khaysuran, the mother of Harun, and his wife, Zubaydah, were exceptions to the general rule, the rule that the wives of the caliph filled essentially the same role as that reserved for the other wives in any harem, namely, to please their husbands and to have children. For this reason wives of lower-class husbands usually enjoyed positions of greater influence in the family since their spouses had perforce to be content with one wife. Such a wife held a place not appreciably different from that of the wife of the Christian in the West, although she did find herself in an odd situation. Were she to seek the material advancement of her husband, as all loyal wives do, he would one day be bringing home another woman to share his bed!

Since chroniclers did not ordinarily move in aristocratic circles—Ibn Khaldun was an exception—they have little to tell of Harun's harem. Mention is made of one slave girl for whom he paid the princely sum of 70,000 dirhams, only to turn her over to one of his servants when she displeased him. It was evidently not this girl but another that had Harun's wife Zubaydah worried. We are told that Zubaydah once made Harun a present of ten ravishingly beautiful girls in order to help get his mind off a beautiful singing girl of whom he had become enamored. One of these ten girls later became the mother of Harun's son al-Mamun.

The homes of the aristocracy during the reign of Harun were richly furnished with rugs, floor cushions, and divans, with a sofa often extending along three sides of the room. Moslems might cool their homes in the summer with ice. Food of the richest variety and from the four quarters of the globe was served from trays of silver and brass that rested on stools or low tables. Sherbets were highly prized as dessert and could be had in a number of flavors. Alcoholic beverages were popular among the upper classes. It was probably only the scrupulous faithful, from choice, and the very poor, from necessity, who observed the Koranic prescription against such indulgence. Christians and Hebrews were the bootleggers of Harun's reign, although bars that dispensed wines were not unknown.

The Moslem had a proverb that resembles the biblical aphorism about cleanliness being next to godliness. His runs "Cleanliness is a part of faith," and such it was. The Moslem must wash himself, that is his hands and face, before he performed his prayer obligation, which meant five times a day. He was to use water, but if the desert made this impossible, then sand. To satisfy this Koranic requirement all mosques were provided with a source or supply of water. Mohammed permitted men to patronize baths but only for washing, not recreation. Contact with more sophisticated civilizations gradually wore down this limitation, however, and in Harun's day Baghdad could boast thousands of baths, so the chroniclers say, with provision for recreation and refreshments. The patronage of the baths must be considered the most popular of men's sports, a wholly understandable circumstance in a land so oppressed by heat and dust. Indoor games such as chess, backgammon, and dice were well known. Al-Masudi says Harun was the first caliph to play chess. More strenuous sports included archery, polo, a kind of croquet, javelin throwing, and fencing. Harun may also have been the first caliph to play polo. Horse racing was also popular and al-Masudi tells of a race which Harun's horse won. Since Harun was greatly gratified at this victory, one must assume that Harun was an honest sportsman.

As in Western Europe, hunting was a sport reserved to the aristocracy. Harun's son al-Mamun, we are told, was a great lion hunter, while one of his brothers was killed hunting wild boar. Hunting with cheetah and falcon were also popular. Game included deer, hares, partridges, geese, and ducks.

NON-MOSLEMS AND THE HARUN CALIPHATE

It was not long after the lands of the unbelievers had been conquered, their cities looted, and many of their inhabitants sold into slavery, that non-Moslems began to live in relative peace in the land of the Prophet. There were, as the Koran put it, "people of the book," that is, Christians and Hebrews who accepted the Bible. This saved them from extermination, but they must still suffer for having corrupted the pure gospel that God had once entrusted to Adam. For this reason these non-Moslems could not testify against Moslems, certain clerical and public offices were closed to them, and they paid a special tax. As time passed the harshness of these discriminatory measures passed too, and it was not uncommon, for example, to find both Christians and Hebrews serving as physicians. Fifty years after Harun's death, a Christian even occupied the office of vizier. On the other hand, Christians could expect outbursts of intolerance at almost any time, such as the decree obliging them to wear distinctive garb which Harun ordered enforced following a defeat by Byzantine armies.

The great majority of Christians living under Abbasid rule were either Jacobite (Monophysite) or Nestorian, not Catholic. A Nestorian patriarch had actually occupied a residence on the site of Baghdad and was permitted to move to the east bank of the river when al-Mansur decided to build his capital there. Throughout the Abbasid period a number of Christian monasteries continued to exist in the city. Harun transported the entire community of Samalu, townspeople and monastery, on the Armenian border, that he captured in 780, to a place north of Baghdad, where he granted it extensive tracts along the river. Nestorian Christians directed vigorous missionary activities from Islam in the countries that lay to the east where Marco Polo encountered them on his journey to the great khan. Hebrews, because of their smaller numbers and their Semitic characteristics, generally found greater acceptance among Moslems than did Christians. Islam in time came even to accept Zoroastrians despite the Koran's denunciation of them as pagans and as fit only to be extirpated. Islam also tolerated such Christian sects as the Gnostics (Sabians), although Manichaeans generally received hostile treatment. Harun enforced earlier decrees aimed at their suppression and appointed a special officer to ferret them out. Whatever the degree of toleration these different groups of non-Moslems enjoyed, the tendency was for their numbers to decrease. There existed strong material inducements for the acceptance of Islam, *viz.,* exemption from a special poll tax and the removal of certain civil disabilities, not to mention greater business opportunities and social acceptance. Repressive measures taken by the Abbasids, including Harun, also accelerated the acceptance of the faith of the Prophet. Granted these pressures, however, there can be no question that many non-Moslems found the relative simplicity of Moslem faith and liturgy attractive and voluntarily accepted the faith of Islam.

ABBASID ECONOMY

The principal economic basis of the wealth of Islam during both the Umayyad and Abbasid periods was agriculture. Of this fact the early Abbasids, including Harun, were fully aware. To foster its development they encouraged the opening of new lands, cleaned out old irrigation canals in Mesopotamia, and provided funds for the construction of new canals, particularly in the southern part of the area. There the land still retained the productivity that had amazed Herodotus in the fifth century B.C. The principal crops included barley, wheat, rice, dates, sesame, cotton, and flax. The area also produced a variety of fruits and vegetables: oranges, apricots, peaches, plums, lemons, figs, grapes, pomegranates, radishes, cucumbers, eggplant, and sugar. The raising of flowers was highly developed in Mesopotamia and in many provinces of the empire. Flowers were in great demand both for private use and by manufacturers of perfumes, unguents, and flavorings for sherbets.

The industry of Islam was principally concentrated in the ancient cities of Egypt, Syria, and Mesopotamia. Iraq and the provinces to the east were famous for the manufacture of rugs, tapestries, embroideries, carpets, satin, and silken, cotton, and woolen fabrics. Sidon and Tyre retained their reputation of ancient Phoenician times as manufacturers of glassware, while neighboring Syria prided itself on its glazed tiles and mosaics. It was during Harun's reign that the paper industry, which had its origin in China, first made its appearance in the Islamic world. Yahya's son al-Fadl is credited with erecting the first paper mill in Baghdad, his brother Djafar with using paper in place of parchment in the preparation of government documents. A lively trade in precious stones lends substance to the many references to jewels, rubies, and sapphires in the Arabian Nights. Al-Masudi tells of an enormous ruby upon which Harun had his name inscribed that would shine like a lamp when placed in a dark room. Harun's sister Ulayyah introduced a dome-shaped cap for feminine wear which might display a band studded with jewels. Harun's wife went her sister-in-law one better and wore shoes studded with rubies.

A flourishing trade between all parts of the empire contributed powerfully to the development of agriculture and industry in the Islamic world. Never before could traders carry in safety such a variety of merchandise from lands so many thousands of miles apart. Of significant aid in oiling the wheels of trade was Arabic, the language of the Koran which all Moslems must learn, together with the sacred charge upon all the faithful to make a pilgrimage to Mecca. Merchants could expect to be understood wherever they went, and also to enjoy the protection which the Koran provided men of their profession. And where travel was a religious obligation, the merchant had no dearth of roads to carry him wherever he might wish to go. Already during the reign of al-Mansur (Harun's grandfather), we read of Moslem merchants traveling to China by way of the Indian Ocean. What especially attracted them to that distant land was silk which ordinarily made its way westward on camel back through Samarkand and Turkestan. Chinese records speak of embassies being exchanged with Islam during the latter half of the eighth century and during the reign of Harun. China was but one country beyond the borders of Islam whose products were displayed in the bazaars of Baghdad. Southeast Asia and India also sent their products, as did the Sudan and tropical Africa. Some goods even managed to slip through hostile frontiers from Western Europe and Russia. Not even the huge cities of China could offer the buyer the variety of goods that he could purchase in the great cities of Islam: muslim (Mosul), damask (Damascus), silks, brocades, rugs, and tapestries; metalware, weapons, steel mirrors, and glassware; jewels, rubies, gold, and silver; perfumes, flowers, and spices; melons, oranges, dates, figs, apricots, and peaches; sugar, cotton, asparagus, spinach, and artichokes; flax, hemp, rice, and wheat; furs and leather goods, not to mention slaves.

HARUN'S BAGHDAD

The capital of Harun's far-flung empire was Baghdad, in his day the largest city of the Western world with the possible exception of Constantinople. Baghdad was essentially a new city which al-Mansur, Harun's grandfather, founded in 762. The site of the city was probably occupied as early as the end of the second millennium (ca. 1200 B.C.), and it is curious that the name borne by this ancient settlement was not unlike the modern Baghdad. This would make it the oldest name site in history. A small community of Nestorian Christians occupied the site during the reign of the Sassanid Persians. When Abu al-Abbas overthrew

Umayyad rule, he had no desire to continue use of Damascus as his capital, but established his headquarters at Anbar on the Euphrates, where he erected a magnificent palace called Hashimiya after his ancestor Hashim. When he died, his brother al-Mansur, who was dissatisfied with Anbar, sent out scouts to seek out a more suitable spot on the Tigris in the vicinity of Baghdad. The story goes that he had members of his retinue spend the night in different villages in the area with instructions to record their impressions. The one, and only one, who reported that he had spent a peaceful night, since mosquitoes that infested the land had not molested him, happened to sleep near the village of Baghdad. There it was that Mansur decided to build his capital.

In building his city Mansur's first consideration, once the site had been selected for its central location within the empire and its unsurpassed advantages for trade, was that of security. His palace was to be not only a home but a fortress. So he laid out his city in a circle with his palace in the center, itself surrounded by an open court over which the imperial guard could enjoy an unobstructed view. In the construction of his capital all cities such as Damascus and Mosul were taxed a quota of craftsmen to help in the work. Because no stones were available in the alluvial soil around Baghdad, a few were brought at great expense from Ctesiphon eighty miles away, but the principal material was bricks. These were made from mud and baked by the sun although some kiln-burnt bricks and tiles were used for facing. Large bricks might weigh as much as two hundred pounds. Mansur laid the first brick in 762, and three years later the city was ready for occupation. The main wall that circled the city, whose inner diameter was approximately a mile, was massive in its proportions. This main wall was ninety feet high. Its towers rose some one hundred feet above the ground. The top of the wall, although only one third the width of the base, was more than forty feet across, sufficiently wide to permit the use of horses and wagons. Four gates pierced the thick walls, each guarded by a heavy iron gate that opened only outward. A second wall encircled this central wall, not quite so thick as the first but protected by a moat. The circumference of this second wall approximated six miles. These circular walls gave it the name of the Round City of Mansur. Four arcades were built to connect these two concentric walls, each equidistant from the other. These arcades were used as bazaars, with a single industry such as the slave dealers or silversmiths assigned to each area. In the open spaces between arcades, the population of artisans, scribes, mullahs, and officials made their homes. The arcades leading to the four gates divided the city into four districts, which were sealed off from one another except at the gates. The purpose of this arrangement was probably the desire to prevent the spread of trouble in case of rioting and revolt.

The dominant structure in the new city was the palace of the caliph. From its gilded entrance it was known as the Golden Gate. It covered an area of eighty acres. The most sumptuous rooms were two large audience chambers, each graced with a dome, the taller one of green rising to a height of 130 feet. Adjacent to this palace and also within the first wall were the palaces of the caliph's children, the royal mosque, and various government buildings. Harun replaced the mosque Mansur had erected with a more stately edifice. Perhaps no great city grew more rapidly than did Baghdad under the Abbasids. Tradesmen, merchants, pilgrims, officials, entertainers, and many other kinds of people who hoped to find or improve their means of livelihood, flocked to the city. So rapidly did the population swell that the fearful Mansur moved the bazaars to the suburb of Karkh outside the city, lest his enemies take advantage of the confusion to hide their treasonable plans amongst the masses. The arcades were then used as barracks for the city police and the horse-guard. The city continued to grow although now outside the two walls, and shortly the city and its suburbs covered the area for miles around. Mansur later transferred some of his troops to the east bank of the river where many Christians also moved. This section subsequently surpassed the older city in wealth and importance. Three pontoon bridges crossed the Tigris to unite the two sections of the city.

HARUN'S COURT

The city of Baghdad provided the stage upon which Harun and the early Abbasids displayed that wealth and splendor which has made their dynasty so illustrious. No court chronicler has left us a good picture of life in the palace during Harun's reign, but that given a hundred years later by Khatib describing the reception of Byzantine envoys of Constantine VII by the caliph Muktadir is probably not far off. The caliph's army of 160,000 men, horse, and foot, was drawn up for the occasion. The caliph's state officers and his favorite slaves stood about him garbed in splendid apparel, their belts glittering with gold and gems. Near them were seven thousand eunuchs, four thousand of them dressed in white uniforms, three thousand in black. The porters and doorkeepers were on hand, in number some seven hundred. Barges and boats adorned with the most elaborate decorations could be seen from the palace as they moved upon the Tigris. Thirty-eight thousand pieces of tapestry were draped about the palace, twelve thousand five hundred of these of silk embroidered with gold. Twenty-two thousand carpets covered the floors. A hundred lions were brought out to grace the occasion, each lion with its individual keeper. Among other spectacles of rare and arresting luxury was a tree of gold and silver that spread its eighteen large and many more smaller branches, on which sat a variety of birds made of the same precious metals. While machinery moved the limbs and leaves of the tree, the different birds warbled their natural harmonies. Through this scene of magnificence the Greek ambassadors made their way, escorted by the vizier, to the foot of the caliph's throne. This almost reads like one of the more extravagant pages of the Arabian Nights.

Over Harun's court consisting of hundreds if not thousands of eunuchs, concubines, singers, dancers, companions, and visitors, presided his wife Zubaydah and his sister Ulayyah. Snatches of gossip telling of friction between the two women can well be accepted. Sisters-in-law have been known to disagree and Zubaydah was of low origin while Ulayyah had a blemish! Zubaydah, despite her humble background, assumed without awkwardness her proper place as Harun's favorite wife. She permitted only gold and silver vessels studded with gems to be used at her tables, and she is said to have introduced the fashion of wearing shoes ornamented with precious stones. Her rival Ulayyah, not to be outdone, began the practice of wearing a fillet on the forehead, adorned with precious stones. For her such a band served a second purpose of hiding the mar on her forehead. Unusually spectacular were the festivities celebrating weddings and the reception of great dignitaries. The marriage of Harun's son al-Mamun to the daughter of his vizier must have marked the epitome of extravagance. It is said a thousand pearls of extraordinary size were showered from a gold trap upon the couple as they sat on a golden mat studded with pearls and sapphires, while balls of musk, each containing the name of some estate, slave, or similar rich gift, rained down upon the royal princes and dignitaries in attendance.

Harun's munificence to those who could brighten his life attracted thousands of singers, musicians, dancers, poets, even scholars and theologians to his court. They came from all over the empire, even from Spain,

Byzantium, and India, some invited, others with only the hope of gaining
fortune by the caliph's favor. Doubtless few went away so blessed as
Marwan, poet and panegyrist who composed an ode in Harun's honor,
for which he received a purse of five thousand pieces of gold, a robe of
honor, ten Greek slave girls, and one of the caliph's best steeds. An uninvited poet was Ibn Jami, the story of whose visit to Harun's court
is told by Abu al-Faraj in his *Kitab al-Aghani* (Book of Songs). It
chanced one day that Ibn Jami heard a Negress humming a song whose
melody so moved him that he paid her four dirhams to teach him the
song. Though she was happy to get the money, she assured him that
some day he would receive 4000 pieces of gold for the song.

So with the song and nothing more Ibn Jami reached Baghdad
hungry and weary. His piety took him to a mosque where he found a
sympathetic soul who gave him lodging, and when he learned that he
was a singer, he took him to the court. There in a room separated from
the caliph by a curtain of silk, he and several other singers took their
turns at "auditioning." No sooner had Ibn Jami sung his song, one of
his own, than several pages came running from behind the curtain to
inquire whose song he had sung. Upon his statement that it was his, he
was told sharply that he lied, that it was a composition of Ibn Jami.

Then after the singers had refreshed themselves with wine, they resumed their singing, following the same order as before. When it came
Ibn Jami's turn, he sang with even greater excellence and volume than
before and precipitating the same kind of excitement as before. Pages
came running out from behind the curtains to ask him whose composition he had sung. When he claimed he had sung one of his own, he
was again accused of lying. Fortunately Ibn Jami now cleared up the
confusion by stating boldly that he was the famous Ibn Jami in person.
Whereupon the curtains again parted, and who should come forward
to accost him but Harun himself on the arm of Djafar. The caliph bid
the singer welcome, complimented him on his superb skill, and assured
him of his good will and generosity.

Then Harun sat down with Djafar and asked Ibn Jami to sing one
of his songs that the caliph had not heard. So Ibn Jami remembered the
melody the Negress had taught him and proceeded to sing this. When
he had finished, Harun turned to Djafar and asked him whether he had
ever heard anything so original. Whereupon Ibn Jami told the caliph
of the Negress and how she had taught him the song, nor did he forget

to mention that she had predicted he would one day receive 4000 pieces of gold for the song. Harun promptly gave Ibn Jami the 4000 pieces of gold and much more in addition: a house richly furnished and fitted with everything his heart could desire, including several male servants and two beautiful slave girls.

There were other poets who graced the court of Harun. The most popular and notorious was Abu Nuwas, rake and skeptic, who helped build the image of the caliph's palace as another Babylon. We are told that he took part in the revelries of the court and joined Harun and Djafar on their nocturnal adventures. That his name in modern Arabic stands for clown suggests the frivolous nature of some of his verse. Wine, women, and song supplied the themes that most frequently attracted his talents, and he might intersperse licentious and even sacrilegious verses to titillate the caliph and his court. There were times when Harun had his surfeit of this kind of entertainment, and in moments of introspection would listen to the sobering verses of Abu al-Atahiyah who warned of the emptiness of all material pleasure. Harun's lavish generosity did not wean Atahiyah from the ascetic life he preferred, and so successfully did he pursue his theme that he is known today as the father of Arabic sacred poetry.

The most popular musician at Harun's court was probably Ibrahim al-Mawsili who as a boy learned to sing the songs of the brigands who had kidnapped him. So sensitive was his ear to dissonances that he is said to have picked out the girl from a group of thirty lute players whose instrument was off and ordered her to tighten the second string of her lute. Rashid paid Ibrahim a handsome salary of 10,000 dirhams and as much as ten times that amount for a single song he might especially enjoy. Another popular singer at Harun's court was Mukhariq, a pupil of Ibrahim's. His father was a butcher, and it was the beauty of the boy's voice in advertising the cuts of meat his father had to sell that first brought him to the attention of a woman singer who happened by. She sold him to Harun, who gave him his freedom and a fortune in addition, even a seat next to himself. So popular was he in Baghdad that people would line the banks of the river to hear his voice as he sang from a boat.

Fortunately Harun did not limit his patronage to artists who could provide him entertainment but extended it to scholars interested in science, mathematics, law, theology, and philosophy. His grandfather al-Mansur had already exhibited great interest in learning. The tradition of the Abbasids as patrons of the muses probably began with him, in particular the practice of having manuscripts in non-Arabic languages translated at government expense. Al-Mansur appears to have requested the Byzantine emperor for certain Greek writings including those of Euclid. Though al-Mansur had no patience with singers and poets, his son al-Mahdi brought them within the circle of his patronage and passed this liberal approach to the arts on to his son Harun. The latter, despite a hedonistic philosophy of life, exhibited a genuine interest in serious learning. Manuscripts captured in Byzantine territory he had translated, as well as works in Syriac, Persian, Indian, and Greek which purported to be of a scholarly character, including the writings of Galen, Hippocrates, Euclid, and Ptolemy. The caliph appears to have possessed a special interest in the advancement of medicine, again a trait that might be traced to his grandfather al-Mansur, who brought in a physician from India to treat his stomach disorder. Islam's first hospital was built by Harun, who appointed a Nestorian Christian schooled in Hindu medicine to serve as its director. This man's son, Jibril, became Harun's private physician. What may have convinced Harun of Jibril's medical talents was his success in restoring to health one of the caliph's concubines who was suffering from some kind of hysterical paralysis, by pretending to disrobe her in public.

Harun encouraged the study of alchemy which was the medieval parent of modern chemistry. His chief librarian, Abu Sahl al-Fadl, translated astronomical works from the Persian. Also benefiting from Harun's patronage were theologians such as al-Shafi and Abu Hanifah who occupied themselves with expressing the ideas of the Prophet in the different languages spoken by the non-Arabic peoples of the empire. A product of their work was the Book of the Letter, the first book on the subject of lexicography. Students of law likewise drew upon the caliph's munificence. Their studies prepared the bases for the four orthodox schools of Islamic jurisprudence which remain in existence today. In view of Harun's example, it is not surprising that his son al-Mamun should bring the history of caliphate patronage of learning to its height. In his House of Wisdom, which was a combination of library, academy, and laboratory, he supported many kinds of scholars—Christians, Hebrews, and Indians, scientists, philosophers, theologians, jurists, translators, and poets—all at state expense.

HARUN AND CHARLEMAGNE

Two thousand miles west of Harun's Baghdad there reigned Charlemagne, another magnificent king. To their subjects there was little question that theirs were kings without peers, and both Harun and Charlemagne would probably have agreed. Both men claimed the right to exercise absolute power, neither recognized a superior authority even in the realm of religion. Both kings led their armies, although Charlemagne campaigned considerably more and won far greater glory. On the other hand, Harun was the better educated, despite Charlemagne's knowledge of Latin and Greek, and if there remains some question as to their intellectual sophistication, the comparative level of learning in their respective courts and capitals permits of no argument. One might equate the learning pursued at Aachen with that of the junior high school, while some of the scholars who visited Baghdad during Harun's reign could occupy professorial chairs in our most distinguished universities. Both kings appreciated the importance of learning, although Charlemagne's motivation in encouraging it was fundamentally religious, not Harun's. While the men in Aachen were learning how to express themselves in Latin and how to conduct logical discussions, the savants at Baghdad were poring over the writings of Aristotle and Galen and pondering philosophical and scientific problems the West would not take up for another four hundred years.

Other comparisons between the two men and their courts, the organization and economies of their empires, and their military strength invite consideration. Did the presence of slavery in Harun's empire contribute to the subsequent decline of Islam or at least to its inability to rise beyond a certain level of industrial development? Did Harun's harem and the life of luxury he and his fellow caliphs preferred lead inevitably to the deterioration of the position of the caliph? Granted the vast cultural and material superiority of Harun's court and capital over provincial Aachen, what about the standard of living that was the lot of the masses in Islam compared with that of the French peasantry? Even the magnificence of Harun's capital and the glamor reflected in the Arabian Nights cannot blot out from view the thousands of beggars who swarmed the bazaars of that city. Though inefficient and arbitrary administration were all too common in Western Europe, there was nothing there to compare with the exploitation that certain provinces in Harun's empire suffered at the hands of their governors if for no more commendable reason than the fact that the natural economy of the West made such exploitation impossible. Whatever the relative strengths and weaknesses of the two empires, both were already in decline when their masters died, and within a century both would crumble into a number of independent states.

Did these two men, Harun and Charlemagne, have any knowledge of the other? Did they exchange embassies? There appears little doubt that they did. Though Islamic chroniclers made no mention of Charlemagne nor of embassies passing between the two capitals, present opinion inclines to accept the positive testimony of Western writers, notably that of Einhard. Einhard has this to say in his biography of his king. "His [Charlemagne] relations with Aaron, King of the Persians, who ruled over almost the whole of the east, India excepted, were so friendly that this prince preferred his favor to that of all the kings and potentates of the earth, and considered that to him alone marks of honor and munificence were due. Accordingly, when the ambassadors sent by Charles to visit the most holy sepulchre and the place of the resurrection of our Lord and Savior presented themselves before him with gifts, and made known their master's wishes, he not only granted what was asked, but gave possession of that holy and blessed spot. When they returned, he dispatched his ambassadors with them and sent magnificent gifts, besides stuffs, perfumes, and other rich products of the eastern lands. A few years before this, Charles had asked him for an elephant, and he sent the only one he had."

It is evident that Einhard's great devotion to his king led him to embellish Charlemagne's eminence. That Harun prized Charlemagne's good will above that of other kings and that he considered him alone worthy of that distinction is innocent nonsense. That a Frankish embassy did go to Baghdad and bring back gifts from the caliph may be accepted as factual. For it appears certain that Charlemagne sent emissaries on three occasions, in 797, 802, and 807. Harun received the first two embassies, his son al-Mamun the third, since Harun had died in the meantime. The first embassy included Sigismund, Lantfrid, and a Hebrew by the name of Isaac, who probably accompanied the other two to act as guide and interpreter. Einhard does not explain the purpose of the embassy. There did exist a number of points of common concern which this and later embassies might have discussed, such as the presence of Umayyad rulers in Spain, the hostility of the Byzantine empire, and the treatment of pilgrims in Palestine. Only Isaac seems to have survived this first trip. He returned to Aachen in 801 with robes of honor from Harun, aromatics, a water clock (not an organ as erroneously believed in the past), and an elephant named Abu Lubabah. Perhaps related to this emissary was the action of the patriarch of Jerusalem in sending Charles two monks with the keys to the Church of the Holy Sepulcher and the city, together with a banner. He would scarcely have done this without Harun's knowledge and approval. This may actually have been part of a broader arrangement between Harun and Charlemagne, which involved giving the latter not only a kind of symbolic protectorate over Jerusalem but over the Abbasid emirs in Spain as well.

A second embassy left Aachen in 802 and returned four years later with one of Harun's courtiers and presents that included a tent and many costly robes. The third mission which left in 807 did not reach Baghdad until after Harun's death. A number of prized articles still remain in Western Europe as mementos of these trips: an ivory horn at Aachen, a sword in Vienna, eight thorns from the crown placed on Christ's head before his death, at Aachen, a gold tray and chessmen in the abbey of St. Denis, and a robe in Durham cathedral. Charlemagne's emissaries carried "to the emperor of the Persians horses and mules from Spain, Frisian robes, white, grey, red, and blue, which in that country were rarely seen and highly prized. He also sent dogs that were noted for their swiftness and ferocity, such as [Harun] had desired for hunting or driving away lions and tigers."

What Harun wanted above all else was a physician who might cure him of his disease, and this neither Charlemagne nor the much further advanced world of Islam and India could do. As noted above, he died in 809 on a campaign against rebels in Khurasan. His two sons fought over the succession, and before al-Mamun had this firmly in hand, his brother al-Amin was dead and one half of Baghdad in ruins. Shortly after Charlemagne died, his son and grandsons were fighting over his empire. Harun and Charlemagne shared a common deficiency in that both preserved a policy governing succession that made civil war almost inevitable. In the matter of reforming such fundamental traditions even great men cannot move far ahead of their times.

Charlemagne

"It would be folly . . . to write a word concerning Charles' birth and infancy, or even his boyhood, for nothing has ever been written on the subject, and there is no one alive now who can give information of it." This is what Einhard confesses in his biography of Charles, and if Einhard knew nothing about the emperor's early years, no one did. For Einhard was a bright young boy of sixteen when Charlemagne, upon the recommendation of the abbot of Fulda, took him to Aachen to live as a member of the royal household. As Einhard says: "No man can write with more accuracy than I of events that took place about me. . . ." It is probable that Einhard spent most of his early manhood at Aachen and may even have married one of Charlemagne's daughters. He took up writing the life of the great Charles after the death of the emperor.

Charlemagne was an imposing figure. He "was large and strong, and of lofty stature, though not disproportionately tall—his height is well known to have been seven times the length of his foot—the upper part of his head was round, his eyes very large and animated, nose a little long, hair fair, and face laughing and merry. Thus his appearance was always stately and dignified, whether he was standing or sitting; although his neck was thick and somewhat short, and his belly rather prominent; but the symmetry of the rest of his body concealed these defects. His gait was firm, his whole carriage manly, and his voice clear, but not so strong as his size led one to expect. His health was excellent, except during the four years preceding his death, when he was subject to frequent fevers. . . ."

Charlemagne's height of approximately seven feet made him stand out above the great majority of his countrymen, since few men in his day even reached six feet. That physical fact alone made him an object of wonder. His physical accomplishments were those his contemporaries considered manly, and in these he excelled. "In accordance with the national custom, he took frequent exercise on horseback and in the chase, accomplishments in which scarcely any people in the world can equal the Franks. He enjoyed the exhalations from natural warm springs, and often practiced swimming, in which he was so adept that none could surpass him; and hence it was that he built his palace at Aix-la-Chapelle, and lived there constantly during his latter years until his death. He used not only to invite his sons to his bath, but his nobles and friends, and now and then a troop of his retinue or bodyguard, so that a hundred or more persons sometimes bathed with him."

Einhard pictures Charles as a warmhearted, manly, and most hospitable person. "He was by nature most ready to contract friendships, and not only made friends easily, but clung to them persistently, and cherished most fondly those with whom he had formed such ties." Strangers he made feel equally at home. "He liked foreigners, and was at great pains to take them under his protection. There were often so many of them, both in the palace and the kingdom, that they might reasonably have been considered a nuisance; but he, with his broad humanity, was very little disturbed by such annoyances. . . ." Einhard says nothing about the sentiments of Charlemagne's cooks!

Despite Charlemagne's great wealth, his robust physique, and the temptations to luxurious living to which many of his Merovingian predecessors had succumbed, he "was temperate in eating, and particularly so in drinking, for he abominated drunkenness in anybody, much more in himself and those of his household; but he could not easily abstain from food, and often complained that fasts injured his health. He very rarely gave entertainments, only on great feastdays, and then to large numbers of people." He appears to have shared the hearty eating one commonly associates with medieval people—when there was enough to eat! "His meals ordinarily consisted of four courses, not counting the roast, which his huntsmen used to bring in on the spit; he was more fond of this than of any other dish." Yet even when enjoying the physical pleasures of the table, he did not forget his soul. "While at table, he listened to reading or music. The subjects of the readings were the stories and deeds of men of olden time: he was fond, too, of St. Augustine's books, and especially of the one entitled 'The City of God.' "

Einhard also judged his lord to be a virtuous man. He "cherished with the greatest fervor and devotion the principles of the Christian religion, which had been instilled into him from infancy. Hence it was that he built the beautiful basilica at Aix-la-Chapelle. . . . He was a constant worshipper at this church as long as his health permitted, going morning and evening, even after nightfall, besides attending mass; and he took care that all the services there conducted should be administered with the utmost possible propriety, very often warning the sextons not to let any improper or unclean thing be brought into the building or remain in it." He shared his age's reverence for relics and made several trips to Rome, all the more willingly because of the opportunity this provided him of praying at the saints' tombs located there. He was also generous to the poor, not only to those in his kingdom, but, according to Einhard, sending food and money to Christians who lived in poverty in Syria and Egypt.

Charles presided over a large household of wives, sons and grandsons, daughters and granddaughters, after the manner of an Old Testament patriarch. His posture was thoroughly paternalistic: usually that of an indulgent father, only on occasion stern, loving all who lived under his roof with him and enjoying their company. He had a great fondness for his children, whether legitimate or illegitimate—this made little difference in his day—and in order to keep his daughters at home, prevented them from marrying "although they were very handsome women . . . saying that he could not dispense with their society. Hence, though otherwise happy, he experienced the malignity of fortune as far as they were concerned; yet he concealed his knowledge of the rumors current in regard to them, and of the suspicion entertained of their honor." For his mother Bertha he had "the greatest veneration and she passed her old age with him in great honor. . . ."

The story of Charlemagne's married life belies the picture of an amiable, patient *paterfamilias,* ruling with considerable dignity and satisfaction a large and, what must often have been, disorganized household at Aachen. His first wife was Himiltrude, a Frankish girl, who was united to him after the Frankish form of matrimony which the Church was seeking to replace with something more canonical. That Charles considered Himiltrude his wife is clear from the name Pepin that he gave their firstborn, which had been the name of Charles' father. Had nothing interfered, Pepin would have succeeded Charles. (Professor F. L. Ganshof refers to Pepin as nothing more than Charlemagne's "favorite bastard.") First to interfere was Charles' mother, Bertha. She persuaded her son to repudiate Himiltrude and marry Desiderata, the daughter of the Lombard king Desiderius, despite vigorous protests from the pope, not over Himiltrude's rights but because the Lombards were Rome's bitterest enemies. Within a short time Charles renounced his friendship with the Lombards and Desiderata as well, and married a thirteen-year-old Swabian girl by the name of Hildegard. By her he had a large number of children, including Louis the Pious who succeeded him. (Pepin, incidentally, became partner to a conspiracy in 792 when he saw how the sons of Hildegard were being preferred to him. Charlemagne nipped the revolt and consigned Pepin to a monastery where he died a monk in 811.) Upon Hildegard's death Charles married Fastrada, of whose evil influence Einhard speaks, whether justly or not is unclear. During her life Charlemagne acquired a concubine, a young woman of the aristocracy named Liutgard, whom he married after Fastrada's death. When Liutgard died, Charlemagne did not marry again although he kept a number of noble girls as mistresses as Frankish custom permitted him to do.

Charles' personal morals will disturb the modern reader more than they should. Contemporaries viewed such laxity with greater complacency then than would critics of similar lapses today, and properly so. For the Franks were scarcely two hundred years removed from barbarism, and a primitive folk usually requires considerable time in which to slough off mores that higher civilizations consider reprehensible. In the matter of morals, Charlemagne did not rise above the level of his age. Einhard does not censure him, although Charlemagne's son, Louis the Pious, surely did not approve. When he succeeded his father in 814, the first change he made was to send packing the loose women about the court.

Actually, to speak of Charlemagne's concubines is as unhistorical as worrying about the sins of St. Augustine's youth. They pale into insignificance, in both instances, before the mammoth contribution each man made to the growth of Western Christianity. Charlemagne's faith was perhaps as deep as that of Augustine following the latter's conversion. It would be difficult to single out any major undertaking of Charlemagne's in which religious zeal did not constitute a powerful, if not the principal, motive. As we shall see below, Charlemagne's concern about reviving learning was fundamentally religious. He was earnestly interested in purifying religious worship, in preserving orthodoxy, and in raising the level of clerical morality. When he died, the Bible was free of many corruptions, the papacy a stronger institution, monastic life immeasurably improved, and the last great pagan German nation, the Saxon, had accepted baptism. Above all, it was Charlemagne who gave the new culture of Western Europe the religious character it retained into modern times. Even his private morals improved as he grew older. If he ordered a regimen of fasting for his subjects to appease God's anger, in the hope of securing divine favor against famine and plague, it only matched the private penances he himself was practicing to expiate his personal transgressions. He appears to have accepted in humility the deaths of his two eldest sons and his oldest daughter as divine chastisement for his sins. Upon news of his death many areas hailed him as a saint. Three centuries later Frederick Barbarossa prevailed upon his pope, Paschal III, to canonize him, and for a time Charlemagne's name appeared in the breviary.

Charlemagne was born in 742, exactly where in the Frankish kingdom is not known. His father was Pepin III, first king of the new Frankish monarchy, known historically as the Carolingian, to which Charles (*Carolus*) gave his name. When Pepin died in 768, Charles and his younger brother Carloman succeeded, Charles receiving roughly the northern and eastern parts (Austrasia and Neustria) of the Frankish kingdom, Carloman the southern part, with Aquitaine in southwestern France being divided between them. In so dividing the kingdom between his sons, Pepin was following the traditional practice of the Salian Franks who viewed their realm as they would any other family possession, and parceled it out among their sons in order to keep it in the family. One other medieval monarch followed this same baleful practice, the king of Poland, and with equally disastrous consequences for his country. For although the theory of one kingdom was preserved, each son ruled his part independently of his brothers. If a king already had difficulty taming a powerful landed aristocracy, and all of them did, dividing the realm among several sons also divided their ability to accomplish this. Furthermore, not once did a king succeed in dividing his country in a manner that pleased all his sons. Charles, for instance, felt Carloman had received the richer portion since it contained the greater share of Carolingian properties. Because of the tradition of dividing a realm, civil war followed inevitably upon the death of a king, and the sons, in their anxiety to strengthen themselves against their brothers, further weakened the kingdom by bartering away precious crown estates in order to woo the support of selfish nobles.

The practice of dividing the kingdom had proved a major factor in the decline of the first Frankish monarchy, the Merovingian, the dynasty Pepin III had replaced with his own. The founder of this Merovingian monarchy was Clovis (481–511), the most successful of all the Germanic chieftains who carved kingdoms for themselves out of the disintegrating Roman empire in the West. At the age of fifteen Clovis was but one of a number of insignificant Salian kings. When he died in 511 he had made himself master of more than half of France, including the cities of Reims and Paris. French historians honor him as the founder of modern France. His name in its more modern form of Louis was as popular with later French monarchs as Edward in England and Otto in Germany. Two circumstances accounted for the success of Clovis: his ruthless ambition and his conversion to Catholic Christianity. This last assured him the vital support of the hierarchy in France and, in the eyes of the saintly historian of the period, Gregory of Tours, atoned for all his savagery. "The Lord cast his enemies under his power day after day," wrote the good bishop, "and increased his kingdom, because he walked with a right heart before Him, and did that which was pleasing in His sight."

True to his tribal traditions, Clovis divided his kingdom among his four sons. For the moment the fatal consequences of that policy were obscured by the success of his sons in extending France to her traditional frontiers: to the Alps, the Rhine, and the Pyrenees. But there the success of the Merovingians stopped. The remainder of the history of their dynasty is a dismal story of civil war, debauched monarchs, and immoral and superstitious subjects. This was the dynasty that sired Brunhild, whose richly deserved execution—carried out by her being tied, hair, arm, and foot, to the tail of a vicious horse—somehow typifies the brutality of the age.

That chaos did not overwhelm France as the Merovingian monarchy decayed was principally due to the work of one of the royal officials, the mayor of the palace. This official's duties in administering the estates of the king and supervising the other members of the court had provided him the opportunity to appropriate the powers of his royal master as these slipped from the monarch's hands. Einhard provides a simple, though vivid account of what happened. "The Merovingian family, from which the Franks used to choose their kings, is commonly said to have lasted until the time of Childeric, who was deposed, shaved, and thrust into the cloister by command of the Roman Pontiff Stephen. But although, to all outward appearance, it ended with him, it had long since been devoid of vital strength, and conspicuous only from bearing the empty epithet Royal; the real power and authority in the kingdom lay in the hands of the chief officer of the court, the so-called Mayor of the Palace, and he was at the head of affairs. There was nothing left the King to do but to be content with his name of King, his flowing hair, and long beard, to sit on his throne and play the ruler, to give ear to the ambassadors that came from all quarters, and to dismiss them, as if on his own responsibility, in words that were, in fact, suggested to him, or even imposed upon him. He had nothing that he could call his own beyond this vain title of King and the precarious support allowed by the Mayor of the Palace in his discretion, except a single country seat, that brought him but a very small income."

To this low state had fallen by A.D. 700 the fortunes of the powerful dynasty Clovis had founded two hundred years earlier. For that reason, when the Moors, after subjugating Visigothic Spain, drove northward through the Pyrenees into France, it was not the king, but Charles Martel, the mayor of the palace, who gave battle at Tours in 732 and drove them back. Charles Martel was content to rule as mayor of the palace, not so his son Pepin. In 749 Pepin appealed to Pope Zachary to correct what his ambitions convinced him was a most unreasonable situation, that is, that the man who actually bore the heavy burden of defending his country's frontiers and of protecting the Church, should be nothing more than a mayor of the palace, while the legal king was sitting on his impotent throne almost forgotten and doing nothing. The pope sympathized with Pepin's plight and announced that, "It is better that the man who has the real power should have the title of king instead of the man who has the mere title but no power." The great assembly of the Franks, thereupon, gave their consent to the dynastic change, and in 751 Bishop Boniface, the papal legate, solemnly anointed Pepin king of the Franks. No one objected when Pepin ordered the Merovingian king to be shorn of his long hair, a Merovingian mark of authority, and confined to a monastery.

This brings us back to Charlemagne and his brother Carloman, the sons of Pepin, who succeeded their father in 768. Charlemagne began his reign unauspiciously. As long as his brother Carloman lived, he appears to have followed a passive policy. Under the influence of his mother, he made peace with Tassilo, the powerful duke of Bavaria, and with Desiderius, king of the Lombards, whose daughter he married to cement the alliance. Then in 771, after a year of marriage, he suddenly repudiated his wife, probably for reasons of personal dislike, denounced the Lombard alliance, and when Carloman died in December of that same year, seized his territories in defiance of the rights of his nephews. If Charlemagne had not known up to this moment what his objective was to be, that had now become clear. He would follow in the firm footsteps of his father (Pepin) and grandfather (Charles Martel).

THE WARS OF CHARLEMAGNE

Charlemagne's military career dates from the first year of his co-rule with Carloman when he put down a serious revolt in Aquitaine. His envious brother Carloman refused to aid him; he argued that the revolt had not spread to his part of Aquitaine. The duke of Bavaria should also have helped, but neglected to do so. The first campaign Charlemagne undertook after his brother's death was a punitive raid against the Saxons who had made one of their predatory incursions into Frankish territory. For the moment he was satisfied with driving them back and establishing a "march" or buffer county to protect the frontier area from that fierce people.

The following year "he was induced by the prayers and entreaties of Hadrian, Bishop of the city of Rome, to wage war on the Lombards." These Lombards were the descendants of the semi-civilized Lombards who had stormed into Italy shortly after the death of Justinian, just two hundred years before. At that time, so savage were they, that the Italo-Romans had looked upon them as the devil's own cousins, and so the pope still considered them in the late eighth century even though they had shed their Arianism during this two-century interval and most of their uncivilized practices as well. But their ambition, which was to subject all Italy, including the city of Rome, to their rule, made them the pope's enemy, and in the Middle Ages, one's enemies were invariably the devil's allies.

Some years before, in 756, Lombard pressure on Rome had impelled Charlemagne's father Pepin to undertake a campaign against them. He had done this upon Pope Stephen II's urgent plea for aid. To press his appeal Stephen had gone to Pepin's court in person, and it was on that occasion that Charlemagne made his first acquaintance with the pope. He was but a boy of eleven at the time, and seeing the successor of St. Peter no doubt left a lasting impression upon him. The pope's visit proved fruitful and Pepin promised military assistance. In acknowledgment of that promise the pope proclaimed him and his two sons, Charlemagne and Carloman, "patricians of Rome and protectors of the Church and her territory." Precisely what this title implied is not clear. Byzantine emperors had bestowed the title of patrician on the Germanic rulers of Italy and Gaul in the fifth and sixth centuries, both to please these barbarians and to preserve the fiction of imperial suzerainty over their territories. In this instance, the pope's bestowal of the title of patrician on Pepin constituted a formal recognition of a *de facto* alliance between the papacy and the Frankish monarchy. Its immediate fruit was Pepin's defeat of the Lombards, whereupon he forced them to surrender Rome to the pope, together with most of the territory to the northeast of the city known as the Exarchate of Ravenna.

Pepin's transfer of this conquered Lombard territory to the pope is known as the Donation of Pepin. It must not be confused with the wholly fictitious Donation of Constantine which probably dates from this same period. This last document records Constantine's purported gift to Pope Sylvester of political control of the West, including Rome, and supreme authority over the entire Church as a token of his gratitude for having been cleansed of leprosy. Although this document has evoked a large literature, scholars are still not entirely certain of the circumstances attending its appearance. It is generally believed that some person or group, perhaps in the papal curia, fabricated it late in the eighth century in an effort to advance the creation of an independent papal state in Italy.

Now it came Charlemagne's turn to defend Rome from the Lombards. Like his father he did so but without enthusiasm. Only after the Lombard king Desiderius had rebuffed Charles' offer to indemnify him for any territory he might surrender to the pope, did he decide on war. He led his army across the Alps in the summer of 773, laid siege to Pavia, and after a year's campaign captured it and Desiderius. This time the Lombards were to have no further opportunity to cause trouble. Charlemagne assumed the iron crown of the Lombards for himself, and at Easter in the year 774 proceeded to Rome where he confirmed the Donation made by his father. But he appears to have retained sovereignty over the city, something his father may not have claimed. He even extended his control in Italy to include for a time the duchy of Benevento, and he annexed Istria on the northern Adriatic after driving off a Byzantine army.

Up to this time, that is, since 771, when he had thrown out his Lombard wife, all had gone well for Charlemagne. Then in 778 he foolishly embarked on a campaign even a less practical man would have rejected as unwise. The year previous the Abbasid governor of Barcelona had presented himself before the Frankish princes at their spring assembly and appealed to Charlemagne for assistance against the Umayyad caliph of Cordova. Charlemagne permitted himself to be dazzled by the prospect of extending his empire into Moslem territory, and in the early spring of 778 led a large army across the Pyrenees. The entire campaign went badly. It began with the capture of Pampeluna which belonged to the Christian kingdom of the Asturias, and ended with the destruction of the rear guard of his army by other Christians, the Basques, as Charlemagne was leading his bedraggled host back to France through the narrow pass at Roncesvalles. The promised Moslem aid against Cordova had not materialized, and Charlemagne was fortunate he recognized his mistake in time before becoming bogged down in a country so far from Aachen.

Although Einhard describes Charlemagne as winning all his battles up to the tragedy at Roncesvalles—"up to the time of his homeward march he sustained no loss whatever"—he was forced to admit this disaster at Roncesvalles. For "on his [Charlemagne's] return through the Pyrenees he had cause to rue the treachery of the Gascons. That region is well adapted for ambuscades by reason of the thick forests that cover it; and as the army was advancing in the line of march necessitated by the narrowness of the road, the Gascons, who lay in ambush on the top of a very high mountain, attacked the rear of the baggage train and the rear guard in charge of it, and hurled them down to the very bottom of the valley. In the struggle that ensued, they cut them off to a man, they then plundered the baggage, and dispersed with all speed in every direction under cover of approaching night. The lightness of their armor and the nature of the battleground stood the Gascons in good stead on this occasion, whereas the Franks fought at a disadvantage in every respect, because of the weight of their armor and the unevenness of the ground. Eggihard, the King's steward . . . and Roland, Governor of the March of Brittany, with very many others, fell in this engagement."

Good Frank that he was, Einhard deplored this disaster. Posterity, however, has less reason to regret Roncesvalles, for the battle provided the theme for the most popular of all medieval epics, the *Song of Roland*.

A few years later Charlemagne had the satisfaction of gaining a foothold south of the Pyrenees. In 793 a Moorish raid into southern France provoked a counterraid by the Franks and the annexation of territory in Charlemagne's name known as the Spanish march. This was later expanded to include Barcelona and Navarre. The people of the Balearic Islands voluntarily accepted Frankish protection against the Moors.

Campaigns such as this one into Spain Charlemagne could ill afford as long as the powerful Saxon nation to the northeast remained unpacified. These Saxons proved the most troublesome of his foes. Their fierce courage, large numbers, the wooded and swampy country they inhabited, and their national paganism made their conquest difficult. "No war was ever undertaken by the Franks that was carried on with such persistence and bitterness," writes Einhard, "or cost so much labor, because the Saxons, like almost all the tribes of Germany, were a fierce people, given to the worship of devils, and hostile to our religion, and did not consider it dishonorable to transgress and violate all law, human and divine."

For thirty-three summers Charlemagne fought the Saxons. Einhard attributes the long war to the latter's perfidy. "It is hard to say how often they were conquered, and, humbly submitting to the King, promised to do what was enjoined upon them, gave without hesitation the required hostages, and received the officers sent them from the King. They were sometimes so much weakened and reduced that they promised to renounce the worship of devils, and to adopt Christianity but they were no less ready to violate these terms than prompt to accept them, so that it is impossible to tell which came easier to them to do. . . ."

Their "perfidy" was the result of their lack of organization and their great hatred and fear of the Franks. No king or chieftain could command the obedience of the four major divisions with which the different tribes were associated, nor enforce the observance of agreements. The fact that the Franks were Christians had also deepened the ancestral hostility of the Saxons. At first Charlemagne was satisfied to drive raiding Saxon parties back into their forests and swamps. A few campaigns convinced him, however, that the portion of his kingdom that faced on their territory would never have peace so long as they remained pagan and unpacified. His campaigns against them followed a fairly constant pattern. He would invade their country, ravage their lands, and slaughter them when they made a stand. They would then submit, do homage, promise to accept Christianity, and hand over hostages for their fidelity. Yet no sooner would Charlemagne and his army retire than they would rise in revolt and massacre the garrisons and missionaries he had left behind. After several such "conquests" of Saxony, Charlemagne divided the country into missionary districts, with a community of monks assigned to each. His next step was to establish counties with native Saxon chiefs often honored with the position of count. These measures had some success, but in 783 a major revolt swept the lands of the Saxons under the leadership of Widukind, the only important chieftain who had not submitted. A principal cause of the revolt appears to have been Saxon resentment at the harsh measures Charlemagne's officials and clergy had employed to enforce baptism and the payment of the tithe. Again Charlemagne returned and put down the revolt. On this occasion he refused to accept new protests of regret and submission. He ordered the different tribes to surrender to him those of their leaders who had fomented the revolt, and he had all 4500 of the men they turned over beheaded. This rash act simply fired Saxon resistance anew, and three more years of bloody and destructive warfare followed before Widukind finally submitted and accepted baptism. Even after this submission sporadic revolts continued until Charlemagne resorted to mass deportations. "He took ten thousand of those that lived on the banks of the Elbe and settled them, with their wives and children, in many different groups here and there in Gaul and Germany. The war that had lasted so many years was at length ended by their acceding to the terms offered by the King, which were renunciation of their national religious customs and the worship of devils, acceptance of the sacraments of the Christian faith and religion, and union with the Franks to form one people."

Charlemagne also incorporated Bavaria into his expanding empire. The early Merovingians had subdued the Bavarians, but they had regained their independence under the later "do-nothing" kings. Pepin forced them to recognize Frankish suzerainty, although when Charlemagne became king, the status of their duke, Tassilo, was that of an autonomous lord. In 787 Charlemagne entered the country with a large army and Tassilo submitted without giving battle. The following year Charlemagne formally accused Tassilo of treason, deposed him, and added Bavaria to his domains. Historians agree that Tassilo's only crime was weakness, and that Charlemagne used not justice but might in removing him.

Charlemagne also defeated the Slavs who lived to the east between the Elbe and the Oder. They agreed to give him hostages, pay him tribute, and accept missionaries. Charles, the son of Charlemagne, carried the war into Bohemia and secured the submission of the Czechs. Charlemagne's greatest effort to the east was against the powerful Avar nation. This was the same Hunnic tribe that had begun to raid Byzantine territory along the Danube shortly after Justinian's death. Their ferocity enabled them to subjugate the Slavic tribes of the area and to establish an extensive empire north of the Danube which they ruled from their headquarters on the Theiss River in Hungary. Despite the passage of two hundred years and repeated contacts with higher cultures, their own level of civilization had not risen appreciably, nor had their brutality abated. Internal dissension had, however, crippled their power. Charlemagne made his first attack on them in 790, followed by others under command of his son Pepin and the governors of the neighboring counties. Their destruction was completed by 796, and what Avars remained were assimilated a few years later by the Magyars, the next powerful wave of invaders from Asia. "All the money and treasure [the Avars] had been years amassing was seized, and no war in which the Franks have ever engaged within the memory of man brought them such riches and such booty."

There were other peoples with whom Charlemagne fought. He forced the Bretons to recognize his authority in Brittany. Against the Danes who were beginning their forays along the Frisian coast during the closing years of his reign he had less success. From Jutland and the islands off the Danish coast they harried the lands along the North Sea and plundered the helpless countryside. They proved an elusive foe, for when serious resistance was finally offered them, they simply took to their ships and sailed off to pillage elsewhere. Charlemagne had a fleet of ships built to defend the coast of Frisia, but this proved generally ineffective. It would require many years before his landlubbers could challenge these Vikings who were even more intrepid mariners than the ancient Phoenicians.

With the two great empires to the east, the Byzantine and that of the Abbasid caliphate, Charlemagne undoubtedly carried on some measure of communication, although its precise nature remains obscure. His contacts with Islam were those he inherited from his father Pepin, whom the Abbasid governor of Barcelona had recognized as protector. This Frankish overlordship is what prompted the governor to enlist Charlemagne's aid in Spain which led to the latter's disastrous expedition across the Pyrenees in 778. Charlemagne's penetration of Italy after destroying the Lombards aroused Byzantine fears, as we have seen, although Constantinople's most dangerous enemy remained Baghdad. It was for the purpose of securing Frankish neutrality, if not assistance, that the empress Irene surrendered claims to Istria and Benevento and suggested the marriage of her son Constantine to Charlemagne's daughter Rotrud. Nothing came of this proposed marriage alliance, nor of feelers that may have passed between Constantinople and Aachen concerning the marriage of Irene to Charlemagne himself. With Harun, Charlemagne's relations do not appear to have passed beyond the point of exchanging friendly embassies.

Charlemagne's military successes and the size of his empire aroused the wonder of his royal contemporaries, from the Anglo-Saxon kings of Britain to the caliph in faraway Baghdad. His was no mere Frankish kingdom. It was an empire that included Spaniards, Italians, Slavs, and Avars. Einhard says Charlemagne more than doubled the territory he had inherited from his father (and brother). In the north he added Saxony and Frisia, Bavaria to the east and the borderlands taken from the Slavs and Avars, to the southwest the littoral of the northern Adriatic with the exception of Venice, two thirds of Italy, Brittany in the west, and the Spanish march across the Pyrenees. Yet he conquered not merely to add to his empire. In his judgment two motives justified his wars: the defense of his people, and the defense and spread of Christianity. The majority of his wars he waged against pagans to the east who menaced his frontiers and against Moslems in Spain. He rarely fought Christians principally, perhaps, because no Christian state threatened his Frankland. That no Christian power menaced him he would have accepted as entirely normal, since he believed Christian nations should live in peace. Between Christians and pagans (and Moslems), however, no coexistence was possible. The Saxons and Frisians he converted, the Avars he destroyed, the Moors he drove back and then established a strong buffer march below the Pyrenees to protect his country from that side. No real threat remained for his people when he died save that of the Danes which would only grow serious after his death.

Few conquerors have been so consistently successful against so many different foes as was Charlemagne. He needed the populous Frankish people and their allies to win his wars, but his victories would have been impossible without his own relentless determination. Though his large empire crumbled into scattered feudal states within a hundred years of his death, a number of his military achievements produced enduring consequences. The pushing back of the Slavs that he initiated would continue and merge in time with the more modern German *Drang nach Osten.* So would also continue the expansion of the Christian holding in Spain where he planted a foothold. The Saxon nation would remain among the family of Christian nations, while the Lombard and Avar peoples, over whose destruction no tears had been shed, would not reappear.

If the story of Charlemagne's wars wearies the reader, how much more must these wars have wearied the emperor! Few men would have persisted so long in the endless task of subduing the stubborn Saxons. They would have been content with establishing a march along the frontier. Yet to Charlemagne that war had to go on until this pagan people had accepted Christianity. One of the moving scenes in the *Song of Roland* is that with which the poet concludes his poem. Charlemagne is now an old, very old, and very tired man. He has just returned from his victorious (so the poet says) campaign against the Moslems in Spain and, after arranging for the punishment of the traitor whose treachery had caused the death of the noble Roland and the other Frankish heroes, he sinks back on his bed and falls asleep. Yet hardly do his eyes close than the Angel Gabriel rouses him and tells him of another campaign he must set out upon immediately. The pious though tired and aged emperor rises up but cannot suppress his feelings. "O God," he mutters to himself, "how weary is my life!"

THE CORONATION OF CHARLEMAGNE

To students of medieval history the high point of Charlemagne's majestic career came on Christmas Day in the year 800, when Pope Leo III crowned him "Emperor of the Romans." Contemporary writers give but brief notice of the event, and how much importance Charlemagne attached to his coronation is not clear. Perhaps the short account in the Frankish royal annals reveals the modest reaction of the Carolingian court. "On the most holy day of the Lord's birth, when the king, at mass before the confession of St. Peter the Apostle, rose up from prayer, Pope Leo placed a crown on his head; whereupon he was acclaimed by the whole populace of Rome: 'To Charles Augustus, crowned by God the great and peaceful Emperor of the Romans, life and victory.' And after

Lauds, he was adored by the pope in the manner of ancient princes; and the title of patrician being dropped, he was called Emperor and Augustus."

Scholars in their endeavor to discover the true significance of this coronation have given close study to the circumstances that attended Charlemagne's journeying to Rome in the late fall of 800. He came upon the urging of Pope Leo, of that there is little doubt. The strong and popular Pope Hadrian I had died on Christmas Day in the year 795, and early the following morning Rome learned of the election of his successor Leo III. Unfortunately Leo enjoyed no important support in the city, least of all among the friends of the deceased Hadrian, who helped swell rising opposition to his pontificate. This degenerated into a brutal personal attack on Leo as he was marching in a procession in Rome in April 799, when he was thrown to the ground and his assailants attempted to gouge out his eyes and cut off his tongue. Somehow he managed to escape and make his way to Paderborn, in Saxony, to lay his cause before Charlemagne. Among other crimes, the pope's enemies had accused him of simony and immorality and, as Leo pleaded with Charlemagne, he could not hope to resume his headship of the Church without the emperor's protection and imperial confirmation of his title. Charlemagne sent Leo back to Rome with a guard, followed himself in November, convoked a synod of ecclesiastics and laymen before which, over the objections of Alcuin that "the apostolic see could not be judged by anyone," he directed the pope to purge himself. Leo was in no position to oppose the emperor's will, although he protested that he was giving his oath of purgation free of all compulsion. Two days later, on Christmas Day, as Charlemagne while attending Mass, was rising from his knees before the altar in St. Peter's, Pope Leo placed a crown on his head, whereupon the assembled people shouted out the acclamation: "To Charles Augustus, crowned by God, great and peaceful Emperor of the Romans, life and victory."

This is how the coronation took place. Now the question that presents itself is: Who was responsible for what happened? Had the pope conceived the idea of the coronation and carried it out on his own responsibility or was it Charlemagne's idea? Did Leo and Charlemagne discuss the matter in relative harmony and agree on the coronation, or was the pope an unwilling agent in the ceremony? There are some scholars who insist that Charlemagne was taken unawares by the pope's action and was quite displeased with the whole episode. The basis of this view is the short but unequivocal observation of Einhard who, after noting that this visit to Rome was the last of four the emperor made to the Eternal City, continued: "It was then that he received the titles of Emperor and Augustus, to which he at first had such an aversion that he declared that he would not have set foot in the church the day they were conferred, although it was a great feastday, if he could have foreseen the design of the Pope."

If Einhard's statement is correct and the coronation of the emperor entirely Leo's work, what had prompted the pope to take the step he did? He surely owed the emperor a great debt of gratitude for the protection he had provided him and for coming the seven hundred miles to Rome just to confirm his title. Investing Charles with the august title of "Emperor of the Romans" would repay part of that debt. On the other hand, if the coronation of Charlemagne was not intended to represent appreciation for services rendered, the pope in his precarious condition may have hoped that this honor might encourage the king of the Franks to continue to afford him his protection. Ever since the decline of Byzantine power in Italy, the pope's position had been insecure, first, because of the Lombards, then because of factional groups within the city of Rome, and third, because of the ability of Constantinople to reassert its authority on occasion, when it was apt to deal harshly with all persons, including the pope, who might in the past have questioned the existence of that authority. Only the king could keep the Lombards out of the city, curb the turbulency of these factions, and permanently end Byzantine pretensions, but how long would he be willing to do this with no more sense of obligation than that deriving from the vague title of patrician? A strong authority must be at hand, somewhere in the West, that would guarantee freedom of papal elections and papal autonomy. What better opportunity than this visit of Charlemagne to abandon finally the theoretical dependence of the papacy upon the Byzantine emperor who had always proved a difficult man to deal with at best. For the greater part of the eighth century he had in fact supported the heretical iconoclasts. Now while orthodoxy had been restored in Constantinople, the ruler there was a woman, the empress Irene. The thought of being the ward of a woman was itself repugnant to the West, particularly so now when the woman was so monstrous a person as Irene who had had her son blinded so that she might rule.

Most scholars reject Einhard's testimony regarding Charlemagne's displeasure over his coronation as faulty. They insist that Charlemagne and his counselors favored the coronation, and they find their best argument in the relationship that existed at that time between king and pope. So much did Leo require the good will and protection of the emperor that it is most difficult to conceive of his doing anything to antagonize the emperor, surely nothing so important as to crown him without full knowledge that he approved. That the crowd assembled in St. Peter's was aware of its part in the ceremony also precludes Charlemagne's ignorance of what was afoot.

If Charlemagne and his counselors had hit upon the idea, what were their motives? They may have been entirely practical, for prudence was one of Charlemagne's virtues. Non-Frankish elements in his kingdom, especially in sensitive areas such as Aquitaine and Brittany, could be expected to find the rule of an "Emperor of the Romans" less distasteful than that of a mere Frankish king. Somewhat akin was the situation existing in Italy, where many peoples now under his control had all their lives been living under at the least the theoretical rule of an emperor (Byzantine). Until there was an emperor in the West to whom they could pay their loyalty, they could be expected to remain restless. Perhaps, too, as his empire grew, so had Charlemagne's vision of his possible role in the West. No important Christian lands remained outside his jurisdiction except across the Channel. Even several of the kings there, as well as the ruler of the Asturias in Spain, had come to address him as "lord" in their letters. Did such deference to him from non-subjects suggest the possibility of his exercising influence over a broader world than his own empire, something he might more properly do in his capacity as Emperor of the Romans?

The man who exercised greatest influence over Charlemagne in the evolution of his ideas regarding his responsibilities as king was the learned and saintly Alcuin. (There will be more about Alcuin later.) To Alcuin we can trace what was probably the principal motive that impelled Charlemagne to accept the title of Emperor. This was the desire to assume the role of protector of the pope and champion of Christianity. Einhard tells of Charlemagne's great admiration for the writings of St. Augustine, above all for his *City of God*. That Charlemagne could have conceived of a higher role than that of a mere earthly king from reading St. Augustine is not at all improbable. He may have seen himself as God's directly appointed agent, with a delegated authority that transcended that of every other Christian, pope included, but an authority that he must use to fulfill God's purpose. There were contemporaries of his who seemed to recognize his messianic role. Just a few days before his coronation on Christmas Day, a delegation from Jerusalem was announced, bearing from the patriarch of that city the keys to the Holy Sepulcher, keys that were to be symbolic of the protection Charlemagne was to assume over the Holy City. To perform such a role Charlemagne's title of king of the Franks and Lombards would not suffice. It was too tribal and too secular, while to most people the title of patrician remained meaningless. "Emperor of the Romans" would clothe him with an aura of grandeur befitting both his achievements and his role as the champion of Christianity and protector of the Church.

A more personal motive for Charlemagne's assuming the new title reveals itself in the strained relations between the king of the Franks and the Byzantine court. These relations had never been cordial, but what had particularly distressed Charlemagne was the inferior position the Byzantine emperor accorded him. In the latter's letters, the Frankish king was always his "son," a paternal condescension that rankled the Western ruler's sensibilities. True, the Frankish king was not quite the upstart of Clovis and Theodoric; yet before the magnificence of Byzantium he counted for little more. Apart from the psychological lift the title "Emperor of the Romans" would provide Charlemagne, that designation would leave him in a stronger position in his dealings with the East. In the judgment of Charlemagne and his counselors, there was no one in the Western world who was his equal, and none in the East who was his superior.

It is probable that both Charlemagne and the papacy agreed the coronation would be of value to both Empire and Church. The pope could assure himself that the new title would not provide Charlemagne greater prerogatives in Rome than he already exercised as patrician. By the same token Charlemagne would find no new responsibilities thrust upon him beyond what he was willing to accept. Given the king's theocratic view of his position, he must have appreciated the usefulness of the title. These different considerations find expression in another chronicler's account of the coronation. "Since, in the land of the Greeks, the name Emperor no longer existed inasmuch as the imperial power was held by a woman, it appeared to Pope Leo and to all the holy fathers who were then assembled in council, as well as to all the Christian people, that it was fitting to give the imperial title to Charles, the king of the Franks, who had possession of the city of Rome, where the emperors had always resided, and of the other cities which they had held in Italy, Gaul, and in Germany. Since Almighty God had chosen to place all those cities under his authority, it seemed only proper to them that with the help of God and in conformity with the demand of the Christian people, he should also bear the imperial title. To that demand Charles did not want to refuse; but, submitting himself in all humility to God and to the request of the priests and the Christian people, he received on the day of the nativity of Our Lord Jesus Christ the title of Emperor with the consecration of Pope Leo."

How then explain Einhard's positive statement concerning Charlemagne's displeasure? He may have been in error, or Charlemagne may have considered the time inappropriate, or he may have objected to the role Pope Leo had assumed for himself, that of himself doing the crowning. To the point of Einhard's accuracy, he is not above error. He prefaces his description of Charlemagne's coronation, for instance, with the flat misstatement that Pope Leo had actually been blinded and that he had had his tongue cut out. As for the inopportuneness of the occasion, Charlemagne may have feared hostile reaction on the part of Byzantium. If so he was correct. Frankish "usurpation" of the title "Emperor of the Romans" did arouse indignation in the East. Only in 812 did Michael I swallow his pride and accord Charlemagne momentary recognition as "brother" instead of "son." Finally, regarding the view that Charlemagne was displeased over being crowned by the pope, there is this clear fact to support it, namely, that Charlemagne had his son Louis proclaimed and crowned emperor in 813 in Aachen without benefit of pope or clergy. In an age when rights were claimed on the basis of custom and precedent more frequently than upon law, Charlemagne and his counselors might well have had a real fear that later popes would point to this coronation as investing them with the right to appoint and dismiss emperors—something they actually did do in time. Charlemagne and Leo had, in all probability, agreed upon the coronation, but the king was not at all willing that the pope should do the crowning. The pope's action must have taken him by surprise and provoked his anger.

The coronation of Charlemagne expressed dramatically the broad role Charlemagne had assumed, or was believed to have accepted, in the direction of Western affairs. It was an event that carried great significance. It formalized the alliance between the Christian Church of the West and the Frankish kingdom that had been initiated by Pepin and had been accepted by Charlemagne. At the same time, it announced the severing of papal dependence upon the Byzantine emperor. By his act the pope proclaimed his decision to turn his back on Byzantium and to cast in his lot with the Franks, a step which surely contributed to the growing estrangement between Greek and Latin Christendom and the coming of the schism in 1054.

What the coronation did not do was to revive the Roman empire in the West. Aachen remained Charlemagne's favorite residence, German continued to be his tongue, there was no attempt to Romanize ceremonials at his court, and he clung to his Frankish dress as before. As Einhard writes: "He despised foreign costumes, however handsome, and never allowed himself to be robed in them, except twice in Rome, when he donned the Roman tunic, chlamys, and shoes; the first time at the request of Pope Hadrian, the second to gratify Leo, Hadrian's successor." In the year 806 Charlemagne, like a true Frank, divided his realm among his three sons (Charles and Pepin preceded him in death).

The empire that was proclaimed at St. Peter's on Christmas Day in the year 800 was a new kind of state. It was a theocratic superstate, a concept and an institution that would contribute significantly to the evolution of that sense of cultural unity which Western Europe has continued to recognize up to the present time. As Professor C. Dawson has pointed out, the Roman empire of the Carolingians was a Roman Empire without Roman law, Roman legions, even without the city of Rome; yet it remained the embodiment and representative of an ideal, which despite its apparent failure, proved more durable and persistent than any of the military or political achievements of the period.

CHARLEMAGNE AND THE CHURCH

This ideal of the religious unity of Western Europe was not the accidental product of Charlemagne's "Empire of the Romans." It was the objective he sought to achieve. Proud as he may have been of his Frankish nationality, he never contemplated using the mores and traditions of his nation as the bond that would provide cohesiveness to his extensive domains. He never forced Frankish ways upon any group. On the other hand, the Christian ethic he did oblige nations to accept, and it was his hope to make this religious faith serve as cement which would bind his empire together. Nevertheless, this objective was purely a secondary one. To have used Christianity to serve even the Frankish state would have been to debase religion. It just so happened that Charlemagne's enemies were also pagans and Moslems, which fact made them equally the enemies of Christianity. What advanced his empire, aided Christianity; what benefited the Church, served his Frankish state. Since his state was a theocracy, there was no separating the two institutions. His enemies were the enemies of God, a claim many subsequent rulers have made, although seldom with so much honest conviction as did Charlemagne. The hope Alcuin expressed in a letter to Charlemagne in 799 was one the Frankish monarch himself entertained, namely, "May God assist you everywhere to subject through the triumph of your might the most unruly spirits to the Christian faith."

The policy of co-operation between the Latin church and the Frankish state that Clovis had accepted and Pepin had revived, Charlemagne adopted as a basic rule of government. Under the first two kings this alliance did not extend beyond the co-operation of two separate institutions, the one the Frankish state, the other the Church. During Charlemagne's reign, the relationship between the two became so close as to approximate the assimilation of the two into one theocracy. As Alcuin assured Charlemagne, his royal dignity exceeded that of all other Christian powers, the papacy and the Byzantine empire included, since Christ had charged the king personally with the leadership of the Christian commonwealth. Charlemagne's responsibility was to God and to no one else, and this responsibility placed upon him the charge of protecting and spreading the Christian religion and of enabling his subjects to practice it in peace. To enable his subjects to live as Christians and in peace, it might be necessary to subjugate additional peoples, for until these non-Christians beyond the frontiers had been baptized they would remain a constant threat. Neither could he permit conquered subjects to remain pagans since their paganism would leave them untrustworthy and dangerous and would, at the same time, be denying God the worship Charlemagne felt God required of all men. So once his armies had defeated an enemy, he divided the subjugated territory into missionary districts, and sent in his monks to proselytize the fallen foe, not by the slow process of instruction and persuasion, but preferably by the more expeditious one of force. To the Saxons he offered the choice of baptism or death. He personally assisted at the baptism of thousands of these pagans in the waters of the Elbe.

This was still an age when the rank and file of a nation followed the lead of their chieftain in matters of faith. When Clovis accepted baptism, three thousand of his warriors were baptized with him. Since each Saxon chieftain, upon his submission, had accepted baptism, Charlemagne naturally assumed their subjects would do the same. His contemporaries thought this was only reasonable. The poet of the *Song of Roland* had Charlemagne applying the same principle in dealing with his captured Moslems. The hundreds of thousands his armies presumably subdued in Spain, all were given a simple choice—baptism or death. Only Bramimonda, wife of the Moslem ruler of Saragossa, in deference to her sex and her high station, was privileged to come to the faith by the slower process of instruction.

Because Charlemagne's state was a theocracy, both bishops and counts were equally his officials. He appointed them both, ordered them to cooperate in governing his people, and dismissed those who failed him. His capitularies deal with secular and spiritual matters indiscriminately, with religious reform, with doctrine, with the liturgy. To him it made no difference whether the recipient of his directive was the steward who needed briefing on the manner in which he should administer his estates, or a bishop who must be reminded what to teach about the Trinity, or an abbot who was warned to mend the evil conditions reported in his monastery. There was no need for Alcuin to have explained to Charlemagne that his position of king made him the guardian of the morals of his people. This Charles assumed. He also accepted Alcuin's admonition that it was his duty to provide his subjects the example of proper Christian living, although here his performance was not entirely commendable. The morals of the royal household at Aachen were low and to this low level Charlemagne himself contributed. Still Charlemagne's age accepted moral irregularity, especially in its kings; furthermore, in its opinion, the king's faithful attendance at divine services, his devotion to the Church, and his charity to the poor, more than covered his moral deficiencies.

Charlemagne viewed his position as king and emperor as investing him with superior authority in both spiritual and secular matters. What convinced him of this superiority was the sacredness of his mission as he saw it, and the simple fact of the pope's political dependence upon him for his existence. He no doubt endorsed the political philosophy of the Byzantine emperor, that the pope was but one of his subjects. In the year 796 he addressed a monitory letter to Pope Leo, part of which read: "It is our duty, with the help of Divine Holiness to defend by armed might the holy Church of Christ everywhere from the visible attacks of the pagans and the ravages of the infidels, and to strengthen within her the knowledge of the catholic faith. It is your duty, most holy Father, to help our armies with your hands lifted up to God like Moses, so that by your intercession, your leadership, and the gift of God, the Christian people may everywhere and always be victorious over the enemies of his holy name."

These words suggest a partnership in the work of God, with the emperor holding the position of senior partner. While the pope could scarcely accept this as their proper relationship, given the circumstances then obtaining, he could do little to change it. Two facts recommended prudent acceptance of the situation: first, that the emperor would not live forever, although the Church would—after the emperor's death the Church could hope to regularize the relationship existing between them; second, that the emperor's motives in interfering in spiritual matters were thoroughly Christian. Until Charlemagne's death, the pope would have to accept his decrees concerning liturgical usages, even his convening church councils in his Frankland to consider the veneration of images and the heresy of Adoptionism. When the council which Charlemagne had summoned to Aachen in 809 declared in favor of the doctrine of the *filioque*—that the Holy Spirit proceeded from the Father and the Son—the emperor remonstrated with the pope for failing to introduce that word in the creed in Rome. He had already ordered its use in the empire! (The pope actually approved the *filioque,* but had withheld its introduction for fear of Greek resentment.)

Because the pope appreciated Charlemagne's sincerity and his power, relations between the two appear to have been consistently cordial. When Charlemagne learned of the death of Pope Hadrian, "he wept as much as if he had lost a brother, or a very dear son." According to Einhard, "he cherished the Church of St. Peter the Apostle at Rome above all other holy and sacred places, and heaped its treasury with a vast wealth of gold, silver, and precious stones. He sent great and countless gifts to the popes. . . ." Medieval popes had seldom had a more devoted royal friend than they found in Charlemagne.

THE GOVERNMENT OF THE CAROLINGIAN EMPIRE

Charlemagne left less a mark on the government of the Carolingian state than one would expect of so powerful and prudent a monarch. His state remained substantially the Germanic monarchy that Clovis had founded three hundred years earlier. The king was pre-eminently a military leader and the group of personal household officials who followed him about wherever he went, constituted his government. The count still directed local government, the land's princes met annually in the spring to consider the business of the summer (usually war), and persons accused of crime were still tried by the unsophisticated processes of compurgation and ordeal.

Though the Carolingian state remained in essence the Germanic institution that Clovis had ruled, it could not have endured for so long a time without accepting significant influences from Christian and Roman (Byzantine) contacts. The older of Charlemagne's subjects whose memories went back a few years must have been disturbed when Bishop Boniface anointed Pepin, the first time the Church had taken a hand in the accession of a Frankish king. And unlike his Merovingian predecessors, Charlemagne no longer appeared at the annual assembly in an ox-cart. The substitution of a horse for the ox-cart they could have dismissed as inconsequential, but the anointing with holy chrism was a matter of great import. Their king was no longer simply their choice, nor was the limit of his power what they had conferred upon him. His authority derived from above and, now that he was an agent of God, he could demand a greater degree of obedience, even subjection, from them than his Frankish predecessors had ever dared ask. The non-Frankish ceremonials at court which derived from Byzantium gave point to the king's elevated state. When a Frank now came to present a petition, even were he a count, he must prostrate himself to the ground and kiss the foot of his lord. Had Charlemagne been less the overwhelming character that he was, and had the shift from Germanic to Eastern etiquette in this respect been less gradual, a similarly defiant group of Frankish princes might have faced Charlemagne as confronted Alexander the Great when he ordered his Macedonian officers to adopt the *proskynesis* (ritual prostration) of the Persian court.

Was Charlemagne an absolute monarch? No, not in the sense of being above the law. He was absolute, however, in the sense that no Frankish institution existed, such as an assembly of princes or positive traditions, that could have blocked his will so long as he did what most of his subjects considered reasonable. Charlemagne and his distinguished adviser and mentor, Alcuin, traced the imperial authority, not to the early German assembly, but to imperial Rome that was ruled by an autocrat. His imperial authority, so Alcuin assured him, was ordained by God. Yet Charlemagne was a practical and shrewd man. He never put his supreme authority to the test of proposing action the majority of his counts and great men would have condemned. In theory there was little difference between the authority of the early Merovingian monarchs and his own, although a great deal in fact. These early kings might aspire to be absolute, but it was an ambition, except in the instance of Clovis, that the poverty of their means and the limitations of their character made almost ridiculous. Charlemagne possessed both the authority and means, by virtue of his personality, to aspire to absolutism, although if this thought entered his mind, he saw no good served by pursuing it.

If Charlemagne's authority was above that of his Frankish predecessors, so were his responsibilities. Clovis promised his subjects nothing beyond law and order within the frontiers of the Frankish state and protection from foes without. Charlemagne promised this and appreciably more, first and foremost, the protection and advancement of their Christian religion. Other responsibilities that he was ready to assume reflect the higher social plane Frankish society had risen to since the sixth century. By the ninth century Charlemagne was prepared to protect his subjects, not only from lawless elements and foreign foes, but from dishonest merchants who might use faulty weights and measures or from landowners who might demand excessive tolls for the use of their roads. He forbade the export of corn in times of crop failure and even made attempts to provide relief for the indigent. Bridges and roads must be built and maintained, principally, it is true, for war purposes, but also for the convenience of his subjects. While these services appear meager by modern standards, most medieval states of Western Europe did not offer much beyond these for another four hundred years.

The most Germanic feature of the Carolingian monarchy was its personal character. The king was the government and wherever he happened to be, there was his capital. So much was Charles the state that he was expected to administer it principally from the income of his private estates. The imprudence of the Merovingian monarchs in permitting their crown estates to slip through their hands accounted in the main for their gradual enfeeblement. Fortunately for Charlemagne, he was the largest landowner in the kingdom. It was equally fortunate that he saw the direct correlation that existed between the efficiency with which his estates were administered on the one hand and his success as monarch on the other. How concerned Charlemagne was about this matter is revealed in his famous capitulary *De Villis,* in which he set down detailed instructions his stewards were to observe in their supervision of his estates. The document also provides an invaluable glimpse at the agrarian kind of life most of Charlemagne's subjects were leading at the time.

"We desire that each steward shall make an annual statement of all our income, giving an account of our lands cultivated by the oxen which our own plowmen drive and of our lands which the tenants of farms ought to plow; of the pigs, rents, obligations, and fines; of the game taken in our forests without our permission; . . . of the mills, fields, bridges, and ships; . . . of markets, vineyards; . . . of the hay, firewood, torches, planks, and other kinds of lumber; . . . of the vegetables, millet, and panic; of the wool, flax, and hemp; of the fruits of trees, of the nut trees and grafted trees; . . . of the gardens, turnips; of the fishponds; of the hides, skins, and horns; of honey and wax; of the fat, tallow, and soap; of the mulberry wine, cooked wine, mead, vinegar, beer and wine, new and old; . . . of the new grain and old, . . . of the hens and eggs, . . . of the geese; of the number of fishermen, workers in metal, sword makers, and shoemakers; of the bins and boxes; of the turners and saddlers; of the forges and mines, that is, of iron, lead, or other substance; of the colts and fillies. They shall make all these known to us . . . at Christmas, so that we may know what and how much of each thing we have.

"The greatest care must be taken that whatever is prepared or made with the hands, that is, bacon, smoked meat, sausage, partially salted meat, wine, vinegar, mulberry wine, cooked wine, garum, mustard, cheese, butter, malt, beer, mead, honey, wax, flour—all should be prepared and made with the greatest cleanliness.

"Each steward on each of our domains shall always have, for the sake of ornament, peacocks, pheasants, ducks, pigeons, partridges, and turtledoves.

"In each of our estates the chambers shall be provided with counterpanes, cushions, pillows, bedclothes, covering for the tables and benches, vessels of brass, lead, iron, and wood; and irons, chains, pothooks, adzes, axes, augers, cutlasses, and all other kinds of tools. . . .

"For our women's work they are to give at the proper time, as has been ordered, the materials, that is, the linen, wool, woad, vermilion, madder, wool combs, teasels, soap, grease, vessels, and the other objects which are necessary."

Charlemagne did give away occasional parcels of crown lands, although only sparingly, and what he surrendered he more than balanced in the way of gifts received, confiscations, and escheat. A variety of other revenues trickled into the imperial strong box. Any land not already in private hands belonged to the crown, as well as possible hidden treasure buried beneath the surface. On the occasion of the meeting of the assembly in the spring, his lords were expected to bring him "gifts." Foreign emissaries also brought him gifts, but he doubtless sent them back presents of comparable value in return. He sent Harun, the caliph in distant Baghdad, horses and mules from Spain, Frisian robes of various colors, and dogs known for their speed and ferocity which were used in hunting lions and tigers. Of the rich gifts Harun's emissaries brought Charlemagne, none was more highly prized than an elephant. Charlemagne became quite attached to the beast and had it accompany him on his travels. Less exotic sources of revenue for the royal treasury included tribute payments from subject lands, plunder, and the bulk of the fees and fines collected in the courts of the land.

Though the total income from such sources might have been considerable, it could never have sufficed in a modern age when the state's responsibilities have grown so enormously. For the relatively simple needs of the Carolingian state these revenues were adequate. The government of Charlemagne made no outlay for education, none for social welfare, for roads, for the army, nor even ordinarily for its officials. These officials provided for their own needs from lands they already possessed or had received from the king. What roads, bridges, and fortifications were constructed were undertaken by the local communities directly served. Counts, bishops, and monasteries provided the king food and lodging when he traveled about the empire, unless he happened to put up at one of his own manors that lay scattered throughout the land.

In theory there existed no limit to the services the king might demand of his subjects. The heaviest and most common charge was military service. Every freeman was required to equip himself with weapons and armor in proportion to his means. This charge constituted a particularly heavy burden on small farmers who found it impossible to hire help to care for their crops during the three summer months when a campaign was usually fought. To furnish such farmers relief and because of the limited demand for foot soldiers, Charlemagne restricted the military obligation to those men best able to afford distant campaigns. These included the larger landowners, although several small farmers might be required to pool their resources and send one of their number to accompany the army. A capitulary of 807 placed the minimum amount of land for full military service at three hides (a hide varied from eighty to one hundred twenty acres).

More critical was the need for horsemen since the majority of Charlemagne's foes were fighting on horseback. What aggravated the problem of recruiting a large force of cavalry was the expensiveness of horses. It is estimated that a horse had a value at this time of approximately two dozen oxen. That fact put military service beyond the ability of ordinary freemen. What Charles Martel had done in order to meet the Moorish cavalry at Tours in 732 on equal terms was to appropriate church lands, distribute these among his followers as benefices, and require them to use the revenues from these lands to equip themselves and their retainers with horses and arms. Charlemagne did not seize church lands. He either used lands of his own or more often simply placed a requirement of cavalry service upon his counts and the wealthier men of the kingdom. So long as the king was sufficiently strong, as was Charlemagne, to demand such levies of his great men and command their allegiance, there was no great danger for him to rely upon a landed aristocracy for his army. The time would shortly come when the existence of bands of horsemen in the service of the powerful men of the kingdom would enable these nobles to challenge the authority of the king. That development would usher in the age of feudalism.

There was another burdensome service which Charlemagne hoped to lighten for his subjects, namely, their duty to attend court. Like the military defense of the land, the giving of judgment was also the business of the people. Charlemagne directed his counts not to summon the freemen to general judicial assemblies more frequently than two or three times a year. Of greater importance was Charlemagne's success in regularizing judicial procedures. He had written law codes provided for those Germanic groups who were still without them, and he decreed that residence, not birth, should determine which law would be applied in individual cases. If a man lived in Bavaria, for instance, he would be tried by the law of that people, even though he were a Saxon. A sharp reduction of the count's unlimited control over judicial administration resulted from Charlemagne's appointment of a select group of prominent men in the county called *scabini,* to serve as professional judges and to supervise judicial procedures. They traveled about the county with the count when he held court and assisted him in the adjudication of civil disputes and the punishment of crimes.

The ordinary methods of deciding criminal cases remained the Germanic processes of compurgation and ordeal. A man might clear himself of the charge of stealing cattle, for example, by means of compurgation. This would entail his swearing an oath that he was innocent of the charge and securing supporting oaths from a number of "oath helpers" who would swear to the validity of his oath. The rank of the "oath helper" determined the number of these character witnesses the defendant would be obliged to produce. The word of a nobleman might be considered the equivalent of the assurances of perhaps six freemen. Should the defendant be of bad reputation or for some other reason be denied the privilege of clearing himself by compurgation, he must submit himself to trial by ordeal. Here the judge was not to be his neighbors but God, and God would manifest the innocence of the defendant by controlling the outcome of the physical test to which the defendant was subjected. A variety of tests were employed: ordeal by hot or cold water, hot iron, and, among Franks of the upper classes, judicial combat. Here follows a description of the procedure to be observed in the ordeal by hot water.

"When men are to be tried by the ordeal of hot water, they shall first be made to come to church in all humility, and prostrate themselves, while the priest says these prayers: 'Aid, O God, those who seek thy mercy, and pardon those who confess their sins. . . .' After these prayers, the priest shall rise and say the mass before all the men who are to be tried, and they shall take part in the mass. But before they receive communion, the priest shall adjure them in these words: 'I adjure you, by the Father, Son, and Holy Spirit, by your Christianity, by the only begotten Son of God, whom you believe to be the Redeemer of the world, by the Holy Trinity, by the holy gospel, and by the relics of the saints which are kept in this church, that you do not come to holy communion and take of it, if you have done this offence, or consented to it, or if you know who committed it, or anything else about it.'

"If they all keep silence and no one makes any confession, the priest shall go to the altar and take communion, and then give it to the men; but before they receive it he shall say: 'Let this body and blood of our Lord Jesus Christ be today a trial of your guilt or innocence.' [There follow more prayers, the blessing of the water to be heated, and still more prayers.]

"Then the priest takes off the garments of each of the men and clothes them in the clean robes of an exorcist or deacon, makes them each kiss the gospel and cross of Christ, and sprinkles them with holy water. Then he makes them each take a drink of the holy water, saying to each one: 'I give you this water as a trial of your guilt or innocence. . . .' [Then follow more prayers, ending with these words by the priest:] 'Let us pray. God, who didst free St. Susanna from false accusation; God, who didst free St. Daniel from the lions' den and the three children from the fiery furnace: free now the innocent and make known the guilty.'

"The man who is to undergo the ordeal shall say the Lord's prayer and make the sign of the cross; then the caldron shall be taken from the fire, and the judge shall suspend a stone in the water at the prescribed depth in the regular manner, and the man shall take the stone out of the water in the name of the Lord. Then his hand shall be immediately bound up and sealed with the seal of the judge, and shall remain wrapped up for three days, when it shall be unbound and examined by suitable persons."

If after this three-day interval the wound was found to be healing properly, the man was declared innocent; if it appeared infected, he was judged guilty. In this event, he would be assessed a fine scaled to suit the offense. Because the maintenance of jails was beyond the ability of ninth-century society, life sentences or sentences running a number of years were impossible. Monasteries might be enlisted to confine erring members of the clergy or aristocracy. For crimes of violence and robbery, the ordinary penalty was death or mutilation.

The royal household that included Charlemagne's principal administrative officials was an inheritance from Merovingian times. These officials included the chamberlain who handled the royal revenues; the seneschal, whose business it was to manage the king's estates; the marshal or constable, whose earlier responsibility for the king's horses opened the way to control of the military establishment; and the butler who had charge of the royal cellar and the vineyards. More influential than any of these major officials was usually the chaplain, often a bishop or abbot, whom the king selected for his learning and prudence. The chaplain's clerks who were responsible for the liturgical services attended by the court also assumed responsibility for keeping legal records and handling the royal correspondence. In time this function of the chaplain's office would develop into the chancery.

The sole potential check on Charlemagne's authority was that latent in the assembly of great men, lay and ecclesiastical, whom he summoned to meet with him in the spring. When Tacitus first described this assembly, it was meeting each month and was sharing control of the tribe with the king, if not controlling the king himself. Since the business of the assembly among the early Germans was almost exclusively military, its membership was limited to those men who were capable of bearing arms. As centuries passed and the business of government ceased being so narrowly and continuously military, the assembly also ceased meeting each month, with the consequence that its control over the king waned proportionately. Nevertheless, it still remained in Charlemagne's day fundamentally a military assembly because of the regularity of a summer military campaign, and when its members assembled in answer to the royal summons at what was known as the Mayfield, they came fully equipped for battle. Now it advised with the king rather than directed his actions, and although Charlemagne would scarcely have proposed action the majority of his princes disapproved, his was the final decision. Other meetings of his great men Charlemagne also summoned, smaller groups, where matters of equally weighty moment might be discussed and decided. And since the king could issue orders on his own authority, it is evident that the spring assembly retained little of its ancient character other than that of discussing matters with the king and representing in theory the voice of the people.

Charlemagne expressed his will and that of his assemblies through the medium of capitularies or royal proclamations which had the force of law. Like early Roman law, those of the tribal Germans were simply customs which were gradually written down as contact with Rome revealed the superiority of written codes. The name Folkright, by which these customs were known, suggests their ancient origin. In the year 802 Charlemagne summoned his dukes, counts, and ecclesiastics to consider with him necessary emendations in this Folkright. Upon completion of this reform, he pronounced this revised Folkright to be the law of the land. As additional changes in the Folkright became advisable or new problems arose that required attention, he would issue capitularies on his own authority in the quiet of Aachen or, after consulting with his counts, before a full meeting of the assembly. If the capitulary was to have wide and immediate application, the practical-minded Charlemagne promulgated it at the Mayfield. In neither case did he anticipate any opposition. Most astonishing to the modern reader of these capitularies is the wide variety of matters over which Charlemagne claimed jurisdiction. Not only did administrative, economic, and military questions receive his attention, but education, liturgy and doctrine, and even monastic reforms as well. They also reveal his careful concern about correcting all irregularities that came to his attention, as the capitulary which warned counts not to postpone sessions of court in order to go hunting.

For purposes of local government, the Frankish empire was divided into administrative units called counties. There were some three hundred of these, each under its own count. Counties lying along a sensitive frontier would usually be more extensive in size and bore the name of marches, from the German word *Mark* meaning frontier. The official in charge of a march was called a margrave (*Markgraf*). Because of the strategic importance of his county and the large number of retainers and fortifications under his command, the margrave ordinarily enjoyed precedence over the count. Charlemagne retained a few dukes in his kingdom, although after the deposition of Tassilo, the duke of Bavaria, none ever again exercised such extensive authority.

Because of the long distances from Aachen, the difficulty of travel, and the non-existence of other officials in the county who might limit the authority of the count, that official's position constituted the weakest point in the administrative machinery of the Carolingian state. So great was the count's (margrave's) authority that even so mighty a monarch as Charlemagne was obliged to keep a vigilant eye on his loyalty. To reduce the danger of revolt, he never permitted the office to become hereditary, and although the count normally held office for life, he might be removed at any time should the king suspect his allegiance. Charlemagne also revived an irregular practice from the past, that of sending out royal inquisitors each year, called *missi dominici* (messengers of the lord), who were to "report to him any inequality or injustice . . . and to render justice to all, to the holy churches of God, to the poor, to widows and orphans, and to the whole people." Charlemagne usually sent out two emissaries, one a bishop or abbot, the other a count, since they were to investigate both spiritual and civil affairs. In order to reduce the danger of collusion between the two of them and between them and the counts whose territories they visited, he always paired them off differently each time they went out and never sent them to the same county twice. He also appointed only men who already enjoyed considerable wealth and who might, therefore, be less responsive to bribes. While the system of annual inquisitors worked satisfactorily for Charlemagne, it could never have done so in the hands of a less powerful and feared monarch. During the feeble reign of his son Louis the Pious, this most vital check on the loyalty of the count fell into disuse.

THE CAROLINGIAN RENAISSANCE

It would be impossible to find a medieval king of Western Europe who ruled so large an empire as Charlemagne. It would be equally difficult to find one who had a more genuine interest in learning. For "he cultivated the liberal arts most zealously, held those who taught them in great esteem, and conferred great honors upon them." Charlemagne, like most Franks of his day, received no formal education. For this reason occasional writers have mistakenly held him to have been uneducated. While Charlemagne could never have passed as a learned scholar, he did acquire an education which for a layman, by ninth-century standards, was considered excellent.

"He took lessons in grammar of the deacon Peter of Pisa, at that time an aged man. Another deacon, Albin of Britain, surnamed Alcuin, a man of Saxon extraction, who was the greatest scholar of the day, was his teacher in other branches of learning. The King spent much time and labor with studying rhetoric, dialectics, and especially astronomy; he learned to reckon, and used to investigate the motions of the heavenly bodies most curiously, with an intelligent scrutiny. He also tried to write, and used to keep tablets and blanks in bed under his pillow, that at leisure hours he might accustom his hand to form the letters; however, as he did not begin his efforts in due season, but late in life, they met with ill success." Given his zeal, however, one may assume that Charlemagne did acquire a reasonably legible hand, not a mean accomplishment in an age when professional scribes did most of the writing.

Charlemagne must have impressed his contemporaries with his ability to express himself, perhaps one of the reasons why he enjoyed engaging in scholarly discussion with his friends. "Charles had the gift of ready and fluent speech," writes Einhard, "and could express whatever he had to say with the utmost clearness. He was not satisfied with command of his native language merely, but gave attention to the study of foreign ones, and in particular was such a master of Latin that he could speak it as well as his native tongue; but he could understand Greek better than he could speak it." How many of those modern scholars who hold Charlemagne to have been uneducated can speak Latin and read Greek!

Charlemagne's interest in education was intimately linked with his interest in Christianity. This was nothing unusual, for in the eighth and ninth centuries, until the close of the Middle Ages in fact, the first purpose of education was assumed to be the service of religion. This, too, was Charlemagne's objective in improving educational standards. Apart from the passing enjoyment a liberal education would provide a few people like himself who might enjoy reading the Latin poets, its principal role was to facilitate the study of the Bible and the church fathers. Few things disturbed him more than to receive letters from bishops and abbots that were "very correct in sentiment but very incorrect in grammar." Such a deficiency in Latin, he feared, would leave the clergy incapable of understanding the Scriptures and of properly teaching the people the lessons of the Gospels.

The fact that Charlemagne's interest in learning sprang from his devotion to Christianity should not disturb the modern reader. For a person to have assigned any other purpose to education at this time in the West would have been inconceivable. Charlemagne's Frankish empire contained no humanists. An occasional monk might read Vergil with real enjoyment, might even try his hand at composing verses, but he remained very much a monk. Such literary ventures were too casual to offer more than momentary satisfaction. Even classical scholars as renowned as John of Salisbury, probably the best educated man of the latter twelfth century, who appreciated the beauty of Ciceronian prose and could almost match it, were primarily churchmen, pretty largely restricted to the discharge of spiritual responsibilities. It is only the later Middle Ages that produced the genuine humanist, a man so enamored of classical thought that he spent his entire day, if he could afford to do so, in literary pursuits and even sought to mold his manners after Cicero. Profane learning for the purpose of serving sophisticated tastes had no place in a time such as the Carolingian age that could boast of no cities, no secular schools, and little cultural intercourse among centers of learning on the one hand and a great measure of turbulency, ignorance, and superstition on the other. Secular education had many centuries to wait.

The cultural darkness of the Carolingian age followed upon centuries that had been equally dark. When in the sixth century Gregory of Tours voiced the lament: "Alas for these our days, for the study of letters is perished amongst us," he was speaking of learning that had already been in decline for a full three hundred years. This cultural decline was linked with Rome's decline, with the decline of her cities, and with the barbarization of the empire by alien peoples who were incapable of, or not interested in, preserving that culture. Had it not been for the rise of the Christian Church which had a need for preserving at least enough of Rome's learning to carry on Christ's mission, the cultural loss would have been almost complete. Yet Christian scholars only preserved learning, they did not promote it. Christians had a more vital responsibility in their judgment, than to foster the arts. They must convert the pagan, they must explain the new gospel, they must preserve the faith from error. Church fathers might employ good Latin and Greek in presenting their views, but they learned classical languages in order to do this, not to read Homer, Cicero, and Horace. Three church fathers, Tertullian, Cyprian, and Minucius Felix, all use the same phrase to express the harsh realities of the times. *Non loquimur magna sed vivimus,* they declared, which in translation reads something like this: "We do not speak of eloquent matters, we are content to live." It was this consideration, not an aversion some Christians entertained for pagan literature, that prevented anything beyond the survival of only a part of classical culture during the difficult centuries ahead.

Toward the close of the fifth century or the beginning of the sixth, Western Europe entered upon the culturally backward period known as the Dark Ages. Except for scattered intellectual centers in Spain and Ireland, war and destruction during the three centuries to come would reduce intellectual endeavor over most of Western Europe to a mere existence. During this melancholy period scholarly activity ceased except on the part of a handful of lonely writers who managed somehow to pursue the study of letters. The first of this hardy group, known traditionally as the transmitters of classical and patristic learning, was Boethius. Yet Boethius was scarcely typical of the group that was to follow him. He was a layman, the only lay scholar for many centuries to come—so much was learning to be confined to monastic and cathedral schools. Because he was a layman, it is also understandable that he should have felt a greater concern for the fate of secular learning than the monastic scholars who came after him. After his death profane learning became a luxury Western Europe could not afford again until the Carolingian age and then only on a very minor scale. Because of Boethius' interest in non-religious learning, he sensed a danger not generally appreciated by his clerical contemporaries, namely, that Western learning would become unsubstantial and sterile if its roots in Greek philosophy and science were allowed to disappear. In order to prevent this tragedy, he set himself the impossible task of translating Plato and Aristotle into Latin. He died before his task was hardly begun, and no one took up the task where he left off.

Following Boethius was his contemporary and countryman Cassiodorus. Like Boethius, Cassiodorus prepared manuals on the seven liberal arts, but unlike him, being a monk, he devoted much time to scriptural and theological studies. (His treatises on the liberal arts were also prepared for the clergy.) His most valuable contribution to Western learning was probably the encouragement he gave to the copying of manuscripts. A few years in time after Cassiodorus, but a great distance in terms of scholarship, was Gregory of Tours, more saintly than learned, whose ungrammatical Latin provided the vehicle for his valuable *History of the Franks*. Markedly superior was the learning revealed in the writings of the Spaniard Isidore of Seville. For the next five hundred years his *Etymologies,* despite their deficiencies, was the Encyclopaedia Britannica of the West. The brightest area intellectually speaking in Western Europe in the sixth and seventh centuries was Ireland. Her sheltered position had preserved her from the Germanic invasions which had devastated the continent and England. The best known of a distinguished group of Irish monks who carried faith and learning to the British Isles and to Gaul were Columba and Columbanus.

This abbreviated list of men who transmitted learning during the Dark Ages ends with its most renowned scholar, the Venerable Bede. Bede was a product of the monastery of Jarrow in northern England. More famous monasteries like those at Lérins, St. Gall, Fulda, and Bobbio also produced scholars but none so famous as Bede. Many monks with scholarly tastes would have envied him his scholarly life. "All my life I spent in that same monastery," he wrote, "giving my whole attention to the study of the Holy Scriptures, and in the intervals between the hours of regular discipline and the duties of singing in the church, I always took pleasure in learning, or teaching, or writing something." Bede knew Latin and Greek, and even Hebrew. To him lay open, therefore, what learning Western Europe possessed at the time. This learning he assimilated, added observations of his own based upon his own study and investigation, then passed this on to others in the form of textbooks and commentaries. His best-known work is the *Ecclesiastical History of the English People*, a living testimonial to the author's deep faith in divine providence and his great love of learning and truth.

One of the principal beneficiaries of Bede's learning was Charlemagne. In the year 781 while in Italy, he happened to meet Alcuin, a monk from York, England, and persuaded him to accompany him back to Aachen. For fifteen years Alcuin remained at Aachen teaching Charlemagne and many others there the learning he owed indirectly to earlier monastic scholars like Bede. Alcuin was the most distinguished of the scholars whom Charlemagne invited to his palace school at Aachen in an effort to raise the level of learning in his kingdom. There were others, all of them from foreign countries since France had few scholars of her own: the poet Theodulf from Spain, esteemed as the leading Latin versifier of his day—his magnificent *Glory, Laud, and Honor* continues to resound through Christian churches on Palm Sunday; from Ireland, Dungal about whom nothing is known except that he was a refugee (Vikings were blotting out intellectual life in Ireland); from Italy, two grammarians, Peter of Pisa and Paulinus of Aquileia, and the chronicler Paul the Deacon who managed eventually to escape with Charlemagne's permission the half-barbarous, loose-mannered court at Aachen for the quiet of Monte Cassino where he wrote his *History of the Lombards;* and two Franks who came to learn rather than to teach: Einhard whom we have met before, and Angilbert who became a writer of Latin verse and eventually lay abbot of a monastery in Picardy.

The most important of all these scholars was Alcuin. His learning, wisdom, and sympathetic nature made him an excellent teacher. Next to Charlemagne, he was the guiding spirit of the intellectual revival that nourished learning throughout the Frankish empire from its center at Aachen. Alcuin compiled textbooks on the liberal arts, training manuals, and commentaries on the Scriptures and on St. Augustine's writings, but his principal role at Aachen was pre-eminently that of schoolmaster, always ready with an apt quotation or maxim. It was in that capacity that he exerted most influence. Those students who sat with him at Aachen carried some of his enthusiasm for learning to their cathedral and monastic schools, where it bore significant fruit among scholars of the next generation. Alcuin was more than Charlemagne's beloved teacher. He was his guide and counselor, at times his critic. His influence is visible in the policies Charlemagne followed toward the papacy, in his stand on doctrinal and liturgical questions, in the evolution of the theory of the empire, and particularly in the emperor's acceptance of heavy responsibilities in the cause of Christianity.

Charlemagne's most dramatic effort in the interest of learning was the assembling of these scholars at Aachen. Einhard does not say whether the emperor ever expressed satisfaction at his success in establishing his capital as a center of learning. He does speak, however, of the great satisfaction these scholarly associates furnished the emperor. Charlemagne liked to join them in learned conversation and discussion, when each would assume a name from the Bible or classical antiquity in order to raise their conversation to an impersonal, more scholarly level. Alcuin was Horace, Charlemagne, King David, because David was the highest king of the Old Testament, and Angilbert was Homer. Together they worked over their favorite Latin authors and the Vulgate. In their study of rhetoric, they must have taken turns presenting short disquisitions, and if Charlemagne was at all vain, his accomplishment here would have filled him with pride. For according to Einhard, "Charles had the gift of ready and fluent speech, and could express whatever he had to say with the utmost clearness. . . . He was so eloquent, indeed, that he might have passed for a teacher of eloquence."

Charlemagne did not stop with his palace school, that was where he began. In the course of his reign, particularly after 800, he directed a series of capitularies to the bishops and abbots of the empire on the subject of education. Those who already had schools were ordered to improve them; those who were without were to establish them. "Let there be schools established in which boys may learn to read," he directed in a capitulary of 789. "In every monastery or bishopric, let them learn psalms, notes, singing, computus [arithmetic], grammar, and let the religious books that are given them be free of faults because often some desire to pray to God properly, but they pray badly because of faulty books. And let care be taken that the boys do not damage them [the books] either when reading or writing." It may have been one of these boys whom Charlemagne himself chastised, either for his poor Latin or for having marred a book.

Monks must not spend their time solely in prayer and physical labor; they must prepare themselves to teach. He ordered them to learn Latin perfectly "because it is proper that men of God should not only live according to their rule and dwell in holy communion with one another, but that they should devote themselves to literary pursuits, each in accordance with his ability, in order that they may be able to prepare themselves to teach others." Charlemagne was particularly disturbed at the existence of variant readings in the Scriptures, the consequence, he was convinced, of the carelessness of the scribes. Monasteries were to take special care in the copying of manuscripts, have several copies of each book on hand, and exchange manuscripts with other monasteries so that more copies of all scholarly writings would become available. Even the script they were using must be improved, for it had degenerated into a scrawl which simply added to the multiplication of errors and complicated the task of reading and understanding. Charlemagne also gave thought to music and "was at great pains to improve the church reading and psalmody, for he was well skilled in both, although he neither read in public nor sang, except in a low tone and with others." He asked the pope to send him clerks who could teach his clergy at Aachen the Gregorian chant he so much enjoyed when he visited St. Peter's.

An indirect but significant impetus to the advance of learning resulted from Charlemagne's practice of appointing educated priests to serve as bishops and abbots. Any priest who had ambitions to become a bishop had best get himself an education. The Monk of St. Gall leaves the impression, indeed, that most Carolingian bishops owed their promotion to their education. Charles at any rate sent Alcuin to the abbey at Tours, to Theodulf he gave a bishopric, while Angilbert he made abbot of St. Riquier.

Charlemagne's enthusiasm for Latin did not extinguish his love of his native tongue. "He also had the old rude songs that celebrate the deeds and wars of the ancient kings written out for transmission to posterity. He began a grammar of his native language. He gave the months names in his own tongue in place of the Latin and barbarous names by which they were formerly known among the Franks." January became winter month, the other eleven in proper sequence being horn-shedding (of stags) month (February), spring month (March), Easter month (April), pasture month (May), break (ground) month (June), hay month (July), ears (of corn) month (August), wood month (September), vintage month (October), harvest month (November), and holy month (December). Unfortunately for the history of old Germanic verse, Charlemagne's son, aptly known as Louis the Pious, ordered the "rude songs" his father had collected destroyed because of their pagan themes.

The influence of Charlemagne's work in reviving learning is seen principally in the improved character of the monastic schools of the empire. Instruction grew more substantial as a result of his efforts, more schools came into existence, and more young men were being educated. The script employed in copying manuscripts was vastly improved and today bears the name of Carolingian minuscule. It is noted both for its clarity and beauty. The monastic tradition of copying manuscripts spread to more monasteries and resulted in the transcribing of the majority of classical manuscripts that are extant today. It is said that Angilbert kept three hundred monks engaged in that activity at St. Riquier. The level of the "low" Latin then in use was radically raised and developed in time into what is known as medieval Latin. This Latin may never have come into existence but for the efforts the Aachen scholars and their successors made to purify the language of non-classical words and usages. Had it not been for their interest in a better Latin, that in use would ultimately have "degenerated" into a Romance tongue, so far removed from the classical, as to leave its parentage concealed except to students of linguistics.

As noted above, Charlemagne's love of Christianity inspired his interest in education. An educated clergy—and this is what he most wanted —could better understand the Scriptures, could participate in the liturgy with greater propriety, could more effectively instruct the laity. A significant result of his renaissance was, nevertheless, the encouragement it afforded profane learning. Boniface, the contemporary of Charlemagne's father Pepin, sought to enlarge his small hoard of books but only with the addition of religious manuscripts. His fundamentally religious orientation might be viewed as representative of the pre-Carolingian age. Yet within fifty years of the death of Charlemagne, Lupus, abbot of Ferrières, could write to Reginbert, a monk of St. Gall, almost as one humanist to another: "Sallust's Cataline and Jurgurtha and the books of the Verrine orations [Cicero] and if there are any others you know we have either in imperfect shape or lack entirely, be good enough to bring to us so that through your kindness those that are faulty may be corrected, and those which we do not have and can never have except through you may be acquired all the more gratefully because unexpectedly." Finally, that Orléans, Tours, Corbie, Fulda, St. Gall, Reichenau, and Lorsch could rise to the level of the centers of learning then existing in England and Italy in the ninth century was in no small measure the result of Charlemagne's work.

Charlemagne was also a builder although nothing on the scale of Justinian. The palace he erected at Aachen has disappeared, but his octagonal church still impresses visitors. It was modeled after the Byzantine church of San Vitale in Ravenna. (The chapel he had erected when he first came to Aachen accounts for the French name of Aix-la-Chapelle.) He "adorned it with gold and silver and lamps, and with rails and doors of solid brass. He had the columns and marbles for this structure brought from Rome and Ravenna, for he could not find such as were suitable elsewhere." The canal he started to dig which would have connected the Rhine and the Danube he never completed, although the "half-mile-long" bridge over the Rhine at Mainz he did finish. This was, unfortunately, "so completely consumed in three hours by an accidental fire that not a single splinter of it was left, except what was under water." Charlemagne died before carrying out his plan to replace it with one of stone. Einhard also credits the emperor with having constructed "two palaces of beautiful workmanship, one near his manor of Ingelheim, not far from Mainz; the other at Nimwegen, on the Waal."

CHARLEMAGNE'S DEATH

According to Einhard, Charlemagne remained in vigorous health until four years of his death when he became afflicted with fevers and "at the last he even limped a little with one foot." Even then he appears to have "consulted his own inclinations rather than the advice of physicians, who were almost hateful to him, because they wanted him to give up roasts, to which he was accustomed, and to eat boiled meat instead." He was on a hunting trip when his final illness struck him down. "As soon as he was taken sick, he prescribed for himself abstinence from food, as he always used to do in case of fever, thinking that the disease could be driven off, or at least mitigated, by fasting. Besides the fever, he suffered from a pain in the side which the Greeks called pleurisy; but he still persisted in fasting and in keeping up his strength only by draughts taken at very long intervals. He died January twenty-eighth, the seventh day after the time he took to his bed, at nine o'clock in the morning, after partaking of the holy communion, in the seventy-second year of his age and the forty-seventh of his reign."

Charlemagne was buried in the church he built at Aachen in a sarcophagus brought from Rome. His remains are still in this church, although now enclosed in a gold and silver reliquary that was constructed in the thirteenth century.

Henry II

"In the year of our Lord 1120, all his enemies being humbled and peace restored in France, King Henry [I] came over to England." He came in his own ship. The young people, most of the royal household, along with other prominent men and nobles crowded on board the *White Ship* which was to bring across Henry's only son and heir, William. This was the proudest ship in the Channel, "better one than which there did not seem to be in all the fleet." Henry's ship made the crossing from Normandy without mishap for the weather was excellent, but the *White Ship,* overcrowded with reveling passengers and manned by a rowdy crew that had imbibed too heavily, struck a rock and all went down save for one lone survivor, a butcher.

This sudden tragedy undid in an instant, so it appeared, the twenty years of long, arduous effort Henry I had expended on molding for himself and his succession a united and peaceful realm. All Henry's hopes for the future of his kingdom and dynasty were gathered in his son, his only legitimate male offspring. When news of the disaster reached him, he fainted away and, it is said, never smiled again. He did attempt to have another son by a new wife—he was a widower—but she bore him none. And so all the solid, untiring work he had expended on the establishment of a strong, just government seemed to have been for naught. Though he was a "lion of justice," and a king of whom the Anglo-Saxon chronicler records laconically, that in his day "no man durst harm another," what would the situation be after his death?

In Henry's age, an able monarch's achievement was apt to die with him unless he left a grown son to succeed. Had William lived, his presence would have prevented civil war and a struggle over the succession. Even across the Channel, the future had appeared bright, for Henry, who was also duke of Normandy, had arranged to have William marry the eldest daughter of the count of Anjou, the man most likely to endanger English control of Normandy. Since Henry already claimed the overlordship of Maine and Brittany, he was looking forward to the day when his son would rule not only England but such extensive territories in France that he would be more powerful than his French suzerain Louis VI himself.

William's untimely death placed this bright future in grave jeopardy. Henry sought desperately to salvage what he could. A second marriage had done him no good, but in 1125 his son-in-law, Henry V of Germany, died and this left his widow Matilda, Henry I's daughter, free to remarry. Upon her father's insistence, Matilda returned to England and upon his further insistence married Geoffrey, the fifteen-year-old son of the count of Anjou who was ten years her junior. Matilda was not the only one who objected to the marriage. Henry's English barons wanted no foreigner on the British throne. When they swore reluctantly in 1126 to accept Matilda in case Henry died without a son, they had elicited from the king the promise that he would not marry her to anyone outside the realm without the consent of the great council. This promise Henry had ignored. The Norman barons hated Matilda's new husband Geoffrey because he was an Angevin, and Normans and Angevins had always been enemies. Even Geoffrey had no relish for a marriage to a woman ten years his elder, and within a year of the nuptials had sent her packing back to Normandy. The passage of two years, and a revolt of his barons quickly matured the young Geoffrey, so he sent for Matilda to return to Anjou. Under such unfavorable circumstances, and from so ill-sorted a pair as Geoffrey and Matilda, was born on 5 March 1133, England's greatest king, the future Henry II.

Had Henry I lived another dozen years, which would have afforded his grandson time to grow up, all conceivably would have been well. Unfortunately, when his grandson was two years old, Henry had a meal of lampreys "though they never agreed with him," chides the chronicler, and died of acute indigestion. Overnight the firm rule England had known for the seventy years since 1066, when Henry's father William the Conqueror had killed Harold, came to an end and "every man who could was quick to rob his neighbor." There was nothing to prevent violence and injustice except the two-year-old boy Henry and his mother Matilda whom few expected would make good her succession. For this was a day when rough feudal nobles took rarely to a female lord, particularly one they had scarcely known, since Matilda had spent the greater part of her life in Germany. What they had seen of her since her return from Germany, her haughtiness and obstinacy, had not engendered any sense of loyalty in their bosoms. There were, in addition, some barons who had grown uncomfortable under Henry's strict rule and wanted no more of that tough Norman dynasty.

Matilda might have saved the crown for herself and her son had she crossed over to England immediately upon news of her father's death, instead of concerning herself with Normandy. Her most dangerous rival, Stephen of Blois, had done just that, even though the Channel had seldom been so stormy. This Stephen was the son of Adela, daughter of William the Conqueror, Henry I's own sister, and therefore Henry's nephew, and his favorite one at that. Stephen had practically been raised at the court where Henry had treated him as his own son. Had Henry I proposed Stephen as his successor, not one nobleman in England or in Normandy would have objected. For Stephen was a brave warrior on the battlefield and a gentleman off it, charming, good-natured, and honorable. He held lands in both Normandy and England, had spent more than thirty years on the island, and had married a wife of solid Saxon ancestry who was even more popular than he was. Stephen's weaknesses would stand revealed later, that is, his lack of resolution and aggressiveness. As a contemporary writer described his character: "It was [his] habit to undertake many projects with enthusiasm, but to pursue them with indolence." To those English barons who may have suspected the presence of these deficiencies, that fact, after thirty-five years of Henry I's stern rule, would have made Stephen all the more attractive.

Dover and Canterbury refused to open their gates to Stephen when he landed, so he hurried on to London which gave him a cordial welcome. The burghers knew and liked the generous Stephen, and, in their concern over peace, greatly preferred the immediate rule of an experienced man to the questionable success of a disagreeable woman and her two-year-old boy making good their claims. So they promptly elected Stephen their king and sent him, with their blessing, to Winchester to take possession of the royal treasury. At Winchester Stephen found both the treasury and his uncle, Henry of Blois, the respected bishop of the diocese, who helped him win over the English hierarchy, including the hesitant archbishop of Canterbury. So on 22 December, scarcely three weeks after the death of Henry I, barons who had solemnly sworn to accept Matilda, attended Stephen at his coronation in Westminster Abbey and swore him fealty.

Though monastic chroniclers have exaggerated the miseries that England was to suffer during the next nineteen years, there was no sadder reign in English history. "When the traitors [that is, Stephen's disloyal barons] understood that Stephen was a mild man, soft, and good, and no justice executed, then did they all wonder. . . . For every rich man built him castles and held them against the king, and they filled the land full of castles. They cruelly oppressed the wretched people of the country with forced labor on the castles; and when the castles were built, they filled them with devils and evil men. Then took they those whom they supposed to have any goods, both by night and by day, laboring men and women, and threw them into prison for their gold and silver, and inflicted on them unutterable tortures; for never were any martyrs so tortured as they were. . . . I neither can, nor may I tell all the wounds and all the pains which they inflicted on wretched men in this land. This lasted the nineteen winters while Stephen was king, and it grew continually worse and worse."

So wrote the Anglo-Saxon chronicler. An even longer tale of woe does the author of the *Gesta Stephani* furnish, although afflictions of the English as described in both accounts, are as suggested, overdrawn. Stephen's reign did start well. Pope Innocent II gave approval to his accession and thereby eased the consciences of those barons who had misgivings over their broken oaths to Henry. At Easter, 1136, a large number of nobles put in their appearance at Westminster where Stephen summoned the great council, although the absence of Robert, earl of Gloucester and Matilda's half brother, aroused concern. Robert did appear a month later, and tendered his oath of fealty. In order to secure Robert's allegiance Stephen made concessions, similar to those he had made to London, to the archbishop of Canterbury, to the king of Scotland, and to the lords who had sworn him homage at Westminster. Stephen was forever making concessions. He preferred this to the hard business of saying no, and then fighting those men who refused to obey. That was his weakness.

Still the fatal flaw in Stephen's rule would become evident only later. For the moment, early in 1137, England appeared sufficiently safe for him to cross over to Normandy in order to thwart Matilda who with her husband Geoffrey was attempting to win over that duchy. In his efforts to block Matilda, Stephen had the moral support of Louis VI, but so few English knights accompanied him across that he had to rely upon Flemish mercenaries and their captains to do the job. These foreigners did more to lose Stephen the duchy than Matilda's troops. His diplomatic efforts to win over the barons proved equally artless, so he left his cause to one of his loyal barons and returned to England. Normandy never saw Stephen again.

Stephen's failure in Normandy provided the signal for revolts to break out in England. The always restless Welsh revolted, the Scots crossed into the northern provinces, and Robert, earl of Gloucester, renounced his recognition of Stephen's claim and declared for Matilda. Then Stephen blundered into adding the powerful English hierarchy to his growing list of enemies. In June 1139 he ordered the bishops of Salisbury, Ely, and Lincoln to surrender their castles. Robert, bishop of Salisbury, was the uncle, the other two were Roger's nephews. As Henry I's justiciar, Roger had acquired considerable wealth and influence which he shared with his two nephews and with his son Roger who was chancellor. He still retained his office of justiciar under Stephen, while his nephew, the bishop of Ely, occupied the office of royal treasurer. Because of their powerful position in the government, as well as their arrogance and greed, Stephen was wise to move against them before they had an opportunity to join his foes. Yet he acted with a ruthlessness that he rarely employed even against lay lords, mistreated them, and threw them into prison. (The elderly bishop of Salisbury he confined for a time to a cowshed.) Even though the avarice and aggressiveness of these men made them more barons than bishops, they remained churchmen nevertheless; consequently, Stephen's act cost him the support of the English hierarchy, the one sure prop his shaky throne could claim.

In the fall of 1139 Matilda and her brother, the earl of Gloucester, landed at Arundel in southern England, and the brewing civil war became a fact. Of the barons who announced their adherence, the most important were the constable, Miles of Gloucester, who was a power in southwestern England, and Brian Fitz-Count who held Wallingford on the Upper Thames. The defection of these barons from Stephen enabled Matilda to gain control of a good part of the country to the west and southwest of London, but that was as much as she could accomplish. The majority of barons remained quiet and uncommitted. For those who planned to enter the war, there was danger in choosing sides before one or the other claimant had established his ascendancy. For those barons who hoped to avoid involvement, neither Stephen nor Matilda had the means to force their co-operation. They had inducements to offer in the way of lands and honors, especially Stephen, yet many who accepted his favors still ignored his appeals for assistance. Until time would reveal the ultimate winner, many chose to improve their condition by raiding the countryside, pillaging helpless towns and villages and holding their inhabitants for ransom, or attacking the less well-defended castles in the area.

Early in 1141 the war spread to Lincolnshire. The earl of Chester, who had married the daughter of Robert of Gloucester, decided to take advantage of Stephen's weakness and establish a state of his own that would span England from coast to coast. He accordingly seized the castle at Lincoln and soon had gathered around him not only his father-in-law Robert, but other barons as well who had lost possessions to Stephen. When Stephen learned of this concentration of enemy forces, he hurried to Lincoln, and there on 2 February 1141 took place the first major battle of the civil war. Stephen fought valiantly, so the chronicler assures the reader, but when the fighting got hot most of his barons fled rather than risk life or limb, and he was captured.

When Matilda learned of Stephen's capture, she was overjoyed. Now nothing could prevent her assuming her rightful place as queen. She hurried to Winchester to claim the royal crown and treasury which were kept in the castle, but had first to win over the town's bishop by promising him full control of the ecclesiastical affairs of the kingdom. Then Winchester castle opened to her and the townspeople proclaimed her "Lady of England." Next she proceeded to London, but there her short triumphal march came to a halt. Within a few days her haughtiness had lost her all she had gained, for "she was elated with unsufferable pride at the success of her adherents in the uncertain vicissitudes of war, so that she alienated from her the hearts of most men." Upon her demand that the Londoners swear their allegiance and hand over a tallage, they rose in tumult and thrust her from the city.

From London Matilda moved northward to Oxford, then turned back south toward Winchester when she learned that the bishop there had again returned to Stephen's fold. During the month of August (1141), while her troops were laying siege to Winchester, adherents of the two claimants kept coming in from all sides, including a large contingent from London that supported Stephen. Finally in September, Matilda and the earl of Gloucester decided they had best retreat before the growing superiority of Stephen's army, but their retreat shortly deteriorated into a flight, in the course of which the earl was captured. When he was exchanged in November for the prisoner Stephen, the situation reverted substantially to what it had been before the two engagements at Lincoln and Winchester. Stephen regained his shaky throne,

Matilda retained possession of a substantial part of the southwest, while scattered barons continued their assaults on towns, monasteries, and countryside. The most infamous of these human monsters was Geoffrey de Mandeville, earl of Essex, whose critical position as constable of the Tower had both Stephen and Matilda showering him with privileges and estates. From his headquarters in the abbey of Ramsey which he had seized, he ravaged the area about Cambridge, burning, torturing, and killing with wanton cruelty and with impunity. In certain localities the countryside became depopulated from such depredations and actual famine struck. "Men said openly that Christ and His saints slept."

Early in 1147 the young Henry came over with a small body of knights in the hope of reviving Angevin fortunes. At Cricklade and Bourton his followers suffered setbacks, whereupon they deserted him. In his plight his mother could not help him, his uncle would not. So in desperation the youthful Henry turned to his kinsman, to King Stephen, for the means of returning to Normandy. True Christian that Stephen was, so the chronicler writes commendingly, he assisted Henry in his need in keeping with St. Paul's exhortation to do good to one's enemies. Less pious contemporaries charged Stephen with having acted both imprudently and childishly.

Matilda followed her son back to Normandy and relative peace settled upon England. The crusade that Louis VII of France and Conrad III of Germany were preparing to lead to Syria also served to reduce fighting in England. Though their armies consisted principally of French and Germans, many English knights took service with one or the other king. Henry was still too young to accompany the crusaders, although sufficiently mature to assist his father in the pacification of Normandy. Because Henry had a Norman mother he proved, indeed, more acceptable to the Norman aristocracy than Geoffrey, and it was not long before his father had entrusted him with the major role in reorganizing the province. In 1150 when Henry attained the age of seventeen, his father turned over to him the entire responsibility of administering the duchy.

Henry should have been satisfied with Normandy, so contemporaries thought. Not only had England accepted Stephen, but it was encouraging him in his efforts to pass on his throne to his son Eustace. The repeated incursions of Matilda had only caused trouble, and how futile Henry's own effort had been in 1147 had been dramatized by Stephen's willingness to help the youth return to Normandy. Yet Henry never once abandoned hope of eventually gaining England which his mother kept reminding him was rightfully to be his. In 1142 he had gone to Bristol, to live with his uncle Robert, earl of Gloucester, and had remained there two years. Five years later had come his first abortive invasion. Then two years later he crossed over to England for a third time, ostensibly for the purpose of being knighted by the king of Scotland (22 May 1149). So inconsequential did Stephen view Henry's coming, that he made no effort to hamper the young man's movements until he learned that the earl of Chester was negotiating with him and that the Scots had promised aid. Then he simply bought off the earl with more grants of land and the possession of Lincoln castle, leaving the discomfited Henry no alternative but again returning empty-handed to Normandy.

Back in Normandy Henry now encountered opposition from Eustace over his claims to that province. Eustace had married the sister of Louis VII, which alliance won him the king's support, who preferred having him in Normandy in the first place rather than Henry, who was the son of the count of Anjou. Henry, however, was so solidly entrenched that he had no difficulty neutralizing Eustace's threat. He ceded Louis several territories which lay on the frontier of the Ile de France, then proceeded with preparations for another invasion of England. Before these had reached their completion, his father Geoffrey died (September 1151) and left him sole ruler of Normandy, Maine, Touraine, and Anjou. This inheritance made him as powerful as his lord, the king of France. Nine months later (18 May 1152), he rose to a still higher position when he married Eleanor, Louis' discarded wife, who brought him all of southwestern France, from the Loire to the Pyrenees, as her dowry.

This marriage of Henry and Eleanor merits attention since England and France would suffer its consequences hundreds of years after man and wife were dead. Back in 1137 Eleanor's father, Duke William X of Aquitaine, had sent his daughter to Paris into the care of Louis VI, as the man most capable of protecting both the girl and Aquitaine. Louis VI could think of no better way of fulfilling this trust than by having Eleanor marry his own son, the future Louis VII. What promised to prove an unusually happy marriage in an age of politically arranged matches, since both people were young and Louis loved Eleanor, turned out to be a failure. The beautiful though strong-willed and sophisticated Eleanor bore Louis two daughters but no son. Equally tragic was the estrangement that grew up between the two, not because of the husband's infidelity which was the usual source of marital incompatibility among medieval royalty, but Eleanor's. At least rumor had it that she had been unfaithful during the Second Crusade when she had accompanied her husband to Syria. All Europe appeared anxious to keep husband and wife together. Even Pope Eugenius III took a hand and had them sleep together when they passed through Tusculum, where he was in momentary exile from Rome, on their return from the East. Suger, Louis' aging counselor, warned the king of the serious injury the French crown might suffer should he have the marriage annulled, and as long as Suger lived nothing was done. When Suger died, and the child that Eleanor was carrying proved to be another daughter, a council of French bishops accommodated and declared the marriage void on the grounds of consanguinity. Eleanor filed no protest. She was thoroughly pleased to be released from her "monkish" husband as she called him.

As soon as the council of bishops had given its judgment on 21 March 1152, Eleanor started off for her domain, the only place a pretty heiress like herself could feel safe. Her trip there turned out to be unusually exciting since there were others, mostly men, who were just as interested in her divorce as Louis and herself. The first eligible bachelor to attempt to waylay her was Count Theobald of Blois. It would be a simple matter to detain her, he decided, as she made her way through Blois toward Poitiers. Fortunately Eleanor learned of his designs in time and fled Blois during the night for Tours. At Tours she discovered that Geoffrey of Anjou, Henry's younger brother, was planning to intercept her on the road she would normally take to cross from Touraine to Poitou, so she kept riding but by another route and finally reached Poitiers. From there she sent word to Henry, whom she had met at the French court, that she was willing to become his wife and bring the great duchy of Aquitaine with her. Henry accepted her offer with alacrity—the romanticist will insist Henry had more interest in her charms than in her duchy —and on 18 May, less than two months after the annulment of her marriage to Louis, Eleanor became Henry's wife.

By the following January (1153) Henry had sufficiently established himself in his new roles of husband and duke of Aquitaine to answer an appeal for help from Wallingford, one of the few towns in England still loyal to the Angevin cause. Four years before when he had last crossed to England, his coming had been no better than a venture. Now in 1153 when he came, he moved with the confidence and authority of a king, of one who ruled over more of France than did Louis VII himself.

Stephen's position in England had meantime worsened even though he had managed to reduce the number of Henry's allies. What caused his fortunes to decline was the estrangement of the English hierarchy. The prelates had not entirely forgotten his harsh treatment of the bishops of Salisbury, Ely, and Lincoln back in 1139. Then in 1148 Stephen had rekindled that resentment by refusing Theobald, archbishop of Canterbury, permission to attend the church council at Reims (the prelate managed to slip across the Channel in a dilapidated boat with Thomas Becket and another companion), and by quarreling with Pope Eugenius III over filling the archiepiscopal see of York. The consequence was a rebuff to Stephen shortly after when he attempted to force the archbishop of Canterbury to crown Eustace his successor, followed by the archbishop's flight to France (again with Thomas Becket), and Pope Eugenius III's injunction that Eustace was not to be crowned since there remained even some question about the legitimacy of Stephen's own rule.

The armies of Stephen and Henry first made contact in January (1153) at Malmesbury, Stephen's troops on one side of the swollen Avon, Henry's on the other. Without attempting a battle, Stephen left the town and castle to Henry and withdrew to London. Henry next marched westward to relieve Wallingford. Again he met Stephen with his royalist army, and again there was no fighting, this time because the barons on both sides announced they wanted no fighting. It was just as well for Henry since time proved very much on his side. Each day more barons defected to his side, while within a few months several hostile earls died. The death that most benefited his cause was that of Stephen's son Eustace. When this young man died, all fight appears to have gone out of Stephen. He was now in his middle sixties, his devoted wife Matilda had died the year previous, and his remaining sons were too young for him to think of pressing their claims against those of Henry.

Not only was Stephen tired of the war, so also were the responsible elements in England. The bishops took the initiative in negotiating a settlement they hoped both Stephen and Henry would find acceptable. Henry's willingness to recognize the rights of Stephen's young son William to the earldom of Surrey and to his father's extensive estates, made their task easy. In November 1153, by the treaty of Winchester, Stephen agreed to recognize Henry as his successor and to co-operate with him in the destruction of the adulterine castles that had sprung up in England during the eighteen years of his troubled reign. Henry swore homage to Stephen, while the barons of both Stephen and Henry did homage to the other. England finally settled down to political tranquillity, although there appears to have developed some trouble between Stephen and Henry over the adulterine castles. In any event, perhaps in some peril of his life, Henry returned to Normandy in the spring of 1154 and remained there until Stephen died later that year on 25 October.

HENRY'S CHARACTER, EDUCATION, AND FAMILY

Upon notice of Stephen's death, Theobald, archbishop of Canterbury, hurried messengers over to Henry in Normandy to bid him come at once to claim his throne. The primate must have recalled how the death of Henry I in 1135 had been the signal for greedy barons to lay their hands on their neighbors' possessions. He had no need for such anxiety now, for the circumstances were wholly different. In 1135, the prospect of a woman's succeeding had given avaricious lords no pause. With Henry as heir apparent, barons knew better and suppressed their greed. Even though a stormy Channel made passage impossible for an entire month, "No man durst do other than good for the mickle awe of him," wrote the observant chronicler. Finally on 8 December, in company with Eleanor, his brothers, and a large group of nobles and troops, Henry landed at Hampshire, moved from there to Winchester, from there to London, where he was crowned in Westminster Abbey the Sunday before Christmas.

Henry was now twenty-one years of age, a strong, stocky, broad-shouldered young man of above moderate height, with thick chest and legs. His was clearly a frame made for physical work and endurance. The garrulous Gerald of Wales likened the muscles of his arms to those of a gladiator. His hands, too, were not those of a king, but rough and reddened, which he never bothered to glove except when hawking. Close-cropped reddish hair which he may never have lost, since no one later speaks of his baldness, covered his well-shaped head. His carriage was not dignified, rather the hurried, vigorous stride of a man who has many things to do. While Henry was not unkempt or untidy, he gave little concern to his personal appearance, neither had he any more concern about personal popularity. His clothes were plain and no better than those of his courtiers. If he gave some thought to avoiding corpulency, a condition which often slowed medieval monarchs, his worry did not rise from vanity but from a desire to retain his health and mobility.

The same interest in health, or it may have been heredity, made Henry moderate in his eating and drinking. It would not have been to his palace, but to that of his chancellor, Thomas Becket, that the visiting gourmet would go for a sumptuous meal. There is even the hint of parsimony about the table he set, undoubtedly from the pen of men who viewed providing a luxurious board to be the peculiar duty of royalty. Among Henry's most valuable gifts were his tremendous vigor and capacity for work. So enormous was his store of nervous energy that he was never tired, even after a long day of hunting when his companions lay around in the straw in a state of exhaustion. When absorbed in some vexing problem he would stay up all night. His restless energy revealed itself even at Mass. (He selected priests known for their speed in saying Mass.) If he did not spend the time at Mass carrying on a low conversation with his attendants, he would doodle in impatience and draw pictures until the service had ended. Henry seldom sat down except at meals, but was forever on his feet. This trait his attendants found wearying, even more so the violent speed with which he traveled about the country, always in haste to reach his destination and often riding far into the night with no adequate lodging awaiting him when he finally stopped. What also vexed his attendants was the suddenness with which he might set out on a trip or, after all preparations had been made, might cancel it. Few men knew his itinerary, perhaps not always Henry himself. His anxious nobles and sheriffs could never be sure when he might turn up.

Hunting, which was Henry's favorite sport, he attacked with the same determination as he did his work. Of dogs and birds his knowledge was that of an expert. He liked especially to hawk, and might indulge this passion when traveling abroad on business of state. During the reign of Stephen the royal forests had suffered considerable encroachment and many acres had been cleared and put to cultivation. Whenever possible Henry reclaimed these areas for the crown and set aside others in addition. As a result of his efforts, royal forests reached their maximum extent during his reign when they covered approximately one third the entire country. Since his forest decrees served to slow the spread of an agricultural economy while at the same time depriving humble folk of the opportunity to brighten their dull fare with game, all for the sake of the royal pleasure, this policy must constitute one of the worst blots on Henry's record. Few practices reveal so graphically the very personal view many medieval monarchs took of their kingdoms as that of reserving so many thousands of square miles of it for their own hunting.

Huge royal reserves were a tradition in the Middle Ages, so it may be unreasonable to take Henry too sharply to task in this matter. Even royal tempers were not unusual, although Henry's was one of the most renowned. He was, fortunately, neither haughty by temperament nor impatient, and usually maintained an amazing degree of equanimity before troubles and vexations which would have tried many ordinary men. When crossed in a matter, however, upon which he had set his mind, or when someone spoke commendingly of a personal enemy, let the culprit beware! In the paroxysms of rage that such circumstances might provoke, he would throw himself upon the ground, curse and moan, and beat the ground in helpless rage. Once when a courtier spoke well of the king of Scotland with whom Henry happened to be feuding, the king tore off his clothes and the covering from his bed, and began to gnaw the straw in the mattress. With respect to friendships and enmities Henry had a long memory. Only after repeated cause would he turn against a friend, while someone he once disliked might be a lifetime endeavoring to prove he was a friend.

Henry was affable and respectful, even humble. He disliked pomp and ostentation and made no pretense to being of better stuff than his people. When he walked about London he permitted men and women to approach him, indeed to jostle him in their eagerness to get close, and he would bear patiently with their questions and importunities. They automatically warmed to his lack of pretense. He earned their respect and loyalty because of the sound, just administration he provided them, even though few took his part in his conflict with Thomas Becket. Yet though he worked long and diligently to establish a strong regime, his first objective was to achieve that power which God and nature had decreed should be a king's. While this necessitated furnishing his subjects peace and justice, in Henry's judgment the attainment of those blessings remained secondary. A contented people constituted the best assurance of a successful reign for himself. That personal affection which Louis IX of France had for his people Henry seems never to have felt.

Henry's devotion to religious duties was not greatly different from that of other monarchs of the time. The chronicler writes of his lack of devotion at Mass, but that was not unusual. He also speaks of his blasphemous rages, but these too were not uncommon. There is little said, on the other hand, of private devotions, of fasts and pilgrimages, of acts of charity toward individuals in want. One chronicler does mention, it is true, that Henry gave much in charity although in secret, "lest his left hand might know what his right gave." Like most Christian monarchs, Henry's nature was not foreign to religious impulses. Shortly after his accession he had a sudden inclination to lead a crusade against the Moslems. Several years later, when he suggested to Pope Adrian that he and Louis VII undertake a joint crusade against the Moors in Spain, Adrian recommended they first ascertain from the Spanish whether they would welcome that kind of interference. Henry and Louis did not sound out the Spanish on this point since by the time the pope's reply had reached them, the impulse had worn off and the two kings were fighting each other instead.

Henry's uncompromising stand on the Constitutions of Clarendon (below) during his controversy with Thomas Becket reflected no intrinsic hostility toward the Church. Saint Louis of France could have pressed the identical program. While Henry might conduct himself unscrupulously in political affairs, in his private conduct he was neither deceitful nor dishonorable. Though he built a good many halls and castles, only six religious houses owe him their foundation, a relatively small number since his century was probably the most active of all medieval centuries in monastic construction. He did expend considerable sums on the construction and maintenance of hospitals for the poor and sick, especially for lepers, although it is curious that these eleemosynary works were limited to his French possessions.

In all of twelfth-century Christendom there was no more learned king than Henry. Both his father and mother gave earnest attention to his education. Quite early they placed him in the care of Peter of Saintes whom contemporaries respected as an excellent poet. During Henry's stay in Bristol with his uncle Robert, he had a Master Matthew as tutor who instructed him "in letters and good manners, as beseemed a youth of his rank." Here at Bristol he met Adelard of Bath, one of the first true scientists of the Middle Ages, who later dedicated his treatise on the astrolabe to the young king. Upon Henry's return to Normandy he studied under the distinguished grammarian William of Conches who was a humanist and, at the same time, a worthy precursor of Robert Grosseteste and Roger Bacon. William compiled a collection of ethical maxims for Henry which he drew from both Christian literature and moral treatises of pagan writers. Walter Map may have been exaggerating when he credited Henry with a knowledge of all the languages spoken from the Bay of Biscay to the Jordan, but there is no question concerning his ability to read and speak both Latin and French. Henry enjoyed reading serious literature, and he liked especially to dispute with the clerks of his court and with scholars who happened by. He was even something of a patron of the arts. The poet Wace composed his epic of the dukes of Normandy upon Henry's request.

In a life beset with more than its share of harassment and disappointment, nothing provided Henry so rich a source of misery and frustration as his own family. "For thirty-six years," wrote one chronicler, he reigned without defeat or injury "except for the sorrows which his sons caused him." Those modern psychologists who emphasize heredity in the analysis of personal traits will have no hesitation positing in the ancestry of Henry's sons a rich assortment of obstinate, unscrupulous, treacherous, unfilial, ruthless, and quarrelsome progenitors. Less sophisticated readers may attribute the lack of discipline and respect in Henry's sons to their father's indulgence as well as to the machinations of their mother Eleanor and the French kings, Louis VII and Philip Augustus. Henry had great love for all his children, most of all for John, his youngest. All four of his sons brought him grief. His three daughters occasioned him no trouble. Girls rarely did in the Middle Ages; their roles were clearly set. Their purpose was to establish diplomatic ties with other regimes and this service Henry's daughters provided without protest. His eldest daughter, Matilda, married the duke of Bavaria; his second daughter, Eleanor, became the wife of the king of Castile, while Jane, the third daughter, married the king of Sicily.

Contemporaries refer to Henry's four sons by contrast as "lion cubs." Henry himself once spoke of them as "four eaglets" bent on destroying him as legend had it young eagles killed their parent. Their quarreling among themselves and with their father is reminiscent of the behavior of the sons of Louis the Pious (814–40). The principal factor in both instances was the same. The sons of Louis the Pious knew they would fall heir to individual shares of the Carolingian empire, but they could not wait until their father was dead to assume control, nor were they generally satisfied with the portion their father had allotted them. In the case of Henry's sons, had their father only England to leave to his eldest son, most of his wars would not have materialized. As it was, he had rich provinces in France to distribute among them, and they could not wait until he died before taking possession.

Henry's firstborn, a boy baptized William, was a sickly child and lived but a few years. His next son Henry was, according to contemporary accounts, a most promising young man, handsome and gallant, and possessing a remarkably charming personality. Before he died of dysentery at the age of twenty-eight while leading a rebellion against his father, he had earned the execrations of thousands of townspeople and peasants in Aquitaine for his ruthless plundering and tyranny. It would be difficult to judge which was the most monstrous of his crimes: his ingratitude toward his father, his treachery which many men experienced, or his sacrilegious violation of sanctuaries. As he lay dying, he sent for his father to come and forgive him his faithlessness, but Henry dared not—he feared his son's "dying" was but another ruse to capture him! Richard, Henry's third son, requires no introduction. A fourth son, Geoffrey, turned out to be as worthless, cruel, and disloyal as his brother Henry. Few mourned his passing at the age of twenty-seven when he died from either a fever or a fall from his horse (in a tournament). This leaves John, the youngest of Henry's children by Eleanor, called "Lackland" by his father at his birth, since there was no province at that time to leave him. John was his father's favorite, which is understandable. Not only was he the youngest, but being the youngest he had less opportunity to offend his father than had his older brothers. The final scene in King Henry's life shows him lying sick to death on his pallet, worn out and old, vanquished by his son Richard and Philip Augustus. He asked that the list of traitors who had joined Richard against him be read. When he heard the name of his son John, number one on the list, he told the reader: "Say no more," turned his face to the wall, and shortly after died.

Eleanor, Henry's queen, brought him Aquitaine, to all appearances a splendid dowry, and in addition gave him eight children including five boys. Under normal circumstances no king could have asked for more. Yet apart from the three daughters, Henry must have wondered at times which brought him more grief, Eleanor's Aquitaine or their children. It would be many years before any duke or king would rule unruly Aquitaine. Its incorporation into Henry's domains netted him only travail. Concerning his relationship with Eleanor, from the large number of children she bore him, one may assume it was as harmonious a union as that which generally exists between strong-willed people, even though she was twelve years his senior. This age disparity probably proved a major factor in their eventual estrangement. When Eleanor gave birth to John, her last child, she was a tired forty-four, he a vigorous thirty-two. He may have been unfaithful to her before John's birth; he surely was afterward. She soon left Henry and removed to Aquitaine where, upon Henry's orders, she took over its administration from her son Richard. She might have continued to rule Aquitaine had she not permitted herself to become partner to the conspiracies of her sons and the king of France against Henry. In the opening weeks of the rebellion of 1173, she was captured trying to make her escape to Paris in the disguise of a soldier, and for the remaining fifteen years of his reign Henry kept her in virtual confinement. Richard released her in 1189 when he took over the throne, and though she was then sixty-seven years old, she still had fifteen years of political activity before her. She died at the age of eighty-two and was buried in the convent of Fontevrault.

HENRY AND THOMAS BECKET

Henry devoted the first years of his reign to establishing royal control over his far-flung dominions. The ties that held the several parts together had loosened during the nineteen years of Stephen's inept rule; furthermore, several new and valuable territories had been added by way of his inheritance in France and Eleanor's dowry. His first move was to complete the destruction of the adulterine castles in England, a project he had begun while Stephen was still king. Some of these castles had once been royal property which local lords had either received from Stephen or had simply seized. Others were new fortresses that had been erected without authorization of the crown. The right to erect castles had been one of the sacred prerogatives William the Conqueror had kept in his possession, and a wise precaution this was especially in any age such as this when a castle was practically impregnable. In the hands of rebellious barons, such fortresses sharply limited, at times even nullified, a monarch's authority. During Stephen's reign adulterine castles had popped up all over England, more than a thousand of them one chronicler declares.

Henry encountered no great difficulty in asserting royal authority over castles he claimed for the crown or in destroying those he wanted out of the way. The wave of enthusiasm with which most groups greeted the new king facilitated his progress, as did the death of six influential earls during the years 1153 to 1155. All English barons accepted his authority, several with reluctance, only one after a show of resistance. The early summer of 1155 Henry spent leveling the castles of the rebellious Hugh Mortimer in the west. William Peverel of Nottingham, another unsubmissive baron, thought it prudent to flee to a monastery while there was still time in order to escape the charge of murdering the earl of Chester. Henry was also successful in recovering most alienations of royal lands and revenues made during Stephen's reign.

Considerable credit for Henry's success in these early years goes to the counselors whom he selected to assist him in administering his affairs. He wisely retained Richard de Lucy, Stephen's justiciar, who continued to serve him and England for a full twenty-five years. Sharing the responsibilities of the justiciar was another able adviser, Robert, earl of Leicester, the most powerful baron of the midland shires. Nigel, bishop of Ely, who had been Henry I's treasurer but had been removed by Stephen, served briefly as Henry's chancellor, then assumed the charge of reorganizing the exchequer whose foundations his uncle Roger of Salisbury had helped lay. The man who replaced Nigel as chancellor was Thomas Becket, one of the clerks in the household of Theobald, archbishop of Canterbury. Theobald had recommended Becket to Henry as an admirable candidate for the post. The archbishop feared that more vigorous counsel would be required to check the ebullient Henry than he could hope to furnish in his advancing years.

Though the office of chancellor ranked behind those of justiciar and treasurer, in Becket's hands it shortly became the most influential in the government. This in itself was no mean achievement since Becket had neither birth nor influential friends to ease his rise. He was born in 1118 of Norman parents who had come to London to ply the merchant's trade. His parents appreciated the value of education and sent Thomas to Merton priory, then to one of the city's grammar schools, and even for a time to Paris. During these early years the Beckets had prospered, then hard times struck, and Thomas had to take employment as a clerk in a counting house. It was while so employed that a happy circumstance brought him to the attention of the archbishop of Canterbury who added him to his staff of clerks.

Thomas possessed both ambition and an amiable disposition, so Theobald sent him to the continent to continue his education, first to Bologna, then Auxerre. Upon his return from the continent, Thomas shortly became Theobald's most trusted adviser, in which capacity he made a number of trips to Rome on the archbishop's business. His influential position and Theobald's favor gained him a number of benefices, which was not unusual, neither was his negligence unusual in providing vicars for several which involved the cure of souls. In fact Becket demonstrated no interest whatever in the priesthood, and the high post of archdeacon to which Theobald advanced him in 1154 carried only secular responsibilities. The office was, nonetheless, the highest ecclesiastical dignity to which a clerk, who was not a priest, could aspire, and one which not infrequently proved a springboard to the episcopacy. It was still as archdeacon that Thomas entered Henry's service as chancellor.

Nature had been generous to Becket. He was tall and handsome. His high forehead and penetrating eyes lent him the appearance of learnedness, and about his manner there was a dignity and grace one would scarcely expect in a merchant's son. No clerk ever made an easier adjustment in moving from the household of an archbishop to that of a king. The pomp and formalities that bored Henry aroused genuine delight in Becket. To him ceremonials, splendor, and display constituted essential perquisites of his new office. The rich gifts which came in from every side from men who sought favors he accepted with a graciousness these donors often considered reward enough. Thomas was ready with his own gifts in return, for munificence was another mark of the perfect courtier. He entertained on a scale only wealthy barons and the king could afford, and to his sumptuous dinners, all served with the most precise decorum, he daily invited a company of important guests, although he did not forget the poor. Some of these daily ate of his abundance as well, for that was also one of the obligations that went with his office. And he could hawk and hound as though he were a true aristocrat. Since he achieved excellence in the accomplishments the aristocracy set store upon, it was no wonder that the sons of more barons and knights grew up under his roof than in the household of the king.

Despite the age discrepancy of fifteen years between Becket and Henry—Becket was the king's senior—the two young men became constant companions, or almost so. When Henry indulged in revelries that dipped below the seemly, Becket either withdrew or absented himself. Henry did not object to Becket's prudishness. His modesty in fact made him all the more interesting, since chastity was not one of the virtues generally exemplified in the courts of the age. Henry also liked Becket for his honesty and sobriety, his industry and efficiency, his loyalty and devotion. He even admired him for his elegance and graciousness and was pleased that he lent the court the dignity aristocratic society demanded. Nor did he begrudge Thomas his more brilliant court and luxurious table, and would often come over uninvited because he enjoyed the older man's company. To Henry these accomplishments were of value but better left to men like Becket who had the time and taste for them. Had Henry not been convinced that he was Becket's superior in intellectual power and in shrewdness, he might have been jealous. Yet, while he was correct in this appraisal, he failed to note in Becket a devotion to duty so strong and unreasoning that it would one day destroy their friendship and bring tragedy into their lives.

Henry's first undertaking, following the destruction of the adulterine castles, was the establishment of his claim to Wales. Ever since the tenth century when the Welsh princes had recognized Anglo-Saxon dominion, English kings had been insisting upon their rights there although no one had had the temerity to attempt the subjugation of that wild country. What forced the early Norman kings to give closer attention to the area were the appeals of marcher lords, those English barons who had carved out estates along the eastern and southern frontier of Wales, for assistance against Welsh chieftains who were resisting their encroachment. Both William II and Henry I had made several expeditions into the country, but neither had done more than humble the Welsh princes immediately involved and force them to render homage. When Henry II was crowned, no Welsh chieftain appeared to do homage. Then when Cadwallader, the exiled brother of Owen, prince of North Wales, appealed to Henry for help in getting back into the country, the king decided to move. He organized a twofold campaign, consisting of both a land force that he commanded and a fleet. It was fortunate that he prepared his expedition carefully, for the Welsh were tough fighters, particularly in their mountainous country. After some stubborn fighting Henry prevailed upon Owen to submit, who then agreed to reinstate his brother, to give hostages, and to do homage in the name of all Wales over which he claimed suzerainty. The prudent Henry did not seek greater authority.

The situation with regard to English claims over Scotland was substantially the same as that over Wales. Here again the hegemony that English kings exercised extended back into the Anglo-Saxon period and remained largely nominal. King Cnut had reaffirmed English claims and so had William the Conqueror when he invaded the country in 1072 and extracted an oath of homage from its king. Whether this homage extended to all of Scotland, or only to the counties just north of the Scottish border, is not clear. Neither is it clear whether Henry II insisted that Malcolm, who had also failed to put in an appearance at his coronation, do homage for all his country or for only the three English shires of Northumberland, Cumberland, and Westmorland. There is reason to believe that the young Henry, upon his knighting by King David of Scotland in 1149, had sworn to leave the Scots in possession of these three counties if and when he became king. If Henry had made such an oath, he now conveniently forgot it or otherwise assumed that the altered circumstances released him from any obligation to honor it. At any rate he now notified Malcolm to come forward with his homage and also to surrender all claims to the three shires and a number of fortresses in the north. Upon Henry's return from his Welsh campaign, Malcolm met him at Chester, complied with his demands, and did homage "in the same manner as his grandfather had been the man of King Henry the Elder." Henry did not feel the time appropriate to demand anything more specific.

Henry next turned to his continental possessions. In 1156 he crossed over to Normandy and did homage to Louis VII for the French fiefs he held there, including Aquitaine. The first trouble to develop here in France came from Henry's younger brother Geoffrey who put in a bid for Anjou, Touraine, and Maine. He claimed that his father's will stipulated he was to secure possession of these once Henry had made good his own claim to England. Henry brushed aside his brother's protest and defeated him without great difficulty. Next he moved into Aquitaine where he received professions of loyalty from that duchy's proud aristocracy. Then he sent Becket off to Paris at the head of a magnificent delegation in order to secure Louis' approval to the betrothal of Louis' daughter Margaret to his own son Henry. He was to propose that Vexin, a strategic bit of territory lying on the frontiers of Normandy and the Ile de France, was to come with the young girl as dowry. Becket's mission was a brilliant success, both in achieving its diplomatic purpose and in impressing the French with the power and affluence of England. Shortly after Becket secured Louis' further approval to Henry's claim to Nantes which his brother Geoffrey, now deceased, had once held. The acquisition of Nantes was of major importance, since the city commanded the mouth of the Loire and also provided Henry a foothold in Brittany which he would later expand to take over the entire county.

From Aquitaine Henry turned his eyes to the east, toward Toulouse, over which he also put forth a claim by virtue of some shadowy right his wife Eleanor had inherited to that rich territory. Eleanor's immediate predecessors had seen the futility of pressing this right since the efforts of a series of able counts had made the county virtually independent, not only of the duke of Aquitaine but of the king of France as well. It was only upon the marriage of Louis VII to Eleanor that the French crown began to take notice of Toulouse, although Louis' demand that the count pay homage went by unnoticed. When Henry, as Eleanor's husband, became duke of Aquitaine, Louis and the count of Toulouse drew together as against a common enemy, and cemented their new friendship with the count's marriage to the king's sister.

Henry appreciated the difficulty facing him in Toulouse and proceeded with caution. He first secured an alliance with the count of Barcelona whose territory adjoined that of Toulouse, then raised a powerful army with the help of a scutage levied in all his dominions, including England. This was a sum amounting to two marks on the knight's fee which the vassal could pay in lieu of the actual military service he owed his overlord. The name scutage or "service of the shield" reveals its military character. Henry had first employed this kind of levy in 1156 when raising troops to fight his brother Geoffrey. He had found the substitution of this tax for personal knight's service eminently successful, since he could use the money he collected to recruit an efficient army of mercenaries to replace what often amounted to an undependable feudal levy of unwilling barons and their followers. Furthermore, his demand for scutage proved palatable to the English baronage which would have objected to crossing the Channel to fight in far-off southern France.

So the lay lords did not object, but the resentment of the clergy was extreme, for they, too, paid the scutage. As long as the man holding of the king had actually fought on the battlefield, as feudal usage required, the clergy had generally escaped that service on the strength of their clerical immunities. Now that the military service was to be compounded by a money payment and this charge was to be levied upon all estates, whether lay or ecclesiastical since all lands were held ultimately of the crown, the Church's treasured immunity had ceased to exist. The man upon whom the hierarchy and clergy heaped their opprobrium for extinguishing this immunity was not Henry but his chancellor Becket, who had probably proposed the tax. At least Becket's zeal in enforcing the collection of the scutage was surely responsible for the enormous amount realized. Several bishops, including Gilbert Foliot, the bishop of Hereford, never forgave Becket. Even John of Salisbury, Becket's close friend, dated Henry's encroachments upon clerical prerogatives to this scutage, and later saw in Becket's martyrdom the satisfaction God demanded of him in expiation of his part in the affair.

If the execrations of the clergy helped draw down upon Henry's expedition the anger of God, that might have been the reason for its failure. A more visible factor was Louis' tardy, and, to Henry unexpected, decision to intervene. When Louis moved into Toulouse, Henry drew back, even though the French army was a paltry force compared to his own. Henry hesitated to make war on his lord, nor did he wish to provide his own vassals justification for attacking him, their overlord, on some later occasion. He left the field to his constable and to Becket, who between them carried on a destructive campaign of burning and plundering, Becket taking particular pride in the thousand troops of his own which he led. Despite the infliction of considerable suffering on the people of Toulouse, Henry's venture there netted him little. He acquired Cahors, but along with this city he gained the enmity and distrust of Louis who would no longer have any reticence about organizing revolts against his powerful vassal.

Other than arranging the coronation of the king's son in 1162, the campaign in Toulouse marked the end of Becket's service to Henry in his role as chancellor. On 18 April 1161 Archbishop Theobald died, and for almost a year Canterbury looked for a new incumbent. Before his death, the saintly Theobald had voiced the hope that Becket might succeed, although that prelate's confidence had counted for little in Thomas' favor except to bring his name forward as a possible candidate. In the judgment of the majority of English churchmen the most qualified candidate for Canterbury was Gilbert Foliot, the bishop of Hereford. Foliot was an acknowledged scholar and a monk of Cluny, who before rising to Hereford had a distinguished career as abbot of St. Peter's at Gloucester. His deep concern for the Church's well-being placed him in the forefront of the reform movement in England. For many years

Theobald had depended heavily upon him in the administration of the western dioceses. Unfortunately Foliot's solid qualities, even a sense of humbleness, were offset by an abrasive temperament and a sharp tongue. No doubt he would have proved a more able than a popular archbishop.

The man whom Theobald, or the English hierarchy, the pope, or even the chapter at Canterbury preferred to succeed as archbishop made little difference. King Henry would decide who the next archbishop of Canterbury would be, and he wanted Becket. Becket had demonstrated his immense value to the crown in his capacity as chancellor. Were he promoted to the primacy and headship of the English church, that value would be doubled since Henry assumed he would continue as chancellor. As archbishop, Thomas would be of particular value in helping the king achieve certain objectives which impinged upon the prerogatives of the Church. For that reason it was imperative that Henry handpick a man for the position who had already proved his devotion and effectiveness. That man was Becket.

Precisely what Becket's mind may have been in the matter of his elevation to Canterbury has remained a matter of controversy. He protested to Henry that he did not want the office, yet was his protest anything more than the usual objection to high office that convention expected of a candidate? He had unquestionably enjoyed the power and perquisites that were his as chancellor, nor is there any doubt that prior to becoming archbishop he gave evidence of any interest in the spiritual life. His protests, therefore, if genuine, may have stemmed from a reluctance to abandon the secular pleasures to which he had grown attached, since abandon them he must if he wished to be a worthy archbishop. Or Thomas may have objected to accepting the office in his conviction that a clash between himself and Henry was inevitable. He knew of Anselm's grievous differences with William II, and of Theobald's, who twice had to flee England in order to thwart the will of Stephen. Could he not expect infinitely greater difficulties with the strong-willed Henry than Theobald had had with the easy-going Stephen? What may finally have persuaded Thomas to accept the office of archbishop, accepting this second analysis of his behavior, was the urging of the papal delegate whose importuning Becket may have considered the voice of God.

The history of the Middle Ages records the names of many bishops who remained quite as unworthy of that high office after consecration as before. That was the reason reformers denounced the practice of lay investiture so bitterly. Consecration invested the new bishop with certain spiritual powers; it did little or nothing to correct vicious habits or weaknesses of character. In Becket's case, these reformers would have had no cause to complain, for upon his consecration the new archbishop became a different man. He had been a deserving chancellor; now he must be a model archbishop. He put behind him the pleasures of court life he had loved, the hawking and hunting that he had enjoyed, the gay, luxurious habits of a rich and popular royal favorite. He put on a hair shirt, took to fasting, scourged himself daily, and spent long hours in meditation, study, and reading the Scriptures. So complete was his transformation and so deliberate, that some scholars have questioned its genuineness.

When Henry learned of the change that had come over Becket, he was puzzled and disturbed. If Becket took his new office so seriously, that might mean trouble. The king had more second thoughts when Becket resigned his office of chancellor. Henry had not expected this; in fact, he very probably would never have raised Becket to the primacy had he suspected this would happen, for both offices were of critical importance in his plans. Henry had simply wanted the one and same Becket who had proved himself so thoroughly capable and co-operative to serve him in both capacities.

Becket threw himself wholeheartedly into his new responsibilities and without delay. As guardian of the English church he proceeded to lay claim to all properties of which Canterbury might have been deprived during the generation or so preceding, also those which his predecessors might have alienated in a manner prejudicial to the see. So thorough was his search and so relentless his efforts that among other important places he recovered for Canterbury was Rochester castle which the crown had considered its own. He withdrew benefices from clerks who were employed in the king's service even though this was a common practice all over Western Europe and one from which he himself had benefited. Because William of Eynsford, a tenant-in-chief of the crown, refused to recognize the archiepiscopal right of patronage over a benefice in dispute, he excommunicated him without first advising with the king. When Henry directed him to rescind the sentence, he informed the king that since the matter was spiritual the crown lacked any jurisdictional right. In 1163 at Woodstock when Henry proposed to the council that the sheriff's aid be paid henceforth into the exchequer, Becket objected so strenuously on the ground that the sheriff was entitled to this fee in return for services rendered, not the crown, that Henry withdrew the proposal.

In the face of such aggressiveness on the part of the new archbishop, the increasingly concerned Henry must have anticipated still greater resistance when at Westminster, the following October, he raised the subject of criminous clerks. No more sensitive issue strained relations between Church and State in England, yet the problem related to a matter over which the Church traditionally had exclusive authority. All clerks, whether priests or merely tonsured young men who lived in the world (just as Becket had done before his ordination), were subject to ecclesiastical control and correction. In view of Becket's firmness, therefore, on all matters falling within the jurisdictional sphere of the Church, Henry was clearly invading "enemy" territory when he now proposed that clerks who were charged with having committed crimes should be formally accused in a lay court, then handed over to an ecclesiastical tribunal for trial, which should then degrade them if judged guilty, and release them to the secular arm for punishment.

It was evident that the king was not objecting to the church court's trying the accused clerk. What he objected to was the practice of the court in imposing such mild penalties that they served as no deterrent and were a scandal to the land. Some men established their right to "benefit of clergy" simply by speaking a few lines of Latin, while the majority of clerks who enjoyed that privilege, never progressed beyond the diaconate toward the priesthood. More than one hundred murders had been committed by clerks during the nine years of Henry's reign, his justiciars maintained. This charge churchmen would not deny, although they continued to insist that the problem was one for the Church to handle, not the State; that a crime, whatever its nature, was a sin, and like a sin could be atoned for by a penance, by some kind of mortification such as living on bread and water for so many years or making a pilgrimage to a distant shrine. In time, with greater care given in the granting of clerical status, the problem would resolve itself.

To Henry's demand, accordingly, that the church courts surrender those clerks whom they judged guilty of felonies to the crown for punishment, the bishops, following Becket's lead, answered that they would not; that God's ministers were subject to no authority other than that of the Church. Since there was a time, before William I had set up separate church courts, when criminous clerks had been punished by the secular authority, Henry now asked the assembled bishops whether they were prepared to swear to obey the ancient customs of the kingdom. To which question all the bishops but one, the bishop of Chichester, gave assent, but qualified it with the clause "saving our order." Their action infuriated Henry who blamed their intransigence on Becket. He accordingly showed his displeasure by depriving the archbishop of several castles and estates he had still been holding by virtue of his former office of chancellor, and shortly afterward withdrew the young Henry from his household where he had been staying.

Though the bishops had blocked Henry's plan concerning criminous clerks, they had done so only because of Becket's insistence. During the weeks following the meeting at Westminster in October, Becket came under sharp attack from several of his prelates, notably from Gilbert Foliot who had been recently translated to London. Beyond the fact that there were canonists who supported Henry's position, prudence recommended making this concession to the king, so Foliot and other prelates argued, the kind of bending to royal wills that the Church had for centuries been doing under similar circumstances. So Becket retreated from his position, and in December at Oxford agreed to accept the customs of the kingdom "loyally and in good faith" without the qualifying "saving our order." Thereupon Henry promptly summoned the council to Clarendon in January (1164) where he called upon Becket and the hierarchy to make a public pledge of their willingness to accept the customs. Becket drew back, fearful of what these customs might be, but after two days of raging by Henry and reassurances from mediators concerning the relative unimportance of such a declaration, the archbishop announced his acceptance. Ten days later Henry formally presented the sixteen articles known in history as the Constitutions of Clarendon.

These constitutions represented the customs Henry had in mind which he now wished confirmed and given legal sanction. As the introduction of the Constitutions declares: "In the year 1164 . . . in the presence of the same king [Henry II] was made this remembrance or acknowledgment of a certain part of the customs . . . of his ancestors, that is, of King Henry his grandfather, and of others, which ought to be observed and held in the realm." Henry's statement was substantially correct, for his Constitutions of Clarendon only presented in legal language customs that had generally prevailed during the reign of his grandfather. Becket and the English hierarchy did not base their subsequent opposition to the Constitutions on the ground that they represented innovations, rather to the fact that these former customs were now being defined. Once customs became laws they could be applied in the courts of the realm with considerably greater ease. So long as they remained practices and had only custom for their warrant, they might be denied to be customs; hope could be even entertained that they might alter their character in time as was the wont with customs. Still Henry's motive in insisting that these customs be enacted into law was not necessarily unfriendly. What he wanted was a precise body of laws upon which to carry on efficient government. Nevertheless, inasmuch as the customs to which he wanted legal status given were not to the Church's liking, the opposition of churchmen like Becket could not be avoided.

Included among the customs which were to become formal laws with the acceptance of the Constitutions was that concerning criminous clerks. There were others equally distasteful to the Church. Article one, for example, provided that disputes over the right of patronage to churches be decided in the king's court. Article four forbade bishops to leave the realm, to go to Rome for instance, without permission of the king. Article seven denied bishops the right to excommunicate any tenant-in-chief or crown official without consent of the king. Article eight provided that, in the event of the failure of the archbishop's court to settle a dispute, the matter "must not go further without the assent of the lord the king," meaning that it could not be appealed to the pope without permission of the crown. One feature of the Constitutions which was relatively new and which perhaps aroused unnecessary uneasiness was that which appointed a jury of laymen to determine disputes concerning land. Actually this was a procedure Henry was shortly to extend to most land disputes in England.

When Henry called upon Becket to give his consent to the Constitutions, the archbishop refused. To justify his refusal, he singled out article three, the one concerning criminous clerks, as being unjust. To have the church court hand over a clerk, whom it had judged guilty and had degraded, to the civil authorities to be punished, would, he maintained, be to punish that clerk twice for the same crime. This clearly violated the justice of God, the archbishop declared, since, as the prophet Nahum had affirmed: "God judges not twice for the same offense." In the end, Becket withdrew his opposition, gave oral assent to the Constitutions and advised his bishops to do the same, although he refused to set his seal to the document. He was clearly buying time in order to lay the matter before Pope Alexander III. That he never had any intention of accepting the Constitutions he made clear when he suspended himself from his priestly functions for having given oral assent.

Becket's obstinacy concerning the Constitutions and his refusal to seal the document completed the alienation of the king. Now Henry set out to destroy him and his methods were rough. The archbishop received a royal summons to come to Northampton to answer to an appeal by John the Marshal, an officer of the crown, against a decision over an estate in which the court of Canterbury had ruled against him. The archbishop was also to answer at this time to the charge of contempt of the crown for having failed to appear at an earlier hearing of this suit when he had excused himself on the plea of illness. When Becket appeared at Northampton, the council which was composed of lay and ecclesiastical lords, judged his illness to have been fictitious, held him, accordingly, in contempt of the king's court, and imposed a fine of five hundred pounds. Then when Becket and his advisers were discussing what action to take in this matter, the archbishop received an order from the king to give an account of the various sums that he had handled as chancellor, including those he had borrowed on the king's security and the incomes from vacant sees and monasteries of which he had custody.

Becket received divided counsel from his bishops as to what to do. Several advised him to put himself in the king's mercy, others to resign as archbishop, a few supported him in his own inclination to defy the king. In his defense Becket protested that the king's demand for an immediate reckoning of the enormous amounts that he had administered as chancellor was unreasonable, that the funds he had expended had been spent for the crown, that he had even used money of his own to meet the crown's needs, and that upon his consecration he had received a release from all secular claims that might arise concerning his previous years as chancellor. When the king brushed these pleas aside and also an offer of 2000 marks to cover all possible deficiencies, Becket announced that he was laying his appeal before the pope. Then in a dramatic gesture that shocked his fellow bishops and infuriated Henry, he entered the council hall where his case was being discussed, dressed in full pontificals and bearing his archiepiscopal cross before him as though calling on God to defend him. When Henry who was in a room nearby learned of this, he sent Becket orders to withdraw his appeal to Rome as a violation of the customs of the realm, but Thomas refused, whereupon a motion was made to try him for contempt of the crown.

This move placed the prelates in a delicate position since Becket had forbidden them to sit in judgment against him. They were fortunate that Henry and the barons finally agreed not to force the issue but rather to cite the archbishop to Rome for having violated his oath to uphold the customs of the realm. When the royal justiciar came forward to announce the decision of the council, Becket, without remaining to hear the judgment, got up and strode from the chamber to cries of "traitor." That night a storm enabled him to flee Northampton, and after three weeks of hiding from Henry's agents, he managed to slip across the Channel to Flanders, whence he hurried to Pope Alexander III at Sens. The pope and his counselors examined the Constitutions of Clarendon and solemnly condemned them. When Henry learned of the pope's action, he sequestered the temporalities of Canterbury and ordered Becket's relatives and friends banished from the kingdom.

Once Becket had escaped to the continent, he ceased being an issue at home. While Englishmen generally sympathized with him as a victim of royal tyranny, their sympathy was a personal one; it did not extend to his cause. To most lay people church courts were no more tolerable than lay courts. Over such issues as the right of bishops to send appeals to Rome or to excommunicate crown officials they wasted little thought. On the matter of criminous clerks they probably agreed with the king that the situation cried for reform.

Even English bishops were inclined to be critical of Becket, especially Gilbert Foliot, the bishop of London, not for opposing the Constitutions which they also found objectionable, but for the methods he had employed in blocking their enactment. Foliot described Becket's behavior in the controversy as that of a man "who was always a fool and one who would always remain one." Though this characterization sounds harsh, Foliot had cause to be bitter. For twenty years he and other churchmen had worked earnestly for the reform and welfare of the English church, during eight of those years while Becket, the "worldly subdeacon," was enjoying himself feasting and hawking. Then upon Becket's sudden and unmerited elevation to Canterbury, he had assumed absolute direction of the English church and by his unrealistic and theatrical performance had brought the fruit of all their hard work into danger. Becket's conduct, some of the bishops maintained, had forced Henry into bitter opposition, when a temporizing policy could have preserved most of the Church's prerogatives.

Becket received considerably greater sympathy abroad than he did at home. The French hierarchy and clergy gave him a warm welcome, while Louis VII derived much satisfaction from the embarrassment the exiled archbishop occasioned Henry. Where Becket was especially concerned about finding support, that is, from Pope Alexander III, he received disappointment. The pope respected Becket deeply for his courageous stand in defense of the rights of the Church, and this he told him. He did not approve of what he considered an unnecessarily inflexible position Becket had assumed in his controversy with Henry. Such an adamant stand was likely to do grave injury to the English church. Yet had Alexander himself been in a strong position on the continent, he would indubitably have thrown his full support to Becket and have employed what ecclesiastical censures he could find in the papal arsenal to bring Henry to heel. The irony of the situation was that in order for he himself to remain pope, Alexander had to defer to critics and conciliate enemies in much the same fashion as he was now urging upon Thomas with respect to Henry. For Alexander was not the only pope at the time. Frederick Barbarossa of Germany had his own pope, Paschall III, whom a good part of Europe was recognizing as the legitimate successor of St. Peter. Were Alexander to condemn Henry and threaten him with excommunication unless he repudiated the Constitutions of Clarendon and restore Becket, he would drive him into Frederick's camp. That might be the end of Alexander's papacy.

Becket refused to listen to the pope's counsel. He would not modify his stand one tittle nor accept any face-saving solution. He did offer to resign his archbishop's office, but that Alexander could not accept without openly admitting defeat for the Church. From the Cistercian abbey of Pontigny in Burgundy where Becket had taken refuge, he conducted a feverish correspondence with pope, kings, religious orders, with all and sundry whom he believed had influence, to recruit their assistance in his battle with Henry. Far from softening his position or moderating the bitterness of his attack, he grew more vituperative, eventually excommunicating the officials who had endorsed the Constitutions of Clarendon, several of the king's principal counselors, including the justiciar, and even threatening Henry himself with anathema. Because of the extreme delicacy of the international situation, Pope Alexander hurriedly rescinded Becket's sentences and, in order to prevent further crises of this kind, appointed legates to arbitrate the controversy. One of these legates was an adviser of Henry's whom the archbishop had just excommunicated.

Several years passed without any appreciable progress in resolving the feud. Then on 14 June 1170, Roger, the archbishop of York, crowned Henry's son Henry at Westminster, and the dispute took on new virulence. Of the most sacred prerogatives claimed by Canterbury, one was that concerning the crowning of the king. Of this fact Henry was fully aware, and to protect himself had first obtained Pope Alexander's permission to have the archbishop of York perform the ceremony. Becket was not alone in denouncing the coronation. Louis VII also resented the fact that only the young Henry was crowned, not Henry's wife who was his daughter. The coronation accordingly weakened Henry's position vis-à-vis Becket, which may have been one of the reasons why he now agreed to a reconciliation. Both men had grown tired of their quarrel. On 22 July they met and agreed to forget their differences. In their conversation together, which no one else was partner to, they apparently avoided the issue of the Constitutions.

Events shortly revealed how empty their reconciliation had been. Henry failed to order the restoration of all archiepiscopal properties that the crown had been holding; Becket kept his hands on letters from the pope authorizing him to suspend the bishops who had taken part in the coronation of the young Henry. (At the last moment the pope had withdrawn his permission to the archbishop of York to do the crowning.) Because Thomas knew his baggage would be searched, he sent the papal letters on ahead, so when he arrived in England on 1 December, the king's agents discovered nothing. Then on Christmas Day in the cathedral at Canterbury he solemnly denounced and excommunicated his enemies from the pulpit, including those bishops who had participated in the coronation ceremonies. Three of these bishops, Gilbert of London, Jocelyn of Salisbury, and Roger, archbishop of York, who knew they were marked for excommunication, had already hurried over to Normandy to lay their case before Henry. When neither they nor the attending courtiers could offer any satisfactory counsel as to how to meet this new problem, the impatient Henry exclaimed: "What a parcel of fools and dastards have I nourished in my house, that none of them can be found to avenge me on this one upstart clerk!" That same day four of his knights left Normandy in secret, crossed the Channel, and cut Becket down in his cathedral where he had taken refuge.

The news of Becket's death shocked Europe. Though Henry was as horror-stricken as the rest of the world, many people held him responsible for inspiring the deed. Pope Alexander placed his continental possessions under interdict and excommunicated all persons implicated in the murder. Henry immediately dispatched emissaries to Rome to make satisfaction for any indirect complicity of which he might have been guilty, but the pope refused to admit them. Instead he sent his own legates to Normandy where they were to dictate to Henry the terms by which he could expiate his part in the outrage. Henry did not wait the arrival of the legates, but wisely withdrew to Ireland which he had been planning to visit. Six months later, when emotions had subsided, he returned, and at Avranches on 21 May 1172 purged himself of his guilt and received absolution. To placate the pope he agreed to adjure what new "customs" he had introduced that were injurious to the Church, to provide for the support of two hundred knights in Syria against the Moslems, to take the cross for a period of three years (he was later exempted from this promise upon agreement to found three monasteries), to allow appeals to Rome, and to restore all properties belonging to Canterbury. There was no direct mention of the Constitutions of Clarendon. It appears Henry made it clear that he would not proceed with any negotiations looking to the settlement of his difficulties with the Church if their repudiation was specifically required.

In the end Henry salvaged a substantial part of his Constitutions. True, he had promised to suppress what new "customs" he had introduced that were offensive to the Church, but as he had always asserted, there was nothing novel about his "customs." Even appeals to Rome to which he had agreed, unless the appellant swore that he intended no injury to the crown or kingdom, Henry did not permit him to leave England. Neither did prelates cross the Channel without first securing his permission. If they ventured to do so without that permission, they might find on their return that the crown had confiscated their temporalities during their absence. Disputes over rights of patronage and similar questions concerning property were regularly decided in the secular courts. On the issue of criminous clerks the church courts did retain jurisdiction, although the secular authorities learned how to make life so miserable and expensive for the obvious felon that he might well wonder whether Henry had not gained that point as well. Between the extralegal measures taken by the king's officials on the one hand and the Church's efforts to suppress the evil features of the practice on the other, the problem gradually passed from the public view. Finally, in the matter of the "free" election of bishops, the crown continued to exercise the powerful influence it had been enjoying before Becket's death.

If in the end Henry secured approximately what he had wanted, so did Becket, that is, if one is to accept the claims of his impassioned biographers. These insist that Thomas knew he was going to his death when he returned to England, and that, furthermore, he longed for that death as a means of preserving the rights of the Church. Such claims most scholars deny. They believe Thomas had no more presentiment of his approaching end when he returned to Canterbury than had Henry. Be that as it may, Christian Europe enthusiastically proclaimed the appearance of a new and great martyr and within three years had importuned Pope Alexander into canonizing Becket. Among the most zealous advocates in spreading devotion to the new saint were the three daughters of Henry II who fostered his cult in the lands of Germany, Sicily, and Spain where their husbands ruled. Within a short time the shrine of Thomas Becket at Canterbury ranked second only to that of St. James at Compostella in Europe. For Englishmen it became, of course, the most popular of all shrines, and men and women

> . . . from every shire's end
> In England, down to Canterbury they wend
> The holy blissful martyr for to seek.

THE GROWTH OF ROYAL GOVERNMENT

Were it not for Henry's dispute with Becket, only students of history would know of the English king whose influence upon the evolution of the English government places him first among British monarchs. Henry's greatness rests upon his work in reorganizing the English government, in establishing royal power, and in creating an effective legal system so solid that its general outlines have carried down to the present. Henry was less a student of politics and jurisprudence than of the actions of men who ruled before him, of Angevin and Norman ancestors, particularly of what his revered grandfather Henry I had done to rule so successfully. Through his mother he inherited the Norman talent for recognizing practices and institutions that possessed promise, which given the proper use and direction would assure an effective government. A study of Henry's work reveals few new ideas, even few new laws, only practices for the most part that others had employed tentatively and irregularly, but which he incorporated into an administrative structure second to none in efficiency in medieval Europe or in the justice it provided its people.

Henry's achievement rested squarely upon the system of royal courts he introduced. These courts furnished the government the means of enforcing its authority while at the same time severely limiting the jurisdiction of the baronial and church courts. Without the support of these royal courts to bolster his authority, Henry's position would not have been appreciably stronger than that of his grandfather. Without these courts England could continue to expect the appearance of weak kings such as Stephen and of reigns when the social and economic fabric of the land might be imperiled. Henry's royal courts, rooted as they shortly came to be in the deep soil of popular support, provided the crown such sanction that from their support any king, excepting only the most incompetent, could hope to rule with considerable success. Henry's expansion of royal government represents, therefore, a major and permanent assault on the power of the feudal aristocracy that had almost destroyed the monarchy during the reign of Stephen.

Among other motives that may have impelled Henry to undertake his work of strengthening royal authority may have been ambition, search for power, and pride in being a strong king. His motivation might have been wholly selfish. Only by curbing the violence and lawlessness of the baronage could he hope to rule in relative security. Only for reasons of personal satisfaction may he have wished to emulate his grandfather Henry I, who had borne the title "lion of justice." He may have sensed the fact that the sturdiest foundation of royal power was popular support. This he could only gain for himself by providing the people a strong and just regime. Whatever Henry's motives, and they were surely not wholly selfish, the power and prestige that his reforms secured him also brought his people peace and justice. In time most Englishmen, in particular the gentry, burghers, and yeomanry accepted him and his work as their best protection against injustice and turbulency.

To provide the bases for his first legal reform Henry seized upon two practices from the past, one introduced into England by William the Conqueror, the other by Henry I. When William the Conqueror introduced feudal rule to England in 1066 he reserved for the crown and its judges the authority to try crimes of violence that threatened the king's peace. Should crimes such as robbery and treason go unpunished,

William realized men would lose faith in his regime and revolt would become inevitable. The precedent from the reign of Henry I that interested Henry II was his grandfather's occasional practice of sending out members of the *curia regis* on missions into the different shires to protect the king's interests. There these royal agents might investigate charges of misappropriation of revenues, or adjudicate disputes over property in which the crown had a right, or simply punish criminals.

In 1166 by the Assize of Clarendon Henry regularized the use of these royal agents, known popularly as itinerant justices since their business was justice and since they traveled about the country. In this assize he delegated these officials with the business of presiding over the trial of men who were accused of having committed crimes against the king's peace "since our lord the king has been king." The specific crimes that were to fall within their purview were murder, larceny, robbery, and the harboring of criminals. Ten years later by the Assize of Northampton Henry added the crimes of forgery and arson to the list of crimes they were to try. From then on the prosecution of these crimes has remained the exclusive responsibility of the royal justices.

The Assize of Clarendon possessed other features equally as important as the extension of royal authority into the area of criminal prosecution. One feature was that of providing a vastly superior system of ferreting out men who might be guilty of these crimes. In the past this matter had been left principally to the individual who had suffered injury or to his relatives, with the result that many crimes had gone unpunished either because of the expense involved in arraigning the guilty or the fear of reprisals should this be attempted. In order to correct this situation, Henry adopted a method that had been employed both in Normandy and England when information had been sought. This was the use of the sworn inquest or testimony of neighbors. In the language of the Assize of Clarendon, the king and his barons "enacted that inquiry should be made through the several counties . . . by twelve of the most responsible men of the hundred [roughly township] and by four of the most responsible men of each village, upon their oath that they will tell the truth, whether there is in their hundred or in their village any man who has been accused or publicly suspected of being a robber, murderer, or thief, or of being a receiver of robbers, murderers, or thieves. . . ."

The twelve men from each hundred and four from each village who were to present these names constituted what contemporaries called a jury of presentment, from the fact that they swore (Latin *juro*, I swear) to give truthful testimony when called upon. The procedure as outlined in the assize directed the sheriff to impanel this jury, ask for the names of men and women under suspicion, and hold these for trial when the itinerant justices should reach the neighborhood on their circuit. (There were five circuits, with three justices assigned to each circuit.) At this point in the prosecution of criminals, Henry had no choice but fall back upon the traditional ordeal, usually that of cold water, to ascertain the actual guilt of the persons under suspicion. Though Henry rebelled at the patent inadequacy of this ancient institution that had survived almost unchanged from the superstitious past, he did require those defendants who had "proved" their innocence by the ordeal, who were "of very bad reputation and publicly and disgracefully spoken ill of by the testimony of many and lawful men," to depart the realm within forty days. Shortly after Henry's death the Fourth Lateran Council in 1215 forbade the clergy to participate any longer in the ordeal, whereupon that system of trying criminals fell rapidly into disuse.

Though Henry had to be content with the ordeal as a means of ascertaining guilt in criminal cases, he was successful in introducing the principle of the jury, more precisely that of the trial or petit jury, in the adjudication of civil disputes over property. The number of such disputes had become legion because of the absence or destruction of records, the turbulency of Stephen's reign when much property had changed hands forcibly, and the division of estates by marriage and sale; nevertheless, the usual method used to secure judgment in such disputes was wager of battle. If the parties to the dispute were themselves unwilling to enter the lists or if they were not of the aristocracy, they hired professional "champions" who threw lances or swung pickaxes at each other until God presumably gave victory to the innocent party.

An infinitely more rational procedure was one that had been employed on occasion in the past when information of a civil nature was sought, namely, the testimony of responsible men in the community who could be expected to have a knowledge of the facts in question. Henry now proposed to offer parties in certain kinds of disputes pertaining to property the privilege of employing the jury method of securing judgment in place of the wager of battle. When the plaintiff claimed to have failed to secure justice from his lord, for instance, or when certain questions existed concerning the right of possession or the nature of the tenure, the case might be transferred from the baronial or shire court to the king's court. In such instances the plaintiff would purchase a writ in the chancellor's office that would direct the sheriff to impanel a jury of twelve good men who would render judgment before the itinerant justice.

The impact of these reforms upon English law, of the introduction of the jury of presentment in the punishment of crime, of the petit jury in civil disputes, was tremendous. Grimly effective was the work of the jury of presentment in ferreting out criminals. On the first visit of the itinerant justices in 1166 in the vicinity of London, fourteen men were hanged and fourteen more mutilated by loss of hand or foot. Equally great was the success of the petit jury in settling civil disputes. Wherever possible plaintiffs preferred to take their disputes to the royal courts which were the only ones eligible to use the jury system. One indirect result of these judicial reforms was that of bringing both the sheriff and the more responsible men of the shire into association with the royal justices and thereby establishing a link between them and the government. Another consequence was the gradual evolution of legal practices and procedures that, as years passed, became increasingly uniform for all England. Because the itinerant justices who applied royal law were all members of the same body (*curia regis*), because they tried the same kinds of cases, employed the same procedures, and appealed to the same body of precedents, local traditions and differences gradually disappeared and gave way to a law common to all England, whence the name common law.

That England today uses common law rather than the Roman law which most Western European nations have adopted may, therefore, be the result of Henry's legal reforms. While countries which are employing Roman law find it entirely satisfactory, it lacks the flexibility of common law since it is based upon legal principles that have altered only slightly since ancient times. Common law by contrast resembles a living organism that constantly adapts itself to conditions and attitudes as these change within the English nation. That history has at hand a clear view of the legal practices of Henry's day is due to the diligence of one of his itinerant justices, Ranulf de Glanvill by name, who prepared a *Treatise Concerning the Laws and Customs of the Kingdom of England*.

When Henry became king, royal justice was practically unknown. When he died, his royal courts had become the popular courts, their volume of business greater than that handled by all other courts combined. This statistic reveals two significant facts: first, that Henry left England a royal government that could call upon an extensive system of courts to provide sanction to its authority; and second, that the justice meted out in these courts was of such a high order that most Englishmen were willing to pay stiff fees for the privilege of using them. This popularity assured the permanence of the royal courts and, indirectly, the permanence of the government. One weakness in the system came to view less than a dozen years after the announcement of the Assize of Clarendon. This was the difficulty occasional citizens living in out-of-the-way places might experience in locating a royal court. One irate plaintiff complained that he had followed in the wake of itinerant justices for five years, only to discover when he finally caught up with them and had won his case, that the money he gained only covered what he had already expended in travel and lawyers' expenses. To remedy this situation Henry established a permanent court of five justices at Westminster "to hear the complaints of the realm and do justice, where justice might be had by those who could not wait the arrival of the itinerant justices or whose case was of such a nature that it might better be tried in or near the presence of the king." Some time after Henry's death this permanent court at Westminster split into three distinct courts: common pleas for private civil cases, exchequer for financial cases in which the government had an interest, and king's bench principally for criminal cases.

Henry's itinerant justices were members of the *curia regis* or king's council that advised with him in matters of major importance concerning the realm. This *curia regis* in eleventh-century England was not appreciably different from those in other countries where feudal institutions maintained. It was composed of the king's direct vassals or tenants-in-chief who were ordinarily summoned to meet with him two or three times a year when questions relating to the common weal came under consideration. When the tenants-in-chief convened in this manner, at Pentecost for example, the body usually bore the name of great council. Chroniclers might also refer to it by the name of *curia regis,* although usage restricted this term commonly to the smaller group of counselors whom the king kept with him to assist in the day-to-day operation of the government. When engaged in counseling the king in administrative, judicial, military, and fiscal matters, they constituted, together with the king, the actual government of the kingdom.

As population increased with the passage of years and civilization grew more advanced, it became inevitable that the business of government should grow proportionately in volume and complexity. The impact of Henry's judicial reforms was especially great. Not only were more men required to handle the judicial business coming before the *curia regis*, but more men who commanded greater knowledge of law than the ordinary tenant-in-chief could be expected to possess. The result was the gradual emergence of a special department from the general body of the *curia regis*, staffed with specialists, who were delegated with the responsibility of handling the judicial business of the crown.

Another offshoot of the *curia regis* that dates from Henry's reign was the royal treasury or exchequer. Just as increasing judicial business had necessitated the establishment of a special royal judiciary, so the growing expansion of fiscal matters led to the emergence of another group from the *curia regis*, this one known as the exchequer. The first suggestion of the eventual birth of such a group appeared during the reign of Henry I when the *curia regis* would meet on certain occasions during the year to devote its entire attention to financial business. It did this customarily twice a year, in the spring (Easter) and fall (Michaelmas), when it met to scrutinize the accounts of the sheriffs who were the principal fiscal agents of the crown and to receive the moneys they brought with them.

When the members of the *curia regis* met to receive the sheriffs' reports, they would sit around a table whose top measured approximately five by ten feet and was covered with a cloth marked off in squares after the manner of a checker board. In this way the table top was made to serve as a sort of stationary abacus, a device whose use was then being introduced into Western Europe. In essence the abacus represented a method of employing Arabic and decimal systems of computation which were vastly superior to the cumbersome Roman system. The squares on the tablecloth represented different values similar to the beads when pushed about on the abacus. The use of this table greatly facilitated the audit of the sheriffs' accounts and eventually gave its name to the modern English exchequer.

Henry was deeply concerned about improving the crown's methods in handling its fiscal business both because this business was expanding and because the efficiency of the government in this matter in Henry I's day had been lost during the reign of Stephen. He therefore appointed Bishop Nigel of Ely, a nephew of the Roger, bishop of Salisbury, who had been responsible for the excellent administration of the exchequer in his grandfather's day, to reorganize the treasury after the manner of his uncle. When Nigel retired, his place was taken by his son, Richard Fitz-Neal, who later became bishop of London. It is largely a description of the work of these three men, uncle, nephew, and son, which one of the officials of Henry II's exchequer has left in his treatise entitled *The Dialogue of the Exchequer.*

Henry needed an improved exchequer in order to handle the vastly increased flow of money in and out of the royal coffers that became particularly marked after the Assize of Clarendon. During Henry I's reign the principal sources of royal revenue had consisted of receipts of the royal manors and forests, fees and fines collected in the hundred and shire courts, feudal aids and incidents, and a variety of irregular and relatively insignificant revenues such as the Danegeld. (This last was not collected after 1162.) The increase in revenues during Henry II's reign can be traced to three developments in general: first, the expansion of the Angevin dominions; second, the expanding activities of the government, particularly its judicial branch; third, Henry's own efforts in increasing the volume of royal revenues. No medieval monarch had a clearer notion than Henry of the direct correlation between the volume of royal revenues and the measure of royal power. Henry also appreciated the near impossibility of augmenting the flow of revenue in an age when the iron rule of custom prevented any innovation. Under the circumstances, he did all his barons would tolerate, that is, he collected with the greatest fastidiousness the revenues tradition granted him, while the new sources of revenue he introduced he permitted to remain optional.

Older sources of revenue included feudal aids and incidents and similar payments from the Church, such as the income of sees and monasteries collected during their vacancies. (Henry never returned the revenues confiscated from Canterbury during Becket's exile.) In place of the ancient Danegeld, Henry imposed a new land tax known as hidage (or carucage), and from towns and tenants on the royal demesne he collected a tallage. At times he demanded special "gifts" from monasteries and Jews. New sources of revenue included scutage which his vassals were generally willing to pay in order to escape actual military service, and the fees which plaintiffs were even more willing to pay for the writs entitling them to take their disputes to the royal courts. Henry continued to collect a share of the fines assessed by the shire and hundred courts and, of course, all the fines and confiscations ordered in his royal courts. The only new tax he imposed which was not voluntary was the direct levy on income and personal property which he ordered in preparation for the crusade he planned to lead to Syria. This was known as the Saladin tithe. Henry's old and new sources of revenue made him the envy of contemporary kings who rightly judged him the richest and most powerful king in Western Europe.

HENRY'S WARS—HIS DEATH

In October 1171 Henry crossed to Ireland in order to give the storm over Becket's murder opportunity to abate. He had long been interested in adding the island to the west to his dominions, first as an appanage for his brother Geoffrey, then later for his son John. The disunity of Ireland promised easy conquest, although the poverty of the natives and the poverty of the land had long discouraged earlier conquerors. The only historical invaders had been the Norsemen who began their inroads in the late eighth century and had eventually established themselves in Dublin, Wexford, Waterford, and other settlements along the coast. That it was through these alien-held windows that Ireland maintained some tenuous contact with the rest of Europe reveals how far the island's culture had fallen since the "Golden Age" of the sixth, seventh, and eighth centuries. Part of this decline was the responsibility of the Norsemen, but the greater censure attached to the Irish for their provincialism which caused their centers of learning to atrophy and the zeal of their clergy to deteriorate.

Ireland was theoretically divided into five major parts, each under the titular authority of a king who fought local chieftains in order to keep his empty title and with the other four kings, over the still more empty title of high-king. For a few years Brian Boru (1002–14) was able to provide the country relative peace. When he was slain in a victory his forces gained over invading Norsemen, the island reverted to its traditional condition of semi-anarchy. In 1166 one Rory O'Connor laid claim to the title of high-king and drove Dermot McMurrough, the brutal king of Leinster, out of the country. Dermot took himself to Henry over in Normandy in an effort to gain his assistance in effecting his return.

Henry had maintained his interest in Ireland and had actually sent John of Salisbury to Pope Adrian to secure papal endorsement for a projected occupation. Adrian responded with the bull *Laudabiliter* which approved Henry's conquest. The pope also sent along an emerald ring betokening that rule, with which Henry might invest his future governor of the island. What had prompted Adrian's favorable action was his concern over the lack of papal ties with the Irish church and with the reports coming out of the island concerning the low state of the clergy. Henry's difficulties with Becket prevented his leaving France when Dermot pleaded his cause, but he gave the Irish chieftain his letters patent authorizing him to recruit what English barons he could for his venture. The most famous of the baron-adventurers to join Dermot was Richard de Clare, earl of Pembroke, a marcher lord, known popularly as Strongbow. Strongbow later married Dermot's daughter Eva and, when his father-in-law died, succeeded to his ambitious pretensions. Strongbow's unexpected success, together with Henry's desire to escape the furore over Becket's death, were instrumental in prompting the king to go over in person in the fall of 1171 in order to block the establishment of an independent Norman state in Ireland.

Strongbow and Henry had no difficulty reaching an agreement, and when Henry appeared in October, he took over Dublin and the surrounding territory, while leaving the Norman chieftain to hold Leinster as a fief. During the six months that Henry remained in Dublin he built himself a royal palace after the Irish style in which he entertained visiting Irish chieftains. Between his hospitality and the impressive size of the army he had brought with him, most Irish chieftains except those in the west and north, saw fit to accept his overlordship. Henry also extended trade privileges to the merchants in Dublin, many of whom had come from Bristol, and in so doing helped lay the foundation for the town's future prosperity. He also initiated a program of reform for the Irish church.

The Irish hierarchy recognized English control as the pope had directed, but the papal admonition to the Irish chieftains that they accept Henry's authority made little lasting impression. No sooner had Henry returned to England than they returned to their ancient routine of raiding each other's herds, scrambling over poor lands and empty titles, and pillaging. In 1177 Henry assigned Ireland to his landless son John and gave him the title "Lord of Ireland." Eight years later he made the mistake of sending John over in person, with a large force of mercenaries, for the purpose of establishing control and uniting the island. This last John almost accomplished: his monumental arrogance, folly, and incompetence constituted such an abomination that Irish and Normans forgot all other considerations that had been dividing them. Henry hastily withdrew his son before all was lost and appointed a justiciar to salvage what he could. In general the English were able to maintain reasonably effective control over Dublin and an area of some thirty miles about the city known as the English Pale. This can be counted as part of Henry's domain.

In the spring of 1173, the year following Henry's return from Ireland, civil war broke out between the king and his sons. The source of the trouble was twofold: first, Henry's initial mistake in assigning his sons provinces and compounding this by withholding from them any voice in the administration of those provinces; second, the aggressiveness of his unfilial sons whose ambition to assume immediate control won the active encouragement of their mother Eleanor and Louis VII. Though Henry had no intention of sharing the slightest measure of authority with his sons until he had grown too decrepit to administer it, he believed it prudent to designate what provinces they could eventually expect to receive in order to prevent civil war. His eldest son, Henry, who was to succeed him, logically received Normandy, Maine, and Anjou. The next largest portion and the most unruly, Aquitaine, just as logically was to be Richard's, the son who had already demonstrated his unique military talent. Geoffrey, the third son, received Brittany. Yet, while the young Henry had already been crowned and all three sons had received oaths of homage from their respective vassals, no shred of authority had passed into their hands, nor could the pensions their father Henry allowed them be considered generous.

The specific incident that fired the revolt was Henry's act in turning three castles in Anjou over to his son John in settlement of the boy's betrothal to the heiress of the count of Maurienne. This betrothal held the key to what proved Henry's most extravagant design. The seeds of the venture were sown some years earlier when Frederick Barbarossa was at war with the pope, and papal supporters had raised the possibility of offering Henry the imperial crown in order to assure the papacy of England's loyalty. It puzzles the reader that the levelheaded Henry should have ever given second thought to the scheme and the possibility of exercising a strong hand in Italian affairs. Yet here he was in 1173–74 arranging this marriage between his son John and the heiress of Maurienne in the hope of one day giving himself (or England) possession of Savoy and Piedmont and control of all the roads leading from France to Italy. Some months after the betrothal the heiress died, so the venture died aborning, but not before Henry had handed over the three castles to John. This act infuriated the young Henry who had been assigned Anjou and who had not been consulted, whereupon he promptly revolted.

When word spread of young Henry's action, other rebels sprang up throughout most of Henry II's empire. Richard and Geoffrey, with some urging from their mother, joined their brother, although Eleanor's plan to meet the conspirators at Paris miscarried when Henry's troops seized her seeking to make her escape disguised as a man. A large section of the nobility of Aquitaine and Normandy who feared Henry's heavy rule, together with many of the leading barons in England who had squirmed over the steady growth of royal authority, threw in their lot with the rebels. Some of the English barons hoped to recover lands, castles, and forests they had seized during Stephen's reign and which Henry had forced them to disgorge. Other barons joined the revolt upon receiving generous bribes of lands and privileges from the young Henry. His promises to William, king of Scotland, of the border provinces his Scottish ancestors had claimed, made him an ally. The young Henry was even able to recruit the assistance of the counts of Flanders and Boulogne for the rebellion.

It was well for Henry that though the rebels constituted a truly formidable group, their strength lay in titles rather than in numbers and resources. They may have boasted a majority of the greater lords, but the larger number of barons, gentry, commoners, and clergy supported Henry. After almost twenty years of peace and justice under Henry, they had no cause to exchange his regime with the kind of feudal misgovernment some of the older heads recalled from Stephen's day. The sturdy peasants of Leicester armed themselves with flails and pitchforks, routed the earl's mercenaries, and helped break the back of what might have developed into a dangerous revolt in the eastern midlands. Even the city of Rouen in restive Normandy refused to yield to the army that Louis and Henry's sons threw around it. The rebels' greatest weakness, apart from their failure to gain popular support, was their woeful lack of organization and leadership. The war consisted of skirmishes, sieges of isolated castles, plundering of countryside, town and village, but no pitched battles or campaigns, only sporadic violence over an enormous area.

Two incidents that occurred during the war are worthy of mention:

Henry's penance at the tomb of Becket and the surrender of the king of Scotland. The pious chronicler sees the first event as accounting for the second. In July (1173) Henry crossed over to England in order to handle in person the grave threat from Scotland. Although he was in a great hurry, he stopped at Canterbury to make his peace with Becket. "On his approach, as soon as he was in sight of the church in which the body of the blessed martyr lay buried, he dismounted from the horse on which he rode, took off his shoes, and, barefoot, and clad in woolen garments, walked three miles to the tomb of the martyr, with such humility and compunction of heart, that it may be believed beyond a doubt to have been the work of Him who looketh down on the earth, and maketh it to tremble. To those who beheld them, his footsteps, along the road on which he walked, seemed to be covered with blood, and really were so; for his tender feet being cut by the hard stones, a great quantity of blood flowed from them on to the ground. When he had arrived at the tomb, it was a holy thing to see the affliction which he suffered, with sobs and tears, and the discipline to which he submitted from the hands of the bishops and a great number of priests and monks. Here, also, aided by the prayers of many holy men, he passed the night, before the sepulchre of the blessed martyr, in prayer, fasting, and lamentations. As for the gifts and revenues which, for the remission of his sins, he bestowed on this church, they can never under any circumstance be obliterated from the remembrance thereof."

Four days later a courier brought Henry the glad news of the capture of the king of Scotland. A small group of Henry's supporters, no more than four hundred, had managed under cover of a heavy fog to slip undetected to the very walls of Alnwick castle and capture the king and a handful of courtiers, while his army of 8000 men was plundering a few miles away. This disaster and Rouen's defiance practically ended the fighting. To all but the king of Scotland, Henry showed himself a benign victor. He surrendered no authority to his sons, but he did increase their pensions and alleviated some of the other of their legitimate grievances. He was also lenient in his treatment of the rebel English barons although their castles he either razed or retained for himself. The king of Scotland, on the other hand, paid dearly for his gamble. By the treaty of Falaise signed in August 1175, he undertook to swear homage to Henry for all of Scotland and to surrender as surety the castles in Berwick, Edinburgh, and other Scottish towns.

Relations with France and with Henry's sons remained quiet for the balance of the aging Louis VII's reign. Then in 1180 Louis' extremely able son Philip Augustus succeeded to the throne and within a short time new trouble developed. The first difficulty rose between the two brothers, Henry and Richard. While the young Henry had still to be content with dreaming of the day he would begin exercising authority in Normandy, his younger brother Richard, with the blessing of their father Henry, was busy at work pacifying Aquitaine. His success in subduing that "hitherto untamed land" aroused both jealousy in the young Henry and fear in the Aquitainian aristocracy who had no difficulty inducing the older brother to join them against Richard. Among the most notorious of the lords of Aquitaine in sowing trouble among the two brothers and their father was Bertrand de Born, lord of Hautefort and troubadour. Dante and Vergil meet Bertrand in the *Inferno*, where they find him carrying his head—the punishment of those who sow discord and turn father against son.

For several months Henry watched his sons fight—Richard against the young Henry and Geoffrey. He feared to intervene lest they turn on him. In February 1183 when he finally took a hand to force an end to their quarreling, this is precisely what the young Henry and Geoffrey did. A few months later the young Henry died, while Geoffrey made peace, and Richard brought his pacification of Aquitaine to a successful end. These developments should have eased Henry's difficulties with his sons, but they did not. When Richard, now heir apparent, was assigned Normandy, Anjou, and Maine, but not given the same authority over these provinces that he had exercised over Aquitaine, he refused to surrender the latter territory to Henry's son John. So fighting broke out again, this time with Richard pitted against his father and his two brothers Geoffrey and John. It soon became evident they were no match for Richard, so it was decided to let him keep Aquitaine with John being compensated in Ireland.

Geoffrey's death in 1186 should have ended Henry's troubles since only two sons remained, Richard who was reasonably content in Aquitaine and John who was in Ireland. Unfortunately Philip Augustus now intruded himself into Angevin affairs. During the six years that had elapsed since his accession, he had consolidated his position in France and was now ready to begin his great project, the destruction of Angevin power in France. He found a willing tool in Richard who though a better warrior than Philip, could never match him in sagacity. Philip now came forward with a number of demands, one that Henry return certain territories the young and now deceased Henry had held title to as dowry of his wife, Philip's sister Margaret. Then he turned Richard against his father by informing him of Henry's alleged plan of handing Aquitaine over to John, of betrothing John to Alice, another of Philip's sisters, and perhaps of even designating him as heir apparent. These charges prompted Richard to demand of his father that he order his vassals to do homage to him as heir, but Henry refused, whereupon Richard renounced his fealty to him and pledged it instead to Philip for the whole of the Angevin continental empire.

Hostilities began in June 1189 despite the pope's frantic efforts to prevent the outbreak of war which would jeopardize the preparations for the crusade in which all three—Henry, Richard, and Philip—had sworn to participate. Richard and Philip entered Maine in pursuit of Henry whom they knew was staying at his favorite city of Le Mans. Though ill and prematurely old, Henry had some fight left in him. He burned Le Mans, then fled southward to Angers where Richard caught up with him. Had he gone north to Normandy which was loyal, he might have escaped. Now worn out and discouraged, he agreed to an interview, when he promised to pay Philip an indemnity of 20,000 marks, to cede Auvergne to him, to recognize Richard as heir of all his possessions, to order the immediate celebration of Richard's marriage with Alice (to whom Richard had been betrothed for a number of years), and to grant amnesty to all lords who had participated in the revolt.

In deep bitterness of heart Henry was borne back to Chinon on a stretcher, where he sent for the names of the traitors to whom he had promised to extend amnesty. Upon his direction, the attendant prepared to read the names, then hesitated. "Our Lord Jesus Christ help me, Sire," he said, "the first name written here is that of Count John, your son." Word that his beloved John had also joined the revolt was too much for the sick old man. He shortly after sank into a coma, revived long enough to have himself carried to the chapel of the castle where he confessed his sins, received communion, and died. This was on 6 July 1189, the twenty-first year of his reign. He was fifty-six years old.

Though Henry died in utter despondency, he had no need to feel discouraged. In England he had achieved his major objectives; in France he left in his son Richard a more formidable foe for Philip Augustus than he could ever have hoped to have been in his declining years. He was buried in the nunnery of Fontevrault where Eleanor later joined him and then Richard.

Frederick II

That men came forward with stories of wonderful things to come when they learned of the birth of Frederick II was not strange. His father, Henry VI (1190–97), was no ordinary king. Henry was the most powerful ruler Western Europe had ever known. He was master of Germany and Italy, and perhaps destined to add even Constantinople and Jerusalem to his domain. There was something unusual, too, about Frederick's mother, the empress Constance. When she bore Frederick, after having been childless for the first eight years of her married life to Henry VI, she was already forty years old. When she gave birth to the boy, there were people who commented on the many years Constance had spent in the convent before her belated marriage to Henry and some who maintained she would probably have preferred to remain a nun. "Ne'er did her heart put off the veil it wore," wrote Dante.

Awesome tales of what the baby would grow up to be—king of the Western world and possibly of the East as well—were mingled with predictions of a sinister kind. The dour Cistercian monk, Joachim of Flora, declared the boy would prove to be the heralded Antichrist. Some of the many men who hated and feared the boy's father, and hoped the emperor's despotic dynasty would die with him, sought to discredit Frederick as illegitimate. He was the son of a butcher they said—a slur that had a long life, for in a fit of rage thirty years later, Frederick's father-in-law damned him as a "butcher's son." Was it to prevent such ugly rumors, which the unusual circumstances of her pregnancy had produced, that impelled Constance to arrange to have her baby born in the bustling market place of Jesi, so it is said, with no fewer than nineteen cardinals and bishops squeezed into the improvised delivery chamber? These prelates would be able to vouch for at least the fact that Constance was the baby's mother.

Who were the parents of the boy Frederick, whose birth in 1194 stirred such universal wonder? His mother was the daughter of Sicily's greatest king, Roger II (1130–54). This was the Roger who helped make Sicily (which, at that time, comprised Sicily and southern Italy) Europe's most advanced state economically, politically, and culturally. Her brother, William the Bad (a name he deserved) succeeded Roger, then her nephew, William the Good (a name he did not deserve). In 1186 this last William agreed to the marriage of Constance to Henry, son of Frederick Barbarossa, king of Germany and Holy Roman Emperor; and though he designated Constance as his heir in the event he had no children of his own, this appeared most unlikely at the time, for William was in his early thirties and his wife was ten years younger. Had it appeared probable that Constance would succeed, powerful foes might have blocked the marriage alliance between Sicily and Germany. Yet, the improbable did happen, and when William died in 1189, Henry promptly claimed Sicily as the possession of his wife.

A year later Henry became king of Germany and proceeded southward to take over his wife's inheritance. This would not be easy. By that time a group of Sicilian nobles had brought forward as their candidate Tancred, an illegitimate grandson of Roger II. Tancred also enjoyed both the support of Richard the Lionhearted, who had stopped in Sicily on his way to the Holy Land, and the blessing of the pope, who wanted no union of Sicily and Germany. Their hopes and efforts proved powerless, however, to stop Henry. Even Richard indirectly aided in his conquest of Sicily. On his return from the crusade, he was captured by the duke of Austria and turned over to Henry, who used part of the huge ransom he exacted from Richard to make good his claim to Sicily. Then, after Henry had established his rule over this southern kingdom, he set out upon what may have been his most ambitious project, the conquest of Constantinople. The ostensible objective of the large host he had gathered was Jerusalem. Part of his army had already sailed, but whether with Syria or Constantinople as its ultimate destination no one will ever know. For it was at this critical moment, on 28 September 1197, that death claimed this ruthless monarch at the untimely age of thirty-one. Nationalist German historians have lamented Henry's death more than did his wife Constance. He might have accomplished, so they believe, that unification of Germany under a strong centralized government which was not destined to come until Bismarck hammered it out more than six centuries later.

All that remained now of Henry's magnificent dream was the little boy Frederick not yet three years old. Frederick had been born the day after Christmas in the year of our Lord 1194, at Jesi in Ancona (some one hundred miles northeast of Rome). Constantine would have been his name had his mother had her way, for she wished his name to honor both herself and the great Constantine. The German princes had indeed hailed him by that name in 1196 when they bestowed upon him the title "King of the Romans." When the boy was baptized in the cathedral of Assisi, however, he received the names of his distinguished grandfathers, Frederick and Roger. In the late summer of 1197 his uncle Philip of Swabia was to bring him from Foligno near Assisi, where his mother was living, to Germany for formal coronation. It was then that news came of Henry VI's death.

Even had Henry been less unpopular, his great empire would have broken up at his death. The universal hatred in Italy of this alien and his tyrannical rule only made it collapse with greater speed. Constance acted even more quickly. She shared Italy's hatred of the proud Germans; she also feared that, of the wide-flung possessions of her husband, she would be fortunate to salvage even Sicily, her own heritage. Prudence warned her to forget Germany. It would prove a millstone about her boy Frederick's neck should she attempt to hold it. So she ordered the many Germans—the notables, officials, and hangers-on—out of Sicily. Then she took the boy Frederick to Palermo where, in the cathedral on Pentecost Sunday, 17 May 1198, he was solemnly crowned king of Sicily.

Meantime Henry's brother, Philip of Swabia, had hurried back to Germany to save at least Germany for his family (Hohenstaufen). There the majority of German princes without hesitation chose him as their king. It would have been unprecedented had they elected the boy Frederick, in view of the strong tradition that the king of Germany must be a mature man capable of ruling and bearing arms. A minority of German princes elected Otto of Brunswick, however, who was the son of Henry the Lion of Bavaria. Their action reopened the traditional conflict that had raged before between those nobles who supported the ambitions of the ducal house of Swabia, the Hohenstaufen, against those who favored the opposing claims of the ducal house of Bavaria. The latter group bore the name of Guelfs, after an earlier duke of Bavaria. Ghibellines was the name given the friends of the Hohenstaufen dynasty. Because the Hohenstaufens had exercised royal power in Germany since the accession of Frederick Barbarossa in 1152, and because it had been the aim of both Frederick Barbarossa and his son Henry VI to rule both Germany and Italy, the Hohenstaufens and their Ghibelline allies had acquired the reputation of being imperialists. That circumstance automatically left their opponents the identification of anti-imperialists, as being friends, therefore, of a king who would be content to reign, not rule, and of a Germany where the feudal aristocracy would retain its dominant position.

Had the prophet who lamented, "Woe to the land whose king is a child," lived in the Middle Ages, he would have bemoaned as equally tragic the land whose ruler was a woman. The empress Constance might order the Germans out, but that did not make them go. Markward of Anweiler, Henry's seneschal in Sicily, declared himself Frederick's vice-regent and announced that he would remain. Most of the other Germans stayed as well. In her helplessness Constance turned to the pope, the aged Celestine III, but he died before he could help her. The new pope, Innocent III, the youngest pope yet to wear the tiara and possibly the most ambitious, expressed his willingness to help her, but his price was high. She must surrender the authority of apostolic legate that her husband Henry had exercised. She must also abandon her power to block appeals to Rome, her right to authorize the holding of synods, and her voice in the election of bishops. These were powers the earlier Norman kings had wrested from the papacy and Innocent wanted them back. Constance was in no position to bargain. Under the circumstances she was fortunate in retaining some voice in the election of bishops. Upon Innocent's insistence, she also released a number of political prisoners and reappointed Walter of Palear, whom she had dismissed, as chancellor and head of the council of regency. Then on 27 November 1198, after announcing that Pope Innocent would serve as her son's guardian, she died.

Innocent accepted, in fact claimed the wardship of Frederick, but papal guardianship did not prevent Sicily from falling into anarchy. Germans, Normans, Saracens, also Genoese and Pisans fought over control of the island and the southern peninsula or simply looted where they could not hope to take possession. In 1201 Markward, with the connivance of Walter of Palear, occupied Palermo and secured possession of the boy Frederick. An eyewitness later described to the pope the poignant scene attending the boy's seizure: the seven-year-old Frederick struck savagely at the man who tried to grab him and then in his impotent anguish tore up his royal tunic and dug his fingernails into his flesh.

The following year when Markward died, another German, William Capparone, took possession of Frederick. Possession of the kingdom he came no closer to achieving, however, than had Markward, even with the help of the German troops Philip of Swabia kept sending south. Now this man, now that group, appeared in the ascendancy. Treachery, violence, and rapine were the order of the day in a land deliberately held on the threshold of anarchy by lords who had more to gain under such conditions. Only the existence of Frederick provided a constant element and the unceasing though generally ineffective concern of Innocent III about his ward. In 1207 when Walter of Palear recovered control of Palermo and of Frederick, conditions began to improve. Two years later, at San Germano, near the Benedictine motherhouse of Monte Cassino, Frederick, now fourteen and an adult according to Sicilian law, took over formal control of the government.

At fourteen, most boys remain boys, but not Frederick. He had grown old faster than most boys. Innocent III even commented how he bore himself like a man. The knowledge of his royal heritage helped mature him, so also his remarkable talents which made him precocious. Most responsible for aging him, however, were the hard circumstances of his early years when he was left to grow up as he could, with little thought given to his proper rearing and development, at times even without adequate provision for his material needs. There were periods when he would have suffered actual want had not sympathetic burghers of Palermo taken pity on the lonely boy and given him food.

The consequences of such neglect in Frederick's early years were not all bad. He developed a spirit of self-reliance, also a confidence in his destiny that enabled him to attack situations less independent men would not have attempted, to pursue with persistence goals prudence would have led others to abandon, and to sustain misfortunes that would have broken ordinary people. Because no one gave thought to his education, he educated himself, and because his school was Palermo, the most culturally advanced city of the West, second only to Cordova, his education was of the best. His insatiable curiosity and interest in learning took him to anyone who had anything to teach, to Moslems, Jews, and to Christians alike, to men who knew something about science, about mathematics and metaphysics, and about history. In order to learn what these men had to say he learned their languages: French, Greek, Arabic, Latin, German, and Hebrew, and probably added to these the dialects spoken in the streets of the great city. In his desire to learn he did not forget his body. Whether to protect himself from the ruffians he met on the streets of Palermo or to possess skills expected of him as king, he trained himself in the arts of fencing and riding and laid the foundation for the strong physique that enabled him later to lead so vigorous a life. His passion for hunting was undoubtedly a product of these early years.

There were other consequences of his neglected youth that were less fortunate. Frederick's pride in his birth, his ambition, and his self-reliance made him self-willed and arrogant. That he frequently suffered the ridicule of men and boys who made fun of him as a "boy king" left him determined one day to rule with a harshness his subjects would not forget. A measure of roughness and uncourtly behavior that he never sloughed off reflected the years he had roamed the streets of Palermo, and the courtliness he never acquired in his youth he was more apt to despise later than regret.

The lack of affection and good will that Frederick demonstrated in his adult life might be traced to these early years when the lonely boy grew up without ever learning the meaning of love. Only toward his two illegitimate sons, Enzio and Manfred, and to one or the other of his mistresses does he appear to have exhibited the tenderness that establishes a bond between two persons. Toward most people, and that included his legitimate children and his wives, he was apt to be unfeeling, if not cruel. The suspicion and unscrupulousness that permeated the atmosphere in which he grew up crushed the roots of softer sensibilities he might have developed and left him skeptical of the existence of unselfishness and truthfulness in others. Reticence and mistrust marked his attitude toward his attendants and associates. His guests might celebrate with him and make merry; they could never feel completely at ease. Only upon Hermann of Salza, the Grand Master of the Teutonic Order, the one person who was convinced of Frederick's honorableness, did he bestow his confidence. Hermann exerted great influence on Frederick. Had he lived, the emperor's life would not have been so tragic. When Hermann died in 1239, Frederick found himself alone, a "wanderer in the world" as Matthew Paris described him.

Though Frederick displayed from the beginning a determination to follow his own counsel, he accepted without demur the wife Pope Innocent III selected for him. She was the sister of King Peter of Aragon, but recently left a widow upon the death of her husband, the king of Hungary. The choice of bride was not a surprise. Even before Frederick's mother Constance had died, there had been negotiations looking to the union of the two families, a plan Innocent heartily endorsed since Aragon, like Sicily, was a papal fief. As this first marriage turned out, Frederick never made a poorer bargain. Not only was his intended— her name was Constance like his mother—ten years his senior, but all she could bring with her as dowry was a paltry five hundred knights. The meagerness of the dowry reveals the poverty of Frederick's prospects, although he might have done appreciably better in point of dowry and bride had Innocent permitted him to push his search to Germany. Innocent preferred keeping the Germans as far from Italy as possible. He might also have hoped that Frederick's wife who had not borne the king of Hungary any children, might continue unfruitful, in which event he could hope to add Sicily to the papal territories.

What must have caught Frederick's eye in the negotiations over his wife to be was the five hundred knights. To his boyish eyes, this number must have appeared a truly formidable force, entirely sufficient to enable him to establish his rule over Sicily. So immediately after his marriage to Constance in August 1209 he proceeded with his plans to pacify the country, only to have pestilence break out among these five hundred Spaniards soon after they arrived. Those who did not die hurried back to Aragon, so that all Frederick could count as fruit of his marriage alliance was the boy that Constance bore him early in 1211. They baptized him Henry.

GERMANY: PHILIP AND OTTO

Up to this time Frederick had kept his attention on Sicily with scarcely an eye for the German part of the patrimony his father had once ruled. There in the north great events were in the making that would shortly cause him to forget the paltry five hundred knights he had just lost. For Italy and Germany could not long stay apart even though Innocent looked upon the Alps as a God-intended barrier to bar one country from the other. Their association went back to Pepin the Short, when he had extricated Pope Stephen II from Lombard power and had made him the "Donation" of Rome. Pepin's son Charlemagne had formally cemented this association of German kings with the papacy on Christmas Day in the year 800 when he accepted coronation as "Emperor of the Romans" at the hands of Pope Leo III. As Holy Roman Emperor, the title the Middle Ages gave him, Charlemagne ruled not only over the lands north of the Alps but over Rome and northern Italy as well.

This fact the Germans never forgot, nor the papacy either, although for a hundred years following the death of Louis the Pious (840) conditions were generally so critical in both Rome and Germany that neither pope nor king had much thought for the other. For the greater part of those hundred years Western kings reigned, they did not rule. Civil war and other circumstances had so weakened them that they could not prevent marauding Vikings, Magyars, and Saracens from overrunning a good portion of Christian Europe, looting the countryside, burning towns and monasteries, and slaying all who could not escape. Before their onslaught large institutions like the State and Church crumbled and all but disappeared. The pope lost his voice, the German kings retained nothing beyond their titles. Local lords, where they were strong enough, seized control of what remained of the Church and of royal authority in their neighborhoods. Such was the feudal period.

The situation improved first in Germany. There the disintegration of the State had never proceeded so far as to shatter the large tribal duchies of Saxons, Swabians, and Bavarians, although even in Germany in 919 the title king lacked substance. The story is told of the election of Henry I that year, how he was out hunting when the messenger arrived to inform him of his election as king. Instead of welcoming the messenger with grateful enthusiasm, Henry berated the puzzled courier for having frightened the quarry away with his noisy approach. Henry, known as the Fowler because of this incident, proved himself an able monarch. Considerably more successful was his son, Otto I (the Great, 936–73), who even aspired to revive the imperial eminence of his predecessor Charlemagne. Like Charles he hurried to Rome to prop up the authority of a pope, this one Pope John XII, and like Charles a grateful pontiff crowned him on this occasion "Emperor of the Romans."

Since the time of Otto I, German kings had made repeated trips to Italy in order to enforce their claims to rule Germany and Italy and to exercise a sort of protectorate over Rome and the papacy. The most persistent monarch in pressing these claims was Frederick's grandfather, Frederick I (Barbarossa, 1152–90). A disastrous defeat at Legnano in 1176, however, forced Frederick I in the end to content himself with a large annual payment from the cities of North Italy (Lombardy) in recognition of his imperial suzerainty. Henry VI, the son of Frederick

Barbarossa, then extended German influence over southern Italy and Sicily after defeating those Norman nobles who had sought to prevent his taking over the inheritance of his wife Constance. That Henry's son, Frederick II, should now find his own fortunes becoming linked with developments in Germany was therefore nothing unexpected.

In Germany incipient civil war had prevailed for most of the ten years following the death of Henry VI in 1197. There the rival factions of Ghibellines and Guelfs were pushing the pretensions of their respective candidates, Philip of Swabia and Otto of Brunswick. Unfortunately for the peace of Germany, neither claimant to the throne was sufficiently powerful to eliminate the other nor possessed privileges and lands enough to purchase the adherence of a preponderant majority of the aristocracy. Beyond Germany's frontiers support for the two pretenders was also divided. John of England supported Otto who was his nephew. This assured Philip, on the other hand, the alliance of Philip Augustus of France since England and France had long been at each other's throats over Normandy. France had also generally encouraged the ambitions of the Hohenstaufens as a weapon against the German princes closer by.

The presence of two candidates and civil war in Germany left the pope not only the logical arbiter under the circumstances, so Pope Innocent III insisted, but the legal one as well. For the pope was more than the spiritual head of Christendom. Under special circumstances he could intervene in the business of kings, and one such circumstance existed now, that is, a disputed election. War among Christians was a travesty of God's will, and Christian society must be protected against such tragedies. If civil or feudal law did not suffice, then appeal must be made to the highest tribunal in Christendom, to the papacy itself, whose jurisdiction over spiritual matters set it above the temporal authority in such situations as this. Furthermore, because the pope had transferred the office of emperor from Constantinople—so Innocent affirmed—and had conferred it upon Charlemagne, the pope possessed the right to anoint, crown, and promote to the imperial dignity the person whom the German princes raised to that honor. And inasmuch as the right to crown carried with it the implicit right to examine qualifications—for if "the princes elected as king a sacrilegious man or an excommunicate, a tyrant, a fool or a heretic . . . ought we to anoint, consecrate, and crown such a man?"—Innocent insisted upon his right to choose between the two rivals.

The German princes left Innocent pretty much to his fine legal spinnings, at least until he revealed his preference for Otto, when the latter's supporters affirmed loudly the propriety of papal intervention. That Innocent should support Otto was a foregone conclusion; Otto was the Guelf candidate and therefore hopefully the more apt to remain in Germany and out of Italy. Otto had also promised to respect papal territories in Italy and the Church's prerogatives wherever they might exist. Philip, on the other hand, made no attempt to hide his position: that Rome was part of the empire and consequently subject to imperial jurisdiction. Under these circumstances, Innocent had no choice.

How inconsequential were Innocent's pretensions to having a definitive voice in the choice between Philip and Otto had become evident by 1204, by which time the great majority of German princes had swung to Philip. Innocent therefore began to reassess his position. The pope was a most practical man. For all his extraordinary talent at finding legal justification for his claims, he never permitted these to block a line of action which prudence recommended and justice and honor did not bar. So once Philip's victory appeared certain, Innocent arranged to have him come to Rome in June 1208 to be crowned. Though admitting defeat in thus accepting Philip, he would at least be re-emphasizing his right to crown the emperor. Then in a moment all was changed. A personal enemy murdered Philip.

Pope Innocent did not approve the murder of Philip, although he saw the working of divine providence in what had happened. For now Otto's election was assured. The German princes were too shocked and too weary to look further. Without much hesitation they agreed on Otto. They only insisted that he marry Beatrice, the eleven-year-old daughter of Philip, in order to unite the two families. Then in 1208 at Frankfort they formally elected him king. Innocent promptly announced his approval of the election, although he demanded that Otto confirm the promises he had made as a candidate. This Otto willingly did and more. He recognized Sicily as a papal fief, acknowledged certain lands in central Italy, including the march of Ancona and the duchy of Spoleto, as papal territories, and extended additional privileges to the ecclesiastical princes in Germany. On 4 October 1209, in St. Peter's at Rome, Innocent with complete satisfaction crowned Otto emperor.

Innocent had little time to enjoy his satisfaction. Within a few weeks Otto demonstrated that such classifications as Ghibelline and Guelf were little better than party labels. Given the opportunity, a Guelf could conduct himself quite as imperialistically as any Ghibelline. And this was Otto's opportunity. Hardly a month after his coronation he was in Pisa working over plans with the city's leaders to oust Frederick from Sicily, with Otto to take over control of the country and Pisa to monopolize its lucrative trade. Insurgent German groups in Apulia also sent their encouragement. Otto could not resist the bait. In the fall of 1210 he marched southward directly across papal territories, Pope Innocent's indignant protests and excommunications slowing him not a whit. As he moved into southern Italy, large numbers of the nobility there and on the island of Sicily flocked to his standards. Even the Saracens offered their support. So desperate was Frederick's position that he offered to renounce his ancestral lands in Swabia and had a galley readied to hurry him out of Palermo. Only the belated arrival of the Pisan fleet, which was to transport Otto's army across to the island, separated Frederick and his kingdom from extinction.

THE EMERGENCE OF FREDERICK

What ultimately saved Frederick was Germany. Otto's mad ambition to take over Sicily had blinded him to the precariousness of his position north of the Alps and to the danger of alienating the pope. True, the pope could be ignored when he had no friends; but when he had friends, let all opponents beware. No one was more persuasive than Innocent in convincing men that what he wished, God also wished, and that they must help him. Though he could offer Otto little resistance of his own, he had bishops in Germany who would listen to him, and a potential ally in Philip Augustus who could not forget that Otto was John of England's nephew. To the German ecclesiastics Innocent sent flaming denunciations of Otto's treachery with acknowledgment of his own myopia in assessing Otto's character. As God had regretted his creation of Adam, so did he now rue what he had done for Otto. To Philip he lamented his failure to fathom Otto's perfidious nature, and he warned him that one day Otto would be assisting his English uncle to get back Normandy.

Otto hurried north, but it was too late. In September 1211 a group of German princes gathered with King Ottokar I of Bohemia at Nuremberg, where they deposed Otto and proclaimed Frederick their new king. Frederick was their logical choice. There was no time for delay and the name of the leader of the Hohenstaufen family was the only one that could command any agreement. The princes' memory of the power, ambitions, and talents of the earlier Hohenstaufens did give them pause, but Frederick's youth and poverty quieted their fears. It was Pope Innocent who was in a real quandary. Even though the names of Ghibelline and Guelf might be meaningless labels, there was no hiding the fact that Frederick was already king of Sicily and that a fundamental principle of papal policy cried out against permitting one and the same man to rule both Sicily and the empire. Still, Innocent had no choice—especially since Philip Augustus also wanted Frederick —so he recommended Frederick to the German princes. He nevertheless made Frederick take two solemn oaths: first, that he would be content with Germany and turn Sicily over to his young son Henry and to an administrator approved by the pope; second, that he would lead a crusade to Jerusalem.

Now it was Frederick's turn to speak of divine providence. Within the space of a brief few weeks, he had found himself suddenly rescued from the very real danger of political extinction as ruler of Sicily and nominated by influential German princes and the pope himself as king of Germany and Roman emperor. His wife Constance sought to remonstrate with him, and so did the Sicilian aristocracy. He should remain in Sicily they told him. There, in relative security and peace, he might have all the power and affluence any man should have a right to expect. Only a fool would jeopardize the loss of these in order to attempt to gain a dangerous throne in Germany.

Frederick never hesitated. To rule as Roman emperor, that was his destiny. For that pre-eminent office he had been born and to nothing less. In March 1212, with only ambition and enthusiasm to sustain him, he left, and after six weeks of perilous travel he managed to slip past his enemies into Rome. There a wildly enthusiastic populace thronged the streets to shout him welcome, while the bells of the Eternal City announced his coming to the cardinals and the great Innocent who awaited him. Never in his turbulent career did Frederick experience so exhilarating a moment—to be acclaimed by the citizens of Rome as their emperor and to be greeted as almost an equal by the most famous man of his age. He wrote later how he had felt on this occasion, as another Caesar summoned by eternal Rome herself to assume command of her empire.

The road from Sicily to Rome had been fraught with danger. That northward to the Alps and Germany was even more menacing. A first stage by ship to Genoa was not difficult, but there Frederick was forced to bide an impatient six weeks before the way appeared reasonably safe for him to proceed by circuitous route to Pavia. From Pavia he got to Cremona, but only after a narrow escape from the Milanese which he effected by swimming his horse across a river to where the Cremonese were waiting for him. Thence, he rode on through Mantua and Verona to Trent, and from there by dangerous paths over the Alps since his enemies were blocking the Brenner pass. His prospects improved perceptibly when a contingent of three hundred German knights joined him at St. Gall, although the real test still lay directly ahead. He must hurry to Constance and reach it before Otto did, or he would never get into Germany. There was no time to waste. Already several German princes, who had earlier announced their support, had defected. Others were unwilling to commit themselves until he reached Germany. Otto also was aware of the approaching crisis. He was hurrying toward Constance from the north with the intention of destroying Frederick before he was able to cross into Germany.

Now occurred one of those dramatic incidents that constantly enliven the pages of history while providing grist for the mills of those who contend that circumstances guide the course of events as frequently as do great minds and greater movements. Constance was momentarily expecting Otto's arrival. The city had been festooned for the occasion, and Otto's quartermaster had already arrived and had given instructions to the cooks to prepare the meal. Then unexpectedly Frederick appeared before the city with his three hundred knights and ordered the bishop to open the gates. The bishop hesitated. He had sworn an oath of loyalty to Otto, and both God and Otto would punish him were he to violate it. Finally, he permitted himself to be won over by the assurances of the abbot of St. Gall and the papal legate, who were with Frederick's party, that he need have no fear of divine retribution since Innocent had excommunicated and deposed Otto. Three hours later Otto rode up, but with so few knights that he dared not attack. "Had Frederick reached Constance only three hours later," wrote the chronicler, "he would never have entered Germany."

After Constance, Frederick's star rose quickly. Southern Germany and Swabia announced their adherence, while a wave of enthusiasm swept almost all but the northern provinces. The glamor of the Hohenstaufen name evoked proud memories of German prestige, while those nobles who had no such memories were taken by the mystical appeal of the blond-haired youth with the thoughtful eyes. They began to speak of him as God's appointed, since his success was nothing short of miraculous. In those parts of Germany where Innocent's denunciation of Otto carried authority, this helped gain Frederick adherents. In fact, so many bishops hurried to his banner that the bitter Walther von der Vogelweide ridiculed Frederick as the *Pfaffen Koenig* (the priests' king).

What ultimately assured Frederick's victory was his alliance with Philip Augustus. That arrangement won him friends among the smaller German aristocracy along the Rhine whose only concern was to be on the winning side. It was also the French army in the end that decided the issue. In November 1212 Frederick met Philip's son, the future Louis VIII, at Vaucouleurs, where the two youths swore eternal friendship and Louis handed over to the near-penniless Frederick the handsome sum of 20,000 silver marks. With this windfall Frederick could assume the role of the traditionally generous Hohenstaufens, a role the thrifty Otto had never assayed. Otto was Walther von der Vogelweide's king, and physically there was nothing wanting in that tall, powerfully built, courageous, though imprudent and somewhat boorish, monarch. But minnesingers like Walther depended upon largess for their existence, and on this score Walther took his king to task. "Had he been as generous as he was tall," he declared, "he would have had many virtues."

Both sides prepared for the battle that would determine whether Otto or Frederick would rule. Had this been the only judgment to be made, however, the military test that came would probably have been as indecisive as most battles during this feudal age, for neither Frederick nor Otto had been able to rally a sufficient number of German princes to provide himself with an overwhelming force. Their contest, however, had become linked with a larger issue, at least in terms of knights, namely that between Philip and John over Normandy. And the battle of Bouvines, in resolving that issue, also decided who would rule in Germany.

John had been able to gather a formidable alliance. His strategy called for an army composed of nobles from Flanders and the Lower Rhine (who liked John's money and feared Philip) to join Otto and attack Philip from the north. Meantime he would invade France from the west. So threatening did the situation look to Philip that he sent an urgent appeal to Frederick to bring up a German army to attack Otto. Frederick did little. Even had he appreciated the full significance of the coming battle, he was helpless. The order he issued to the German princes to assemble at Coblenz passed unheeded, and the battle that decided his fate was fought at Bouvines, in July 1214, without his being there. Several weeks after the battle he turned up with a handful of German knights, in time to receive from Philip the imperial banners his French knights had taken from Otto. The German chronicler expresses the shame of his country for having let another king fight its battles; and he notes, as if in punishment of that infamy, how German arms from now on moved in the shadow of the French.

The battle of Bouvines proved a truly decisive encounter. John had already suffered defeat, early in July, west of Paris at La Roche aux Moines. When his allies also went down at Bouvines (between Reims and Aachen), he lost Normandy and almost lost his crown. Only his acceptance of the Magna Charta at Runnymede, in June of the following year, saved him his throne. For Otto, however, the loss was irretrievable. He had fought valiantly at Bouvines—fighting he could do—until a lance knocked him out of his saddle. On the horse his squire gave him, he decided to flee rather than continue to fight. Still, one must pity him. For a few years yet he struggled on, while losing what friends had not already turned against him. The appeal of his representative at the Fourth Lateran Council (1215) for removal of the Church's anathema fell on Pope Innocent's deaf ears. He died in May 1218 at the age of thirty-seven, his death apparently brought on by some medicine that he had imbibed too freely. Despite his serious illness, he had himself beaten with rods as penance for his sins and succumbed just after the bishop of Hildesheim granted him absolution. Before he died, he directed his brother to surrender the imperial insignia to whomever the German princes would choose as their ruler.

The beneficiary of Otto's misfortunes was Frederick. On 25 July, at Aachen, he was formally crowned king of Germany—although with makeshift insignia, since Otto had the official ones in his possession. But Frederick's gratification was so great he did not mind the missing regalia. Here he was, just twenty-one years of age, now at last king of Germany. The world lay before him, for he would use that glorious position as a key to still more glories which he dared not reveal until later. Pope Innocent had given him his blessing now that he had surrendered his regalian rights in the episcopal lands of Germany. Before he left Germany he would secure the adherence of its princes with a grant of similar privileges for them.

On the day of the coronation, when the ceremonies had been concluded, Frederick mounted the scaffolding in the cathedral at Aachen, upon which rested the newly completed shrine enclosing the body of his illustrious ancestor Charlemagne, and nailed shut the door. For the moment, the ceremonies and honors of the occasion, the adulation of princes, prelates, and attendants, and the impact of his newly established link with the great German monarchs of the past, carried Frederick away. As he was listening to a monk appealing to the crowd to join the crusade, Frederick suddenly took the cross from the monk's hand, announced that he would shortly lead a crusade himself, and asked the Cistercians, whose community he then joined, to begin praying for the success of the undertaking. Was Frederick sincere? Pope Innocent, wise man that he was, must have wondered, as have historians ever since.

After his coronation Frederick traveled about Germany confirming titles and conferring honors, holding diets and courts, and granting rights and lands. He must show himself to his Germans, he must establish himself in their thoughts as their king and gain their good will before returning to Italy. Germany was not to be his home, since he would rule his empire from Sicily, but it must remain loyal. He asked nothing more. The experience of his predecessors convinced him that no king could rule Germany as the king of England might rule England, or the French king, France. The vast open spaces of Germany made him shudder, as did its forests and swamps, its lack of roads, and even more so its bristling fortresses and powerful aristocracy. And the weather appalled him, accustomed as he was to balmy Sicily. He did nevertheless enjoy many months in the palace at Hagenau which his grandfather, Frederick Barbarossa, had built. The scenery of the place and its great hunting reminded him so much of Sicily.

Frederick might be content with German loyalty, but he knew that, for loyalty to survive, it must rest upon a stronger base than the memory of a Hohenstaufen king living in far-off Sicily. To provide that base he decided to make use of his friendship with two orders, with the Cistercian monks and with the Teutonic Knights. The Cistercians, those austere, hard-working brothers of St. Bernard, had their communities scattered all over Germany, where their unobtrusive piety made them popular. Their ubiquity and their independence of local princes appealed to Frederick. By giving them lands and privileges, by himself becoming a sort of lay brother or oblate of the order, Frederick hoped to gain their loyalty and make for himself a powerful ally in his efforts to hold Germany.

The other community that was to provide a glue for the unsubstantial fabric of decentralized Germany was the Teutonic Knights. This was a military religious order that had come into existence about the time of the Third Crusade (1189–92). It was the smallest of three such orders, the other two being the Templars and the Knights of St. John, and the least distinguished. But whereas the two other orders had been forced into virtual retirement with the loss of Syria to the Muslim, the Teutonic Knights still had a promising future fighting the heathen Slavs to the east of the Oder. Like the Cistercians, the Teutonic Knights constituted a kind of supranational community which, while identified with Germany, owed allegiance only to the papacy. So Frederick wooed the Knights with gifts and privileges, and they repaid him with a devotion the emperor could count on from no other group.

The medium through which Frederick dealt with the Teutonic Knights was Hermann of Salza, who was Grand Master of the order from 1210 until his death in 1239. The paternal affection Hermann showed Frederick is difficult to explain, yet even more difficult the filial respect Frederick extended to Hermann. The fact that so honorable and universally respected a man as Hermann of Salza could serve Frederick prevented many people from subscribing to the flood of charges, both true and untrue, made against the emperor. Beyond the success of the Teutonic Order, which Hermann gained by his statesmanlike administration, he devoted himself wholeheartedly to the preservation of peace between the papacy and Frederick. Without his constant intervention, the final break between pope and emperor would have come considerably earlier. He died on Palm Sunday of 1239, the day Pope Innocent IV placed the emperor under the ban.

The most important measure Frederick accomplished during these eight years in Germany (1212–20) was the election of his son as "King of the Romans"—i.e., heir apparent to the empire. Though Frederick had sworn a holy oath to Pope Innocent that he would remain in Germany and turn Sicily over to his son Henry once he had been crowned emperor, there is no reason to believe that he ever had any intention of doing this. The manner in which he had distributed lands and privileges to the German princes, the autocratic bent which the mere position of suzerain in Germany could never have satisfied, his love for the culture and land of Sicily where he had spent almost all his life, all these considerations precluded such a possibility.

Whether Frederick could have effected the exchange of Sicily for Germany as his immediate domain only as long as Innocent lived is doubtful. He did possess a powerful lever for breaking down Innocent's resistance, namely the threat of delaying his crusade, although that resourceful pontiff could probably have thwarted such obstructionism. With the aging and gentle Honorius III, who succeeded Innocent in July 1216, Frederick had no need for vigilance. He was, in fact, barely courteous. When Honorius notified Frederick and the other rulers of Christendom of his election, as was Rome's custom, Frederick was nine months before acknowledging receipt of the message.

Frederick's first overt act of defiance was to bring Henry to Germany in 1217, when he had him created duke of Swabia. Next, he neutralized the opposition of the powerful ecclesiastical princes, who might have been sensitive to papal pressure, by granting them such broad privileges —*viz.*, surrendering the imperial right to erect castles on their lands and to impose tolls—that they became, in effect, territorial sovereigns. With the ground thus prepared, there was no objection in Germany when the diet at Frankfort elected Henry "King of the Romans" in April 1220. When Honorius protested from Rome, Frederick assured the pope that the German princes had done this "without his knowledge and in his absence." Honorius was a charitable soul and may have believed Frederick. If he did not, he did not dare force the issue for fear of endangering the crusade. One last precaution Frederick took before leaving Germany in August 1220; he appointed the most powerful of the ecclesiastical princes, Engelbert, archbishop of Cologne, as guardian of his son and as his vice-regent while he was away. He made it quite clear that he intended to unite Germany and Italy, whether Honorius approved or not.

Frederick proceeded south to Rome, where Pope Honorius crowned him and his wife Constance on 22 November. No jarring note marred the meeting of king and pope or the coronation ritual that followed. When Frederick met the pope in St. Peter's, he bowed down and kissed his foot, whereupon the pope saluted him with the kiss of peace. At the high point of the service, after the pope had crowned Frederick and had given him a sword to symbolize his new role as the champion of St. Peter, the assembled Romans shouted out: "To Frederick ever glorious, of the Romans the unconquered emperor, be life and victory."

When the pope departed the church and was about to mount his horse, Frederick held his stirrup, an act expressive of feudal subordination his grandfather Barbarossa had once refused to perform. And both Frederick and Honorius departed feeling satisfied. Frederick was now Roman emperor and king of Sicily. Honorius drew satisfaction from the fact that never before had a vassal of the pope's been crowned Roman emperor. He was also pleased with Frederick's announcement that he would send assistance to the crusaders in Damietta at once, and that he would himself be leaving on the crusade in August 1221.

FREDERICK AND SICILY

Frederick wasted no time in idle celebration. The situation in Sicily and southern Italy demanded his immediate attention. He had chosen Sicily over Germany because in that southern kingdom he could rule as an autocrat. Yet there appeared to be a real danger that he had lost, without hope of recovery, what little authority he had exercised there since he had left the area eight years before. Rebellious Saracens held most of the island of Sicily, while powerful nobles ruled large portions of southern Italy as independent princes. Frederick's first move was to promulgate a number of assizes from Capua in December 1220. "We who have received from the hand of the Lord the sceptre of the empire and the rule of the kingdom of Sicily," he boldly announced, "do declare to all our faithful subjects of the aforesaid kingdom what is our will and pleasure." Among these decrees were two which struck at the heart of feudal power: first, that all adulterine castles must come down; second, that all titles to land must be scrutinized before the king would confirm them.

Though a pretense at justice and legality was made in implementing these decrees, Frederick's policy in essence was to destroy the castles of his enemies or of those men he did not trust and to deprive these lords of their lands. To accomplish this he used the power of the lesser aristocracy; then, with that unscrupulousness Machiavelli sanctified almost three centuries later as the proper policy of the successful prince, he humbled the smaller lords in their turn. Those towns that held out, he leveled, and he directed their now homeless inhabitants to start new settlements elsewhere. Western Europe had never known so ruthless a king, and in Sicily men from now on would think long before defying the rule of Frederick.

A full two years were required before the stubborn Saracens of Sicily submitted to his rule. Behind their hostility was less hatred of Christianity than fear of what a Christian victor might do to them—and they had good reason to fear Frederick. One of their emirs he had kicked so viciously that they left him for dead. But this was the kind of brutality Frederick was apt to visit upon anyone who opposed him. To the Saracens in general he offered not only their lives but freedom to practice their religion. He moved thousands of them to depopulated Lucera near Foggia, where he made his favorite residence. The local bishop might protest over the number of mosques gracing the skyline of the community, and the pope and curia at Rome grow nervous at the proximity of this Moslem nest, but this did not dissuade Frederick. From his knowledge of Moslems he knew how loyal they could be to enemies who had befriended them. No shrewder move did Frederick ever make than when he took these people under his protection. They proved his most faithful allies in the dangerous years ahead. From them he recruited the majority of his household servants, his imperial bodyguard, and the core of his army.

Frederick next turned his attention to the "reform" of feudalism. Such feudal practices and prerogatives as he found distasteful he extinguished, either by simple fiat or by appeal to some ancient tradition from the past. The total number of vassals he greatly reduced, and from those that remained he extracted a personal oath of loyalty. There would be no mediate vassals in his Sicilian state. He even suppressed the fundamental feudal principle that fiefs were hereditary. No son could expect to inherit the estates of his father unless the father had a record of loyal service. The right of the lord to control the marriage of his vassals he insisted upon claiming. As a consequence of these and similar "reforms," Frederick's aristocracy remained feudal only in name. It depended upon the king for the continuation of its attenuated existence. His counts lived in unfortified residences, not in castles. He made of his Sicilian aristocracy a medieval prototype of that splendid but impotent French nobility immured by Louis XIV in the halls of Versailles. (Incidentally, there were castles in Sicily, but these were fortresses, nothing more. They were ordinarily left unoccupied except in time of danger.)

Still another group beyond the feudal aristocracy enjoyed a position in Sicily which Frederick deemed incompatible with the absolutism he planned to exercise: the maritime states of Pisa, Genoa, and Venice.

Frederick resented their lucrative trading privileges and the powerful economic position that they could have used to throttle the state any time they chose. Of these states, Genoa was the most firmly entrenched, as well as the most confident of the future because of the critical assistance she had given the emperor a few years before when he was trying to make his way northward into Germany to claim his kingdom. Frederick thought differently. Nothing could interfere with his goal of absolutism, at least not gratitude for past services. Those Genoese who did not leave Sicily voluntarily, he imprisoned; and those properties they did not surrender, he confiscated. From now on, all maritime states would pay handsomely for the privilege of using Sicilian harbors and wharves. To protect himself against the danger of a future boycott by these states, as well as to have a fleet to carry his own commodities and troops, he began building his own fleet. He bought some ships, he seized others, and he laid heavy demands upon cities for seamen, shipping materials, and laborers to help in the construction of shipyards and ships. Landowners were required to send him lumber. What shortly grew into the first German imperial fleet in history he placed under command of an ex-pirate, William of Malta, who had behind him a long history of preying on Genoese ships.

The well-ordered state Frederick had in mind demanded the elimination of an autonomous aristocracy and the repossession from foreigners of valuable maritime privileges. Such a state also required laws which had as their purpose the maintenance of public morality and the protection of religion as a force working for social tranquillity and preaching obedience to constituted authority. So decrees were enacted to control the behavior of those who played at dice. Dice playing itself was not forbidden, since it served as an amusement; but those who played must restrain themselves from imprecations—apparently as traditional a way then as now of cursing misfortune. Towns must expel whores, forbid them the use of the baths of the community, and bar them from the company of respectable women "since a mangy sheep frequently infects an entire herd." Even minstrels drew the emperor's ire for their scurrilous and libidinous verses. Men who sang such songs were to suffer punishment. And lest Christians, being unable to tell a Hebrew from a Christian, be scandalized at the failure of Hebrews to observe Christian regulations, it was decreed that Jews must leave their beards grow and must stitch a patch of yellow to their clothing. (This regulation lapsed after a few years.)

Up to this point the bulk of Frederick's legislation had been largely negative. Its object had been the removal or suppression of practices and privileges which would have impeded the establishment of royal absolutism. But what about the men who would man the administrative machinery of this new state and operate it efficiently and faithfully? Whence were they to come? Frederick was certain he had the answer when, in 1224, he founded the university of Naples. This was to be the first secular university in the West, perhaps in the world. Its first and only purpose was the training of loyal and competent men for the imperial civil service. Frederick could have obtained all the legally trained men he needed from Bologna, the foremost law school in Christendom, but he wanted none of its products. Bologna was heavily influenced from Rome; the law taught there had a clerical orientation. Sicily must not only be free of clerical influence, but its judges and officials must reflect an absolutist, secular philosophy in the execution of their responsibilities. To nourish this fledgling university Frederick forbade any of his subjects to attend foreign universities and ordered home all students who were elsewhere. (Those seeking medical training could go to Salerno.)

While one must admire Frederick's sagacity in recognizing the need for a secularly trained bureaucracy to administer his absolutist state, and also commend him for the means he employed to provide these men, it was his misfortune that his experiment in secular education came a century too early. Despite strenuous efforts, he failed to attract either foreign students or a sufficient number of scholars to staff his faculty. The university of Naples scarcely rose above the level of a preparatory school whose function remained that of training the officialdom of Sicily. Frederick was often tempted to close its doors.

FREDERICK AND THE CRUSADE

Meantime, pressure had been steadily building for Frederick to honor his promise to Pope Innocent III to go on a crusade. When the crusaders set out for the East in 1217, Otto of Brunswick remained a theoretical threat in Germany, and Frederick used that as an excuse for not accompanying them. A year later Otto was dead. Now Frederick requested Honorius' further indulgence, on the plea that he had still enemies in Germany as was evident from the refusal of Otto's brother to surrender the imperial insignia. Gradually, even the mild Honorius' patience at Frederick's procrastination grew thin. "What ships, dearest son," he wrote the emperor, "what galleys have you made ready?" Then in 1220 Frederick emerged from Germany and was crowned that November in Rome. He again pledged himself to a crusade—surely the following summer. But nine months later Frederick was too busy establishing absolutism in Sicily to go, although he appeased Honorius to a degree by sending a relief fleet of forty galleys to Egypt. These ships reached Damietta too late to do any good, for the Fifth Crusade had already come to its tragic end. In September 1221, the entire crusading army had surrendered to al-Kamil, the sultan of Egypt.

It is not easy to reckon the degree of culpability attaching to Frederick for his failure to accompany this crusade. Had he never promised to go, the crusading army might have delayed putting out until a more formidable host had gathered. The expectation of Frederick's coming which never materialized surely held up operations in Egypt. Yet, whether his appearance during those years (1219-21) would have prevented the debacle, or whether the crusade might have succeeded in 1219 had its leaders not wasted valuable time waiting for Frederick, are questions that have no answer.

Several reasonably positive assertions concerning this crusade may be advanced: that Frederick probably never had any intention of going— that is, apart from passing gusts of emotion that momentarily beclouded his vision; that the inept leadership of Pelagius, the papal legate, was in large measure responsible for the complete failure of the crusade, although more prudent leadership may not have brought victory; that al-Kamil was willing to release Jerusalem to the crusaders together with a corridor to Acre, but Pelagius spurned the offer in his conviction that he could gain total victory; that Frederick warned Pelagius and the other leaders not to leave the protecting walls of Damietta until he arrived. These are strong probabilities. What is certain is that the crusading army did precisely what Frederick may have warned against. In the heat of August 1221 the crusaders left Damietta and marched against a much larger Moslem army to the south. No sooner had they departed the city than al-Kamil ordered the dykes destroyed to their rear. Within a few hours the Christians found themselves bottled up between the flooding Nile to the rear and flanks, and the attacking Moslems to the front. That al-Kamil would have honored his promise to permit Christian use of Jerusalem as long as he lived is borne out by his refusal to massacre the Christians as his counselors urged. Instead he gave them their freedom. Thus, a month after the proud Christian host had sallied out of Damietta confident of destroying the sultan's army, the last forlorn crusader limped out of Damietta to board ship for the West.

Among those people who laid the failure of the crusade at Frederick's door was Pope Honorius. This is understandable since Frederick, instead of devoting earnest efforts toward organizing a crusade in Sicily, expended his efforts on establishing autocratic rule, refugees of which harsh policy kept streaming into Rome to appeal to Honorius against the emperor's tyranny. Innocent III would have used the threat of excommunication to force Frederick into taking up the cross; Honorius, however, decided on a milder though hopefully equally effective kind of prod. The empress Constance had died in June 1222. The pope now proposed that Frederick marry Isabella, the daughter of John of Brienne, who through her mother was heiress of the kingdom of Jerusalem. Frederick grabbed at the opportunity this gave him of gaining territory in the East. He insisted, however, that John surrender his title of king of Jerusalem the moment he married Isabella; furthermore, that all conquests he might make on the crusade must accrue to the kingdom of Jerusalem.

In November 1225 Frederick married Isabella (by proxy), but still no crusade. The pacification of Sicily had not been completed, neither had Frederick secured anything approaching the control of the Church in his kingdom that his father Henry VI had enjoyed. In the course of negotiations with Honorius, Frederick had discovered how powerful a weapon the promise of leading a crusade could be in extracting concessions. Until he had forced all possible concessions from Honorius, he would keep that arrow in his quiver. So Frederick began to insist now that the crusade he was to lead become a general undertaking for all of Western Europe, not just a Sicilian enterprise that would drain his kingdom of men and money. Not only should knights come from Germany in such number as to provide the bulk of his army, but also contingents from England and France and from Lombardy as well.

Frederick warned Honorius that Christendom lacked the pope's interest in a crusade. Nations had awakened to the existence of national interests, kings to dynastic ambitions, individuals to the heavy cost of such undertakings. The duke of Bavaria had expended, it was said, the equivalent of 7000 ounces of silver to meet his costs on the Fifth Crusade. Despite the promise of generous indulgences, the mendicant friars whom Pope Honorius had sent to preach the crusade could arouse little enthusiasm. In France, Philip Augustus lay on his deathbed. His son, the future Louis VIII, was busy preparing plans, not for the recovery of Jerusalem, but for reopening the war with England. Hermann of Salza, the Grand Master of the Teutonic Order, did manage to stir some response in Germany, but about all John of Brienne could bring back from Paris and London was a new wife for himself (something of an accomplishment, nonetheless, in view of his seventy-five years). Not all was dark, however. When Philip Augustus died, Louis VIII indeed resumed the conflict with England, but he also honored the promise his father had made and sent 157,000 silver marks for use in the Holy Land.

What proved the principal obstacle to the crusade was not so much the lack of response on the part of Western Christendom as the demands Frederick kept making upon Honorius whenever he wished to slow down the preparations or whenever he felt he could blackjack the pope into new concessions. The most persistent of his demands concerned a greater voice for himself in the selection of Sicilian bishops. The one demand most unpalatable to Honorius, at least immediately, was that he surrender the duchy of Spoleto and other territories that Henry VI had once ruled but which Innocent had reclaimed from his widow Constance. Frederick's most dangerous and ambitious demand he never expressed, although Honorius and the emperor's enemies must have sensed it; namely, the extension of imperial rule to Lombardy.

At San Germano on 25 July 1225, Frederick finally agreed to a definite date for leaving on a crusade. He had made similar promises before. This time he offered sureties that he would keep his pledge to leave no later than August 1227. He would send 1000 knights to Syria immediately; he would deposit 100,000 ounces of gold, in five installments, with Hermann of Salza, with the patriarch of Jerusalem, and with the king of Jerusalem, which he would forfeit should he evade his promise; and he would accept automatic excommunication for failure to honor his vow. And in order that there would be no mistake about who was the king of Jerusalem who should hold part of this pledge, he had Isabella brought from Syria to Brindisi where he married her the day she arrived. Immediately following the ceremony he demanded that his new father-in-law surrender title and crown forthwith. Since this was hardly the proper decorum for such festive occasions, one can appreciate the wrath of John, although one would wish that he would have carried his complaint to some less harassed person than Pope Honorius. John was a gigantic person, a veritable Samson on the battlefield, and he had a temper to fit his frame. Now that he stood to be deprived of his kingdom by his son-in-law, the latter must have appeared all the more despicable for his non-warlike physique and his less than open appearance and policies. No wonder John is said to have referred to him as nothing better than a "butcher's son." In the end Honorius was able to placate the irate father-in-law with a pension and the government of Tuscany. He later became Latin emperor of Constantinople.

Frederick was now finally ready to go on his crusade. He had pacified Sicily and he was king of Jerusalem. His next move would be to the East, to drive the Moslems from his kingdom. He sent out summonses to his son Henry and the German princes to meet with him at Cremona at Easter (1226) together with representatives from the duchy of Spoleto and from the communes of Lombardy. The purpose of the gathering was ostensibly that of making final preparations for the coming crusade. Yet, why convene at Cremona which was the leading imperialist city in the north and the hated rival of Milan, the bitterest foe of imperial ambitions? And by what authority had Frederick ordered the knights and cities of Spoleto to send representatives? By summoning these last, was he not clearly announcing to the pope that Spoleto was from now on to be imperial territory? And was he really planning a crusade and not hoping rather to employ the large concentration of German knights which would assemble at Cremona to establish the same kind of autocracy in Lombardy as he had forced upon Sicily?

Milan had no doubt what was in Frederick's mind. The emperor had in fact listed among other matters to be discussed by this diet at Cremona that of restoring imperial rights to northern Italy. Even if Frederick did not contemplate an absolutism as in Sicily, but only the recovery of the rights guaranteed his grandfather Barbarossa by the Treaty of Constance in 1183, this would entail a painful readjustment on the part of Milan and its fellow communes. Much water had flowed under the bridge since 1183, particularly during the period following the death of Henry VI when imperial authority had practically lapsed. During the fifteen years since, Milan had been the most aggressive of the cities of Lombardy in appropriating imperial properties and rights. So when orders arrived that they send their representatives to meet at Cremona, the cities of Lombardy—Milan, Bologna, Brescia, and others —met in March 1226, reorganized the Lombard League that fifty years before had thwarted Barbarossa's ambitions on the battlefield at Legnano, and dispatched troops northward to block the passage of German troops through the Alpine passes.

Now followed six months of charges and countercharges between Frederick and the Lombard League, with poor Honorius caught in between. Frederick demanded that the pope excommunicate Milan and the other Lombard League cities because their open defiance was endangering the crusade. This the pope hesitated to do, even though he had himself repeatedly denounced these same cities for their negligence in suppressing heresy and for their anti-clericalism. Frederick protested to Honorius that his only concern was the crusade—but could the pope believe him? If Honorius were to place the Lombard cities under the ban of the Church, that would be the end of the crusade, for Frederick would feel justified in marching against these enemies of the Church, rather than against the Moslems, and then would claim the blessing of the Church for his conquest of North Italy! Eventually the Lombard cities, pope, and Frederick hammered out a compromise. The emperor agreed to revoke the ban of the empire he had placed upon these cities, all parties promised to forget their mutual grievances during the coming crusade, and the Lombard cities contracted to supply four hundred knights for a period of two years. Then, on 18 March, Honorius died and all this difficult negotiation came to naught.

For Frederick the character of the new pope would prove of decisive importance. That any pope would be suspicious of so ambitious a monarch as Frederick, and that the policy of the papacy would remain generally hostile, this much the emperor was ready to accept. Yet the personality of the new pope could make a great difference in the measures Rome would employ to influence the emperor. The tolerant Honorius, for example, though as committed to papal independence and to the crusade as Innocent III, had been conciliatory in negotiations with Frederick where his predecessor would have been unbending. What would the new pope be like?

The cardinals convened the day following Honorius' death and gave their votes to the peaceable Conrad of Urach, the only German cardinal in the college. Conrad declined the honor, whereupon the cardinals switched to the strong-willed Hugo of Segni, cardinal of Ostia, nephew of Innocent III, a man who could be expected to follow a firm line in dealing with the emperor. Hugo's choice of name, Gregory IX, may have been significant. Pope Gregory VII (the famous Hildebrand) had earlier fought a bitter battle with an earlier German emperor. Though Gregory was the cardinals' second choice, his record was an impressive one. He earned his spurs under Innocent III, who had sent him to Germany to press papal interests during the struggle between Philip of Swabia and Otto. After Otto's defection, Gregory had strongly urged Frederick's candidacy upon Innocent who was suspicious of all Hohenstaufens. Since time had proved Innocent's suspicions well founded, the least Gregory could do to rectify his error was not to permit himself to be fooled a second time by this ingrate. It was no accident, therefore, that already during Honorius' pontificate, Gregory had headed the group in the curia that advocated a strong policy toward the emperor.

This phase of Gregory's early career was known only to an inner circle. What the world knew as his great accomplishment was the vigorous endorsement he had given the mendicant orders. Gregory admired the friars for their self-abnegation, their love of God and neighbor, and their dedication to the sanctification of souls. Francis of Assisi had been Gregory's friend. No wonder he had proved the most persistent advocate of the cause of the friars in urging Innocent to allow them a place in the Church. Gregory had been wrong about Frederick but eminently correct about the friars. In the coming battle between papacy and Frederick, these friars would prove themselves the pope's most devoted allies. After their early experience with Frederick in Sicily, they were in full agreement with Gregory that the emperor posed a truly dangerous threat to the freedom of the Church. To pope and friars, Frederick was the Antichrist.

Frederick sensed that Gregory would be less flexible than Honorius, especially on the matter of the crusade. Honorius had pressed the crusade for the purpose of gaining possession of Jerusalem. For Gregory, a crusade would serve a second purpose, one equally important, that of removing Frederick to Syria where he could not pursue his dangerous Italian ambitions. Fortunately for the cause of peace between the emperor and new pope, Frederick was now actually committed to going. What had brought him to this point was not so much the approaching expiration of the two-year period he had agreed to at San Germano, nor even the accession of the unbending Gregory. It was rather the happy fruition of the negotiations he had been secretly conducting with the sultan of Egypt, al-Kamil, over the surrender of Jerusalem. Because war seemed imminent between this Kamil and his brother, the sultan of Damascus, the former had offered Frederick Jerusalem, in fact the whole of the former kingdom of Jerusalem, in a bid for the emperor's alliance. So now Frederick would be going east, not to fight a crusade for which he had no stomach, but to take over his kingdom. Meantime, knights and pilgrims kept streaming into Brindisi whence Frederick had announced the crusade would put aboard ship for Syria. Some 70,000 gathered there, many too many thousands for the area to sustain. Food was scarce, the heat of July and August intolerable to the many crusaders who had come from north of the Alps, and sanitation provisions were non-existent. Under the circumstances it would have been a miracle had no epidemic struck. There was no miracle. Thousands died of the fever, many more thousands fled the area. Nevertheless some 40,000 crusaders remained and early in September embarked for the East, with Frederick boarding the last galley. He sailed on the eighth in the company of the patriarch of Jerusalem and Count Louis of Thuringia. The latter, the only German prince to join the crusade, was already ill when he boarded the ship. Two days later he died, and Frederick, quite shaken by his death and himself sick with the fever, needed little urging from his companions to turn about and return to Brindisi. He sent the galley on its way, forwarded a message to Gregory explaining his reason for not going but assuring him that he would be joining the crusade in the spring, and went off to the baths of Pozzuoli to regain his health.

Pope Gregory had been following the events of the summer with the closest attention. Just as soon as news reached him that Frederick had turned back, and without waiting for the emperor's personal message, he proclaimed his excommunication (20 September). The pope's precipitate action and the manner in which he justified the excommunication are significant. He seemed almost relieved that Frederick had provided him cause to pronounce the anathema. He did not explain his condemnation as following automatically upon Frederick's broken vow, which would have been sufficient. Instead he took the occasion to loose a flood of vituperation and even calumny. He accused Frederick of having deliberately selected the most unhealthy place in Italy for the crusaders to assemble, of having chosen the dangerous month of August for the same reason, and of having wasted valuable weeks hunting in order to delay the crusade and precipitate the plague. To Frederick's offer to do penance in order to secure removal of the ban, Gregory answered no. Officially it was Frederick's failure to go on the crusade that had evoked the papal anathema. Actually it was the emperor's Italian policy. The broken vow simply provided Gregory the pretext he was seeking.

Christian Europe must have marveled over the curious situation provided by pope and emperor during the winter of 1227–28. For generations popes like the last two, Innocent III and Honorius, had devoted themselves unsparingly to the cause of the crusade. To Christendom nothing was made to appear so important, no act of piety carried such rich indulgences. To give one's life for the cause of Jerusalem was for the layman the highest spiritual goal to which he could aspire. Yet, here in the early months of 1228, Gregory was doing what he could to block the crusade Frederick had announced he would lead to Syria. He encouraged the emperor's enemies to revolt, he forbade the clergy to co-operate with the crusade in any way, and he directed the cities of Lombardy to deny passage through the Alpine passes to crusaders planning to join Frederick. Gregory must prevent the crusade at all costs. If Frederick did go to Syria, Gregory would have no choice but remove the ban of excommunication. If Frederick's crusade proved successful, the glory would redound to the emperor alone. His influence and position would grow all the more menacing to the Church in Italy. Furthermore, if Frederick did persist in going, that would give the lie to the charge of insincerity the pope had hurled at the emperor in September.

For the opposite reasons a crusade had become a necessity for Frederick. Only by going to Jerusalem could he convince the people of Europe that it had been illness, not designs on Italy or lack of faith, that had prevented his departure in September. If he could convince Europe of this, it would be inclined to believe him and doubt the pope in the case of future conflict with the papacy. Furthermore, if he went on the crusade Gregory could not withhold removal of the ban. Early in 1228 Frederick accordingly sent on five hundred knights, appointed a regent for Sicily, and himself embarked at Brindisi with forty galleys on 28 June. On the way to Acre, where he landed 7 September, he stopped at Cyprus long enough to establish his claim to suzerainty over the island. This proved a mistake, since the Ibelin family that he dislodged from control enjoyed powerful influence in Syria. He could ill afford any more enemies in Syria, for once Gregory's emissaries put in their appearance, the majority of the clergy, the Templars, and the Hospitalers turned against him. Among his adherents he could count only his Sicilians, the Germans, and the Teutonic Knights.

Frederick was less concerned over the manner Christians would receive him when he landed at Acre than over the position of al-Kamil. Since the original pact between himself and the sultan had been agreed upon, the sultan of Damascus had died, poisoned it was said by al-Kamil. Would al-Kamil continue to honor his promise to Frederick to turn over Jerusalem now that the alliance had lost its meaning? For Frederick the situation was critical. Even had he wished to fight al-Kamil, which he did not, he could pit only a handful of knights against the might of Islam. Every day his position worsened as more people hearkened to Gregory's threats and denunciations and dissociated themselves from him as a pariah. Failure in Syria most probably would cost him his throne in Sicily, for news was arriving from Sicily telling of how papal armies were overrunning his kingdom. All the emperor could do was to put on a bold front in order to impress both al-Kamil and the emperor's Christian enemies with the strength he did not have. He gave orders that fortifications be repaired and even moved his camp closer to Egypt where some skirmishing took place between Christian outposts and the Saracens.

Frederick's only hope lay in the success of his negotiations with al-Kamil. That these negotiations had continued at all did credit to the sultan. He had given his word to Frederick and he also had a high personal regard for the emperor. Each admired the other for his tolerance in matters of religion and for his interest in learning. Even now, when Frederick's situation was desperate and his future hung by a thread, they passed queries and answers back and forth dealing with scientific and metaphysical problems that bothered them. What led al-Kamil to honor his promise to Frederick in the end, in the face of bitter opposition from his own counselors, was the fact that he had made Frederick this promise. Were he to break his word, Frederick his friend might well lose his throne in Sicily. In this event, too, a papal commander would take over in Syria and war would surely follow.

Al-Kamil, however, modified the terms he finally offered Frederick. The return of the entire kingdom of Jerusalem was now out of the question. He might even have lost his throne had he attempted this. But he did offer Frederick the city of Jerusalem except for the Mosque of Omar to which Moslems should have access, also Bethlehem, Nazareth, and a corridor to Acre, together with the port of Sidon. This last dominated trade routes to Damascus and its surrender was an earnest of the sultan's good faith. Frederick snapped at the sultan's terms and with Hermann of Salza swore on 18 February 1229 to honor the agreement, known as the Treaty of Jaffa. The treaty was to endure for ten years and might be extended.

On 17 March Frederick entered Jerusalem and on the following day a solemn mass of thanksgiving was celebrated in the Church of the Holy Sepulcher. Because Frederick was excommunicate, he could not be present at the mass; but he entered the church after the service and placed the crown of the kingdom of Jerusalem on his head. It would have been difficult to find a high ecclesiastic to do this in view of Frederick's excommunication, although the emperor's action may have been intended as an announcement to the world that he owed his crown to no earthly intermediary. God had made the Christian occupation of Jerusalem possible, so he assured the assembled pilgrims. Only with the divine assistance had he been able to accomplish what kings and armies had for so long striven in vain to do.

Frederick's words may have edified his friends, but they only sharpened the hostility of his enemies, including the archbishop of Caesarea who laid Jerusalem under an interdict. When the patriarch of Jerusalem recruited an army—ostensibly against Damascus, actually against Frederick—the emperor drove him and the Templars out of Acre. On 1 May an angry Frederick left Syria. He could not afford to tarry any longer to straighten out affairs there. His kingdom of Sicily was in jeopardy, if it had not already been lost. War had broken out there almost the moment he left when his regent, anticipating attack from the north, had invaded the march of Ancona. Papal troops attacked Sicily in three places and Pope Gregory called upon France, Spain, England, and Lombardy for men and money. His appeal aroused no response. As it turned out, he needed none. So heavy had Frederick's rule weighed upon the country that, apart from the monastery of Monte Cassino, almost no one offered opposition. The large cities revolted within a few months. To weaken what support Frederick retained and to reassure those who feared the emperor's vengeance should he return, Gregory helped spread the rumor that Frederick was dead. What a topsy-turvy world! An excommunicate crusader no sooner recovering Jerusalem for Christian pilgrims than the patriarch placed the Holy City under an interdict, while papal armies overran the crusader's kingdom in Italy, than which there was no more heinous offense in Christendom!

Frederick landed at Brindisi on 10 June (1229). Although he was without an army he stood in no danger. The townspeople were overjoyed at his unexpected appearance; they had thought him dead. When

his overtures to Gregory were rejected, he organized an army of Saracens, Sicilians, and returning crusaders, and proceeded to the reconquest
of his kingdom. Within six weeks papal armies and resistance had melted
away, and he stood at the frontiers of the Patrimony. There he stopped.
Any intrusion of papal territory would have cost him what sympathy
or neutrality he enjoyed among the rulers of the West. The pressure was
now on Pope Gregory, and much against his will the pope had finally
to negotiate. He demanded a high price for the absolution Frederick
wanted. On 23 July 1230 they agreed to terms, and a month later Frederick was absolved. In exchange for absolution and papal recognition of
the emperor's authority over both Sicily and the empire, Frederick promised to return properties he had taken from his enemies and, what hurt
him a great deal more, surrender his voice in the election of Sicilian
bishops and his right to tax the Sicilian church. For both proud men
the peace went down hard. Gregory had lost the papacy much prestige;
the emperor had surrendered a significant portion of his absolutism.

THE "MODERN STATE" OF SICILY

After Frederick had completed the pacification of Sicily he and his
advisers, notably Peter della Vigna, set about drawing up a new system
of law and government. The former system in Frederick's opinion had
been a patchwork of laws and customs that had demonstrated its inadequacy by the manner imperial rule had collapsed during his absence in
Syria. After two months of work the new code was ready for promulgation and went into effect 1 September 1231. It bore the title *Liber* (*Lex*)
Augustalis. Because of its proclamation at Melfi, it is commonly known
as the Constitutions of Melfi. The new code represented a blending of
old Norman ordinances, earlier decrees Frederick had enacted, and a
group of new laws, all carefully integrated to constitute the first systematic body of law possessed by any Western nation. Its most significant
feature was the manner in which the principles of Roman jurisprudence
pushed into the background the traditional law based upon custom and
feudal practice which was common to the West. This was no accident.
Frederick admired the highly organized character of Roman law, its
centralizing, autocratic philosophy, its emphasis upon authority and
justice. It was his ambition to rule like another Roman emperor, hence
the deliberate introduction of aspects of Justinian's codification and, of
course, the use of the title, *Lex Augustalis*.

According to the new dispensation, the ruler exercised his absolute authority through a hierarchy of officials whom he appointed and who were responsible to himself. These officials did not inherit their positions; neither wealth nor birth qualified them for consideration, but only the preference of the king. As noted above, most of them were to receive their training in the university of Naples. They were to consider their office a responsibility, not a benefice or a mark of favor, and surely not an opportunity for personal gain. Frederick paid his officials and he retained them so long as they proved faithful and efficient. All officials must present annual reports which would cover both their activities and the activities of their subordinates. The principal officials numbered seven, as had been the case with preceding kings of Sicily. They included the chancellor, who drafted laws and handled correspondence; the constable and admiral, who were in charge of the army and navy respectively; the justiciar, who was the minister of justice; the chamberlain, who handled finances; the seneschal, who was responsible for the royal residences and forests; and the prothonotary, or logothete, who handled non-judicial business and served as the king's leading counselor. Except for two or three lords, the feudal aristocracy was excluded from the government although the four leading bishops of Sicily helped constitute, with the principal officials noted above, the council of the crown.

The kingdom was divided into eleven provinces, each administered by a justiciar who was appointed by the king to serve for one year. The justiciar might continue to hold office for annual terms upon the wish of the ruler. The judges and all other major officials who served under the justiciar were nominated by the king. To remove circumstances which a dishonest official might employ to cover irregularities, he was not to be a native of the province he served nor hold property there, nor was he to marry without approval of the king. Though officials were omnipotent within their jurisdictions, the reports which their superiors were to supply the king served as an effective check upon their tyranny. Any malfeasance would result in confiscation of property, imprisonment, or death. Frederick's officials were servants of the state almost to the extinction of their individuality. No bureaucracy in the West could compare with Frederick's in efficiency and service. His officials did not dare give him anything less.

The ultimate test of any government's authority is its ability to raise money. It is no exaggeration to say that the very slow emergence from feudal helplessness, which was the lot of kings of the tenth century, to the absolutism several of them were enjoying at the close of the Middle Ages, can be traced directly to their inability to expand the financial resources they had at their disposal. The ability to increase such resources significantly explains in large measure the success Henry II of England, Philip Augustus of France, and now Frederick of Sicily. Though Frederick had deprived the feudal aristocracy of its autonomous position and had reduced the independence of the Sicilian church, those steps of themselves would not have enabled him to establish autocratic rule. For that he needed money.

Frederick discovered in the monopolies that his Norman predecessors had exercised a favorable foundation upon which to erect his new fiscal system. Even the ancient tradition of state regulation, which had characterized the economy of the island of Sicily from the tyranny of Dionysius down through the period of Roman and Byzantine domination, prepared the climate for Frederick's considerably more extensive measures. New monopolies to supplement older ones gave him control of salt production, iron and steel, hemp and tar, silk, and the dyeing of cloth. Because Frederick raised huge quantities of grain on the imperial estates which he could transport free of cost, he also enjoyed a virtual monopoly in the production of grain. While the administration of these monopolies might be entrusted to a particular group, such as the dyeing of cloth to Hebrews, the bulk of the profits accruing from such exploitation went to the state.

Frederick expected trade to provide the state a constant and large flow of revenue. For that reason he suppressed the collection of internal customs which impeded commerce on the one hand while enriching local lords and towns on the other. In their place he introduced an efficient system of state warehouses through which all goods entering and leaving the country must pass. No goods could be imported or exported except by way of these warehouses where a duty was collected on all commodities. Duty rates were not so high as to slow the movement of goods except in time of local shortage or war when the export of certain articles might be reduced or even embargoed. These warehouses served a second purpose. Since they were located in harbor cities and on frontier roads, government agents at these posts could control communications with foreign countries and prevent the arrival of unwanted legates or the escape of political refugees. In an effort to stimulate the growth of trade Frederick also had roads and bridges constructed, encouraged immigration, and founded a number of new towns. Mention should also be made of commercial treaties the emperor negotiated with Tunis and Egypt and of his minting the first gold coin in the West. These coins were called *Augustales*. On one side appeared the image of Augustus, with Frederick's name on the other. The implications were manifest.

The prosperity of most states in the Middle Ages depended principally upon the exploitation of its agricultural resources. The only exceptions were the mercantile communities of North Italy and the Low Countries. Since Sicily was no exception to the general rule, Frederick gave earnest attention to increasing the productivity of the Sicilian soil. That he owned more land than any other proprietor furnished him both a personal and a national interest in such development, although the distinction may have been only technical. To the task of increasing Sicily's productivity he brought a knowledge of soil, seed, and livestock that was extraordinary for his time, and a willingness to experiment that was equally unusual. He encouraged the raising of sugar cane and established refineries to handle the crop. He experimented with the production of cotton, henna, and indigo, and even sought to acclimatize the date palm. He took measures to eradicate pests and injurious animals. That the means he employed to cope with a plague of caterpillars involved each farmer's turning over a daily quantity of insects reveals how many centuries removed was even the precocious Frederick from modern insecticides. Farmers who neglected to cultivate their soil might find their acres turned over to some landless person, although no farmer caught in arrears could be deprived of his oxen or farming implements. And Frederick permitted forests on the royal demesne to be cleared to make room for vineyards.

The most unmedieval measure Frederick enacted to strengthen his kingdom was the decree prohibiting the marriage of Sicilians to foreigners. It had often grieved him, the emperor explained, to see how his people had suffered corruption from foreign manners and peoples. "When the men of Sicily marry the daughters of foreigners," he warned, "the purity of the race degenerates, evil and sensual weakness increase, and the integrity of the people is contaminated by the speech and by the habits of others." Frederick's efforts to keep his Sicilians pure anticipated those of more modern rulers, although one may doubt whether ever a ruler had so "impure" a people to start with as did the emperor: Carthaginians, Greeks, Romans, Moslems, Jews, Normans, Germans, and what-have-you! Frederick's aim was a national state of Sicilians bound to him body and soul, completely dominated by the state, trained by the state, their goal in life the service of the state. In approximating this goal for his state Frederick provided the closest parallel the Middle Ages had to offer to ancient Sparta and modern dictatorships. As Pope Gregory remonstrated: "In your empire no one may dare, without your leave, to move hand or foot."

FREDERICK'S PERSON AND CHARACTER

Frederick was now thirty-six years old, the age when many men attain the peak of their physical and mental powers. The addition of some pounds since his youth gave him the appearance of being shorter than he was. His beardless face and balding head had disappointed the Saracens. On the slave market, one Moslem chronicler doubted he would have brought two hundred drachmas! Yet, an active life had given him vigorous health and a powerful physique. Though not unacquainted with the sensual luxuries of Oriental courts, he never permitted himself to succumb to their debilitating influence. He may have been the only European to take a bath daily, almost a sin in the Middle Ages. Most remarkable about his appearance were his clear, penetrating eyes. A friend likened them to the eyes of a serpent. They made most men feel uncomfortable.

Frederick's character was more enigmatic than his eyes. Peter della Vigna, who knew him better than any man, would have avowed his inability to fathom his master's nature. Proud he was, and ambitious, although not vain nor even arrogant in a small sort of way. As the scion of the emperor Augustus, he was aspiring only to what was rightfully his when he demanded a rank and authority above that of any man, pope included. Not even a wife would dare share the pinnacle with him, just as no woman shared Augustus' glory. The drive within him to become master of the empire was relentless. It died only when he died. Even had he been able to foresee what a tragic and barren course his ambition would lead him, he would not have turned back. His destiny was to rule.

The world accepts Frederick's ambition and his love of power as the ordinary characteristics of great men. It admires the emperor's love of learning and his use of the scientific method. It also approves his tolerance of Moslem and Hebrew. What it condemns are his selfishness, cynicism and unscrupulousness, his tyranny and cruelty. He may have distributed charity for humanity's sake, but there is no record of this.

His was an unsympathetic nature. Most eloquent testimony to his lack of affection, his unhappy wives could have provided. His callousness to human suffering and his cruelty were common failings among the aristocracy, although the savagery he displayed at times even John of England would have had difficulty matching. His materialism shocked the West and drew criticism from Moslem observers. How deep-seated were the skepticism and agnosticism of which his enemies, including the pope, accused him, one hesitates to say. His interest in science made him suspect, as did the Oriental aspects of his court and his fraternizing with Moslems. He may have been the only Christian prior to modern times to enter the Mosque of Omar. No doubt Frederick liked to titillate the people about him with irreverent observations, as when he passed a wheat field and wondered aloud how many gods might be growing there. Even innocent queries, such as what the saints and angels might be doing all day, did him no good. There is, on the other hand, no reason to suspect the sincerity of his attraction to the Cistercian order, nor the genuineness of his piety when he helped translate the body of St. Elizabeth to a permanent shrine. In his will he gave generously to the crusades for his soul's sake, directed that the cathedrals at Lucera and Sora be rebuilt, and died after receiving the viaticum.

Frederick's contemporaries hailed him "the wonder of the world." Of a number of accomplishments which gained him this praise none was more unusual than his extraordinary intellectual development. There was, for example, his contribution to Italian literature. Before his day Italian literature scarcely existed. It was he and his circle of scholars at Palermo and Foggia who first composed poetry in the Italian language. The form they cultivated was that made famous by the troubadour whose lyric poetry had traditionally been composed in Provençal. Frederick's group also introduced a more concise form of this poetry. The leading member of the emperor's circle, Peter della Vigna, reflected some of Frederick's versatility. He was a distinguished jurist, something of a poet, and especially renowned for the eloquent manifestoes he produced in the emperor's name. Their brilliant though precise and logical Latin style were the envy of the Christian chanceries in the West.

Frederick's curiosity about what might pass for science, mathematics, and metaphysics impresses the modern reader. There was nothing he did not wish to know, whether the knowledge concerned the stars, diseases of horses, quadratic equations, or the existence of the soul. Supplementing this curiosity was a critical spirit not common to his age, of insisting upon confirming information and phenomena by observation or experimentation. For this reason he refused to follow Aristotle when writing about falconry, not only because he was sure he knew more on the subject, but because the Greek philosopher had had little or no actual experience with falcons. When he heard tell that the hot sun of Africa caused ostrich eggs to hatch, he sent a group of zoologists to al-Kamil to study the phenomenon. On the basis of the information they brought back, he set up incubators in poultry farms in Sicily. He sewed up the eyes of falcons to disprove the common notion that falcons depended upon sight to locate their food. Yet how elementary his scientific posture may still have remained is revealed by the story that he sent to the king of Norway to verify the belief that objects thrown into a certain spring in that northern country turned to stone.

Frederick corresponded with some of the leading scholars of his day including Leonard of Pisa, the foremost mathematician of the Middle Ages. The emperor arranged for the translation of scientific, geometric, medical, and philosophic writings from the Arabic, Greek, and Hebrew, including treatises by Averroës for whom he had the greatest reverence. The leading scientist at his court was Michael Scot, who exerted considerable influence upon Frederick by virtue of his office as chief astrologer. In his reverence for the claims of astrology, Frederick was very much the child of his age.

Of the many stories told about the emperor's scientific curiosity, there were some that suggest the deliberate distortion of malevolent tongues. Did he, as charged, have a man sealed in a barrel in order to prove that there was no such thing as a soul since none could be found when the man's dead body was removed? Or, in his desire to learn more about the body's digestive processes, did he have two men eat full meals, then have one rest while the other hunted, after which he ordered their stomachs cut open to ascertain whether rest or activity were more conducive to digestion? He is also said to have undertaken an experiment similar to that Herodotus recounts, of having two children raised by nurses who had strict orders not to speak to them, so as to ascertain, once they started speaking on their own, which was the language that Adam had used? The children died before they had learned to talk, and the critical chronicler observed that children obviously needed conversation and love in order to survive as much as they needed food. Then there is the story, this not a disparaging one, how he once asked Michael Scot what the distance might be from the floor of the room in which they were standing to the sky. After Michael had carefully computed the distance, Frederick removed to another residence for several months, meantime giving orders that that particular floor be lowered several inches. When he later brought Michael back again and posed the question a second time about the distance to the sky, that extraordinary astronomer observed, after completing his reckoning, that either the sky had moved or the earth had sunk!

What is fact, what fiction, about Frederick's scientific experiments remains debatable. There is nothing dubious, however, about the scientific character of his well-known book on falconry entitled *On the Art of Hunting with Birds.* The emperor wrote the book to please his son Manfred who was also interested in the sport. Actually it was more an art than a sport. There was something mysterious, Frederick maintained, about the power that would cause the proud, fierce falcon to return to captivity on his master's arm after soaring aloft in complete freedom. Only an aristocrat with the skill and patience to train such a noble bird could hope to exercise such authority over it. "It is for that reason," the emperor wrote, "that while men of aristocratic birth learn the art, the uneducated seldom do so. Hounds and hunting-leopards can be tamed by force, falcons can only be caught and trained by human skill. Hence a man learns more of the secrets of nature from hawking than from other kinds of hunting!"

Frederick's treatise on falconry was definitive, so he affirmed. "Our intention is to set forth things which are as they are." There was little point in looking further. Aristotle was useful although deficient because of his lack of experience. Here was the product of almost thirty years of loving, meticulous study of the bird, supplemented with an exhaustive knowledge of the literature on the subject and the experience of working personally with all the different kinds of falcons that could be brought to Sicily. He had falcons brought in from places as distant as Iceland and India. In his study Frederick discussed the different kinds of falcons, their habits, feeding and breeding, their physical composition, organs, and plumage, how they could be captured, reared, and trained. Some of the remarkably accurate drawings that illustrate the treatise may have been Frederick's own work. The clear, affirmative style is unmistakably his.

Frederick's passion for falconry reflected the emperor's broad interest in zoology and in nature in general. His knowledge of horses and dogs was considerable. At Lucera he maintained the first zoo in European history. Some of the animals he received as gifts from his friend al-Kamil. It may have been the emperor's curious interest in animals, more probably his desire to impress people, that led him to have his giraffe, elephant, and assorted panthers, lions, leopards, monkeys, ostriches, peacocks, parakeets, and eagles accompany him whenever he traveled. To the majority of ordinary folk who had never been away from home, this menagerie alone would have made Frederick "the wonder of the world." Near his residence at Foggia he established a preserve for waterfowl, while game preserves, hunting lodges, and foresters' houses could be found scattered about the kingdom.

Frederick deserves a page in the history of medieval architecture. He proved himself a great builder, not in grandiose structures, rather in the large number and simple beauty of the multitude of villas, strongholds, watchtowers, and hunting lodges he had erected. Because these structures were not churches nor located in cities, they have disappeared almost without trace and little remains today to bear witness to this facet of his genius. For he was his own architect and what testimony there remains suggests his taste to have been a happy blend of the functional and artistic. The first evidences of Gothic in Italy appeared in his Sicily, the work probably of Cistercians who were among his favorite builders. He erected a single church, the cathedral at Altamura. Only on his deathbed did he remember his promise to rebuild the cathedral of Lucera, which his Saracen workmen had razed because of its ruinous condition and because he needed the stone for a project of his own.

Frederick's interest in occult sciences and his flippant comments about religion facilitated the work of his enemies in blackening his name. Much of what they said and wrote was sheer calumny. Their sharp criticism of the Oriental treatment he gave his wives on the other hand and their attack on his own personal morals were probably deserved. In addition to four legitimate children by his three wives, all three spouses properly succeeding one another, there were a dozen illegitimate sons and daughters born of several mistresses. Historians have identified an Italian, a Saracen, and a German mistress. That he showed these mistresses the affection he never bestowed upon his wives is a failing other men have shared. The spectacle of wives shunted off to live out their lonely lives in some out-of-the-way villa in Sicily guarded by black eunuchs, however, is one the Middle Ages had as much difficulty accepting as the modern world, whatever the particular Oriental conventions that may have obtained in southern Italy. Equally repugnant to

Christian contemporaries were the dark-eyed Saracen dancing girls who graced Frederick's residences, some of them the gift of al-Kamil. These girls, together with the pretty Moslem weavers from Lucera who worked the looms and provided for the needs of the court, supplied the basis for the charge which only Frederick's friends could deny, that the emperor maintained a harem. This, too, would have made him "the wonder of the world," at least in Western eyes.

GERMANY AND LOMBARDY

An uneasy peace hung over Italy following the reconciliation of Pope Gregory and Frederick in July 1230. What they had said when they broke bread with Hermann of Salza on that occasion at Anagni no one knows. Nothing has been recorded. Hermann must have looked upon the past as a closed book which pope and emperor would not reopen. The other two knew it was not to remain closed. They were probably thinking about the future. Gregory knew that Frederick was not satisfied, not satisfied with the powers he had surrendered to the Sicilian church, not satisfied with certain territories that had been incorporated into the Papal States, and certainly not content with the defiance of his imperial rights in Lombardy. The pope may even have suspected that Frederick aimed to revive the ancient authority of Augustus over Rome and the papal territories. Under the circumstances, therefore, the conflict was bound to continue. This meeting and agreement in 1230 represented but a truce.

Frederick made his first move in the fall of 1231 when he summoned the German princes to a general diet at Ravenna for 1 November. At least the Lombard cities suspected his intentions, whereupon they revived their league, and blocked the Alpine passes. So November came but no diet, while Frederick fumed and Pope Gregory protested, protested the defiance of the Lombard League but only protested. He did not dare antagonize his only allies in the north, not even several years later when he learned that they had encouraged Frederick's son Henry in Germany to revolt.

The story now shifts to Germany. Henry was eighteen years old, no longer under the supervision of a guardian and, like most young men, anxious to prove himself. He was perceptive enough to fear the gradual extinction of royal rights in Germany if the ever growing power of the princes was not halted. He lacked, however, the prudence and self-discipline to see a task through that would have tried the sagacity of a much wiser man, nor had his unsteady character won him many true friends. In order to erect a counterforce to the princes, he allied himself with the lower nobility, the *ministeriales* or civil servants, and the towns, and began extending the latter important rights. This policy the princes could not tolerate, so they turned on Henry and in May 1231 forced him to extend them substantially the same privileges Frederick had given the ecclesiastical princes in 1220. To all intents and purposes, these rights left the princes territorial sovereigns, and Frederick had no choice but confirm these privileges a year later.

Relations between Frederick and his son grew progressively more strained. The fault was the young man's, although Frederick had done nothing to gain his son's affection and respect. So, in spite of paternal remonstrances, Henry continued his intriguing with the enemies of the princes, coupled this dangerous conduct with extravagant living, and even sought to divorce his Austrian wife in order to marry an early love. In the spring of 1232 Henry was prevailed upon to meet his father at Aquileia where he promised on his oath never again to disobey imperial orders nor to molest the princes. Back in Germany he reverted to his old policies and in the fall of 1234, upon the promise of the Lombard cities to block the Alpine passes to his father's troops, raised the standard of revolt.

As it proved, Frederick needed no troops. Once news reached Germany of the emperor's arrival in Regensburg, Henry's allies melted away. After the failure of a forlorn attack on Worms, the unfortunate young man listened to the advice of Hermann of Salza and submitted unconditionally to his father. At the diet held in Worms in July 1235 he knelt before the emperor, laid down the crown, scepter, and sword, and begged his father's pardon. Frederick left him his life but not his freedom. Henry was taken first to Heidelberg, then to more secure confinement in Apulia. In February 1242, as he was being transferred to another prison, he either slipped from his horse into a mountain gorge or more probably precipitated himself into it. Henry's defection and death were Frederick's first great sorrow.

Henry's revolt was not permitted to interrupt preparations for Frederick's third marriage, which was solemnized at Worms on 15 July. This time his wife was Isabella, sister of Henry III of England, twenty-one years old and a strikingly beautiful and charming young woman, if we are to believe the German chroniclers. What most recommended the marriage alliance to Frederick was the effect it would have in neutralizing what remained of anti-Hohenstaufen sentiment in northern Germany, where Guelf loyalties had once been strong. Frederick may have admired Isabella's beauty, intelligence, and prudence, but these were qualities he was less concerned with than the children she might bear him. Her fate was to be similar to that suffered by his first two wives. After ten days of brilliant celebrations, Arab eunuchs took her in tow and she spent the six years remaining to her life in lonesome isolation in southern Italy. She did on occasion—rare occasion—appear with Frederick in one of his southern residences, but it was deemed a most special privilege when her brother was once permitted to pay her a private visit. She bore Frederick a daughter and a son. Her brother Henry III once complained that his sister never wore the crown of empress. His poor sister had infinitely more than this about which to complain. She lies buried next to Frederick's Syrian mistress in Andria.

Before leaving Germany, Frederick held a great diet in August 1235 at Mainz. The main matter of business was the proclamation of a land peace. This proclamation included both old and new legislation. Those men who could not prove self-defense for taking up arms would suffer sharp penalties from their lord. Frederick retained the right to judge princes and to impose the much feared ban of the empire upon those who defied this land peace. In the emperor's absence, a grand justiciar would enforce the peace. This law has some significance apart from being the first to be written in both Latin and German. Because it received periodic confirmation from later kings, it served as a basis of subsequent peace legislation. Frederick liquidated his own family feud with the Guelfs when he created Otto, nephew of his erstwhile opponent, Otto IV, first duke of the new duchy of Brunswick-Lüneburg.

Now that Germany could be counted on as remaining within the imperial fold, Frederick turned to his major project, the pacification of Lombardy. Its defiance of his imperial authority in closing the Alpine passes to him and in supporting the revolt of his son provided him ample justification. Pope Gregory attempted to head off his move since it would place him in a most delicate and dangerous position. While he could not condone the defiance of the Lombard cities, neither could he employ the weapon of excommunication against them as Frederick insisted he do. This would have assured Frederick's triumph, and once Lombardy had been subjugated, the papacy would be left to face Frederick alone. All Gregory could do was to affirm his right to arbitrate the dispute on the basis of the Donation of Constantine and the pope's transferal of the empire from Constantinople to the Germans in the person of Charlemagne.

Late in 1236 Frederick led his army southward from Germany and captured and destroyed Vicenza. A revolt by Duke Frederick of Austria, the only German lord who had refused to swear loyalty, forced him to return to Germany; there, he humbled the duke and had the German princes elect his nine-year-old son Conrad king of the Romans. Then in the late summer of 1237 he again crossed the Alps. The army he was able to gather around himself numbered some 15,000 men and included Sicilians, contingents from loyal cities in the north, German knights who hoped to make their fortune in Italy, and some 7000 Saracen archers. Mantua surrendered without fighting, but Brescia proclaimed its defiance with the encouragement of an army of about 10,000 allies, principally men from Milan which stood by. When this army refused to leave the protection of the city to do battle, Frederick resorted to a stratagem. He moved his army in the direction of Cremona and set up camps here and there in order to leave the impression that he was going into winter quarters. Instead, he doubled back toward Brescia under cover of reed-filled marshes and waited for the Lombard army to move west. Toward the evening of 27 November he caught this army completely off guard at Cortenuova and won a tremendous victory. Of the enemy who were not slain more than 4000 surrendered, including 1000 knights, among them the general in command, Pietro Tiepolo, who was the *podestà* of Milan and the son of the doge of Venice. Something equally prized that fell into Frederick's hands was the *carroccio,* or standard-bearing chariot of Milan.

Cortenuova was Frederick's greatest victory and he celebrated it as had the victorious generals of ancient Rome, with a triumph. He selected the loyal imperial city of Cremona for the celebration. Never had the Cremonese seen the like as they waved their banners and shouted their exultation while the procession marched by. First came Frederick, a green mantle over his shining armor, then his Saracen archers marching immediately behind in their colorful uniforms, followed by musicians with trumpets, cymbals, and drums. The emperor's menagerie of exotic animals was there too, along with their black guards. Then wagon upon wagon rolled by laden with the immense booty taken at Cortenuova. Pietro Tiepolo had a special place of ignominy reserved for himself. He lay bound in chains to the shattered mast of the proud *carroccio* which was dragged past by an elephant. From the wooden tower of the *car-*

roccio black trumpeters proclaimed the triumph of the new Augustus. The fallen enemy brought up the rear: knights, nobility, and soldiers, barefooted and downcast.

The victory at Cortenuova appears to have beclouded the vision of Frederick. For the moment he seems to have lost his sense of reality. As Florence and some other cities announced their submission, while Milan and others asked for terms, Frederick assumed mistakenly that Italy lay at his feet and was ready for the plucking. He seems to have forgotten that one defeated army was not all Lombardy, that its walled cities remained as formidable as ever to a thirteenth-century army. For the moment, too, he forgot his most deadly enemy, Pope Gregory, who was not asking for terms, only looking on anxiously. So instead of giving long thought to how he might most prudently exploit his victory, the emperor permitted the exhilaration of the moment to put himself in one of his most arrogant moods. He would humiliate the fallen enemy. To Milan's plea for terms he demanded unconditional surrender, to her prayer that he show mercy, he returned the cryptic reply that he would do what he would do. To warn the pope what was in store for him and to apprise the Roman populace of the glory his victory would bring them, he had the *carroccio* taken to Rome as imperial spoils, much like Pompey had brought back from Jerusalem the candlesticks and trumpets from the Hebrew Holy of Holies.

Because Milan feared the worst, it refused to surrender. "We fear your cruelty," the city notified him, "which we have experienced; so we prefer to die under our shields by sword, spear, and dart, than by trickery, starvation, and fire." Milan's defiance heartened Brescia, Bologna, and other cities. To trample out this last flicker of independence, Frederick mounted what he expected would be an overwhelming attack. He demanded knights from Germany. He even appealed to his brother kings to send aid since he was fighting their battle. "This matter touches you and all the kings of the earth," he warned them. Should his rebellious subjects succeed in their revolt, how long could they expect to maintain their thrones?

His efforts did raise a huge army. There were Germans who came, Sicilians, Italians, and Saracens, and contingents from France, England, Hungary, and Castile, even from Constantinople and from al-Kamil's army in Egypt. Frederick's immediate objective was Brescia. Once he had captured that city, Milan would be isolated. From Spain he imported a famed Arab engineer to direct his siege engines. How it happened no one tells, but the Brescians spirited away both engineer and prison in which he was chained, then used him effectively against Frederick's engines. As weeks passed without any success, Frederick stooped to savagery. He had captive Brescians bound to his engines to protect these machines from missiles fired against them from the city. When it became manifest that the siege would be a long one, Frederick made overtures, only to have the Brescians reject these with scorn. Bad weather, then disease finally compelled Frederick to give up his siege. He burned his siege engines early in October and withdrew to Cremona.

Frederick's repulse at Brescia had serious consequences. All Italy had been awaiting the outcome. Those cities that would have submitted, now determined to continue resistance, while several cities like Genoa which had announced their adherence to the emperor, withdrew their allegiance. The pope, too, who had been completely passive since Frederick's victory at Cortenuova, began to stir again, slowly at first then with a burst of indignant vigor when he learned that the emperor had arranged a marriage between his illegitimate son Enzio and the widowed heiress of Sardinia. For Sardinia was a papal fief. Gregory immediately sent his legates off to Genoa and Venice and concluded a secret treaty by which these maritime states pledged themselves to carry the war to Sicily, while the Lombard cities would pin down imperial armies in the north. Then on Palm Sunday, 20 March 1239, Gregory formally excommunicated the emperor—because of his policy toward the Sicilian church!

THE DEATH STRUGGLE

Each side girded itself for the deadly struggle that would mean the end of one or the other. Each side sought to justify its position before Christian Europe, the pope to arouse a crusade, the emperor to gain a sympathetic neutrality. Gregory denounced Frederick for his harsh policies toward the Church and for his agnosticism. He had denied the virgin birth of Christ and far worse. "In truth this pestilential king maintains," so the pope affirmed, "that the world has been deceived by three imposters, Jesus Christ, Moses, and Mohammed: two of these died in honor, the third was hanged on a tree." Gregory also dusted off the old charges that Frederick had deliberately caused the deaths of thousands of crusaders at Brindisi in 1227 and that he had negotiated terms with the Mohammedan sultan at the expense of Christians. Frederick charged in reply that if Gregory was himself not a heretic, he at least consorted with heretics, for a number of Lombard cities, notably Milan, were known to harbor heretics. Concerning the other charges brought against him as well as the conflict with the papacy, Frederick announced his readiness to lay his case before a general council composed of princes and prelates.

Such propaganda served little beyond neutralizing the other's charges. Europe was in no mood for a crusade, certainly none in Italy. The situation there was muddled to say the least. How could Gregory call Frederick an agnostic when the empire and Sicily had proof of his harsh legislation against heresy? And had not the emperor undertaken the only successful crusade most people could remember? The English chronicler must have expressed the misgivings of many when he wrote: "We know he faithfully set out to war for our Lord Jesus Christ and exposed himself to the dangers of the sea and of the faith. Up to now we have not observed an equal piety in the Pope." That no love of the faith motivated Frederick's decrees against heresy, only concern about peace in his realm, and that he would never have undertaken any crusade except for selfish, material reasons, they did not know. Nor would they have believed the pope had he told them that the fundamental reason for his war on Frederick was the emperor's aim to subordinate all Italy, including Rome and the Church, to his will. And why should they have believed Gregory? Had he not told them once that Frederick was dead? And why suddenly charge Frederick with dark policies toward the Sicilian church, the very moment he had his son marry the heiress of Sardinia?

So Europe left Gregory, Frederick, and Lombardy to their own quarrel, and these three went at it in dead earnest. The pope raised funds in his territories and obtained heavy tribute from Lombardy and some financial assistance from sympathetic bishops outside Italy. Frederick levied a tax on the Sicilian church, embargoed money leaving the realm, confiscated the possessions of his enemies, and expelled all foreigners. Because of the traditional loyalty of the friars to the pope, he expelled them as well. Actually it required only a few weeks to prepare Sicily for war, so efficient was the administrative system Frederick had introduced. To discourage cities under his control from revolting, the emperor demanded hostages from those communities and threatened to execute them should these communities rebel. One of the first "hostages" to suffer that fate was the son of the doge of Venice who had been captured at Cortenuova. He was strung up when news reached Frederick of Venetian attacks on Sicily.

Meantime the war raged with increasing fury in central and northern Italy. Allies shifted as the winds of fortune changed direction, now this way, now that. What concerned most communities was not which side won but that of being on the side that did. Cities did not fall easily, only the small towns did. Siege equipment was impotent before the massive walls of the larger cities and Frederick lacked the money and manpower necessary to conduct long sieges. But this impotence only made the war more savage. So the war went on and on, and no one could be sure where it would end. If Ferrara and Ravenna turned against the emperor, Tuscany and Viterbo welcomed his arrival, and the duchy of Spoleto fell without a fight. For the moment Frederick was winning and on 22 February 1240 he marched on Rome where the imperial party was in control. It had the city festooned awaiting his triumphant entry. Nothing it seemed could avert catastrophe for Gregory and his cardinals. As a last desperate maneuver Gregory had the reliquaries containing the heads of Sts. Peter and Paul and other relics carried in solemn procession from St. Peter's. As he reached the throng gathered in front of the basilica, the aged pontiff stopped to harangue them over the crimes of Frederick, placed his tiara on the relics, then prayed aloud: "May you holy ones protect the city now that the Romans no longer choose to do so." At these words the doubtful crowd caught fire, shouted out their support of Gregory, and hurried to bar the gates of the city. With the city barred to him, Frederick continued on southward into Apulia. Never had he come so close to victory.

Meantime pressure was building up for negotiations, exerted notably by Louis IX and the ecclesiastical princes of Germany. Negotiations did actually get under way. Then suddenly Gregory announced that he was summoning a general council to meet in Rome at Easter (1241). He decided he could not permit negotiations since out of these some compromise must eventuate, and he was unwilling to accept any compromise. A general council, on the other hand, would do his bidding, condemn and depose Frederick, and proclaim the perfidy of the emperor and the Christian world's responsibility to destroy him. Frederick appreciated the mortal danger in the pope's move. He promptly notified the rulers of Europe that since the pope's motive for summoning the council was strictly political, that is, to settle the question of Lombardy, the pope was not justified in summoning it. He would therefore block it, and, since he controlled both the water and land approaches to Rome, this he could very easily do. Kings had best keep their prelates at home.

The German prelates did remain home. Those of England, France, and Spain started out for Rome but never reached the city. The pope had directed them to gather in Genoa and he had paid this city an enormous sum to provide them transport and armed escort to Civitavecchia (just above Rome). At the last minute, the English prelates thought better of it and remained behind in Genoa. The others embarked and had almost made their destination when a combined imperial and Pisan fleet attacked. The latter sank three ships, three swift galleys managed to escape back to Genoa with mostly Spanish prelates, but the remaining twenty-two ships were captured. Never in history had there been such a capture: over one hundred prelates, including two cardinals who were Frederick's archenemies, and three papal legates! Frederick hustled his captives off to filthy jails in Apulia where several of the older bishops died. The French prelates he released so as not to alienate Louis.

Frederick's act shocked Europe. To capture an entire church council! Even had a Moslem infidel done the deed, Europe would have been horrified. Though Frederick had announced that he would do exactly this, no one had believed him. Now, for the first time, many men began to ask themselves whether some of the damning accusations the pope had made about the emperor's diabolical nature were perhaps true. But worsening opinion abroad could do Frederick little damage. Had he done worse, were this possible, Christian Europe would probably not have lifted a finger. They did nothing, for example, to meet the truly great peril of the Mongols that now appeared to the east. Genghis Khan, the world's most ruthless conqueror, had overrun a great part of Asia before he died in 1227. His sons and grandsons had continued his fearsome progress and overran Russia, Poland, and Hungary. Tens of millions of people had been slaughtered by these Mongols in the course of their conquests and now Batu, the grandson of Genghis, was nearing Vienna!

Europe was terrified and even Frederick was alarmed. Emissaries kept coming from across the Alps, the king of Hungary in person, to implore him to hurry north and unite Europe behind him. He alone could possibly meet this terrible threat. Frederick protested he dare not leave Italy. The last time he had left Italy to go on a crusade to capture Jerusalem, the pope had unleashed his armies on his kingdom. He must remain where he was. He would send appeals, however, to the kings of

Spain, France, and England, to arouse them to the gravity of the situation and implore their assistance.

Even this was more than Pope Gregory did. For him the most deadly enemy of Christendom was not the savage Mongols across the Alps who were approaching Vienna but Frederick who was right on the doorstep of St. Peter's. The pope had not even permitted Moslem occupation of Jerusalem in November 1240 to divert his attention from Frederick, and had actually turned back crusaders who were minded to go to Syria to help retrieve the situation.

Then a miracle happened. Of their own accord the Mongols suddenly wheeled about and withdrew toward the east. What saved Vienna was the death of Ogodai, the Great Khan in far-off Mongolia. Upon news of his death Batu and the other leading members of the family started off there to elect a new khan. The news that the Mongols had pulled out must have left Frederick with mixed emotions. On the one hand he was relieved that Germany was safe. He must surely have regretted, on the other, that he had not hurried to Germany, assumed command of a crusade against these onrushing savages, and reaped the glory of this "victory." That would have done much to refurbish his image as Holy Roman Emperor which the capture of a church council had so sadly tarnished. As it was, many Germans never forgave him for having left their country to its fate.

Frederick was never one to lose sleep over what might have been. His image in Germany and elsewhere would take care of itself once he had Gregory in his grasp, and this no earthly power could any longer prevent. In June 1241 he loosed the attack he was confident would end in the occupation of Rome and the capture of the pope. While his army mopped up what resistance remained in Romagna, one of the cardinals, John of Colonna, who hated Gregory as much as did Frederick, seized points nearer the city. Then on 21 August just as the emperor was about to close the vise on Gregory and win his final victory, the pope at the very last moment snatched it right out of his hands. He died.

For almost three years an unreal calm settled upon Italy. Now that Gregory was dead, Frederick had no one to fight. To have taken Rome and St. Peter's would have netted him nothing but the opprobrium of the Christian world. What he wanted was a pope who would make concessions and release him from the ban of excommunication, but the cardinals could elect no pope. They did agree on Celestine IV shortly after Gregory's death, but Celestine was already tottering to the grave and died after reigning seventeen days. So Frederick fumed, importuned, and threatened as month after month passed with no pope. Finally on 25 June 1243, the ten cardinals announced their choice, the cardinal of Genoa, who took the name of Innocent IV. Frederick proclaimed his joy over the election of an "old friend." It is true the new pope's aristocratic relations were among the emperor's most loyal adherents in Parma. Still Frederick did not let this mislead him. He knew that Innocent's talents and conviction were similar to those of the great Innocent whose name he had selected. He also knew that the new pope had been Pope Gregory's closest adviser. His subsequent comment that "No pope can be a Ghibelline" expresses his correct appraisal of what was in store.

They did reopen negotiations, Pope Innocent IV and Frederick, and there were moments when agreement appeared almost within reach. Frederick was growing weary of the war and his Sicily was on the verge of bankruptcy. Innocent was under pressure from Christian Europe, from Louis IX in particular who was planning a crusade. Yet neither pope nor emperor trusted the other and after so many years of bitterness, bloodshed, and suffering, neither could bring himself to accept a reasonable compromise. The cities of Lombardy also proved an obstacle. The pope needed them, they had need of the pope, but they could not agree on how to handle Frederick. Even as hostilities broke out anew, plans were arranged for a personal meeting of pope and emperor, when Innocent abruptly fled Rome in the disguise of a soldier and escaped by ship to Genoa. Frederick had lost his most precious advantage.

After this no peace was possible. Innocent continued on to Lyons where he felt secure, summoned a general council for June 1245, and directed the emperor to appear for trial. Frederick closed the Alpine passes to prevent the prelates from Italy from attending, although he delegated proctors to present his case, among them the patriarch of Jerusalem who pleaded the critical need of a general crusade against the Moslems. Of the near two hundred ecclesiastics who gathered at Lyons, the great majority were from Spain and France. On 17 July, after several near-violent discussions, the council declared Frederick guilty of perjury and sacrilege, of breaking the peace and of heresy, and solemnly deposed him.

Now the war entered its final and grimmest phase. Innocent called on the German princes to elect another king, declared the throne of

Sicily vacant, and directed the friars to preach rebellion in the imperial domain. Frederick countered with an appeal to the cupidity of the kings of Christendom and urged them in the name of reform to appropriate the wealth of a corrupt Church. As Frederick sensed the slow worsening of his position after the proclamation of his deposition at Lyons, he grew increasingly distrustful of his associates. Several of these turned against him, including Peter della Vigna, his most trusted counselor. Frederick accused the pope of having corrupted Peter and of having bribed him to poison his emperor. Frederick had his old friend blinded, who, perhaps to escape worse, killed himself by breaking his head against the wall of his prison. Dante met Peter in the *Inferno,* consigned there not because of treachery, which he denied, but for his suicide.

As imperial and papal factions fought over cities from without and their factions strove for mastery within, the war grew more savage. Those who lost could expect torture, mutilation, and death. Even prisoners who felt fortunate in having their lives spared were not safe. When Milan held out against Frederick's repeated attacks, he relieved his frustration by ordering the right eye of his Genoese captives gouged out and their right hand cut off. The Saracen leaders of the revolt in Sicily he had sewn in bags with deadly serpents and thrown into the sea. For the emperor, as with the Mongols, terror was to serve as a weapon to cow the opposition and to deter those from defecting who might have been tempted to do so. Yet terror was more than policy with Frederick. He hated his enemies. Had he one foot already through the door of Paradise, he once declared, he would return to earth, given the opportunity, in order to revenge himself on Viterbo!

Still the winds of fortune also blew Frederick's way. Where he and his sons campaigned, the war went well. True, tragedy almost struck early in 1248 during his siege of Parma. He was out hunting with his falcons on that occasion when the Parmesans suddenly counterattacked and captured or destroyed almost his entire force of five thousand men. Only he and a dozen men managed to cut their way out of the trap. The following summer (1249) the Bolognese captured his son Enzio, a truly painful blow for the emperor. Then fortune smiled again. The Genoese suffered defeat on the sea, several important cities including Ravenna, Piacenza, and Parma, either joined Frederick or were captured, and the dispirited Bolognese opened negotiations. Diplomatic help was also coming from Louis IX. The Saracens had captured him and his army at Damietta and Frederick had used his influence with the sultan to secure his release. Whereupon Louis sent to Innocent to demand that he make peace with Frederick since only the emperor could restore the kingdom of Jerusalem. If the pope refused, Louis would have him and his curia expelled from Lyons. Innocent's frantic appeal to Henry III of England for asylum went unanswered.

If Frederick's fortunes were mending, fate refused him time to use them. It chanced that while out hunting near his favorite palace at Foggia he suffered such a severe attack of dysentery that he could not make it back to his palace but took to bed at Fiorentino. A premonition that he would die led him to send for notaries and for the archbishop of Palermo. He died on 13 December 1250, after drawing up his will, putting on the grey habit of the Cistercians, and receiving the last sacraments from the hands of the archbishop. His body was taken to Palermo and interred in the cathedral beside that of his first wife, Constance, in a sarcophagus of dark red porphyry which he had had prepared for himself. The man who has been called the greatest king between Charlemagne and Napoleon, whom Matthew Paris described as "the wanderer of the world," was finally at rest.

Louis IX

Louis IX was a saint. His piety was so manifest, like that of St. Francis, that men who knew him were convinced he was a man of God. Good men, Henry III of England for example, fought him, and on several occasions groups of Louis' own nobles took up arms against him, but there was always something strange about their opposition. It appeared to lack spirit and conviction, as though these opponents feared they were opposing not only Louis but heaven as well. French noblemen who bitterly resented certain ordinances Louis promulgated which impinged upon their traditional rights were reluctant to defy him, for was he not a saint? Louis might be imprudent at times and even unreasonable, as his devoted biographer Jean de Joinville was willing to concede, but this made him no less a saint. To the poor and oppressed Louis was the man whom God had sent to succor them in their distress. And because those writers who have left memoirs of Louis considered him a saint, the modern reader has no choice but accept him as such if he is to understand the man, his policies, and his place in men's hearts.

BLANCHE OF CASTILE AND LOUIS' MINORITY

The person most responsible for forming the character of Louis was his mother Blanche of Castile. The great devotion Louis felt for her as a boy he continued to give her as a youth and as king. In fact it may be no great distortion of history to speak of the co-rule of Blanche and Louis until 1252, when Blanche died, or even to list her among the monarchs of France. During Louis' minority (1226–34) she governed France and again when her son was on the crusade (1248–52), while during the years intervening he constantly appealed to her for counsel. In the literature of the day, Blanche is consistently identified as "Blanche of Castile," as if to remind good Frenchmen that she was a foreigner, not a true Frenchwoman. She was Spanish, Joinville writes, "and had neither kindred nor friends in all the realm of France." Yet to charge her with disloyalty to France as her enemies did was slander. No native-born king could have served France more devotedly than did Blanche during her son's minority, even though she never forgot her beloved home beyond the Pyrenees. The women of her court and her servants were Spanish, and the faith she instilled in her son bore that intensity which the long centuries of warfare between Christian and Moslem had bred in Spain.

Blanche came by her strong character honestly. Eleanor of Aquitaine was her grandmother, than whom both Louis VII of France and Henry II of England, Eleanor's successive husbands, would have sworn that there was never a more headstrong woman in the whole of Christendom. Eleanor never ruled, but not because she did not try. Her granddaughter Blanche did have that opportunity, and the courage and knowledge of statecraft she demonstrated would have aroused the admiration of the later Louis XI, although of his unscrupulousness she possessed none. What motivated her was her sense of duty to the France her husband had given her to rule until their son came of age, and the conviction that God would hold her responsible for ruling his people well.

Louis VIII's death in 1226 set two precedents. Never before had a Capetian king died before his son was of age. This Louis could not help. The second precedent he set himself, however, when he appointed his wife Blanche to act as regent for their twelve-year-old boy Louis. For a woman to rule France was unprecedented, but Louis VIII knew what he was doing. Only his strong-willed wife, not his untrustworthy half brother Philip Hurepel, could prevent ambitious feudatories from exploiting the absence of a strong king to carve for themselves generous slices from the royal domain. Blanche's first move, taken upon the advice of the cardinal legate, was to have Louis crowned as quickly as possible, in the very month that Louis VIII had died (8 November 1226). The ceremony took place at Reims on 29 November, with the bishop of Soissons officiating since the archiepiscopal see was vacant. No feast followed the coronation either at Reims or Paris. The absence of many lords from the ceremony where they should have come to pay their homage made it more an occasion for concern than celebration. Still Blanche took the opportunity to show her spirit. She informed Thibaud, count of Champagne, that because he had abandoned Louis VIII during the recent siege of Avignon, he was not welcome and should have remained away until he had made satisfaction for his treachery.

No sooner had Louis VIII died than feudal opposition began to stir. Such restiveness was not uncommon upon a king's death, although it was greater now because the ruler was a woman. That fact alone seemed to justify revolt. At any rate it did provide French nobles an issue upon which they could agree, that is, villifying her for being a woman and a foreigner. Among the less opprobrious terms by which they referred to her was Dame Hersent, the she-wolf in the *Roman de Renart*. One potential opponent, Ferrand, count of Flanders, who had been captured at the battle of Bouvines (1214) and had been in prison, she released in January and so bound him to the regime. Another count, Renaud, count of Boulogne, who was also captured at Bouvines, she decided would be safer in prison where he shortly died. Philip Hurepel she placated with the surrender of several castles, and where she deemed this necessary, she made like concessions to several other lords.

Peter of Dreux, count of Brittany, proved himself the most dangerous vassal. In an age when a majority of lords were haughty he was known for his insolence and brutality. It may have been his cruel treatment of the clergy of his province that gave him the name of Mauclerc (the wicked clerk), more likely the fact that he had once been a clerk who had turned sour. His ambition was as great as his cruelty for he claimed descent from the firstborn son of Louis VI whom he held had been unjustly deprived of his throne. Mauclerc was assured the support of Thibaud, the count of Champagne, in any revolt he might undertake, of that of Raymond VII, count of Toulouse, as well, and above all of the assistance of Henry III, king of England, who would jump at any opportunity to recover what he could of those lands Philip Augustus had taken from his father. Rounding out the opposition was an assortment of nobles in Poitou and Gascony whose co-operation could be counted on so long as they expected to gain more by opposing Blanche than by remaining neutral.

This group made up the first coalition of nobles who fought Blanche, but their opposition melted away almost before it had taken form. When the queen refused to bend to their demands and threats but assembled an army instead, Thibaud of Champagne weakened, announced his adherence to the crown, and revealed the plans of the rebels (whatever these might have been). Shortly after at Vendôme Mauclerc submitted along with the others, although Blanche had eased

Mauclerc's action by turning over to him the strategic fortresses of Bellême and St. James de Beuvron on the frontiers of Normandy and Brittany which Louis VIII had given him to guard.

Though this first rebellion dissolved early in 1227, rebel nobles came within an ace a few months later of capturing the king. Joinville has this simple description of the incident. "After the King was crowned, there were some of the barons who requested the Queen to grant them certain large territories; and because she would do none of it, they gathered themselves together, all the barons, at Corbeuil. And the holy King told me, that he and his mother, who were at Montlhéry, durst not return to Paris until the men of Paris came under arms to fetch them. And he told me how all the way from Montlhéry to Paris, the road was thronged with people, armed and unarmed, all loudly praying Christ to give him health and long life, and to defend and keep him from his enemies." So early in Louis' life the Parisians may not have had special reason to love him. They did, however, have a real knowledge of what a resurgent feudal nobility would do to their rights. Louis, too, appreciated the importance of their loyalty to the crown. On his deathbed he warned his son Philip to preserve the towns "in the same estate and in the same liberties in which they were maintained by thy predecessors . . . for it is by the strength and wealth of the big towns that thou shalt awe and hold in check both friends and strangers, and particularly thy nobles and barons."

The fighting in Toulouse, the former stronghold of Catharism (Albigensianism), which had not completely ended with the collapse of the first coalition against Blanche, burst into flame in 1228. Raymond, the count of Toulouse, was, however, left to his own resources which were no match for those of the crown and he had no choice but accept the terms the queen offered. While these terms were severe, they were only the logical culmination of the long efforts Blanche's predecessors had given to acquiring that powerful fief. The first move had come with Louis VII (1137-80) who had stepped in to block English expansion into the area. Louis' son Philip Augustus was tempted to interfere directly in 1208 when Pope Innocent III called for a crusade to eradicate Catharism, but he preferred to leave this to his nobles in the north. In 1219 he finally authorized his son, the future Louis VIII, to lead a royal army into Toulouse, where this son gained considerable success, especially on his second campaign. Had Raymond not joined the coalition against Blanche, he might have salvaged a good part of his domain. Now he had no choice. In the treaty of Paris in April 1229 Blanche forced him to cede a large part of his domain to the crown while agreeing to the marriage of his daughter Joan to one of her sons, that is, one of Louis' brothers. It was expected that this marriage would ultimately mean the absorption of Toulouse by the crown, which it did.

In the northwest Blanche was also victorious against Peter Mauclerc who was causing new difficulties. Both she and Louis were on hand to witness the surrender of the castle of Bellême. Then the situation suddenly worsened. The embittered Mauclerc sailed to England, repudiated his fealty to the French crown, and did homage to Henry III. The grateful but foolish Henry responded by landing an army at St. Malo in Brittany. It was fortunate for Blanche that several of the nobles who had earlier been allies of Mauclerc were now busily engaged in plundering Champagne in order to punish its count for having abandoned their rebel ranks several years before. The logic of the situation should have drawn together the two groups, Mauclerc and the English and the nobles overrunning Champagne; but the reverse happened. So hesitant were the latter nobles to defy the French crown, that when Blanche demanded of them aid against Mauclerc and the English, they responded with a few knights for the prescribed forty days, after which they withdrew. But the short time they had left Champagne enabled the count to re-establish himself with the help of royal troops, so when Henry III decided that he had enough of a campaign that had gone wretchedly from the start and returned to England, all fighting ceased. Peter Mauclerc made one last futile attempt to retrieve his fortunes in 1234, then he too submitted. On 25 April 1234 when Louis attained his twenty-first year, Blanche turned over to him a throne even stronger than that she had received in trust from her husband Louis VIII a dozen years before.

LOUIS: HIS CHARACTER AND PERSON

Now with Louis safely on the throne, let us take a long look at this remarkable man. The existence of what for the Middle Ages is an unusually large volume of contemporary evidence makes this possible. There is no medieval man of whom we have a clearer picture. We see him not darkly as in a mirror, which is the case with other men of the times, but almost face to face. The modern biographer is, nevertheless, not entirely happy with the character of much of the written evidence that time has preserved. It smacks so much of hagiography. Once a man had become a saint, contemporary writers were apt to notice or imagine only what was good in him. Louis had an unusually good press. His contemporaries considered him a saint, and hardly had he died than efforts got under way to speed his canonization. For this reason the modern reader is doubly grateful for the prosaic but honest reminiscences of Jean de Joinville. No man knew Louis better than did Joinville, nor would Joinville have considered it honorable to have written anything less than the truth.

Louis was born at Poissy just outside Paris on 25 April 1214. The château in which he was born his father had received from Philip Augustus and there Louis was baptized. No event of his life, no honor or dignity, Louis declared, could compare in importance with his baptism which made him a member of the kingdom of God. Philip the Fair, during whose reign Louis was canonized, founded a monastery of Dominicans on the site of the château and dedicated it to his sainted grandfather.

Little is known of Louis' youth other than that his mother Blanche kept him firmly in hand. The king recalled in later life how his mother accompanied him to the woods and the river when he wished to play, that she taught him his letters, and that she disciplined him when he needed correction. As was traditional in aristocratic circles, the boy Louis spent his early years in the company of the women of the court. Joinville writes how Louis learned of God through "the good teachings of his mother, who taught him to love and believe in God, and who set men of religion about him. Child as he was, she used to make him repeat his Hours and hear the lessons on feast-days, and often told him, as he recorded later, that she would rather he were dead than that he should commit a deadly sin."

Louis continued the pious devotions of his childhood throughout his life. He usually attended more than one mass each day, the first a low mass for the dead, then a high mass, so solemn and prolonged it is said, that most people became wearied. Louis insisted on having a fine choir, supported by musical instruments, and he would on occasion join in the chant with a fine voice of his own. The divine office required of monks and friars he also recited. At midnight he would rise from bed for Matins and Lauds, after which he might remain for a long time in prayer either in the chapel or on his knees in his chamber. He recited these Hours in a low voice so as not to disturb his sleeping attendants, but he would waken them for Prime, and so quickly did he dress himself and go off to church, that not infrequently the less alert of his valets had to hurry after him in their bare feet. After dining at noon he would recite Terce, Sext, and None, rest for a time in his chamber, then say with one of his chaplains the Office of the Dead and Vespers. Compline he would customarily recite in the Sainte Chapelle, after which he would remain in prayer for a long time before retiring. On a journey he would say the Hours on horseback.

A canon of the Fourth Lateran Council (1215) made it obligatory for Christians to receive communion once a year, although reception beyond that point was not encouraged. To contemporaries, therefore, the fact that Louis received six times a year was counted extraordinary. The six occasions on which he elected to receive were Easter, Pentecost, the Assumption of Mary (15 August), All Saints' Day (1 November), Christmas, and the Purification of Mary (2 February). The nature of the king's preparations during the weeks preceding these occasions must have been great although nothing is recorded. We are told that before communicating, he would wash his hands and his mouth, remove his hood and coif, and proceed to the altar not walking but on his knees, where he would recite the confession with great devotion before receiving. Each Friday he confessed his sins.

Louis had a particular love for sermons and often invited priests and monks who were known for their eloquence to visit the palace. Whenever he stopped at a monastery, something he regularly did in his journeys about the kingdom, he would request a member of the community to preach a sermon for him. He took these sermons seriously and would often explain the points the preacher had made to his attendants who, he knew, could not understand the matter so well as he. Nor did he object when the preacher's words struck close to home. On one occasion he sent for a Franciscan friar named Brother Hugh who happened to be nearby, to preach a sermon for him, which the friar did. In the course of his remarks Hugh took those monks to task who were staying with Louis when they should have been in their cloisters. "And if they say, that in this cloister [that is, the king's court figuratively speaking] one can live a strict life for the salvation of one's soul—then I do not believe them; for when I have dined with them, it was off divers sorts of flesh, and good strong wines; wherefor I am quite sure that had they been in their cloister, they would not have been so well off as they are with the king." Though Louis pleaded with

Brother Hugh to stay with him a while, he refused, saying: "I shall not remain, Sir. I will rather betake me to some place where I shall be more pleasing to God than in the king's company."

During Lent and Advent Louis observed a strict fast, while on vigils, ember days, the days before the feasts of the Blessed Virgin, and on Good Friday he took only bread and water. After his return from the crusade, he also fasted five days before Pentecost and on all Mondays, Wednesdays, and Saturdays of the year. Abstaining from wine constituted a real sacrifice in the Middle Ages when even monks and nuns received a daily ration. Instead of wine Louis drank beer during Lent, so Joinville says, because he did not like it and could only swallow it with a grimace. The king would also dilute delicious sauces with water to the disgust of his chefs, and he would turn over to the poor large fish and lampreys which he especially prized.

Louis slept on a simple mat of cotton, not on a mattress or bed of feathers. He wore a hair shirt but took such pains to keep knowledge of this a secret that even his grooms who lived with him knew nothing of it. He also received the scourge regularly from one of the chaplains at court. Knowledge of the king's mortifications did not ordinarily become public until during the canonization proceedings following his death, although many of his contemporaries marked how he never laughed on Friday nor wore a hat on that day out of reverence for the crown of thorns.

Louis' generosity to the poor left a deep impression upon his people despite the tradition, as true in the Middle Ages as in antiquity, that being a king must make a man wealthy. That Louis was not. He had nothing approaching the revenues of the caliph Harun al-Rashid, for instance. Like all medieval kings of this period, the principal source of his income was his own estates whose extent was not large nor whose productivity great. Nonetheless the king gave generously from his means. As Joinville writes: "From his childhood up, he was compassionate towards the poor and the suffering; and it was the custom that, wherever he went, six score poor should always be replenished in his house with bread and wine, and meat or fish every day." His manner of giving was personal. He would wait upon the poor as they sat about his table, cut the meat for those incapable of doing so, and give them money when he dismissed them.

Louis' benefactions to the poor were not solely of this personal character. He probably expended considerably larger sums in gifts for the construction of almshouses and asylums and for their maintenance. "Also he founded the Blind Asylum (*Quinze-Vingt*) near Paris to receive the blind of the city of Paris. . . . Shortly afterward he had another house built outside Paris, which was called the House of the Daughters of God, and caused a great number of women to be boarded there, who by reason of poverty had fallen into the sin of wantonness, and granted them four hundred pounds worth of revenue to support them. Also in many places of his kingdom he founded houses of female Beguines (lay nuns) and gave them revenues to live upon, and gave orders to admit such as gave promise of a chaste life." Poor girls who had no desire to remain unmarried he provided with dowries to enable them to find husbands.

Probably every religious order in France benefited from Louis' charity, although he lavished gifts of clothing, food, and money especially upon the friars. He might pay for the construction of a dormitory or a chapel, at times finance the cost of the entire community. Of the monasteries he built his favorite was Royaumont in Paris. In this abbey he had a room built especially for himself, serviced by a private stairs, from which he could assist at the divine office during the night. When his relatives and courtiers grumbled over his excessive liberality, he answered: "I would much rather be extravagant in alms for the love of God, than in the pomp and vainglories of this world." Nevertheless, so Joinville assures the reader, "the hospitality of his [Louis] palace was so courteous, generous, and plentiful that nothing like it had been known for a long time past at the courts of his predecessors." Other contemporary writers would not agree.

Among Louis' acts of generosity toward the poor and despised, none left so deep an impression upon contemporaries as the attention he gave those most wretched members of medieval society, the lepers. Joinville narrates an incident touching himself which reveals the horror he and most people felt concerning those unfortunates. On one occasion Louis asked him which he would rather be, a leper or a person who had committed a deadly sin. To which query the honest Joinville promptly replied that he would rather have committed thirty deadly sins than be a leper. Whereupon Louis chided him for his foolishness and pagan sense of values. "For there is no leprosy so foul as deadly sin," he told him, "seeing that a soul in deadly sin is in the image of the devil. And truly when a man dies, he is healed of the leprosy of the body, but when a man dies that has committed a deadly sin, great fear must he needs have lest such leprosy should endure so long as God shall be in heaven."

The most moving incident from the life of Louis that tells of his love of lepers concerned the leprous monk he visited at the abbey of Royaumont. The leprosy of this unfortunate brother had progressed so far—eyes and nose gone, lips almost eaten away—that his appearance was nothing short of hideous. When the abbot brought Louis, upon the king's request, to the leper's cell, they found him nibbling as best he could on a piece of pork. The king immediately fell to his knees before the leper as before a saint, cut the meat into small pieces, and handed them to the leper. Then he sent to the palace for some baked partridges the leper had indicated he might relish, cut up the wings and salted them, and put these pieces in the mouth of the sick man. When Louis found that the salt irritated the mouth wounds of the leper and made them bleed, he removed the salt and continued with his feeding. Then he comforted the leper assuring him that if he bore his sufferings with patience, he would have his purgatory already behind him when he died. After this when Louis visited Royaumont, he always dropped in to comfort and feed the leper.

Louis also visited the hospitals of the city where he would often perform the most disagreeable tasks. Because the king realized that many of his people would consider some of his acts of mercy as degrading and take offense, he kept them as much a secret as possible. For this reason he preferred to wait upon blind people who could not recognize him.

The king observed strict moderation in both eating and drinking. Like most men he added water to the wine he drank, and he warned Joinville that he was simply building up troubles for his old age by taking his wine straight. For when he was old, he could not drink un-watered wine without becoming intoxicated, and "it was a passing foul thing for a gallant gentleman to get drunk." Louis never made food a topic of conversation as was the wont of wealthy folks, nor did he ask his cooks to prepare special dishes for him. As for clothes, he once told Joinville that men should so dress "that sober men of the world might not deem us overnice, nor young men deem us slovens." Yet when Robert of Sorbon attacked Joinville for his "goodly dress," Louis came to his friend's defense and observed that, "You should dress well and neatly, so that your wives may love you the better, and your people esteem you the more."

Louis abominated the habit of cursing even more than drunkenness and "if anybody within his reach used any foul language or lewd oath about God or His Mother, the King caused them to be severely punished." The king never used any kind of an oath or strong language. Joinville says that during the twenty-two years he was in his company, he "never heard him swear by God, nor by His Mother nor by His Saints; but whenever he wanted to affirm anything, he used to say, 'Truly it was thus,' or 'Truly it shall be thus.'"

It is rare for medieval documents to speak of so incidental a matter as the education of a prince and the case of Louis is no exception. There is nothing beyond the reference to his mother's supervising his early education. That Louis was able to understand sermons preached in Latin indicates he had both a good education and that he was an apt scholar. He was also well versed in the knowledge of Scriptures and in patristic literature. When in Syria he was disturbed at the large number of excellent libraries the Moslems were maintaining. So on his return he proceeded to gather a library in one of the rooms of the palace (the origin of the *Bibliothèque Nationale*). Among other books that Louis ordered copied were the writings of Augustine, Ambrose, Jerome, Gregory, and other church fathers. The scribe notes that Louis preferred to have copies made rather than acquire the manuscripts in order to increase the number of volumes in existence. It is said he loaned Vincent of Beauvais some 1200 manuscripts to assist him and his staff in compiling the *Speculum maius,* the most distinguished encyclopedia of the Middle Ages. Louis encouraged juristic studies and may have been responsible for the translation of the *Digest* and for the establishment of law schools at Orléans and Angers. A provision of the treaty he negotiated with Raymond of Toulouse in 1230 was one requiring the count to provide salaries for fourteen professors at the university of Paris.

Robert of Sorbon, who founded a college (*la Sorbonne*) for indigent students in 1250, with some assistance from Louis, tells of an incident which reveals the king's unusual knowledge of St. Augustine. A learned clerk, while discoursing on Christ's death, mentioned that the apostles had abandoned Christ at the crucifixion and that for the moment their faith in him was extinguished. Upon hearing this, an eminent ecclesiastic rose to object. He insisted the Scriptures said only that the apostles had abandoned Christ physically, that they had run away and not that they had repudiated him in their hearts. But Louis interposed and defended the preacher. To prove his point, he had Augustine's commentary on the Gospel of St. John brought from his library, then turned to the pertinent passage where Augustine states quite clearly that the apostles had fled "leaving Christ in both body and soul."

Of this kind of disputation was Louis particularly fond. For this reason he preferred dining at table with serious and learned people rather than with his barons, because they were more scholarly and because they spoke of religious matters. And Joinville notes how the king liked to engage in spirited discussions after dinner in preference to listening to a good book one of the friars might happen to recommend.

In view of Louis' admiration for the friars and his interest in religious learning, it is not surprising that he knew Thomas Aquinas, the eminent Dominican scholastic, and that Bonaventure, the distinguished Franciscan theologian, preached at his court. On one occasion it happened that Aquinas received an invitation to dine with the king and other guests at the palace. The learned friar sought to excuse himself to his prior on the plea that he was busily working on the *Summa theologiae,* but his superior was insistent. So Aquinas obeyed and came, but only physically. His mind continued to ponder the particular problem with which he had been wrestling. For as he sat at the banquet table absorbed in his thoughts and mulling over this problem, he suddenly struck the table with his great fist and exclaimed, "That will refute the heresy of the Manichaeans." His shocked prior who was sitting next to him grabbed him sharply by the arm to shake him out of his abstraction and to warn him not to forget that he was in the presence of the king. Whereupon Aquinas rose and bowed toward the king to offer his apologies for having been so rude. But Louis was all admiration at the scholastic's behavior, and lest the thought that had so excited the scholar be forgotten, he sent one of his secretaries to where Aquinas was sitting to make a note of it.

Louis considered the most sacred of his royal responsibilities that of ruling justly. It was no accident, therefore, that his love of justice was the virtue his own people and foreign rulers especially admired in him. Wealth and territory did not interest him, and even the exercise of royal authority he would have considered a vanity except that it provided the means by which he could give his people justice and peace. If he ruled justly and forced his subjects to deal justly with their fellows, then God would bless France with peace. It was this kind of rule he had in mind when he admonished his son: "Fair son, I pray thee, win the love of the people of thy kingdom. For truly, I would rather that a Scot should come out of Scotland and rule the people of the kingdom well and justly, than that thou shouldst govern them ill-advisedly."

Louis set his judges a good example that they never permit fear or favoritism to influence them in the administration of justice. No worse offender had Louis on this score than his harsh brother, Charles of Anjou. On one occasion he ordered Charles to pay the Parisian merchants the debts he owed them, on another to disgorge an estate he had seized, on another to free a knight whom he had arbitrarily imprisoned. Charles was not to forget, Louis told him, that though he was his brother, France had only one king, and so long as he was on the throne, he would require his subjects, noble or commoner, to respect the rights of others. Then there was a noble woman of Pontoise who had persuaded her paramour to slay her husband. She confessed her crime, and, according to the custom of the time, was to be burned at the stake. The queen, the countess of Poitou, even the friars in the area begged the king to mitigate the harshness of the punishment in view of the woman's manifest remorse. Her relatives and friends asked that, if she must be burned, at least the execution be carried out in some place other than Pontoise. Louis was adamant, both that the woman die and that she be executed in Pontoise, "for he wanted that all justice concerning malefactors be administered openly before the people and that no justice be handled in secret."

Louis showed even greater devotion to the cause of justice in the case of three youths, students who were staying at the Benedictine abbey near Coucy. They had gone hunting one day on the abbey grounds, shot a few rabbits, then inadvertently strolled on to the neighboring estates that belonged to Enguerrand, lord of Coucy. The lord's wardens seized the three boys, threw them in jail, then upon orders of the irate lord who did not waste time on an investigation, hanged them on the spot. Upon the abbot's appeal, Louis summoned Enguerrand to come to Paris. Enguerrand came, but he brought with him an imposing group of nobles: the king of Navarre, the duke of Burgundy, and the counts of Brittany, Blois, and Champagne among others. These nobles first insisted that Enguerrand be tried by his peers, then after further consultation decided that inasmuch as the defendant was now denying he had even ordered the three youths hanged, that the simple issue should be whether he was telling the truth. That issue touched his honor and he should, therefore, have the privilege of clearing himself by wager of battle. Louis said no, that this privilege did not extend to instances where the aggrieved parties were the poor or members of the clergy. He maintained that his predecessors had disallowed wager of battle in similar instances because of the difficulty such people would have in securing a champion who would be willing to contend with a nobleman. In the end Louis accepted the advice of his counselors. He deprived Enguerrand of his right to punish anyone caught hunting or fishing on his estates; the particular estate on which the youths had been apprehended, he ordered him to turn over to the abbey; he also required Enguerrand to spend three years in Syria as a crusader, which he did; and he forced him to pay a heavy fine of twelve thousand pounds which he then expended on monastic buildings and an asylum.

That Louis in these and similar cases assumed the right to impose his own judgment followed logically from his view concerning his position. He was God's highest representative in the temporal order. As king he was also the father of his people. For this reason he might at any time bypass conventional procedures, assume the role of judge, and settle disputes for people who sought his good offices. "Many a time it chanced in summer, that he would go and sit in the forest of Vincennes after mass, and all who had business would come and talk with him, without hindrance from ushers or anyone. . . . I have seen him," writes Joinville, "sometimes in summer, when to hear his people's suits, he would come into the gardens of Paris, clad in a camel's-hair coat, with a sleeveless surcoat of tiretaine, a cloak of black taffeta round his neck, his hair well combed and without a quoif, and a white swansdown hat upon his head. He would cause a carpet to be spread, that we might sit round him; and all the people who had business before him stood round about, and then he caused their suits to be dispatched—just as I told you before about the forest of Vincennes." The best proof of Louis' justice was the frequency with which nobles, even foreign princes, accepted his arbitrament.

Louis was anxious to eliminate the use of force to satisfy wrongs, and to this end issued orders for the suppression of practices that were at least as old as feudalism. He forbade the use of the duel before royal judges which was accepted as a method of ascertaining the truthfulness of a witness accused of falsehood. The right of vengeance which an individual might appeal against another or one family against another family, he found equally intolerable. In order to end such practices he enacted or revived laws aimed at punishing persons guilty of participating in such feuds, then went to the length of forbidding all private warfare, and finally banned the carrying of weapons altogether. These measures struck down prerogatives the aristocracy considered as sacrosanct as their privileged status itself. Understandably, Louis' actions aroused much resentment among the aristocracy.

Louis has suffered censure, both from contemporaries and from modern critics, for the excessive devotion he had for his mother and for the lack of consideration he occasionally showed his wife. In both instances he may merit some blame, as Joinville is ready to concede. Louis' deep attachment to his mother can be traced to the devotion she gave him during his childhood. Then during the years of his minority, his admiration for her deepened as he witnessed the courage and firmness with which she handled the many critical problems facing the regime. When news reached him on the crusade that his mother had died, so poignant was his grief that he took to his room and remained there isolated for two days. When he finally emerged and saw Joinville, he ran to him and announced with great emotion that his mother had died. At which information Joinville observed drily: "Sir, I am not surprised at that, for she was bound to die; but I am surprised that a wise man like you should make such mourning. For you know, the sage says, that whatever trouble a man may have at heart, it should not show in his face; for thereby he rejoices his foes and grieves his friends."

Joinville did not share the depth of Louis' admiration for his mother and he disapproved especially of the manner Blanche sought to keep Louis from seeing his wife. Such was the "harshness that Queen Blanche showed to Queen Margaret," he writes, "that Queen Blanche would never, if she could help it, suffer her son to be in his wife's company, unless at night, when he went to bed with her." Joinville is our source for the one romantic episode that time has preserved from the life of Louis. He tells how the two young people, already husband and wife, managed to meet by stealth during the day despite Blanche's sharp eyes and, one may assume, some misgivings on the part of Louis' tender conscience. It so happened that Blanche had her rooms beneath those of the king, but above those occupied by Margaret, the three floors connected by a spiral staircase. So the young couple worked out a plan "that they could talk together on a spiral staircase which led down from one floor to the other; and had so laid their plans, that when the doorkeepers saw the Queen coming to the apartments of her son, they would rap on the doors with their rods; and the King would come running into his rooms, so that his mother might not catch him; and the ushers of Queen Margaret's apartment did the same when Queen Blanche was on her way thither, so that she might find Queen Margaret in them." The reader may find this incident amusing, not another when Margaret was deathly sick and Louis properly beside her, when Blanche suddenly appeared and ordered him out of the room. Whereupon Margaret exclaimed, "Alas! neither dead nor alive will you let me see my lord!"

That the relationship between Louis and Margaret shed in time the romance of the spiral staircase era one would expect, but that he came to treat her with a measure of severity requires explanation. She did accompany him on the crusade, as did the wives of a number of the nobles, and Joinville notes how the news of Blanche's death also set her to weeping, which puzzled the gruff crusader and he asked her why all the tears for a woman who had caused her so much bitterness. Margaret explained that she was not weeping for her mother-in-law—she was no saint!—but for the king whom she knew would be in great sorrow.

Joinville had great admiration for Margaret and rightly so. Despite her faults, she proved herself a loyal and energetic wife and a thoroughly heroic woman on the crusade when the crusading army departed from Damietta and left her in complete control. Because Joinville found her such an admirable person, he could not comprehend Louis' lack of sentiment. He tells on one occasion that the king, knowing that he (Joinville) had just seen the queen, asked whether Margaret and the children were in good health. (This was while they were on the crusade.) Joinville assured him that they were, but he adds this observation for the reader's information. "I have recorded this because I had been already five years about his person, and he had never yet mentioned the Queen or his children to me, nor to anyone else, in my hearing; and it was not a good fashion, it seems to me, to be so reserved about his wife and children." Margaret bore Louis six sons and five daughters.

Margaret would undoubtedly have preferred a more demonstrative husband, but then she could always derive comfort from the conviction that no wife ever had so faithful a spouse. And when husbands are kings, this is a particularly rare boast. What lay at the root of the difficulties between Louis and Margaret was Margaret's fondness for political meddling. Margaret had a passionate and ambitious nature and often permitted her emotions to urge policies upon Louis which he considered unwise. Her favorite sister was Eleanor, wife of Henry III of England, so she constantly intrigued in behalf of the English. The sister she had least love for was Beatrice, wife of Charles of Anjou, so she was forever at odds with that brother-in-law over political matters.

Margaret's most reprehensible power play came shortly after the death of her eldest son, Louis, who died at the age of sixteen. The mother had never attempted to gain this son's confidence, probably because of the close association between the boy and his father. No sooner was the boy Louis dead, however, than she approached her next eldest son, Philip, then fifteen, and persuaded him to make her several promises, confirmed by a sacred oath: that he would remain under her tutelage until he reached the age of thirty; that he would never make an alliance with Charles of Anjou; that he would have as counselors only men she approved; that he would reveal any hostile moves that might affect her; and, of course, that he would keep these promises a secret. Somehow news of this understanding got out, whereupon Louis immediately secured a papal bull dispensing the boy from his vow. Louis had already issued several orders which limited the expenditures of the queen and prohibited her from issuing instructions to any of the crown officials. He even forbade her to take anyone into her personal service without first receiving his approval. When Louis left for Tunis on his last crusade, no one but Margaret and her friends objected that he placed not his wife but two of his counselors in charge of the government.

Louis' attitude toward his wife and children was correct without being warm. It is also easy to err in judging him and his times by the standards of today. In an age when the children of the aristocracy were customarily reared elsewhere than at home, family ties were seldom so close as they are today. That Louis was human enough to consider one of his daughters a favorite suggests that he may not have been greatly different from most fathers. This daughter was Isabella whom he hoped would become a nun. But she preferred to remain in the world and became the wife of the king of Navarre. We also know that the death of his eldest son Louis, a charming and upright youth, proved a heavy blow, and that among those who came to comfort the parents was Bonaventure. What little information there remains concerning Louis' attention to his children we must again credit to Joinville. "Before he [the king] went to bed," he writes, "he used to send for his children, and would tell them stories of the deeds of good kings and emperors; and he used to tell them that they must take example by such as these. He would tell them, too, about the deeds of wicked rich men, who by their lechery and their rapine and their avarice, had lost their kingdoms. 'And these things,' he used to say, 'I tell you as a warning to avoid them, lest you incur the anger of God.'"

Another side of Louis' character, which along with his attitude toward Margaret, has drawn unfavorable comment was his unfriendly attitude toward Jews. Joinville gives the incident upon which this view is principally founded. The occasion was a disputation between Christian and Jewish scholars at the monastery of Cluny, a kind of debate which was not uncommon at this time. In the course of the exchange, a knight stepped forward and asked the leading Jewish scholar present whether he believed that Mary was the mother of God. When the rabbi replied that he did not, the knight smote him a hard blow under the ear with his staff, and the debate broke up forthwith. The abbot who had presided upbraided the knight for having acted so foolishly, only to have the knight denounce him in turn for having permitted such a meeting in the first place since the cleverness of the rabbi could have weakened the faith of unlettered Christians who might be present. So Louis commenting to Joinville on this incident told him that he agreed with the knight, and that only skilled scholars should attempt to argue with Hebrews. A layman, "if he hears the Christian law defamed, should undertake its defence with the sword alone, and he should use it to run them straight through the body as far in as it will go!"

These are harsh words, indeed, although they bear no trace of anti-Semitism. So deep was Louis' faith and so profound his reverence for his Christian faith, that he would have recommended cutting down any person, Jew, Moslem, or pagan, who might dare question it. While on the crusade, one of the Moslems who came to arrange terms for the ransom happened to be able to speak fluent French. Upon learning that the man had once been a Christian, Louis ordered him out. "Get thee hence," he told him, "for I have no more to say to you." To Louis all non-Christians were enemies.

The laws Louis enacted against usury struck directly at moneylending in which many Hebrews were engaged. Yet Christian moneylenders were also affected. Because usury on the part of Christian moneylenders was considered a sin, their guilt and punishment was left to bishops. Royal officials enforced the law against Hebrews. Like Frederick II Louis ordered Jews to sew a piece of yellow cloth to their clothes to protect Christians from scandal. He also ordered the Talmud burned because of what he considered the anti-Christian spirit in which Jewish leaders administered its regulations. All his animosity toward Hebrews disappeared, however, when they became Christians. Both he and the queen frequently acted as godparents for converted Jews, and he also gave employment to some of these in the government. No doubt he would willingly have immured himself in a prison for life if Hebrews would have accepted Christianity, as he declared his readiness to do if the sultan and his subjects became Christian.

According to the chronicler Salimbene who saw Louis as he was about to leave on his crusade, the king was tall though thin, had warm eyes, and was gracious in his bearing. Louis' attitude toward men, whether important or humble, suggests the approach of St. Francis who looked upon all men as children of God, although Louis would have restricted that condition to Christians. There were occasions, not many, when he displayed the existence of a temper which his chroniclers say he kept well in hand: when after waiting six years for a child, his wife Margaret gave birth to a girl; when just after he and his fellow crusaders had been released from captivity and he was still weak from his serious illness, he staggered into the room where his brother Charles, the count of Anjou, was playing dice and "took the dice and the tables and flung them into the sea; and was very wroth with his brother for so soon taking to dice-playing." (Louis had forbidden playing with dice.)

Louis showed no interest in the hunt, the most popular sport indulged in by the aristocracy. His love of asceticism might have precluded that activity if not his frail constitution and frame. It is true that his duties took him on many trips about his kingdom and there is no hint that he ever found himself unable to discharge his royal responsibilities because of lack of health. Nonetheless he was often in poor health, suffered occasional attacks of erysipelas, contracted a malarial infection in 1242 which he never entirely threw off, and almost died in 1244. In view of his poor health he was imprudent in attempting his first crusade and suicidal in undertaking the second. Doubtless his rigorous fasts and bodily mortifications contributed to his frail health. At fifty he was a prematurely old man. In the eyes of his contemporaries, these physical weaknesses were the marks of a saint.

HIS EARLY YEARS AS KING

When Louis assumed control of the government on 25 April 1234, there was no evidence of any significant shift in policy from that his mother Blanche had directed. She continued, as a matter of fact, to give counsel to the young king, and the dutiful Louis seems to have always given it earnest consideration although he did not always follow it. As long as she lived, Blanche preserved a hand in the public acts of the court and assisted Louis in his negotiations with foreign powers. During the early years of his reign she blocked several marriage alliances that would have weakened the crown. One of these concerned Flanders. Louis' brother, Robert, had married Marie, the daughter of the count. Her dowry was to be Flanders. But her mother, Jeanne, now a widow, decided to shed her widow's weeds and had her eye on the younger Simon de Montfort (son of the Simon who fought in Toulouse). Blanche nipped that project in the bud, probably with a measure of personal satisfaction. In view of Simon's later career as the aggressive organizer of a baronial revolt against Henry III in England, France could count herself fortunate in not having this ambitious lord within her frontiers. Blanche also prevented Raymond VII, the widowed count of Toulouse, from remarrying, a step that might have endangered the passage of the Toulouse heritage to Alphonse, one of Louis' brothers.

Though Blanche handed her son a peaceful realm when he became twenty-one, it was not long before trouble appeared. The first coalition to oppose the young king fortunately evaporated almost as soon as it took form. Its architect was Thibaud, count of Champagne. His objective was the recovery of certain ancestral possessions, including the counties of Blois and Chartres, which he had been obliged to cede to the crown. Now without first obtaining Louis' permission, he espoused his daughter to the new count of Brittany (the son of Peter Mauclerc). The effect of this maneuver was to establish an alliance between two of Louis' most powerful feudatories, one to the west the other to the east. But before these two lords and several others who were contemplating revolt could move, information reached them that the royal army was gathering at Vincennes. At the news the coalition melted away and Thibaud had no choice but go to Paris to seek Louis' pardon. At first he attempted to escape punishment by claiming immunity on the grounds of being a crusader, but Louis brushed this aside despite the threat of ecclesiastical censure. So Thibaud begged his king's forgiveness on his knees. Louis left him in possession of Champagne, although he ordered him to choose between spending the next seven years of his life in either his distant kingdom of Navarre or in Palestine. Thibaud elected to do the latter. Further humiliation awaited him as he was leaving the palace. With the encouragement of Robert, Louis' brother, several servants threw soft cheese, tripe, and ordure in Thibaud's face, while others were busy cutting off the tail of his horse. Upon the enraged Thibaud's complaint, Louis imprisoned the culprits, but released them when Robert assumed responsibility for what they had done.

A woman's pique provided the spark for the first revolt to actually materialize during Louis' reign. The woman was Isabella, mother of Henry III of England, once King John's wife, and before that the espoused of Hugh of Lusignan. This espousal John had ignored back in 1202 when he decided to marry the young miss of thirteen himself. For this grave breach of feudal rights the aggrieved Hugh had appealed to Philip Augustus, who was both his and John's suzerain. Philip summoned John to Paris to explain his breach of fealty, and when John ignored the summons, declared Normandy and other Angevin lands forfeit and made good that forfeiture with his victory at Bouvines. Now here was Isabella back in the news again in 1241, this time the wife of Hugh, count of La Marche, the son of the Hugh to whom she had been once betrothed.

Time and her once high status as queen of England had sharpened Isabella's proud, imperious nature, and it was only with difficulty that she had brought herself with her husband Hugh to Saumur in 1241 to do homage to Alphonse, brother of Louis, for possession of the fief of Lusignan. Alphonse had just recently assumed his new role as count of Poitou and as such was Hugh's suzerain. If what Isabella claimed was true, Blanche and Margaret, that is, Louis' mother and wife, deliberately set out to humiliate her. When she entered the reception hall at Saumur, they did not rise, "not even a little," nor did they ask her to sit with them as an equal. So mortified was Isabella over this slight that when she returned to the château she ordered all the furnishings of the rooms that Louis and his brothers had occupied during the past few days to be thrown out: drapes, furniture, even the liturgical ornaments of the chapel, in order to efface the last trace of their having been there. Then when Hugh, her husband, returned in the evening, discovered her and the house in such turmoil, and humbly asked her what the difficulty might be, she presented him an ultimatum: he would have to choose between her or doing homage to Alphonse. She utterly refused to live with any pusillanimous husband who would bow to people who had humiliated her!

Poor Hugh had no choice but get busy organizing a conspiracy. He found this easier than he had anticipated since many Poitevin nobles much preferred a foreign lord in England, particularly a weak and improvident king like Henry III, to a vigorous monarch near at hand. Henry III also joined the group upon assurances from Hugh that a great army of knights would be on hand to support him. The king of Aragon also joined and so did the count of Toulouse. Though the count of Toulouse was Alphonse's father-in-law, this relationship had been forced upon him, and here he was desperately grabbing at this chance as perhaps his last opportunity to escape the inevitable absorption of his lands into the Capetian domain. By Christmas 1241, when all appeared in readiness for a successful revolt, Hugh formally repudiated his oath of homage. Louis summoned him to Paris and upon his refusing to appear, declared his fiefs forfeit and ordered up his knights to carry out his judgment.

Louis' army moved so fast that by the end of spring 1242 all the Poitevin strongholds had fallen into his hands. Henry put in a belated appearance in May and then with only a pitifully small force of three hundred knights, all he could raise among Englishmen who were indifferent, if not opposed, to his efforts to recover his lost possessions. Henry's mother, the angry Isabella, was there to greet him and not much else. The many knights the count of La Marche had promised were nowhere to be seen. Isabella tried to help the cause by hiring some men to poison Louis and his brothers, but they were apprehended in the kitchen. On 21 July the two armies faced each other across the wild Charente River near the bridge at Taillebourg. So disturbed were the English at the sight of the French camp—"it resembled a large and populous city"—that Henry asked for an armistice. The next day a skirmish between the two forces led to a battle, then the rout of the English with Henry himself giving the signal for flight. He had packed his baggage just in case of such an emergency the night before. With their allies all gone, no alternative remained for Hugh and Isabella than to make their submission to Louis. The bent, though not broken, Isabella stuck to her threat. Rather than go back to her husband, she took the veil. Louis moved in pursuit of the English, but the marshy land in the area caused him and many of his troops to contract malarial fever. Thousands of his men died and he himself became seriously ill.

Before news of the collapse of the rebellion in Poitou reached Raymond of Toulouse he had committed himself to revolt. One can sympathize with his action even though judging it foolhardy. Raymond remained the last hope of the native aristocracy of the area to retain their autonomous position against the inexorable extension of royal authority. Normally royal administration could have been counted a blessing under Louis, but this was not the case in Toulouse. Because of the distance from Paris and the difficulties that kept the crown busy nearer home, the royal seneschals whom Louis had appointed had become a law to themselves. Under the cloak of eradicating the remnants of Albigensianism, they and their lieutenants had co-operated with the inquisitors in eliminating all who might oppose them in their ruthless pursuit of power and wealth.

Raymond moved too late. Hardly had he occupied Narbonne and Béziers than news reached him of Henry III's debacle near Taillebourg, which resulted in the defection of the last remaining allies. All Raymond could do was to throw himself on Louis' mercy. Louis was reasonable. He required the count to swear to carry out the terms of the Treaty of Paris of 1229 and to actively support the inquisitors in their suppression of heresy.

Though this revolt of 1241–42 cost the crown little effort to suppress, its collapse meant a great deal for Louis. For the remainder of his reign, he experienced no further unrest in either the west or south. What must have pleased the king even more was the rapid disappearance of the last islands of Albigensianism, to which end Raymond co-operated as he had promised. In 1249, for example, he ordered the burning of eighty Cathari to whom the inquisitor had given milder punishment.

LOUIS AND HIS GOVERNMENT

Though Raymond and other nobles had revolted against Louis, they knew he was no tyrant. Neither did he wish to destroy feudal institutions nor deprive them of the considerable autonomy these left them. Louis inherited a position in terms of authority approximately halfway between that of the first Capetian, Hugh, who in 987 exercised little authority and that of Louis XI in the fifteenth century who almost attained the position of an autocrat. When the French princes elected Hugh their king in 987, it was understood that he would be content to bear the title, that he would not aspire to rule them, that he would be king in France rather than king of France. Hugh had understood his position. Though he had his great officers, as did the other magnates, their actual authority extended no further than the frontiers of his own family territories, now known as the royal domain. If and when he wished his vassals, as the other territorial lords of France were known, to agree to some action, his only recourse was to summon them to his court and appeal to them for their support. This support they would be willing to give him provided what he had in mind also served their interests. The execution of royal justice, royal revenues, and the use of royal troops outside his own domain were unheard of. A more decentralized system of governing France could hardly be imagined. Such was the nature of the early feudal kingdom.

The administrative machinery that operated within the royal domain, that is, the small fraction of France known as the Ile de France with its center in Paris, which belonged to Hugh before he was elected king, reflected the primitiveness of the political institutions of the period. The names of the king's principal officials continued to be those of Carolingian days: constable, butler, chamberlain, seneschal, and chancellor. Here in Hugh's kingdom they held their offices for life, which was the next step to their becoming hereditary. Of these royal officials the seneschal was the most important. He supervised the king's household as well as the prevôts who were scattered about the royal domain and handled the king's business. He also controlled royal finances, commanded the army, and shared judicial powers with the other great officers. Hugh's highest official in theory was the chancellor who supervised the central administration, authenticated all royal acts with the seal he kept in his possession, and acted for the king in the royal absence. For more personal assignments and those Hugh hesitated to entrust to his independently minded higher officials, he might delegate to members of the petty aristocracy called *palatini*. Since these possessed little importance in their own right, they could be expected to be more faithful.

Such was the modest administrative machinery Hugh and his immediate successors had at their disposal, and this explains the relative ineffectiveness of the French monarchy during the first century of its existence. Over what Hugh's accomplishments might have been, history is silent. His magnates must have been satisfied with him, however, for they accepted his son Robert when he died. Robert the Pious (996–1031), the chroniclers called this king, but apart from a certain measure of virtue suggested by the title, he remains quite as much a cipher in the history of France as his father. He reigned for thirty-five years, then passed the crown on to his son Henry I (1031–60), who after another twenty-nine years left it to his son Philip (1060–1108).

Little good have historians said about this Philip and a good deal that is uncommendable: that he was fat and greedy and hardly better than a rake in his private life. It was during Philip's reign that William, duke of Normandy, added England to his domain, a development for which Philip receives censure even though he might have lost his throne had he dared interfere. He may deserve credit, on the other hand, for beginning the pacification of the turbulent nobility of his domain which his far abler son Louis VI (1108–37) completed.

Historians customarily date the rise of the French monarchy with this Louis, in fact pass over his four predecessors as having accomplished little beyond producing sons and living long, but otherwise useless, lives. As indicated, Louis completed the subjugation of the feudal aristocracy within the royal domain. This he accomplished despite his enormous girth. So fat was he, it is said, he could not mount a horse once he reached the age of forty-five. Louis recognized the value of having the Church on his side. In return for the protection he gave her, he received much more in return, namely, the loyal services of Suger, the abbot of St. Denis, who was the first of a series of distinguished church statesmen who have served France. Louis was perhaps the first Capetian to recognize the value of towns to the growth of royal power. He protected them and granted them charters; they gave him money and troops wherewith to weaken the feudal aristocracy. In the opinion of contemporaries Louis' greatest accomplishment was arranging for the marriage of his son, the future Louis VII, to Eleanor, the wealthy heiress of Aquitaine.

Louis VII (1137–80) has had few friends among historians. They link his name with two misfortunes, the one, Eleanor, the other, the Second Crusade, though neither was entirely his fault. Whether it was because of unfaithfulness on Eleanor's part, or her failure to give him sons, or the sheer impossibility of living with so strong-willed a woman, Louis divorced her and sent her home to Aquitaine. Whereupon—it may have been pique—she promptly married his most dangerous vassal, Henry of Anjou and Normandy. Within a few months of the marriage, this Henry became king of England, and France and England settled down to at least two Hundred Years' wars before the English were finally expelled from France. Historians have never forgiven Louis for divorcing Eleanor although when he shed her, he had no idea she would marry Henry. There is also the question of how much he really lost when he gave up Aquitaine. Aquitaine proved just as indigestible to the English as he had found it, and Henry must often have rued the day he ever heard of either Eleanor or Aquitaine. Meantime Louis went on to be a good king, almost a proto-Louis IX in his love of justice and his gentleness. He continued the friendly policy of his father toward the Church and towns, and, it is said, was even tolerant toward Jews.

Historians may disagree over the merits of Louis VII; they never disagree over those of his son Philip II (Augustus, 1180–1223). That France superseded Germany during Philip's reign as the first power of Christian Europe provides proof of the measure of his achievement. When he died the king was the strongest and wealthiest lord in France. Philip lacked the virtues of his father, or at any rate, most of them. He was cynical, untrustworthy, and unscrupulous, although toward the majority of his subjects he was just. It was his shrewdness, his energy, and his ambition that brought him his great success. Because of the magic of Richard the Lionhearted's name, Philip's own significant contribution to the modest success of the Third Crusade has passed unnoticed. Against Henry II and his son Richard, Philip managed to hold his own, which was about all anyone could expect. John's blunders simplified Philip's seizure of Normandy, Anjou, and other French possessions the king of England held in fief, but full credit for a brilliant victory at Bouvines (1214), no one can take from him. His policy in permitting northern nobles to begin the destruction of the powerful aristocracy in the south prepared the way for the eventual incorporation of that part of France into the royal domain.

The reign of Louis VIII (1223–26) was most noteworthy for its exceptional brevity. Most of the Capetians had reigned for many years, Louis' own father and grandfather for more than forty years apiece. So brief was Louis' reign, indeed, that there was ugly talk of his having been poisoned. Louis' principal achievement was the establishment of royal power in Poitou and Languedoc, a step that led to the early absorption of Toulouse.

Meantime a great deal had happened to the simple administrative machinery with which Hugh had started the Capetian regime back in 987. Because it is usually impossible to state precisely when certain new officials and procedures came to be introduced, one may safely conclude, when there exists no evidence to the contrary, that the growth of royal administration took place just as unobtrusively as the word growth suggests. Royal power assumed new forms, powers, and responsibilities as altering circumstances recommended change, and when this change took place, it usually came about in so gradual a manner as to elude the notice of contemporary writers. It was circumstance not plan, for example, that led the king's judiciary to become localized in Paris some years before the royal government itself ceased being peripatetic. Because of the grave inconvenience of transporting the accumulating mass of records that it needed to do its business, the judiciary found travel too much of a hardship some time before the rest of the government did so.

The force of tradition exerts a powerful restraint upon change even today when many men consider the acceptance of tradition as the mark of the reactionary. Infinitely more powerful was its influence in the Middle Ages when men respected tradition as the source of law and when few men even imagined that change could be a necessary prelude to progress. Because of this medieval respect for tradition, change in royal administration came slowly during the early Capetian centuries. In fact only with Philip Augustus may one speak of change rather than growth. Then the introduction of two factors forced a significant expansion of the machinery of government: first, the inclusion of Normandy and other English possessions into the royal domain; and secondly, the acquaintance these lands brought the king with the more efficient methods the English had been employing in those territories. A possible third factor making for change was the ambition of Philip Augustus to exercise a greater measure of authority than that with which his predecessors had been content. Yet in all this change there was ordinarily less planning than accident and more expediency than principle.

During the reign of Philip Augustus there were two developments in particular that marked and made possible the growth of royal power. The first was the appointment of new provincial officials, called bailiffs and seneschals, who gradually replaced the prevôts as the principal agents of royal authority in the royal domain. The second development was the selection of specially trained men to handle the judicial and financial business of the government at Paris. The early Capetians had never found the prevôts satisfactory. These officials were often simple farmers and usually lacked administrative ability; they might also have been tempted to give more thought to furthering their own fortunes than those of the king since they had come by their offices by outbidding others for the dignity. The prevôts might also hold office for life and even pass their positions on to their sons. Under the circumstances, only occasional prevôts proved themselves both loyal and efficient administrators. They help create the popular image of the royal agent who, with relative immunity, plundered Church, townspeople, and peasantry alike.

Philip Augustus was well aware of the inadequacy of the prevôts, therefore all the more interested in the bailiffs and seneschals he found serving the English crown in Normandy and the other former Angevin possessions. Within a short time he introduced them to the rest of the royal domain. Because he paid them salaries, they remained in his service as long as they pleased him, a fact that made them immeasurably more sensitive to royal instructions than the prevôts had been. Though their initial purpose was to check on the loyalty and efficiency of the prevôts, they had soon assumed the management of the royal estates and began discharging the crown's judicial and financial responsibilities. Their appearance marked the real advent of French royal authority in the provinces.

The acquisition of Normandy and the Angevin territories necessitated a comparable expansion of the royal government within the circle of the king and his counselors. These counselors, who included the great officers of the past such as the seneschal, chancellor, and chamberlain, had become hereditary. This normally meant they were inefficient if not irresponsible. Unless the king could effect some kind of transformation that would breathe new vigor and purpose into this central office, the value of the bailiffs and seneschals would be largely wasted. What the king required was a body of trained and devoted men, specially equipped to handle the judicial and financial business of the crown. Only then could he hope to rule.

Up to the time of Philip Augustus royal government remained substantially the traditional *curia regis* which for centuries had been assisting the feudal lord in ruling his land. The word *curia* may be translated council, which illustrated the first duty of the vassal, namely, that of taking counsel with the king and the other vassals. Giving advice, however, represented just the first responsibility of the *curia regis*. A second might be that of assisting the king in the actual discharge of administrative duties. To the chroniclers of the age the *curia regis* could therefore mean several different kinds of bodies, some large, others small, their common element being that of counseling and assisting the king. The *curia regis* might be the gathering of all the king's vassals at Paris or elsewhere, wherever the king designated, not unlike in constitution and purpose the Mayfeld of Charlemagne's day, or the *curia regis* might be the handful of advisers who stayed with the king to provide him counsel on a semi-permanent basis and to help him handle the business of being king. The *curia regis* might even be a specially summoned group, whether large or small, which had been assigned a specific financial, judicial, or ecclesiastical responsibility.

Whatever the *curia regis* might have been under the earlier Capetians, by the time of Philip Augustus' accession it had proved itself increasingly incapable of satisfactorily handling the problems of royal government as these had grown in volume and complexity. The king needed an experienced and trained group of men, a kind of permanent staff, for this work. To fill this need there slowly emerged during the reign of Philip Augustus the outlines of two groups of specialists which gradually became distinct from the *curia regis* proper and took form during his later years and the reign of Louis IX as independent bodies, namely, the *parlement de Paris* and the *chambre des comptes*.

The first writers to employ the term *parlement* appear to have had in mind a meeting of the *curia regis* when its business was principally judicial, to distinguish it from the same *curia regis* when it was gathered to handle more routine matters. During the ninety years that intervened between the accession of Philip Augustus and the death of St. Louis this term *parlement* slowly assumed a more distinctive connotation. It gradually acquired an identity almost apart from that of the *curia regis,* as a separate body possessing its own rules and procedures and functioning as a purely judicial authority. (Only during the reign of Philip III, Louis IX's son, was it officially organized as the judicial section of the *curia regis*.) The catalysts in this evolution were: first, the growing volume of judicial business which resulted from the expansion of the royal domain and the activities of the new group of royal officials within that domain; and second, the advisability of establishing a permanent headquarters for an agency which needed to maintain extensive records. In time, the officials and clerks who did this business, perhaps some twenty or thirty in number, were obliged to acquire legal training, information, and skills in handling judicial responsibilities. This set them apart from the other members of the *curia regis*. Simple membership in this *curia* no longer sufficed, special training in law became a requirement.

The origins of the *chambre des comptes,* the other group of counselors to separate from the mother *curia regis,* are equally obscure. Like the *parlement* its emergence and maturing straddle the reigns of Philip Augustus and Louis IX although it was only officially organized as a formal independent body in 1320. Where the *parlement* originated in the need for more judicial experts to handle the growing mass of judicial business, so the *chambre des comptes* was born of the need of a similar group of fiscal experts who could devote its time to handling the crown's financial operations. Both *parlement* and *chambre des comptes* met irregularly as had been the case with the *curia regis,* although a permanent staff handled their business and prepared their work for them when they were not in session.

The fiscal business of the crown increased as a result of the incorporation of Normandy and the Angevin territories as well as from the greater exploitation of the regular sources of revenue. Louis continued "to live of his own," as feudal tradition required, although the inadequacy of the revenues realized from his own estates grew every year more apparent. Feudal tradition permitted him to supplement these with the usual aids and incidents. Louis imposed a special aid, and a heavy one, on the occasion of his two crusades. A significant increase in revenues resulted from the growing efficiency and authority of the royal judicial officials in collecting fees and fines. The privilege of offering money in lieu of the military service and the hospitality that the feudal aristocracy owed the crown, Louis extended to commoners for what services they might be responsible. Like his predecessors he collected payments from towns, placed assessments upon moneylenders, principally Italians and Jews, and realized significant revenues from his control over tolls and coinage.

During these years when royal administration expanded, it is seldom possible to detect at any time the hand of either Philip Augustus or Louis as directing this growth. Where Louis' hand is clearly evident, however, is in the addition of a new royal official called the *enquêteur.* Louis was not the first king to send out inquisitors, but he was the first one to do this in the interest of his subjects and not of the crown. For Louis in appointing these officials was not concerned with protecting the crown's rights, but rather with learning of grievances his subjects might have against the crown's agents. In January 1247 Louis gave these *enquêteurs* orders "to receive in writing and examine all the complaints which can justifiably be brought against us and our ancestors, as well as statements concerning the injustice of which our bailiffs, prevôts, foresters, serjeants, and subordinates have been guilty."

This is a most unusual order. Had time preserved no other echoes of Louis' reign, this document alone would have marked him as a "good" king.

Nevertheless it comes as something of a shock to learn that so extensive an investigation into the working of royal administration had become necessary in view of the many generations France had been blessed with good kings. Every king, beginning with Louis VI in 1108, had proved himself well above average both in efficiency and in his interest in sound government. Philip Augustus dealt harshly with officials who were proved guilty of maladministration, and so had his son Louis VIII, while no one could accuse Blanche or Louis IX of having been tolerant of corruption. Yet the fact remains that the growth of royal administration during those years had often proved a mixed blessing. In certain places, especially in southern France, it had approximated a tyranny. Though the majority of bailiffs and seneschals were reasonably honest and efficient, a substantial number soon discovered that the absence of any agency to check on their activities and the many miles the king was away in Paris enabled them to practice their iniquities with impunity.

The deficiencies of the crown's agents usually took one of two forms: one, the tendency of even honest bailiffs and seneschals to expand the area of their competence at the expense of the rights of local lords and communes; second, the practice of dishonest officials, most frequently the lower ones, to abuse the farm they had purchased. (The farm was their right to collect taxes for themselves, wherewith to cover the cost of their services to the crown. This long continued to be the manner royal agents in France received their pay.) Royal agents were guilty of outright thefts and usurpations, of demanding fines and bribes from men they arbitrarily arrested, and of using torture to enforce payment of taxes and extortions. The area which suffered most grievously from the tyranny of royal government was the south where the royal agent could cloak his vicious practices under guise of suppressing heterodoxy. Even Joinville speaks of royal tyranny when he excused himself from accompanying Louis on his second crusade. He must remain, so he told the king, in order to protect his people from the "serjeants of the King of France" and the count of Champagne, who had "destroyed and impoverished" his people during his absence on the earlier crusade.

Joinville's testimony indicates that the use of *enquêteurs* lapsed while Louis was away in Syria, and that is true. Louis revived the practice of sending out these men upon his return and placed the institution on a permanent basis. The first inquisitors Louis employed were usually members of the clergy, often Franciscans. He may have used them to save money, more probably because he considered them less open to bribery. He soon discovered, however, that whatever their other virtues, they lacked the sophistication to deal with crown officials, so he began to recruit members of his own court staff for the job who had greater experience in conducting inquests and in dealing with royal agents.

On the basis of the information reported by these *enquêteurs,* Louis issued ordinances in 1254 and 1256 for the guidance of seneschals, prevôts, foresters, serjeants, and other officials in the performance of their duties. Their first charge was to take a solemn oath "that so long as they shall hold office of bailly, they will do justice to every man without exception of persons, to poor and rich alike, to stranger and friend alike, and will maintain such usages and customs as are good and tried." In order to reduce the opportunity to misuse their offices, they were prohibited from owning property in the area they served or from marrying a son or daughter to any person living within their jurisdiction. They must also remain in the neighborhood for a period of fifty days following the termination of their duties in order to facilitate their prosecution for possible misconduct. They were warned against accepting bribes, against denying anyone justice, and against levying taxes beyond those authorized by the crown. They were to avoid swearing and to eschew games of dice, while enforcing the laws against the manufacture of dice and against prostitution. They were enjoined from arresting anyone for debt or crime or from imposing a fine "save it be tried and assessed in full court," nor were they to sell offices or forbid the export of corn, wine, and other commodities for the purpose of selling licenses to those willing to purchase them. The work of these *enquêteurs* in investigating and correcting abuses on the part of crown officials and in forcing them to carry out the ordinances noted above contributed significantly to Louis' reputation as the guardian of justice and the protector of the weak.

Louis viewed his position of king as one combining the office of feudal suzerain with the role of father of a Christian people. As the latter he considered himself under sacred obligation to work unceasingly for the sanctification of his subjects. As feudal monarch he recognized his obligation to respect the rights which tradition accorded his vassals. When these two obligations came into conflict, however, he showed no hesitation whatsoever in doing God's will as he saw it, whatever the sanctity of feudal traditions. If his vassals lost prerogatives under the circumstances, they should never have had those rights in the first place. The right of private warfare was a case in point. Only those privileges would he tolerate which were in keeping with his views of Christian justice. When his vassals gave him counsel as feudal tradition required, he might follow their counsel or he might not. The final arbiter would be his conscience. His vassals grumbled, on occasion they even moved to revolt, but so universal was the conviction that Louis served only God, not ambition, that such resistance never mounted sufficient enthusiasm to succeed. Still it is a curious fact that in a history of the growth of royal despotism in France, one encounters the contribution of the saintly Louis IX alongside those of the unscrupulous Philip IV and Louis XI.

Since feudal confusion was the alternative, most historians approve the advance of royal power during this period although they regret certain concomitants of that advance. That it advanced by royal fiat set a dangerous precedent, whatever the justice of the king's motives. Less worthy monarchs who lacked Louis' virtue would profit by his example. Furthermore, the methods employed by such an institution as the court of the inquisition which only functioned in France with Louis' leave, exerted a baleful influence upon the growth of criminal law which was then in its formative stage. In an age when heresy was a crime and even a Frederick II executed heretics, no one can accuse Louis of undue severity or intolerance in seeking to eradicate Albigensianism. Neither can he be held responsible for the excesses of occasional inquisitors. Yet the secrecy which shrouded the operations of the court and its arbitrary character provided the background to the judicial despotism later practiced by Philip IV.

LOUIS AND THE CHURCH

Louis' attitude toward the Church and papacy have attracted considerable attention. What position did this saintly king take toward papal practices and policies to which less pious kings made vigorous objection? Did he permit without protest, for example, the excommunication of royal officials, the filling of French benefices with Italian clerks, the imposition of financial exactions upon his clergy, or the appeals of disgruntled citizens to the papal curia? It goes without saying that Louis harbored no ill will toward the clergy, quite the contrary. "The King loved all people who devoted themselves to the service of God and wore the religious habit. . . ." This devotion Louis extended in a special way to popes and papal legates. Though he might disagree with them, and he did so on a number of occasions, never did his difficulties with the papacy reach the point of bitterness. Such hostility, of course, the popes on their part could not permit. They were engaged in a deadly struggle with Frederick II and the Hohenstaufens for most of Louis' reign, and they had no one else to turn to had they broken with him.

While Louis treated clergy and papacy with great respect, he knew that human passions could throb as fiercely under clerical robes as under lay cloaks, and that certain bishops could be as proud and unscrupulous as other vassals. Joinville notes the names of several prelates whose aggressiveness Louis repelled with as much firmness as had they been laymen. A particularly sensitive point in Church-State relations during Louis' reign concerned obstinate excommunicates, that is, men and women who had suffered ecclesiastical censure but who refused to take the steps necessary to removing that censure. No longer did excommunication provoke the spiritual anguish it once had done and popular indifference to this kind of pressure was worrying the hierarchy. So they turned to the king and begged him to instruct his officials to lay hold of such excommunicates once they had remained obdurate for a year and a day, and force them to make their peace with the Church. To this request Louis replied that he would willingly issue the necessary orders but only if the bishops permitted him first to review the justice of the original censure. This privilege the bishops replied they could not permit him since the matter touched religion. Whereupon Louis told them flatly that he would not co-operate with them. "For if I did so, I should be flying in the face of God and of justice; and I will give you this as an instance: the bishops of Brittany kept the Count of Brittany no less than seven years under sentence of excommunication, and in the end the Court of Rome absolved him. Now, if I had put compulsion on him after the first year, I should have done so wrongly."

This dispute with his bishops over excommunicates who refused to submit occasioned Louis little anguish. What did was the bitter struggle between the papacy and Frederick II. What position should he assume? The sight of the papacy under attack caused him much grief. His own faith called out to him to intervene, precisely what the pope repeatedly reminded him was his Christian duty to do. Yet Louis hesitated. He knew that popes were human, that they fell into the easy error of dignifying anything they chose to undertake as God's will and of denouncing their opponents as tools of the devil. He could not forget the precipitate manner Gregory IX had excommunicated Frederick when he turned back on his crusade in 1227 nor how papal armies had overrun Sicily during the emperor's absence in the Holy Land in 1228-29, than which, in his eyes, even with all his hatred of the infidel, there could be no greater crime. He also had difficulty accepting the pope's protests that Frederick's aim was to conquer Italy and to make the holy see his agent. Appreciably less difficulty, however, did he have in dismissing Frederick's warning that the pope's objective, on the other hand, was the destruction of royal power wherever it existed and the establishment of papal political supremacy all over Europe.

So Louis was prudent and decided that a policy of strict neutrality was the wisest under the circumstances. He would not permit his brother Robert, count of Artois, to assume the imperial crown the pope offered him, nor would he allow another brother, Charles of Anjou, to lead an army into Italy as long as Frederick and his son Conrad lived. It was only in 1262 that the pope finally broke down his scruples to the point where he permitted this. Papal demands upon the French clergy for financial assistance he discouraged until after his return from his crusade when he no longer offered any resistance. He never permitted knights to leave France for Italy, and if ever the pope sought permission to make his headquarters at Reims, as some writers believe, he refused him upon the advice of his barons. Yet when Frederick seized his bishops on their way to Rome in 1241, he demanded that the emperor release them without delay. Also when Frederick made preparations to march against Innocent IV in Lyons in 1247, though the king refused the pope asylum, he gave Frederick to understand that he would protect the pope. Yet throughout the entire period of Frederick's difficulties with the pope, Louis remained on amicable terms with the emperor in defiance of the papal excommunication. He even permitted the emperor to communicate with certain French barons in 1246 who had formed a league to oppose what they claimed were encroachments of the Church.

Louis had a number of reasons for deploring the war between the papacy and Frederick. One was the threat it posed to the success of his crusade. After 1244 this crusade had become almost an obsession with him, so convinced was he that God was insisting that he lead one. Yet how could it succeed with the pope and emperor carrying on their own war in Italy. He repeatedly offered the contestants his good offices to bring their dispute to an end, but all to no avail. Frederick was eager for the emperor's arbitration, in fact, several times asked him to intervene. But the pope was adamant. To permit a secular ruler to arbitrate a dispute involving the papacy would set a dangerous precedent; furthermore, the pope, especially Innocent IV, was convinced that there was no trusting Frederick, for which reason he was unyielding in his determination to destroy him and his entire dynasty. To the pope they represented incarnate evil itself. So long as they existed, at least in Italy, there could be no hope for the Church. Though Louis failed in his efforts at reconciling the two, he remained the man both pope and emperor turned to consistently, not only because France was a great power but because Louis, its king, was a just man whose judgment all Christendom respected.

At home Louis' policy toward the Church did not differ substantially from that of other Christian kings. His mother Blanche had already shown him the necessity of resisting churchmen when this became advisable and to have no fear of ecclesiastical censures whenever the legitimate rights of the crown were involved. In the presentation of priests to benefices, Louis exercised this right in a manner some bishops could well have used as a guide. "When any of the benefices of Holy Church escheated to the King," writes Joinville, "he would first take counsel with good persons of religion and others; and after consultation he would bestow the benefices in good faith, honourably and according to God. Nor would he give any benefices to any cleric, unless he resigned all the other church benefices that he might hold." The French clergy looked to Louis for protection against papal exactions, to the pope against those of the king. The demands of both were heavy, for Louis needed money to finance his crusades, the pope needed money to fight Frederick. This was a situation not peculiar to France, nor was the lot of the clergy in France greatly different from that in other Western Christian countries during these centuries. The clergy everywhere was caught in a vise. The only two people from whom they could hope to secure protection, that is king and pope, were themselves normally their greatest oppressors.

LOUIS AND HIS NEIGHBORS

Louis' desire for peace and his love for justice stood out most vividly in his dealings with other powers. His two most powerful neighbors, Henry III and Frederick II, were in deep trouble for a good part of his reign. Louis' grandfather Philip Augustus and his grandson Philip the Fair would have had no compunction about exploiting these opportunities in order to push back French frontiers at their neighbors' expense. Not so Louis. For territory he had no more love than for power. His only desire was to live in peace with his fellow kings, all of them fortunately Christians, since that is what God demanded. The only war Louis could contemplate was one against the infidel, and for that kind of war he was always ready, again since that is what God wanted. But "Beware," he cautioned his son Philip, "of going to war with Christians save after great deliberation. . . ."

Louis' renown for justice brought him a number of disputes to arbitrate. In 1264 he arbitrated the conflict between the two families of Marguerite, heiress of the count of Flanders and Hainaut, over her possessions. Marguerite had married young, which was not unusual, and when she was fifteen and had two sons, her husband went off to Rome to defend the validity of his marriage against the charge that he had once been a subdeacon. Rome often took a great deal of time to resolve marital problems, particularly when they were enmeshed in politics as was this one. So after a few years, Marguerite tired of waiting for her absent husband and married again; nor did she wait long before she had another family, this one consisting of three sons and two daughters. Now the question arose, who would inherit Flanders and Hainaut, the sons of the first marriage whose legitimacy depended upon Rome's decision, or those of the second? As fortune would have it, one of the families had taken possession of Flanders, the other of Hainaut, so Louis did what reason and expediency suggested and assigned the two provinces accordingly. All appeared settled until he left for the crusade, when war broke out and continued until his return when he forced the two parties to recognize his original settlement.

Louis had less difficulty over the question of succession to Navarre which he arbitrated and other disputes as well that were referred to his judgment. The most famous controversy which he was asked to arbitrate was the quarrel between Henry III of England and his barons led by

Simon de Montfort. As usual the trouble was largely of Henry's own making and again as usual, it was a case of Henry's overreaching himself. He had permitted his son Edmund to accept the crown of Sicily from the pope even though the pope was in no position to give him Sicily. It was still firmly in Hohenstaufen hands. Yet the pope had already spent a huge amount of money in his efforts to dislodge the stubborn Germans, so when Henry accepted Sicily for his son, he also made him agree to assume the papal debt. When Henry shortly after fell behind in his payments and the pope threatened to use ecclesiastical censures against him, he had no choice but summon the great council. Instead of money, however, the barons countered with a series of demands, known as the Provisions of Oxford, which they forced him to accept. The effect of these was to deprive Henry of control of the government and place it in the hands of a council of fifteen barons whom the barons themselves would select and whose consent Henry must have before undertaking any important action. The Provisions did not bring tranquillity to England, and after several years of continued confusion, Henry and the barons in 1264 asked Louis to pass on the legitimacy of the experiment. Since the Provisions would have made a figurehead of the king, Louis, quite logically in keeping with the traditions of the age, found them invalid (Mise of Amiens), whereupon the barons repudiated his judgment and revolted against Henry.

Louis fared more successfully in dealing directly with Henry over the thorny problem of John's lost provinces. Though Henry had made no new incursions into French territory since his forlorn effort of 1242, he had never ceased to protest and to intrigue. During the fifties, while Louis was in Syria, he renewed his demands on Blanche who was acting as regent. Though Henry's position was weaker than it had been in 1242 since English interest in recovering the former Angevin territories had meantime practically disappeared, nor could Henry have possibly financed any kind of war, Louis decided that in the interest of peace he would meet him more than halfway. He agreed with his counselors that Henry had no basis in right for the claims he was making. Nevertheless, he felt peace and good will between his France and England were worth the small price he would have to pay. Personal considerations also recommended conciliation. Henry was his brother-in-law, Henry's wife was the favorite sister of Louis' wife. Louis also admired Henry's piety. So after several years of weary discussion an agreement emerged known as the Treaty of Paris (1259). By the terms of this treaty Henry renounced all claims to Normandy, Anjou, Touraine, Maine, and Poitou. In return Louis surrendered to him small territories along the eastern border of Guienne and undertook to finance for two years the cost of maintaining five hundred knights that Henry needed so desperately in his Sicilian venture.

Historians have criticized Louis for giving Henry territory when in their judgment he should rather have pushed him completely out of France and thereby precluded the tragic Hundred Years' War. To critics of his own day who argued in much the same vein, Louis admitted that he had turned over these lands, not because Henry had a valid claim to them, "but to put bonds of love betwixt my children and his who are first cousins. And methinks that what I give him is well spent; for whereas he was not my liege-man, now he comes into homage to me."

Some time previously Louis concluded a similar treaty of friendship with the king of Aragon which involved the exchange of territory. By the Treaty of Corbeil (1258) he renounced his claims to Roussillon and the county of Catalonia which were parts of Charlemagne's empire, while the king of Aragon relinquished in turn his claims over Toulouse. The marriage of the latter's daughter Isabella to Philip, Louis' son, cemented the treaty.

LOUIS' FIRST CRUSADE

Louis would have considered his greatest undertaking and his greatest failure the crusade he led against the Moslems in Egypt in 1248. The circumstances of his going were not unusual: a grave illness, followed by a vow to go on the crusade should God give him back his health. Louis had always shown interest in the Holy Land and had been sending money and troops to the Christians in Syria and to the Latin emperor of Constantinople. The hard-pressed emperor had expressed his appreciation by offering Louis the crown of thorns (for a price) and other relics of the crucifixion in the hope of keeping them out of the hands of the greedy Venetians, his creditors. No doubt Louis' great devotion to these relics, for which he had the exquisite Gothic church of Sainte Chapelle constructed, heightened his interest in Jerusalem. Still it was his near-fatal illness in December 1244 when he almost succumbed to a malarial infection that prompted his taking the cross.

Blanche, Margaret, Louis' counselors, and his prelates all begged the king not to go, but he was adamant. Preparations got under way immediately and in August 1248 a formidable host sailed from southern France. Besides Louis it included his brothers Robert of Artois and Charles of Anjou, together with a number of French dukes and counts, and Sir Jean of Joinville, the seneschal of Champagne, who left posterity an account of the undertaking. Some Englishmen joined the crusade and later some Germans. Many more might have come from north of the Alps had the pope not secretly forbidden preaching the crusade there lest it interfere with his own crusade against Frederick.

The crusaders made for Cyprus which most of them reached in September. Cyprus was to serve as a base of supplies for the attack on Egypt. For it was Egypt, rather than Syria, which Louis and his advisers believed would provide them easiest access to Jerusalem. Though the ill-fated Fifth Crusade had planned to follow the same route but had foundered in Egypt (1221), they attributed that debacle to mistakes they would be careful not to repeat. While waiting in Cyprus for supplies, two Nestorian emissaries arrived from the Mongol general at Mosul bringing feelers for an alliance against the Saracens. Louis who was probably more interested in converting the Mongols than in gaining their assistance sent back an embassy headed by three Dominicans. The portable altar, pictures of saints, and liturgical articles they took with them ended up in faraway Mongolia where they aroused interest but little else.

On 15 May 1249 a huge fleet, the largest crusading flotilla ever assembled, left Cyprus and, after buffeting a severe storm, arrived 4 June off the Egyptian coast at Damietta. Next morning the first crusaders fought their way ashore in the face of strong opposition. The landing of the Christians seems to have sapped the courage of the aged general in charge and he gave orders to evacuate the powerful and well-stocked city of Damietta. Whereupon the happy crusaders occupied the city, reconsecrated the mosque into a cathedral, and had Margaret and the other ladies who had accompanied the crusade brought in from Acre. Hopes ran high as the crusaders settled down to wait for the flooding Nile to subside. The sultan after executing some fifty of his generals for having permitted the Christians to occupy Damietta opened negotiations, repeating substantially the same offer made by the sultan to Pelagius, the leader of the Fifth Crusade, only to be rebuffed in much the same fashion by Louis as the foolish Pelagius had done some twenty-five years before. The sequel was also the same, the destruction of the crusade. History has seldom repeated itself so emphatically.

As weeks passed and then months, supplies at Damietta began to run low, then disease made its inevitable appearance. Finally in October, upon arrival of Louis' brother Alphonse with reinforcements, the crusaders moved southward toward Mansurah with Cairo as its major objective. Most of the crusaders and the Templars preferred an attack on Alexandria, but Louis chose to follow the advice of his younger brother Robert who maintained that Cairo held the key to Egypt. So in November the army started forward, slowly but steadily, and under Louis' prudent leadership besting the enemy whenever he made a stand. In late December the crusaders found themselves before Mansurah, but there a wide canal held them up for six weeks. Finally a Bedouin appeared with an offer to show them a ford where they might cross. Louis appointed Robert to go forward with a sizable number of knights and Templars, but not to engage the enemy until the main army arrived. Robert crossed the ford, then in order to catch the enemy by surprise, disregarded Louis' orders and attacked the main Egyptian camp. His plan worked and, had he stopped with occupation of the enemy's camp, all would have been well. In spite of the urgent pleading of the Templars who had long experience behind them, Robert ordered his group to follow after the fleeing enemy right into the city of Mansurah. The city proved a death trap. The Egyptians simply let the knights and Templars pour into the city—they numbered some five hundred—then cut them down almost to a man in the narrow streets where they were helpless.

Robert's rashness deprived Louis' crusade of any hope of success. It is doubtful whether the crusaders could ever have stormed Cairo and Alexandria with what equipment they had, but more was building and more being brought in. If nothing more, the capture of Mansurah, which would have opened the way to these cities, would have provided Louis a stronger hand in negotiating with the enemy. After the disaster at Mansurah came famine, dysentery, then despair. On 5 April 1250, the bedraggled crusaders turned back to Damietta under heavy attack by the Egyptians to whom they finally surrendered. Had they waited any longer dysentery would have killed them all, including Louis.

Louis blamed no one for the disaster but accepted the calamity as the working of God's inscrutable will. To Louis himself no blame attaches. Apart from undertaking what may have been a foolhardy venture from the beginning, he had conducted the campaign well. He had planned it carefully, made ample preparations, and had led the crusading army with prudence and courage. Nor was there anything lacking in valor or determination on the part of the crusaders themselves. But famine and disease were two enemies with which crusading armies had never learned to cope. Few crusading endeavors suffered so catastrophically as this one of Louis'. Thousands died in the fighting, more thousands from dysentery, and still more after their surrender. Those Christians who were sick, the Egyptians slew immediately and during the weeks following many more who could not hope to raise ransom. Louis and his nobles suffered constant harassment and abuse. Had it not been for the ransom they could pay, not one man or woman would have lived to return to France. For money told in the end, together with the deep impact the king's honorableness and courage made upon the enemy. There was even light talk of asking him to become their sultan. (They had slain their own.) In the end Louis and the Egyptians worked out terms: Louis was to ransom himself by restoring Damietta. For his army he would pay the huge sum of a million besants. Finally the evening of 6 May 1250, Louis, together with what was left of his army, and the ladies who had been in Damietta all this time, left for Acre.

The majority of Louis' counselors and his nobles were for leaving immediately for France, but Louis refused. Louis realized that if he left, no more prisoners would be released; furthermore, that what territories remained in Christian hands would rapidly melt away. Many of the defenders of this Christian outpost in Syria had died in Egypt, many others had decided to leave the moment the king pulled out. So a sense of duty held Louis in Syria, together with the knowledge that his crusade had resulted in a serious weakening of the Christian position in the East. Until he had restored the morale of the Christian defenders and repaired their fortresses, he could not afford to leave. So he busied himself with securing the defenses of Acre, Haifa, Caesarea, and Jaffa, all of which he accomplished with little interference from the Moslems. He was even able to relieve antagonisms which traditionally separated Templars, Hospitalers, Venetians, Genoese, and Pisans into hostile groups. He managed to exploit the hostility between Cairo and Damascus to the extent of persuading the Mamluk ruler of Egypt to release the last of his crusading prisoners and to remit the balance due on his ransom. He might have wished to do more, but neither his brothers in France nor the pope in Italy would send reinforcements. So on 24 April 1254, with the assurance of the patriarch of Jerusalem that his remaining any longer was not necessary, Louis embarked for home.

Joinville's memoirs describe some interesting, several harrowing incidents that Louis and his shipload of crusaders experienced on their return voyage. Near Cyprus their ship ran aground and all believed the waves would shortly destroy the vessel and they would perish. One of Joinville's knights hurried to bring the seneschal a coat as he stood there on deck in his night clothes awaiting the end. When Joinville gruffly asked what need he had for a coat at such at time as that "when we are going to be drowned," the knight replied: "Upon my soul, Sir! I had rather we were all drowned, than that you should take a chill and die of it!" In the morning divers examined the damage and warned Louis to continue on in another ship since they doubted his ship could withstand the heavy seas they might encounter. But Louis refused to leave the ship. Had he gone on and left the five hundred or more passengers to remain in Cyprus, they would have had to stay there for a year and possibly longer before getting back to France. "And so," the king explained, "I prefer to trust my life and my wife and children in God's hands, rather than cause such injury to such a vast number of people as are here on board."

Another incident that Joinville relates reveals Louis' warmheartedness as well as his firmness. As the ship was nearing the island of Pantelleria, the queen asked Louis whether some galleys might be sent ashore to get fruit for the children. The king agreed and sent off three boats, but with strict orders to their crews to arrange to meet the ship again as it passed the main harbor. When the ship reached that point, there was no sign of the galleys. The sailors were for continuing on as quickly as possible since, in their judgment, the men who had gone ashore had been captured by the Saracens. They were fearful that they themselves would be attacked if they tarried. Louis ordered them to turn the ship about. He would not leave his men on the island without first ascertaining what had happened to them and making an attempt to rescue them. So the sailors proceeded to turn the ship about and shortly after spied the galleys. To Louis' query to the men who had gone ashore why they had failed to show up when agreed, they laid the fault to six youths who had accompanied them but who had refused to leave the island until they had eaten their fill of fruit in the gardens. So despite the pleading of the queen and the others, Louis ordered the six boys consigned to the brig for the balance of the trip. "And it served them right," observed Joinville, "for their greed injured us so much as to delay us for full a week, because the King had made the ship put about."

Another incident on the return trip illustrates Louis' willingness to
seek counsel while in the end doing what his conscience and reason
recommended. Ten long weeks of sailing since leaving Acre had finally
brought Louis and his ship to Hyères off the coast of Provence, whereupon the queen and Louis' counselors urged him to give orders to land
there rather than continue on to Aigues-Mortes, more than a hundred
miles to the west. Louis stubbornly refused. He wanted to put ashore
in his own territory he said. (Provence was his brother Charles' territory,
while Aigues-Mortes was the port of embarkation he had especially built
for this crusade.) Then after refusing to reconsider his decision for
more than a day, he called Joinville aside and asked him what he
thought about the matter. "I said to him," writes Joinville, " 'Sir, it would
serve you right, if the same thing happened to you as it did to my Lady
of Bourbon. She would not land at this port, but put out to sea again
for Aigues-Mortes, and at sea she remained for seven weeks afterwards.' "
So Louis called another meeting of the council, and Joinville adds: "The
King yielded to our advice, whereat the Queen was greatly delighted."

Louis returned to France in July 1254. He had been away for six
years, during which interval Blanche had served as regent until her
death late in 1252, then his brothers Alphonse and Charles. Though no
serious developments had taken place during Louis' absence, the situation was not good. A civil war was under way in Flanders, Henry III
was in Gascony intriguing with the king of Castile, while some of
Louis' nobles were talking revolt. The strangest event that had occurred
during his absence was the appearance of a kind of peasant crusade
that somehow took form in northern France in the spring of 1251, born
of compassion over the news of the king's misfortunes in Egypt. Its
membership was composed of peasants and poor laborers, men, women,
and children, who set out somewhat aimlessly toward Paris on their
way presumably to Egypt to rescue Louis. Somewhere they found a
leader, a mysterious old man, pale and gaunt, with a long beard, who
called himself "Master of Hungary," and who claimed to have received
a personal commission from the Blessed Virgin to lead the crusade. As
the horde moved across France he would preach to his followers,
distribute crosses, and even work miracles, it is said. Despite the mob's
religious fanaticism they were hostile to the clergy since they laid
the king's sufferings to the failure of the priests and monks to support
the crusade. Blanche initially sympathized with the movement, but when
it grew more violent after leaving Paris and began to break up into

companies, she ordered its suppression. Almost as quickly as it appeared, it disappeared, to take its place in history alongside other half-mad, half-religious mass movements that had a way of cropping up during the Middle Ages.

LOUIS' LAST CRUSADE AND DEATH

When Louis departed Syria in 1254 he not only left behind a force of knights that he continued to maintain but he also promised the Christians there that he would be returning. In 1267 he began serious preparations for what he hoped would be as powerful a crusade as the earlier one. Again he refused to be dissuaded from undertaking what the state of his health alone should have prevented his doing. Joinville tells how he, at one point in Louis' preparations, had to support him in his arms, so weakened was his condition. Those people "committed a deadly sin who encouraged his going," Joinville declares. For himself, he could give no account of this crusade, "because," as he explains, "I was not there, thank God!"

The principal culprit in this most lamentable of enterprises was Louis' brother Charles of Anjou. This hard, ruthless man was now in possession of Naples and Sicily. He had captured and executed Conradin, the sixteen-year-old grandson of the great Frederick II, the last remaining member of the illustrious and feared Hohenstaufen dynasty. Even this did not satisfy Charles. He wanted more: Tunis, then Constantinople perhaps, and Syria. That his pious brother should waste French lives and resources on a crusade Charles could not permit. So he persuaded Louis that he would best serve his hope of taking Jerusalem by attacking the emir in Tunis. (The emir had just suspended tribute payments to Charles!) The emir, Charles assured Louis, was on the point of becoming a Christian. A little pressure would suffice to win him over, then the road to Egypt from the west would be open.

So at the last minute Louis diverted the crusade from Egypt to Tunis. Early in July 1270 he sailed with a large host that touched first at Sardinia, then landed on the eighteenth of the month in Africa. The emir had abandoned Carthage as not worth defending, which the French found only too true. From Carthage they stumbled on through the hot sands toward Tunis with only light resistance from the enemy. The emir saw no point in opposing the Christians since the heat and desert would do his work for him. With no tents to protect them from the blazing sun and with insufficient water and food, the crusaders were already succumbing when dysentery struck. First Louis' son Jean-Tristan died, then on 25 August, King Louis himself. Before he died he made his will and gave his last earnest instructions to his son Philip on how to be a good king.

That the death of no medieval king evoked such sorrow as did Louis' is the strongest testimonial to the man's goodness. The French people forgave him the dreadful cost of his two crusades—crusades and suffering were the soul of the Middle Ages—they only remembered the strict justice he rendered, the love he had for the poor, and his devotion to peace. What man can do more?

Louis XI

Physically, Louis was an unattractive king. There was little dignity about his appearance. Had he not been king, no one would have paid him the compliment of a second look unless to stare. He was below medium height and walked a halting, ungainly gait on legs that looked longer than they were because of their scrawniness. As he grew older and heavier these physical deficiencies appeared more marked. Nor would a glance at his face have relieved the generally unfavorable impression the man created. His eyes were deep-sunken and lacked warmth, and as he grew older they grew more suspicious and distrustful. The sense of general disproportion left by heavy jaw, large forehead, and long, thin nose led his enemies to liken him to a buffoon. Louis' barbers kept him clean-shaven and his hair short, although all their ingenuity could not prevent him from balding. In a man seemingly indifferent to what others thought, he appears to have been sensitive about his lack of hair. When he commissioned the sculptor to carve the effigy for his tomb, he directed him to show him in possession of a full head of hair.

A prudent man might have compensated for the physical deficiencies an ungenerous Nature had provided by wearing well-tailored, attractive clothes, but not Louis. He seemed almost to take pride in his ill-favored appearance. Instead of obscuring its lack of elegance he aggravated it. So he wore a short coat after the manner of Italians which helped reveal his legs in all their ungainliness when long coats were actually fashionable in France. There hung about him a general air of shabbiness which his preference for black, brown, and gray colors and for fustian and serge tended to accentuate. It was only during the last years of his life that he dressed with a measure of extravagance. His motive for doing this was to give the lie to rumors about his impending demise. Since rich colors were so much out of character with him, this alone should have convinced his subjects that something was wrong. Perhaps because of his distaste for splendid clothes and for splendor in general, he chided his nobles for wasting their substance and their subjects' on extravagant attire.

Most distinctive about his apparel was his hat, a heavy bonnet of beaver or wool, with brim broad enough to protect him from the sun and rain. Some writers have made much of the leaden images of saints Louis occasionally had suspended from the brim, as evidence of his extreme superstition, but this may be doing him an injustice. The hat seldom bore more than one image at a time. When one hung from his hat, it indicated that the king was returning from a pilgrimage to the shrine of the saint whose image he displayed. It was customary to do this. Whether it was the knowledge of his unprepossessing appearance or his dislike for pomp, circumstance, and speeches, Louis had a habit of entering cities as unobtrusively as possible when he traveled, preferably by some side gate.

Louis may have dressed shabbily, but he was not untidy. His château at Plessis where he spent a good deal of his time he had furnished with a specially equipped bathroom that enabled him to take regular hot baths. And like many members of the upper class he was generous in his daily use of rose water. When he became king he preferred to eat alone, but as he came to find pleasure in conversation, he customarily invited guests to dine with him. Eating never became a passion with him, and if he ever made requests upon his cooks, it was for a special kind of meat. Where most kings on their travels gave long notice of their arrival so that nothing would be lacking their comfort, Louis traveled almost incognito with a small escort and stopped by some tavern along the way rather than put up with one of his nobles. When Louis found himself without pressing problems and in convivial company, he not infrequently ate heavily and consumed more wine than sobriety allowed.

Commines observed that Louis' "chief pleasure was chatting with his friends," and diplomats also commented about the king's garrulity, a trait that must have struck them as most unusual in view of his usual secretiveness and his devotion to business. Unfortunately the chatting Commines speaks about apparently never rose above the level of chatter, unless it dipped, as it frequently did, to mere scurrility and abuse at the expense of enemies and of women. Of women Louis had a low opinion. He held them to be weak both physically and morally. The only woman he might except from that ungenerous appraisal was his daughter Anne whom he appointed regent on his deathbed. "Anne is the least foolish woman of France, for I know of no wise ones," he declared. How he came by this low opinion his contemporaries do not explain. There were low women at court when he was a boy, including Agnès Sorel, one of the most famous of French royal mistresses. Still Louis' mother, Marie of Anjou, was a gentle woman and pious, nor would any sane man accuse either of the two women Louis married of moral irregularity. His wives and mother may have been submissive, but that was expected of medieval women. That Louis regaled his table companions with coarse talk about women, among these even his mother and wives it seems, remains a black mark on his character.

No trait of Louis' was more unconventional than his preference for the company and counsel of commoners. That medieval kings appreciated the wisdom of employing men below the rank of noble as trusted officials was not unusual. What was unusual about Louis' policy was that he appointed such men to high posts in the government and depended upon them for his counsel. Louis explained to Commines that he preferred to use small men to do his work, even to give him advice, in order to keep them under obligation. Their loyalty he could always count upon, for without his favor they amounted to nothing, and he could dismiss or punish them if they proved inefficient or derelict. There was also a personal reason for his use of commoners. He felt comfortable in their company, could laugh and jest freely without fear of suffering the ridicule hostile members of the haughty nobility might make at the expense of his unchivalrous deficiencies. So he selected men like the notorious Olivier le Daim (the Evil), his barber, gave them titles and pensions, acted as godfather for their children, and found them wealthy heiresses to marry.

Louis would have attributed his lack of popularity among the aristocracy to his policies which endangered their privileged position and to his contempt for the gay, frivolous lives they led. The aristocracy would, on the other hand, have pointed to Louis' unpleasant, irascible disposition, to his cynical, suspicious nature, and to his dangerous ambitions as constituting the basis for their hostility. That the commoners in whose society Louis mixed never accorded him complete acceptance either would appear to bear out the validity of some of this indictment. They shared the mistrust felt by the aristocracy. They sensed the fact that his friendship was accidental, that it sprang less from a respect for them than a contempt and fear of his own class. Louis trusted no one, neither father nor wife, nor was any one safe from his venomous tongue. A sneer became him more than a smile, and if he asked about someone it was not sympathy that fathered his concern but search for information he might use to advance his projects. His suspicions grew with his age. The extreme measures he took to protect himself in his favorite castle at Plessis provide a prototype of those that twentieth-century military dictators have found necessary to employ.

This picture shows Louis at his worst and the picture is probably overdrawn. In his day most writers who dealt with his career were Burgundian in sympathy. They hated and feared him, and modern writers have tended to use their accounts without considering the circumstances. They have also failed to judge Louis in the political and social context of his age. They have made much of his cruelty, for example, of the iron cages he had fashioned to keep his political prisoners secure, of the enemies he tortured and hanged. Yet Charles the Rash of Burgundy, Louis' principal opponent, enjoyed the sympathy of both fifteenth-century chroniclers and more modern writers despite the fact that he was at least as cruel as Louis and on occasion vented his spleen on helpless men and women, something Louis never did. If Louis employed torture, so did other kings of the period. If he chained his prisoners, so did the English captors of Joan of Arc. If he used iron cages, these actually amounted to small rooms, their only fearsome feature being the virtual impossibility of the prisoners breaking out. That is why Louis used iron, although he undoubtedly hoped that word of these adamantine prisons would discourage potential traitors from carrying out their designs.

The story of Louis' relations with members of his immediate family is not a pleasant one. The annals of kings tell of many unnatural sons but of only a few who joined conspiracies to unseat their fathers as did Louis. His father, Charles VII, even feared his son it is said, and the thought that his son may have poisoned him may have darkened the last months of his life. This may be said in extenuation of Louis' behavior toward his father: Charles had done little to earn his son's affection or respect. Louis was, furthermore, convinced, and with reason, that he could serve France more effectively than could his father in the latter's declining years. There is nothing, however, to offer in extenuation of the cruel manner Louis treated his first wife Margaret of Scotland, as we shall see. Most shocking to modern sensibilities is the heartless manner he forced the duke of Orléans to marry his hunchbacked daughter, Jeanne, whose deformity he was sure would prevent her having children and thus cause the duke's fief to escheat to the crown. "The children they will have," he is said to have observed with a chuckle over his diabolical cleverness, "won't cost them much to raise."

In an age when political expediency, not romance, dictated marriages among the nobility, contemporary opinion would have excused Louis the two or more mistresses he had, particularly since these appear during the interval between his two marriages. In the illegitimate daughters he sired he appears to have taken a truly paternal interest and when they grew up arranged advantageous marriages for them. He had six legitimate children of whom three survived. We are told of the great joy he experienced at the birth of these children and how he sat in disconsolate silence for six hours when his one-year-old son François died. It was in order to comfort his wife on this unhappy occasion that Louis is supposed to have promised her to remain faithful, a promise Commines says he kept. Louis gave special attention to the rearing and education of the dauphin. The boy appears to have had a weak constitution, which may have been the reason why Louis gave instructions that he was not to learn how to hunt. Louis considered that a dangerous sport.

Even Louis' enemies, including Thomas Basin, the bishop of Lisieux, whom he eventually exiled, admitted that the king was not all bad. One virtue that all granted him was his courage on the battlefield. Commines declares Louis' army would have suffered defeat at the battle of Montlhéry had the king not mingled with his men and urged them to continue the fight. In the attack on the fortress of Dambach in Alsace he risked his life and suffered the shot of an arrow bolt directly through his knee. From his youth he showed an enormous capacity for work which he maintained until the end of his life. Seldom, if ever, did he permit personal comfort or pleasure to call him from his responsibilities, not even his one passion for hunting. In the execution of his plans he displayed consummate patience and persistence and a methodical fastidiousness that left no room for chance. No man could read the minds of his opponents more successfully. His skill in this respect he attributed to his reading of history which, according to his adviser, held the master key to the variety of frauds and deceits perpetrated by men since the beginning of time. No one matched Louis' skill in the art (or science) of diplomacy, and no one, affirmed Commines, "was more capable of extricating himself from a difficult situation in time of adversity." Louis' skill in diplomacy and the expectation of his ultimate triumph over his enemies was what presumably induced Commines to leave the service of the duke of Burgundy for that of the king.

Nothing so pleased Louis as to engage in intrigue and embroil his enemies in webs he had woven. Quite apt was the Burgundian poet Molinet's reference to him as "the universal spider." Commines tells of one trap Louis set for a man he had long hoped to ensnare. This was Louis of Luxembourg, count of Saint-Pol and constable of France, one of the more slippery nobles who sought to outwit the king. The wily Saint-Pol occupied strategic territories to the east of Paris and in an effort to exploit that position soon found himself engaged in the dangerous game of keeping the kings of France and England and the duke of Burgundy all convinced that he was their loyal ally. How the constable hoped to dupe such a master spy as Louis appears incredible. At any rate, the constable came to feel in time that some fence-mending had become necessary in order to disabuse Louis of any possible suspicion he might be harboring concerning his fidelity, so he sent an embassy, headed by one Louis de Sainville, to convince the king of his complete devotion. Louis happened to have with him at the time an old Burgundian nobleman, the Seigneur de Contay, who was a friend of the duke of Burgundy. So he arranged to have the seigneur and Commines slip behind a screen in the room where he planned to receive Saint-Pol's emissary to hear what the latter had to say.

When Louis de Sainville was ushered into Louis' presence, he found him sitting on a stool immediately in front of the screen, a spot Louis had chosen to make certain the aged seigneur would hear everything. The emissary convinced that only he and Louis were present in the room began to speak quite freely, telling Louis how Saint-Pol had recently sent him to the duke of Burgundy to persuade him to abandon his alliance with the English, how the duke had stormed and ranted in his fury, and how he had villified Edward, referring to him as "that Blayburgh" (rumor among the enemies of Edward had it that he was a bastard and that his real father was a common archer by the name of Blayburgh). "And to please the king the more, as he thought, when he spoke these words, the said Louis de Sainville, in imitation of the duke of Burgundy, stamped his foot, swore by St. George . . . with as many invectives besides, as could possibly be used against any man. The king pretended to be highly pleased at the relation, and desired him to tell him it over again and to raise his voice, pretending that he was somewhat deaf; which de Sainville was quite ready to do, beginning again and acting it all out with good will." Some time later the irate duke of Burgundy had the satisfaction of handing Saint-Pol, who had taken refuge in his dominions, over to Louis who had him beheaded.

Louis was undeniably a hard man. Yet here and there, almost hidden among records of weightier matters, appear references to incidents that reveal the presence of warmth underneath his unattractive exterior. If, as Molinet observed, Louis would rather lose 10,000 gold crowns than one archer, that might reflect less personal consideration for his men on the king's part than sound policy. That Louis also rehabilitated the family of Jacques Cœur, the wealthy merchant prince, who had been jailed and his property confiscated on the preposterous charge of poisoning Agnès Sorel and the more plausible one of malfeasance— this, too, a skeptic might count simply as consistent with Louis' policy when he came to the throne of reversing everything his father had done.

Still there is no justice in denying the genuineness of the alms Louis gave to the people of Languedoc and the Loire Valley when they suffered loss of their harvests, or his charity to the lepers of Amboise, Cléry, and Orléans, or the money he presented poor girls so that they might provide themselves with wedding gown or dowry. When Louis was out hunting and his hounds killed some peasant's lambs or geese, he paid generous damages, the kind of consideration few nobles would have felt worthy of their notice. Louis arranged for an archer who had lost a leg in his service to continue on garrison duty as a crossbowman in order to provide him a livelihood. The story is told how on one occasion when Louis was on his knees in his favorite church at Cléry, a clerk interrupted his prayers to tell him how he had been released from prison to raise 1500 livres he owed, but that his jailers were about to apprehend him for his failure to do so. Whereupon the king congratulated him on his fortune in coming to him at that precise moment when he himself was asking God to do him a favor. When on his arrival in Toulouse in 1463 he chanced to meet several men being marched off to the gallows, he pardoned them. His payment of 50,000 crowns to Edward IV for the ransom of Margaret of Anjou, ex-queen of England (more below) when she could no longer be of any use to him, was a true act of charity.

Louis' one passion, apart from his driving ambition to establish royal power throughout France, was the chase. That he constantly indulged in that sport strikes one as remarkable, even though hunting was first in popularity among the recreations of the male members of medieval aristocracy. For Louis had no time, it seems, for anything but work, and especially none for the traditional diversions of the social elite. Yet it was not unusual for him to go off for a day or two of hunting even in the midst of important negotiations, although one may assume that he was able to convince himself on those occasions that a slight delay might work to his advantage at the bargaining table. Louis would even drag himself out of a sickbed early in the morning to be off after stag and wild boar when any normal person would have heeded his physician and rested. The reader is torn between laughter and sympathy to learn how in Louis' last illness, when even he was too incapacitated to hunt, he had dogs and cats chase rats and mice around his room while he watched the excitement from his sickbed.

Louis' love for hunting dogs provided nobles and foreign princes the one chink in the king's armor through which they might get to this most impervious of men. Where other kings warmed to presents of jewelry or weapons, Louis welcomed dogs. Lorenzo the Magnificent sent him sporting dogs, as did the king of Scotland and the English ambassador. Had Charles the Rash, the duke of Burgundy, been as much a dog fancier as Louis, perhaps the two might have been friends despite Louis' determination to unite France at Charles' expense. When one of Louis' favorite hunting dogs fell ill, he made votive offerings to St. Hubert, the patron of medieval hunters. Contemporaries found this less curious than the strict injunction Louis gave to the aristocracy to stay out of the royal forests. He may have wanted the game for himself or he may have wished to protect the poor peasantry who watched helplessly as the aristocratic huntsmen trampled their crops. Louis even liked to raise dogs, scarcely a proper avocation for a distinguished medieval monarch, and for his kennels he collected all the different kinds of breeds he could acquire. For his tomb he arranged to have an effigy carved of himself, showing him in a kneeling position, dressed in hunting garb, with sword, horn, and rabbit dog at his side, with his eyes fixed on the statue of the Virgin. Odd though such a pose might be, in no other could the Virgin have found less pretense.

Louis also collected birds and maintained a huge aviary near his castle at Plessis. There the privileged visitor might find magpies, canaries, goldfinches, linnets, larks, eagles, owls, pheasants, herons, crows, ostriches, and, of course, falcons. Louis would even take birds with him on his travels and would permit them to fly around in his chambers, much to the annoyance of his host. He also maintained a zoo where he kept a lion, leopard, elephants, camels, and monkeys. Another medieval king, Frederick II, kept a zoo and with Louis, liked dogs. It has been said that some men who have a fondness for dogs show less affection than they should for their wives. If this is true, both Frederick II and Louis XI are cases in point.

Among the astonishing facets of Louis' life is his devotion to religion, that is, astonishing to the reader who ordinarily learns only of the king's cruelty and the utter unscrupulousness with which he sought to attain his objectives. Yet a cursory glance at his devotions suggests a miniature St. Louis. Each day he attended Mass and recited the Hours. On Wednesdays and Fridays he abstained from meat. Like Louis IX he washed the feet of the poor on Maundy Thursday. When on his travels about France he came to a town, it was his wont to go directly to the church where he would attend Mass or take part in the divine office. He was generous in his contributions for the construction and repair of churches for which there was a great need following the devastation of the Hundred Years' War. Like his contemporaries, Louis showed excessive interest in relics, frequently made pilgrimages to shrines within the limits of France, and set up chantries for his spiritual welfare after death. One tradition that carries back to him in those parts of France where some of the pious customs of the Middle Ages still linger, is the recitation of the angelus at noon. This devotion Louis ordered established throughout France in 1470 when the Virgin answered his prayers and blessed his wife with a son.

Most writers who have commented on Louis' piety have dismissed it as mere superstition. Even the archbishop of Tours attacked him for giving so lavishly to churches when God would have been better pleased had he reduced proportionately the heavy burden of taxation he had imposed upon the people. In 1482, the year before he died, his offerings are supposed to have exceeded 12,000 livres. That so parsimonious a person as Louis ordinarily was could expend such huge amounts for spiritual favors, demonstrates at least the depth of his faith. Critics have accused Louis of placing his dealings with heaven and the saints on a profit-loss basis, that he prayed and made votive offerings as a kind of enticement to procure material blessings, that he discontinued praying to those saints who appeared unresponsive, and that he even asked divine assistance for schemes that were scarcely commendable.

Louis prayed like most medieval Christians, more frequently for God's help in attaining some material end, *e.g.* good health or victory, than he did for the advancement of the City of God or the correction of his own moral deficiencies. In common with late medieval Christians, he had great devotion to the Virgin Mary and credited her favor with his successes over his enemies. The victory he gained as dauphin over the English at Dieppe, for example, he laid to her intercession, and to show his gratitude rebuilt the church at Cléry which was dedicated to her. In accord with medieval tradition, he ordered Te Deums and processions in thanksgiving to God when he gained a victory or negotiated a favorable treaty. A medieval theologian could question the purity of his faith, not its existence, although he might smile at the king's naïveté in arranging to have his tomb set at an angle in the church of Cléry so that the Virgin could keep his effigy constantly in her gaze from her niche in the wall.

For the greater part of his life, Louis suffered poor health. Indeed, a list of his ailments would appear to qualify him as a fit study for the medical profession. From his youth he suffered from hemorrhoids, was afflicted at irregular intervals with gout, and for most of his life with a painful skin disorder that he imagined to be leprosy. He suffered recurrent fevers and stomach ailments and in time appears to have contracted epilepsy. Though Louis was inclined to be skeptical of men's abilities and even their intentions in ordinary affairs, he never lost his faith in his physicians in spite of their inability to help him. The one man to whom he listened in his last years, from whom he even accepted a measure of abuse, was his favorite physician Jacques Coitier.

Among the unusual remedies Louis sought for his catalog of ailments—at least they sound bizarre today—was that of bathing in the blood of turtles. The times held this to be an effective cure for epilepsy. One reads that Louis may have even drunk the blood of infants, presumably to cure the same malady! This remedy sounds immeasurably worse than it should. If he actually did this, we may be sure the infants were not slain, only bled, and we should also remember that bloodletting was so common a practice in the Middle Ages as to pass as routine. Another measure recommended for epileptics was that of avoiding sleep, and for this purpose shepherds were brought in to play their pipes under the king's window. Contemporaries mention that in other instances his head was chilled in order to provoke sleep and that he also suffered himself to be cauterized with red hot irons. Under the circumstances, even the religious cynic would have commended Louis for placing greater faith in prayer for recovering his health as at least a less painful means. Between Louis' bodily ailments and the long, dangerous contests he had with his nobles, one can accept the truth of Commines' observation: "I think that if all the good days he enjoyed during his life, days in which he had more pleasure and happiness than hard work and trouble, were carefully numbered, they would be found to be few; I believe he would find twenty of worry and travail for one of ease and pleasure."

Despite Louis' many maladies, no French monarch traveled so much since the time of Charlemagne nor worked so industriously at the business of being king. The operations he carried on in his task of building royal power resembled those of a general who conducts an active campaign along a long front. He traveled unceasingly, up, down, and across France, stopping at some inn when he needed food, sleeping where few kings would have stooped to stay, and up and going the next morning before the roosters were sufficiently awake to crow. So fast did he move and so frequently without apparent itinerary, that emissaries had as much difficulty tracking him down as they did in catching him. One clerk of the bishop of Evreux was sixty days in locating him. All the while, whether at home or on his travels, he carried on a furious correspondence with the army of agents he had scattered about France and in the countries along France's frontiers.

Although Louis selected his emissaries with extreme care, even his most successful agent could not match him in making friends or in seducing enemies. "He was above all the seducer with the sweet, honeyed voice," never pompous or arrogant, always treating foreign emissaries as acquaintances, calling them by their first names, and offering money to those he felt he could buy. Two bourgeois ambassadors from Catalonia he embraced as though they were his peers. When deputies arrived from Amiens in 1473, his words of greeting were: "I wish to speak to my good friends of Amiens not as ambassadors, but as my friends." The best of food and lodging was provided his foreign guests. Where presents and money might gain him his end, he was liberal in their use, a method of buying favor he found more effective and less expensive than the elaborate fêtes and displays most princes put on for visiting dignitaries. For in Louis' judgment, money was the one, universal solvent, and no one could blame him for being cynical, since his experience had demonstrated how ready most people were to sell their principles for a fee.

Louis revealed his true statesmanship in his anxiety to secure the most competent counselors and officials. Though he was as industrious and as ubiquitous as any French king of the Middle Ages, he realized that the efficient administration of a country as large and populous as France required the assistance of able and faithful public servants. He looked everywhere for talent, both among the aristocracy and bourgeoisie, even in places where he should not have looked. For he was not squeamish about a man's past or even what his private conduct might continue to be, so long as he served him well. One of his advisers, Jean de Doyat, was an embezzler, another, Ambroise de Cambrai, had forged a papal bull. Louis' first grave mistake, as he later admitted, was in dismissing his father's trusted counselors. He eventually took most of them back into the royal service. As Commines writes: "And for such as he had discarded in time of peace or prosperity, he paid dear, when he had occasion for them, to recover them again; but when he had once reconciled them, he retained no enmity towards them for what had passed. . . ." Commines only entered Louis' service after the king's repeated attempts to lure him away from the duke of Burgundy, for Louis was most persistent, "the most diligent and indefatigable to win over any man to his side that he thought capable of doing him either mischief or good. . . ."

CHARLES AS DAUPHIN

Louis was born 3 July 1423 at Bourges where his father, still only dauphin, had fled after the English and Burgundians had occupied Paris. Not much is known of Louis' early years. His parents gave him little personal attention, so he grew up in the care of servants in a lonely establishment of his own. His father entrusted his education to John Gerson, the distinguished chancellor of the university of Paris, who drew up the course of study Louis was to follow. Gerson's friend, Jean Majoris, a master of arts and licentiate in canon law, taught Louis his seven liberal arts and also supervised his religious instruction. Of particular interest did Louis find the lives of the saints and the history of France and of its early kings as recorded in the chronicles kept by the monks of the abbey of St. Denis. Commines writes commendingly of Louis' education as different from that of most nobles who "are brought up to nothing but to make themselves ridiculous, both in their clothes and their discourse; they have no knowledge of letters . . . no wise man is suffered to come near them to improve their understanding. . . ."

In the world of today, marriage becomes the concern of the young man in his late teens or early twenties. In the Middle Ages a boy's parents, if they were of the nobility, were apt to have picked out a wife for him before he was six. In the case of Louis, his father had decided on a future wife for him when he was five. She was to be Margaret Stuart, daughter of James I of Scotland. At the time Charles' situation was desperate. Only part of the French people accepted his claim to the throne. Burgundy and the northern and western provinces recognized Henry VI of England as their king. Under the circumstances, the Scottish alliance was the best Charles could hope for, although this may sound disparaging to a sturdy nation such as the Scots who had stood long and steadfastly by the side of the French against their common foe, the English.

Margaret was to bring a dowry of 15,000 livres and 6000 men in exchange for the county of Saintonge which was still in English hands. Though the initial treaty had been signed in October 1428 when Charles' situation appeared hopeless, as his fortunes mended after the appearance of Joan of Arc, he permitted the matter of the marriage to lag, as was the way with Charles, and the agreement was only ratified some years later. On 25 June 1436 the marriage of Louis and Margaret was solemnized at Tours in the presence of the archbishop of Reims, and a year later, when Louis was fourteen, it was consummated.

In the long history of unhappy marriages among members of the royalty, this marriage of Louis and Margaret proved one of the most pitiful. Charles and his good-natured wife, Marie of Anjou, were pleased with Margaret, which may have been the only reason Louis had for disliking her. For Margaret was an attractive young woman and had a beautiful face and an amiable disposition. But as Commines says simply, Louis "was married to the daughter of Scotland to his distaste; and as long as she lived he regretted it." Commines might have added that Margaret also regretted the marriage and for much greater reason. The only weeks the lonely miss enjoyed in France were those she spent with the queen prior to the consummation of the marriage. Soon after her marriage, she took to composing verse, probably in order to relieve the dreariness of her existence. Her detractors charged her with spending too many hours at that unhealthy pastime when she should have been sleeping. What may have kept her awake was the knowledge that her suspicious husband had set a spy on her trail, undoubtedly the most despicable thing he ever did. This spy, Jamet de Tillay, manufactured irregularities his master expected him to discover, the result being growing despondency on Margaret's part and growing resentment on Louis' when nothing really incriminating turned up. (She was extravagant, but given Louis' penurious disposition, what wife would not have seemed so!) Because Margaret had nothing to live for and was barren in addition, she permitted a heavy cold or pleurisy to carry her off at the age of twenty-one. Louis' conduct in the entire affair appears unusually shabby, and those writers who have attempted to portray his life in the best possible light, have made no attempt to gloss over his baseness in this episode.

Shortly after Louis' marriage, his father Charles VII had him join him in the campaign then under way against the English in Guienne. This war had been in progress longer than anyone could remember, ninety-nine years in fact, as modern historians reckon the Hundred Years' War (1337–1453), and it had still seventeen years to run before the English would be expelled from France. Guienne, that part of France the king of England had ruled in 1337 as a vassal of the king of France, was the root cause for this most tragic of medieval wars. For an English king to be a duke of Guienne and therefore a vassal of the king of France had been tolerable back in the feudal age. In the fourteenth century when feudalism and its conventions were rapidly disappearing, it was no longer admissible. The trend toward centralization in the late Middle Ages left any state and its king increasingly hostile to the acceptance of such foreign-held fiefs. For this reason the French wanted this English duke, his English officials, and soldiery ousted ere they made permanent their hold on the country. The English on their part felt they must make good their possession of Guienne before the French forced them out. Because France was many times wealthier in resources and population than England and because logistics were in her favor, she should have won the war in short order. The reverse was the case. Fortune in one of her most capricious moods smiled rather on the smaller English armies at Crécy (1346), Poitiers (1356), and Agincourt (1415), and in those encounters had given the English smashing victories over French forces that were considerably larger. Scholars have attributed the debacle of French arms to the consummate overconfidence of their leaders, to their consequent indifference to military tactics, and to the longbowmen upon which the English, in their desperation, had to depend.

Although the English won these great battles, they lacked the money and men necessary to nailing down their victories. For this reason the war had continued on and on, its origin so far back in time no one could remember when it had started. There were, fortunately, extended periods when fighting lapsed, for which the English at least could be grateful. For the French countryside, these intervals of peace had brought little respite. When war raged, both French and English soldiers lived off the country. When fighting ceased, the French and their unpaid mercenaries continued to live off the country. Our modern image of a soldier is that of a young man who serves his country in a reasonably unselfish fashion and who observes the rules of humane warfare. Men-at-arms in the late Middle Ages were ordinarily mercenaries or at least adventurers; they fought for pay and for loot. As some writer has graphically painted their character, they represented "the sweepings of the streets and prisons of Europe."

Because of the bankruptcy of the French government and its inability to maintain law and order, its soldiers continued to live off the countryside, to loot, burn, and pillage even when hostilities had temporarily ceased. After a battle they simply turned marauders. Because they had a price on their heads and could expect no mercy if caught, they gave none. Their names reveal their ferocity. One group bore the name of *écorcheurs* (or flayers). They stripped people to their skins. Another group of marauders were the *tard-venus* (late-comers), who followed in the wake of earlier human wolves to pick up or destroy what might have remained. During these terrible years the word brigand acquired the connotation it has today. It derives its meaning from the brigade or company of which these men were members, whether legitimately fighting a battle or looting the countryside. There was no getting rid of these marauders except to pay them to leave, when they would go elsewhere to pillage. Hardly any part of France remained unscathed. The horror of the situation lends credence to the answer Joan of Arc gave her inquisitors at her trial when they asked her why God should have sent her to help the French. Her answer was, "Because He had pity on them."

France's misery did not all stem from military catastrophes. Part of its origin was accidental, namely, the mental illness of Charles VI (1380–1422) whose periodic fits of madness kept the government in a constant state of turmoil. The antagonism already existing between the two powerful lords, Louis, duke of Orléans, a brother of Charles VI on the one hand, and Philip, duke of Burgundy, an uncle of Charles VI on the other, developed quickly, once he became ill, into a rough contest between them for control of the crown. When Philip died in 1404 his even more aggressive son, John the Fearless, assumed his ambitions and his hatred for the duke of Orléans. On the evening of 25 November 1407, a band of assassins in the pay of John fell upon Louis of Orléans and murdered him. This brutal act did not end the feud, it only embittered it. The slain duke's son married the daughter of the count of Armagnac, a powerful lord in southern France, who shortly had a strong group of ambitious nobles behind him, eager to challenge the bid of Burgundy for supremacy. When virtual civil war broke out in 1411, John the Fearless opened negotiations with the English, which after Henry V's brilliant victory at Agincourt, almost led to an alliance. What caused John the Fearless to hesitate was his reluctance to ally himself with the English, France's ancient foe. On 10 September 1419 he went to meet the dauphin, the future Charles VII, to discuss the possibility of a reconciliation. As he knelt before the dauphin on the bridge of Montereau to make his obeisance, several "unknown" assailants rushed in and slew him. His indignant son Philip (the Good), the new duke of Burgundy, promptly concluded the Treaty of Troyes with the English (1420). This treaty provided for the disinheritance of the dauphin Charles, for the appointment of Henry V of England as regent for the mad Charles VI, and for the marriage of Henry to Catherine, the daughter of Charles. The succession to the thrones of both France and England, following the death of Charles VI, was to pass to Henry V and his children by Catherine.

The only people to protest the Treaty of Troyes were the dauphin Charles who had fled to Bourges and the Armagnac group in the south who continued their defiance of the English and the Burgundians. In 1422 both Henry V and Charles VI died. Charles' death was a blessing, that of Henry a calamity. While Henry's brother, the duke of Bedford, who assumed the regency in the name of the eight-months-old Henry VI, proved himself a capable administrator, he could not prevent the rise of factions in England which seriously crippled English war efforts. For the moment he continued to gain victories over the dwindling numbers of soldiers still fighting the cause of the dauphin. In the fall of 1428 the English began the siege of Orléans, the key to what remained of the dauphin's France. Even the dauphin was on the point of abandoning the struggle. His cause appeared hopeless; he was even beginning to entertain doubts concerning the legitimacy of his birth and his rights to the throne. It was at this point, when French fortunes had reached their nadir, that Joan of Arc appeared, assured Charles that God wanted him to be king, drove the English from Orléans, and cleared the way to Reims where the dauphin was crowned King Charles VII on 18 July 1429. The year following, the Burgundians captured Joan, sold her to the English for a king's ransom, and the English burned her at the stake as a witch.

The English might burn Joan; the nationalism she had stirred among the French they could not extinguish. Now the fortunes of war swung to the side of the French. Nothing seemed to go right for the English. As they suffered reverse upon reverse, the duke of Burgundy began to ask himself whether he had done the wise, even honorable, thing in allying himself with the English. A week after Bedford died in May 1435, Charles VII and Philip, duke of Burgundy, ratified the Treaty of Arras. This agreement took Burgundy out of the war. Charles denied any complicity in the murder of the duke's father (John the Fearless), promised to hunt down the murderers, agreed to dispense Philip from doing homage for Burgundy, and turned over to him a number of counties and towns, above all the towns that lay on either side of the Somme and between the Somme and Flanders. Charles did retain the right to redeem these towns for the sum of 400,000 gold crowns. It was the year after the ratification of this treaty in 1435, that Charles sent for his son Louis and directed him to join in the campaign against the English in Guienne.

The young Louis took this campaigning most seriously, more seriously perhaps than his father wished. He asked and received command of the military operations in the Upper Loire Valley against Château-Landon. When his troops captured the fortress, Louis in his youthful exuberance was for executing all the French and English he had captured and only with difficulty was prevailed upon not to issue those orders. From there he accompanied Charles to Paris whose cold welcome he never forgot. Years of English and Burgundian rule and recurrent bloody riots and rebellions had benumbed the townspeople. They did not quite know what to think of Charles and the dauphin. Charles then assigned Louis the pacification of Languedoc. Here for the first time the young man demonstrated his talent for forcing taxes from estates and towns that had sworn not to give another sou. This money assured him success. He used it to buy off those *routiers,* mostly marauders, who would accept his money. Those who refused, he destroyed. Within a few months he had given Languedoc the first peace that part of France had known in generations. Then his father sent him into Poitou where he repeated the measures he had employed in Languedoc and with the same success.

Now Louis involved himself in a second disgraceful episode. (The first concerning his wife Margaret was still in progress.) In 1439 Louis gave ear to the treasonable plans several lords had hatched to overthrow Charles and put him in his father's place. Charles' continued success against the English had made these lords uneasy. They feared that in a short time the king would have grown so powerful as to be able to turn against them and force them into submission. Like most feudal vassals, they were willing to respect their oaths of fealty to Charles up to a point, to the point where their own autonomy appeared endangered. Then neither considerations of honor or of loyalty to France would prevent their conspiring against the king, even with a foreign foe like the English if necessary. By the late 1430s it had become the conviction of these powerful vassals, notably the count of Alençon and the dukes of Bourbon and Brittany, that any further successes by Charles would threaten their own positions. He had already forbidden them to maintain companies of their own soldiers; his next move would be to humble them.

Early in 1440 the revolt known as the *Praguerie* jelled. The duke of Bourbon and count of Alençon, who had assumed its direction, had no difficulty convincing Louis that he would make a far better king than his aging father. Charles VII had some knowledge of what was afoot. At the first overt act of the conspirators, he moved with a speed he had never shown when Joan of Arc was alive. Upon his appeal, the towns flocked to his support. They had long memories of the anarchy, devastation, and bloodshed that feudal supremacy had meant. Fortress after fortress fell quickly to the king's armies, and within a few weeks the rebels were left no alternative but to submit. Charles proved reasonable. Since his own son was so deeply involved, he could scarcely have done otherwise. Three times the duke of Bourbon and Louis knelt before him to ask his forgiveness. Louis also asked pardon for his accomplices; he had promised them this, he informed his father. But Charles refused to extend them his pardon, told Louis he had no right to have made such a commitment, and granted him leave to go if he chose. There were other princes of the blood, he warned him, who would readily take his place as heir apparent. In the end Louis submitted, but his father thought it prudent to assign him the province of Dauphiné to give him something to keep him out of mischief.

For the moment, Louis left Dauphiné to his and the king's agents while he continued his campaigning against the English and against the marauders that operated in their wake. The *routiers* he found in Champagne he defeated and disarmed, their leaders he executed. Then he hurried to Dieppe which was under heavy English attack. Here he personally led the successful assault on the enemy fortress that was throttling the city. Next he moved southward against the rebellious nobles in Toulouse. He captured their leader, the count of Armagnac, and hurried him off to prison in Carcassonne. On his last assignment, during this period of his apprenticeship as it were, he led an army composed principally of freebooters to assist the emperor of Germany against the Swiss who were attacking Zurich. Here in the siege of Dambach he received a painful wound when an archer shot an arrow through his knee. When he returned to France, he left the greater part of his force of outlaws in Alsace.

This was 1446, the year Charles VII hurried him off without further ado to Dauphiné. His father had caught him again at his game of plotting. For the next ten years Louis devoted himself to the task of ruling his appanage. The ministers his father had given him he replaced with men of his own choice whom he drew for the most part from the petty nobility. He forced all feudal lords of the area to do homage and to pay aids, including several bishops who had always considered themselves independent. He recruited an army of his own by offering some captains exemption from taxes, others patents of nobility. He coined money, levied taxes, and created a *parlement*. In the interest of industry and commerce, he ordered the repair of roads, established a number of fairs, reduced imposts on goods to facilitate their movement, and extended protection to Jewish bankers. In other efforts to modernize Dauphiné he founded a university at Valence with all four faculties of arts, law, medicine, and theology. Withal he found time to indulge his passion for hunting, and he also found himself two mistresses. If only his father had died and let him be king, his satisfaction would have been complete.

During these ten years in Dauphiné, Louis never forgot what his future role would be. Against the day when he would be king, he began courting the friendship of the duke of Savoy, his neighbor to the east. Savoy blocked the road to Italy. In order to earn the duke's friendship, Louis agreed to a treaty which provided free trade between the two provinces, the extradition of criminals, and mutual military assistance. Louis was also interested in the duke's daughter, at least when he learned the size of the dowry her father had promised to give her. But when Louis broached the matter of this marriage to Charles VII, his father would have nothing of it. France was already allied with Savoy, he explained; furthermore, Louis could make a more advantageous marriage with a Portuguese or Hungarian princess. Louis was adamant, however, and since he was already almost twenty-eight years old, modern opinion for once would be on his side. So in 1451, despite his father's objections, he married Charlotte. From now on his relations with his father deteriorated rapidly. Charles did not trust his son. He had again discovered evidence of his conspiring with the duke of Burgundy and the count of Alençon. As a warning to Louis he dispatched troops to Lyons, a city on the border of Dauphiné. A year later, in August 1456, Louis abruptly left Dauphiné and fled to Burgundy. In a message to his father he explained that he had learned the duke of Burgundy was planning to lead an army against the Turks and that he was going to Burgundy to join him on the crusade!

Philip the Good, the duke of Burgundy to whose protection Louis had fled, was Louis' uncle. His first wife, Michelle, had been Charles VII's sister. When he learned of Louis' arrival in Louvain, he sent his son Charles (the Rash) to bid him welcome. Then he waited for word from Charles VII, but none came. So after some hesitation, since he did not wish to anger the king, he decided to give the fleeing Louis a haven, assigned him the castle of Genappe together with a handsome pension of 36,000 francs. Both he and his duchess sought to make the dauphin's stay pleasant, while their son, the young Charles, who was ten years Louis' junior, accompanied him on his hunting expeditions. When Charles' wife bore a daughter, Mary of Burgundy, Louis served as godfather. He also acted as conciliator between Philip who had an evil temper and his son Charles whose was equally bad. A few months after his arrival in Burgundy, he sent for his wife Charlotte who was now of canonical age. In due time she bore him a boy whom they baptized Joachim. The child lived just a few months. Two years later Charlotte bore a daughter, the Anne whom Louis designated as his regent on his deathbed.

Charles VII finally sent Philip a protest over having given his truant son a home, although his objection must have been merely formal. Since he trusted the sixty-year-old duke more than he did most of his vassals, he should have considered Louis safer with him than plotting trouble elsewhere. And it appears that apart from several instances when Philip felt embarrassment over the presence of his distinguished guest, he drew much satisfaction from his role as protector. He felt certain his favor toward his young nephew would surely bring rich dividends the day Louis would become king. No doubt he would then assume the position of first royal counselor, a role he had expected Charles to have given him following the Treaty of Arras.

That Philip did harbor such sentiments about Louis' future benevolence would alone have confirmed stories about his growing senility. Charles VII who knew Louis' lack of generosity, his ambition, and his covetousness as only a father can know his son, must have smiled to himself over Philip's fatuity. The observation he is supposed to have made on this matter may have been apocryphal, though Charles was perceptive enough to have made it. "My lord of Burgundy," he is said to have declared, "knows little of what he is about, to harbor the fox that will devour his chickens."

Meantime Louis was behaving himself reasonably well, was bearing himself with great consideration toward his host, and was even learning to stomach the rudeness of his cousin Charles. In his *Memoirs* Commines speaks of the disciplinary value this period of exile had for Louis in building his character, "for he was obliged to adjust himself to the humor of those he stood in need of, which singular misfortune taught him." During this period of exile he undertook no overt conspiracy, although he waited with growing impatience the death of his father. Loudly and repeatedly he assured Philip of his profound gratitude to him for his beneficence, while he no doubt was considering all the time the rich, populous cities that graced the duke's expansive domains and the ease with which he would one day take these from his slow-witted son Charles. The astrologers and the spies he had in his pay in his father's palace assured him Charles' condition was bad and that the king could not hold on much longer. (Charles' malady was probably cancer.)

Toward the end he refused to eat anything, probably because of an infection in his mouth rather than fear of being poisoned. On 17 July 1461 the king's counselors sent a message to Louis to inform him of the imminence of his father's death. Even before death finally came on 22 July, Louis was on his way to Reims for his coronation.

Louis had waited a very long time for this coronation, although not for the pomp and fêtes that accompanied it. He would be done with such pageantry as quickly as possible. So he asked Philip, than whom there was no more magnificent lord in Western Europe nor one with a greater passion for display, not to celebrate the event with excessive solemnity, but the duke refused. The coronation was to be as much his day as Louis'. He too had been looking forward a long time to this event as the day when, as favorite uncle of the new king, he would assume the leadership in French affairs to which his wealth and might, his loyalty to the crown and to the dauphin, and the traditional eminence of Burgundy entitled him. The circumstances of the coronation would make that leadership manifest. He brought with him some 4000 troops, a veritable army of attendants, with the gentlemen of his household garbed in the most resplendent of uniforms, while a long baggage train of wagons followed behind bearing his horde of gold and silver plate and many barrels of Burgundy's best wines to give all good men cheer. He himself was fitted out in rich black velvet studded with rubies, while the white horse he rode carried a small fortune in gold trappings and precious stones. His son Charles was dressed in crimson velvet. There was no lord, least of all Louis, who approached the splendor of the duke of Burgundy and his court.

On the evening before the coronation Louis entered Reims dressed in the red and white satin of the French royal house. He stopped at the cathedral for a brief prayer, then repaired to the palace, but returned to the cathedral at midnight where he remained at his prayers until five. Then he returned to the palace and slept until eight, when he rose to prepare himself for the coronation. The ceremonies began at nine. Their most solemn moment came when Louis, stripped to his waist, received the holy oils on his eyes, mouth, navel, armpits, shoulders, and loins. Then he was clothed in his coronation robes, took his seat on the throne, whereupon the duke of Burgundy, as *doyen* of the French vassals, placed the great crown upon his head and called out: "Long live the king! Mountjoy Saint Denis!" The crowd immediately took up the cry and added their "Noel!" after which the festivities got under way.

Louis had had enough. He excused himself from most of the events and banquets celebrating the event and, already that afternoon, got down to the hard business of governing. To others, especially to the duke of Burgundy, he would leave the pomp and circumstance they so much enjoyed. He had a different sense of values.

LOUIS' EARLY CAREER

The accession of a new ruler usually brings change. In this respect Louis' accession set no precedent. The degree to which he dismissed his father's officials, however, the grounds he employed to justify their dismissal, and the manner of men he selected to serve him in their place were unusual. In view of Louis' aversion to his father and his policies, it was generally assumed that his accession would bring extensive changes in administrative personnel. "From the beginning," wrote Commines, "he thought only of revenge." Philip, duke of Burgundy, sensed what was coming and at the coronation banquet asked Louis to do what most new kings did on such occasions, which was to extend a pardon to his enemies. Louis said he was willing to forgive all save seven persons, although he did not tell the duke which seven he had in mind. If he actually planned to punish just seven, these surely included Pierre de Brézé and Antoine de Chabannes, both of them counselors who had served Charles VII faithfully and efficiently. That they had been loyal to his father was cause enough in Louis' judgment for their removal, although Antoine de Chabannes on one occasion had actually defied him in the presence of the king. Louis had charged Chabannes with having given him treasonable advice only to have Chabannes flatly deny the charge to his face. Louis ordered both Brézé and Chabannes outlawed. They were seized and imprisoned and their property confiscated along with the possessions of several of Charles' other counselors. Among the beneficiaries of their impoverishment were the children of Jacques Cœur.

If loyal service to Louis' father might condemn an official to dismissal, the converse was also true. Several of the men Louis took into his service could claim little qualification other than that they were in Charles' disfavor. For chancellor Louis selected Pierre de Morvilliers, a man Charles had expelled from *parlement* for corruption. As first chamberlain and marshal he appointed Jean de Lescun, known as the Bastard of Armagnac, who had conspired with him against his father. Another trusted adviser was Jean de Doyat, an embezzler, while his most trusted confidant was his favorite barber, known popularly as Olivier le Daim (the Evil) whom he ennobled and permitted to grow enormously wealthy by means ordinarily disreputable. His new admiral was Jean de Montauban who once had captained a gang of marauders. Least reprehensible of Louis' appointees were the clerks who had served him in Dauphiné, whom he raised to responsible positions as bailiffs and seneschals. As noted above, Louis shortly realized his folly in dismissing his father's counselors and eventually took most of them back into his service.

Louis' appointments created uneasiness which other of his first moves did not allay. Here and there he did alleviate the burden of the taille and salt tax, but this he did in a haphazard manner and only for a brief time since the enormous sums he soon found himself in need of in order to redeem the Somme towns, necessitated a general increase in taxation. The net result was confusion and resentment. The clergy and hierarchy, too, were uneasy despite his abrogation of the Pragmatic Sanction of Bourges (more later). He ordered them to file an inventory of their goods under pain of confiscation, while he abolished the general exemption they enjoyed of selling the wine produced on their own lands without paying a tax. The university of Paris resented in its turn the king's foundation of a new university in Bourges.

The nobility was the class for which the accession of Louis boded least good. That he cared nothing for the pomp and glitter of court life, for pageants and fêtes which he considered wasteful of time and money, they already knew. That he did not plan to continue to preside over a brilliant court at the palace became clear when he cut off the pensions of the nobles who were living there. They would have to return to their châteaux where they belonged and where they would cost the crown no money. Louis also ordered the nobility out of the royal forests. Still two lords had reason to welcome his accession. These were the counts of Alençon and Armagnac. Charles VII had had them lodged in prison because of their treasonable behavior, whence Louis promptly released them.

Louis' reign of more than twenty years proved an unusually full one, as one would expect of so ambitious a monarch. Louis insisted on ruling and any medieval king who wished to do more than reign, even as late as the fifteenth century, was likely to have his hands full. Though the virtually independent position that the feudal aristocracy had enjoyed in France in 987 when Hugh Capet was elected had eroded measurably under the persistent assault of the later Capetians, notably Philip Augustus, Louis IX, and Philip IV, a great deal of the progress these kings had achieved in subordinating this aristocracy had been lost during the calamities of the Hundred Years' War when royal power had all but collapsed. Charles VII had managed to bring France out of anarchy and had even expelled the English from France, but he had done little to humble a number of powerful feudatories. On the contrary, his victory had been purchased in large measure by granting the duke of Burgundy an autonomous position. To force Burgundy back under royal authority and to reduce a half-dozen other proud vassals, this was Louis' first ambition when he became king. It would take him a lifetime to accomplish this goal.

His first important act as king was a step in the direction of this objective. In September 1463 he turned over the sum of 400,000 gold crowns to Philip the Good of Burgundy in purchase of the Somme towns. The privilege to do this had been provided by the Treaty of Arras. No one imagined Louis could scrape up the money, but desperation provided the spur. Louis appreciated the critical importance of these towns to France and the equally critical importance of purchasing them without delay. In the hands of the duke of Burgundy they menaced Paris; in his own, they provided Paris an effective barrier against attack from his most dangerous enemy. As long as Burgundy held these towns, Louis would find it impossible to deal authoritatively with his other feudatories since the duke could always be expected to intervene in their behalf. These towns held the key to Louis' future, but he must work fast. Philip was in poor health and aging. Were he to die it would be impossible to secure their purchase since Philip's son Charles (the Rash) was entertaining plans even more ambitious than Louis. He planned to sever all ties between Burgundy and France and to establish Burgundy as an independent, mighty kingdom, even more glorious than it had once been centuries before.

The origins of Burgundy went back far in time, as far back as those of France. Semi-civilized Burgundians and Franks had both crossed into Gaul from Germany and fought the armies of the dying Roman empire. One of the first dates in Burgundian history was A.D. 437, when a Roman army had administered a bloody defeat to the Burgundians, echoes of which slaughter are heard in the German national epic, the *Nibelungenlied*. The Burgundians eventually settled in the area of Lake Geneva and westward into the valley of the Rhone River where they constituted an independent Germanic kingdom until absorbed by the sons of Clovis. Burgundy was part of Charlemagne's empire and when that empire was divided three ways by the Treaty of Verdun in 843, the province was also divided. Part of it, the future duchy of Burgundy, went to form the kingdom of Charles the Bald, the future France. The other part, the later county of Burgundy or Franche-Comté, became part of Lothair's kingdom. Lothair's portion, or what might be called Lotharingia, constituted roughly the block of lands extending north and south between the Rhine and the Rhone rivers and including Belgium, Holland, Luxembourg, Alsace, Lorraine, southeastern France, and Italy. It was this ancient kingdom, minus only Italy, that Charles (the Rash) in his wildest moments hoped to revive, with himself as king.

The duchy of Burgundy continued part of France during the reigns of the Capetians. A branch of the Capetian family actually governed it. Then in 1361 this branch became extinct, whereupon John the Good of France set up Burgundy as an appanage and gave it to his capable son Philip (the Bold) to administer. (By appanage is meant a fief that the king of France gave to one of his younger sons. They might pass the fief on to their heirs but with the provision that it return to the crown when the male line became extinct.) To men who urged the strengthening of royal power, John's act in handing Burgundy over to his son appeared preferable to surrendering it to some alien family, since the royal family would remain in possession. The addition shortly after of Franche-Comté to Burgundy, which the duke would hold as a fief of the Holy Roman Empire smoothed the way for the prominent role Burgundy was destined to play during the next one hundred and fifty years. Overnight Burgundy had become a power and its duke the most powerful of royal feudatories. In time some duke of Burgundy would surely conceive the idea of using this solid, compact territory as the basis for an autonomous state.

For the moment that danger was too remote for anyone to sense, not even Charles V (1364-80), known as the Wise, who encouraged the expansion of Burgundy northward into the Low Countries in order to bar possible English expansion. Through the efforts of Charles V, Burgundy gained several important territories in the north, including Artois and Flanders. During the tragic reign of Charles VI (1380-1422), though France itself hovered on the brink of disintegration, Burgundy acquired additional territories through the aggressive policies of duke Philip the Bold and his son John the Fearless. The real architect of the Burgundian state was, however, Philip the Good, Louis XI's former host and protector.

Philip the Good (1419–67) was a distinguished gentleman, tall, handsome, and powerfully built, at the same time gallant and urbane. For forty years he presided over the most magnificent court in Europe which his patronage to scholars and artists also made the cultural capital of the West. It was only fitting that this near perfect embodiment of the ideals of chivalry, as claimed by his champions, should have founded the most exclusive of all chivalric orders, the Order of the Golden Fleece. Philip's life of pleasure and display made him the idol of the aristocracy. Though he kept a bevy of mistresses about him most of the time, he proved an unusually energetic and capable prince. Had he been in his prime when Louis came to the throne in 1461, the cause of French royal absolutism would have had to wait for a later king.

Philip was even popular with the commoners who filled the large, flourishing cities in his scattered possessions. They too were pleased that he should rule in such magnificence since the prosperity of Burgundy enabled him to maintain a lavish court and still keep taxes at a reasonable level. The murder of his father John the Fearless had forced him into an alliance with the English from which he extricated himself by the Treaty of Arras in 1435. He had never felt comfortable about the English alliance since he considered himself pre-eminently a Frenchman. As his domains continued to swell with the acquisition of Brabant, Hainaut, Luxembourg, Zeeland, and Friesland, his appetite for bigger things seems to have been whetted. Toward the end of his life he was contemplating the acquisition of Champagne, Alsace, and Lorraine. These provinces would give him a continuous block of territory stretching from southern France to the North Sea. This Middle Kingdom between France to the west and Germany to the east, he would some day rule over as king, so he hoped. The neutral position he assumed during the closing campaigns of the Hundred Years' War represented his first step toward independence.

It was with this Philip, prematurely old because of the full life he had led, that Louis negotiated the return of the Somme towns. The king employed as his intermediaries the members of the Croy family which had gained an ascendancy over the duke and whose co-operation Louis very probably purchased. It is possible that Philip permitted himself to be misadvised since he needed money to finance a crusade in which he appears to have been sincerely interested. But Philip's son, Charles (the Rash) was furious over the proposed sale of the cities, and Philip, too, had he not been approaching senility, would surely have seen the folly of the step and have found some way around the provision permitting Louis to purchase them. Too late he realized his mistake, whereupon he dismissed his Croy counselors and handed over the direction of Burgundian affairs to his son. When Philip died on 15 June 1467, this Charles, known in history as both Charles the Bold and Charles the Rash, the least competent of the great dukes of Burgundy, fell heir to his impressive domains and his ambitions.

Charles was now about thirty years of age, physically strong and well-proportioned, though not so handsome and tall as his father. He also lacked his father's attractive personality and his popularity as well, nor could men easily break through the man's melancholic reserve and gain his affection and confidence. Charles did share his father's violent temper, yet unlike his father who was warmhearted, Charles was apt to be cruel and vindictive. Charles' finest qualities were his faithfulness to his wife and his authentic interest in liberal studies. The study of history was his favorite subject and he appears to have found in Alexander the Great the man whose accomplishments he was fated to emulate. There was something prophetic, he thought, about the fact that his father and Alexander's both bore the name Philip. Why should he not also be an empire builder? "Even half of Europe would not have satisfied him," observed the shrewd Commines, who left his service when he saw the tragedy to which Charles' madness would inevitably lead. Of the two titles history has given him, Charles the Rash fits his character the better. He reminds one of a figure from Greek tragedy, a medieval Oedipus as it were, who permitted his mad obstinacy to sweep him to his doom. The wily Louis only speeded his fall.

Charles the Rash was not the only feudatory from whom Louis could expect trouble. To the west was Francis II, duke of Brittany, who had his own army and government. Like Charles, Francis was also an ambitious young man who regarded himself quite as independent as did the duke of Burgundy to the east. At the moment Francis' relations with the English were understandably friendly since England was in the throes of virtual civil war and he had nothing to fear from across the Channel. That circumstance usually guided Brittany's policy. When England had a strong king, Brittany inclined toward the French as the less dangerous of its two powerful neighbors. Now that Louis was king, Francis naturally gravitated toward the English. He barred his territory to Louis' officials, maintained an alliance with the English, and even established an understanding with Charles the Rash. He also infuriated Louis by blocking his attempt to nominate to the abbeys and dioceses of Brittany.

There were other feudatories who were eager to join Charles the Rash and Francis of Brittany against Louis. The duke of Bourbon who dominated the Upper Loire region and Auvergne was his enemy since being deprived of the governorship of Guienne. Louis had also antagonized the powerful houses of Orléans and Anjou by pursuing a policy of friendship toward Francesco Sforza, the duke of Milan, and a policy of neutrality in Italy where Orléans and Anjou had ambitions. In Spain Louis pressed claims based upon his mother's rights as granddaughter of the king of Aragon, and though he managed to secure control of Roussillon and Cerdagne, he also inherited the enmity of dangerous lords south of the Pyrenees.

Louis' fishing in the troubled waters of English politics had also netted him the hostility of Edward IV. What had prompted his interference there was the hope of replacing Edward on the throne with the unfortunate Henry VI who was languishing in the Tower and of getting possession of Calais for himself in return. Henry VI, it will be recalled, was the boy whom Henry V had left to succeed him when he died so prematurely in 1422. The regency that had ruled England during Henry's minority had not worked satisfactorily. When Henry VI assumed control the situation went from bad to worse. In his lucid moments Henry proved too gentle a monarch to deal with England's unruly nobles; when he was insane—he had inherited this malady from his maternal grandfather, Charles VI of France—he was helpless. Two factions struggled for control, the Yorkist and the Lancastrian. When Louis came to the throne, Edward IV, the Yorkist, was on the throne, the Lancastrian Henry VI in the Tower, but Henry's resolute wife Margaret (of Anjou) was in France importuning Louis to intervene. He had finally agreed to do this, at least orally, and this made Edward his foe.

In the spring of 1465 Louis suddenly found himself confronted with a dangerous coalition of nobles who called themselves somewhat generously, the League of the Public Weal. The principal adherents were the embittered feudatories of the houses of Orléans, Brittany, Bourbon, and, above all, of Burgundy. For their official leader they selected Louis' younger brother Charles, the duke of Berry, a sickly, ill-looking, and none too bright young man of eighteen. Until his death, this Charles, wrote Commines, was a tool in the hands of Louis' enemies. When he died a few years later, they accused Louis of poisoning him. Had Charles been of better stuff, had he been something like his brother Louis, for instance, this revolt might have achieved permanent results. What sired it was basically the fear these nobles had of Louis, not so much of what Louis might do to them individually, rather what the fruition of his policies would do to their collective positions. His obvious contempt for their way of life, the measures he had already adopted to restrict their privileges, above all his evident determination and ability to accomplish his principal goal of centralizing the government of France under his authority and of subordinating all French aristocrats to his will—these were the considerations that motivated their revolt.

Despite the sweeping charges the League made against Louis' tyranny which all classes had suffered, so they proclaimed, few individuals or groups rallied to their standards. Even the majority of the members of the aristocracy, particularly those of the petty nobility, saw no point in risking lives and fortunes in a war whose principal benefactors would be the great lords. Three bishops joined the League, one of them the able and courageous bishop of Lisieux, Thomas Basin, who considered Louis a potential tyrant. The other bishops contented themselves with praying for peace. The towns in general (except those in Normandy) supported Louis, and this included Paris which refused to open its gates to the rebels. What proved the major weakness of the League was, however, not lack of popular support but the traditional inability of feudal lords to agree on strategy and on terms. Louis first marched against the duke of Bourbon and would have crushed him completely, but had to hurry to Paris when word reached him that the other rebel leaders were approaching the city. Then Charles the Rash, now given control by his father, foolishly attacked Louis without waiting for the arrival of his allies. The result was a confused and indecisive battle at Montlhéry, just south of Paris. Next when Charles (Louis' brother) and the duke of Brittany did appear, they and the duke of Burgundy could not agree on what concerted action to take. Louis wisely let them argue. The reinforcements he had secured might have given him victory, but he was not one to risk his throne on the outcome of a single battle. He much preferred to negotiate, at which game few could match his talents.

The terms Louis and the rebel feudatories agreed upon at Conflans and finally at St. Maur in October 1465 suggest near complete capitulation on the part of the king. Louis agreed to hand over to his brother Charles the governorship of Normandy. The possession of this province, just across the Channel from England whence they could expect help, was of critical importance in any plan the feudatories might have of permanently crippling Louis. Louis also agreed to appoint as constable of France the count of Saint-Pol who had led part of Charles the Rash's army. And to Charles himself he returned the Somme towns for which he had paid the princely sum of 400,000 gold crowns just nine months before! The extent of Louis' concessions, which also included grants of money or rights to all his foes, appears astonishing. He may have overestimated the strength of his enemies. More probably he doubted the wisdom of staking his future on the uncertain fortunes of war when he could safely temporize. He would make time his ally. Once his enemies had separated, he would proceed to undo the damage they had temporarily done him.

If Louis believed time would destroy the organized opposition of his enemies, he was correct. Almost immediately the duke of Brittany began to quarrel with Charles, the new duke of Normandy, which estrangement Louis promptly exploited by taking back Normandy. As a lesson to future provincials who might join rebellious groups, he purged all Norman officials who had supported the League of Public Weal. Some he exiled, including Thomas Basin, the bishop of Lisieux, others he executed. All suffered confiscation of their possessions. He also had his agents in Burgundy challenge the right of Charles to exercise such powers as raising troops and taxes on the ground that these were royal prerogatives. At the same time he sent emissaries to Liége, a city that had always been restive under Burgundian control, to incite the townspeople to revolt.

For once in his life Charles the Rash demonstrated an ability to do something other than swing a battleaxe. No sooner had he forced Louis to accept his terms at Conflans than he proceeded to negotiate a treaty of alliance with Edward IV. This was not difficult to do following Louis' promise to Margaret that he would help get her husband Henry VI back on the throne. On 3 July 1468 the new Anglo-Burgundian alliance was cemented with the marriage of Charles the Rash to Margaret, the sister of Edward. To Louis this was a setback of major proportions and the blow may have momentarily befuddled him. At any rate his next move, as Commines says, was one of the gravest mistakes he ever made. He decided to go to Péronne (near Amiens) where Charles the Rash was staying to discuss their differences in person. That he traveled into "enemy" territory with a small escort was itself imprudent. What made his act criminally foolish was the near fatal miscalculation he made regarding the ability of his emissaries in Liége to stir up trouble. For scarcely had the somewhat puzzled Charles the Rash opened conversations with Louis, puzzled, that is, over the king's astonishing visit with so few men, than fleeing Burgundian soldiers brought in news of the revolt of Liége, of the massacre of the bishop and many Burgundians, and, worst of all, of the work of Louis' agents who had stirred up the people.

Louis never came so close to destruction. The news of Liége put Charles in one of his greatest furies and for two days he stormed about like a mad man. He ordered the gates of Péronne closed and had his soldiers surround the castle where Louis was lodged. Louis was his prisoner and, for perhaps the first time in his life, Louis was genuinely frightened. In his desperation he turned to the one weapon he had learned resolved most situations, to money. To Cardinal Balue, one of his company, he confided 15,000 gold crowns with instructions to distribute the money where it would do the most good. What Balue kept for himself did only the cardinal some good, but enough passed into the hands of Charles the Rash's counselors to induce them to urge moderation upon the duke. They may have convinced the duke that he could not violate the safe-conduct he had given the king. Commines speaks of a "friend" as having been the principal intermediary, and historians have assumed the friend was none other than Commines himself since it was shortly after this incident that he left the duke's service for Louis. In any event terms between Louis and Charles were finally agreed upon and incorporated in the treaty of Péronne. To mollify the duke Louis agreed to turn over additional cities to add to his domains, to exempt the duke from military service, to give to Charles, Louis' brother who had been driven from Normandy, the county of Champagne instead, and, most onerous of all, to accompany the duke on a punitive expedition against the rebellious people of Liége. As Commines writes, Louis said "yes" to all the duke's demands. He had no choice but eat very humble pie.

About ten days later Louis accompanied Charles and his army to Liége. Since the city's walls had been destroyed some time before in punishment of an earlier revolt, the citizens could offer little resistance. The duke's army seized and executed the leaders of the revolt, then for four days gave the city over to systematic destruction. After burning and smoldering for seven weeks, nothing remained of Liége but its churches and they had been looted. Charles had never shown himself in a more savage mood. Louis' humiliation on the other hand had been profound. Commines writes how he had to pretend to approve of Charles' vindictive measures, how he even on occasion shouted out a laudatory "Long live Burgundy!" From now "he hated Duke Charles with deadly venom."

Louis returned to France a much chastened man. He had committed the kind of stupid mistake fools are apt to make, and he found himself the laughingstock of Europe. The duke had also revealed to the world how faithless the king could be to his promises. For several years Louis' situation remained critical. He did manage to force his brother Charles to accept Guienne in place of Champagne, but this did not greatly exercise Charles the Rash since the latter promptly arranged the betrothal of his daughter Mary to Charles. Louis' English venture also backfired. The revolt of Margaret and the duke of Warwick, which he had helped finance, was indeed successful and Edward IV had been forced to flee the country. Six months later, however, Edward returned to England with men and ships Charles the Rash supplied him and he destroyed the Lancastrians once and for all. Now Edward was fully committed to war against Louis. In the fall of 1471 a new coalition took form against Louis, this one composed of the kings of England and Aragon, the duke of Burgundy, and several powerful French feudatories. Louis' blunders had revived the old Anglo-Burgundian alliance.

THE DESTRUCTION OF BURGUNDY

In May 1471 Louis' brother Charles, duke of Guienne, the man who was to marry Charles the Rash's daughter Mary died. This death jolted Louis' enemies and the indignant duke of Burgundy decided to use it as a *casus belli*. Historians doubt that Louis was in any way responsible for Charles' death, but the duke was probably convinced that the king had had him poisoned. Such was the duke's charge at least as he called upon his allies to destroy this monster. Without waiting for them to move, he invaded Vermandois, took Nesle and put its population to the sword, then turned against Beauvais. Here he ran into that fierce resistance with which the towns of northern France and Flanders had repeatedly defied aristocratic armies. Among the women who helped their fathers and husbands man the defenses was one Jeanne Laisné who took her place in history alongside other legendary heroines as "Jeanne Hachette." Beauvais' defiance may have saved Louis. It surely started Charles down the road to ruin.

The repulse at Beauvais led Charles to agree to an armistice with Louis. He should have used the respite to ponder his reverse at Beauvais and especially the failure of his allies to join him. Instead he appears to have turned his back on Louis and the trouble he could cause him in order to bring to fruition his grandiose dreams to the east. Not only would he make Burgundy a kingdom, but he felt the time had now come to unite the northern and southern parts of his divided dominion by conquering the lands that lay between, principally Champagne, Alsace, and Lorraine. The treaty of Péronne had to all intents and purposes established the independence of Burgundy. Now secure in the alliance of the kings of England and Aragon and several French lords whom he felt confident would immobilize Louis, he would proceed to make his dream to the east a reality.

This is where Charles made his fatal mistake. Though his armistice with Louis, and especially his alliance with England and Aragon, may have removed the threat of direct attack by the French army, they could not protect him against Louis' diplomacy and his money. These could prove more dangerous than the king's army. As Commines writes of Louis at this time: "He made greater war upon him [Charles the Rash] by letting him go his own way and in secret creating enemies for him." An instance of this came in the fall of 1473 when Charles the Rash met Frederick III of Germany at Trier in order to discuss the marriage of Charles' daughter Mary to Maximilian, the emperor's son. In return for his daughter, Charles was to receive the title of "King of the Romans" and in time perhaps even the imperial crown for himself. During the night of 25 November, before final terms had been agreed upon, Frederick stole silently out of Trier with not a word of explanation to the duke and without even paying his debts. These debts he should have been able to pay if, as scholars believe, it was Louis' money that had led him to break off his talks with the duke so abruptly.

Even this rebuff did not disconcert Charles. On 23 January 1474 he publicly proclaimed his intention of restoring the ancient kingdom of Burgundy. Six months later he signed the Treaty of London with Edward IV which pledged both men to attack Louis in the summer of 1475. Edward's price for bringing an army of 10,000 men across the Channel was recognition as king of France, that is, over all of France that Louis presently ruled minus Champagne and a few small counties that Charles would annex. The destruction of France as an independent state, a destruction that Henry V of England and Philip the Good, duke of Burgundy, had contemplated following the Treaty of Troyes in 1420, was now to be attempted by Edward and Philip's son Charles.

There is good reason to doubt whether either Edward or Charles was entirely serious about destroying Louis. It is difficult to conceive of the ease-loving, yet shrewd Edward, on the one hand, generating sufficient zeal to undertake the hardships of a long campaign whose objective the energetic duke of Bedford had failed to accomplish fifty years before. Perhaps all Edward had in mind from the beginning was to blackmail Louis into paying him a huge amount to return to England. The duke of Burgundy, on the other hand, had his eyes on his future state of Lotharingia, not on Louis directly. If he accomplished his goal of founding a new powerful and independent kingdom, and he had no doubt he would, his position would be so formidable it would be a matter of relative indifference to him whether it was Louis or Edward who was king of France.

Louis probably had no difficulty assessing his two opponents for the mutually distrustful allies that they were. He had no real fear of Edward, but Charles and his ambitions constituted distinct threats to himself and to France. Even were he, Louis, to remain king of France, should Charles achieve his dream of establishing a Burgundian kingdom that would include the huge block of territory running from north France (Artois, Flanders, and Picardy) and the Low Countries to Dauphiné and Provence in the south, his own France would have been reduced to a minor state. Burgundy would then be the leading power of Western Europe. So Louis got busy with his agents and his money. Among the first allies he procured were the Swiss. These mountaineers with their pikes and halberds could withstand any feudal army Charles might send against them. Many of them already feared Charles since their communities lay in the path of his expansion. Those who did not fear Charles, Louis bought. Then he reconciled these Swiss with their traditional enemy Sigismund of Austria and united them all in a common cause against the duke. "It was one of the wisest things that he did," observed the perceptive Commines.

There was yet time for Charles to avoid disaster. Had he now adopted a defensive policy in the east and delayed his hopes there until, in conjunction with Edward, he had crippled or destroyed his real enemy, Louis, he might have achieved his ultimate goal. His fatal mistake was in failing to realize how his entire future depended upon Louis' defeat. He should have joined Edward in northern France, as he had promised, with 10,000 men of his own when the English king landed his army there in July 1475. Instead, he had his army besieging the city of Neuss on the Rhine in order to force that city to accept a relative of his as archbishop of Cologne. No other act so reveals the ineptitude of the duke, that is, to extend his activities to the Rhine which would drive the emperor and the German princes of the area into Louis' arms, while at the same time defaulting on his agreement with Edward, the one man whose assistance might have won him his crown. Commines can find no other explanation for the duke's blunder than the work of divine providence. "And God had allowed his mind and judgment to become disordered, for all his life he had striven to open a way into France for the English, yet at this moment when the English were ready, he remained stubbornly determined to embark on an impossible undertaking."

Misfortunes had already begun to dog Charles. Alsace had risen in revolt against the tyrannical governor he had placed in charge, had executed him, and had driven out the Burgundian troops. By May 1475 Louis XI had persuaded Frederick III and the duke of Lorraine to join his alliance against the duke. If it was not divine providence, as Commines suggests, it was the duke of Lorraine's defiance, engineered by that "universal spider" Louis, that led Charles to move ever deeper into the morass of Rhenish affairs when he should have been preparing to meet Edward in Calais. To further harass the duke, Louis now marched an army into Picardy. He hoped his presence there might discourage Edward at the last moment from honoring his agreement with the duke to land an army.

Edward did, nevertheless, land his army as he had promised, and a splendid army of 10,000 it was, the best the English had ever brought to France, according to Commines. Edward had hoped to make contact with Charles the Rash and his army, but he saw no sign of either.

Several days later Charles did put in a belated appearance, but he came alone. He assured Edward, however, that his army was on its way, that while it would be moving northwestward through Lorraine (Lower), Edward's army should march southward through Saint-Quentin and into Champagne where the two armies would meet. Thence they would march together against Louis.

So Edward, somewhat reassured, started forward, captured several cities on the Somme, and reached the vicinity of Saint-Quentin in early August. Meantime his enthusiasm for the war had been steadily ebbing. He kept wondering why he heard no news of Burgundians approaching, wondering, too, why no French nobles were defecting, not even the duke of Brittany who had promised to join the campaign. (Louis was busy buying off the duke.) Soon Edward began asking himself, too, whether Charles the Rash had left him to fight the duke's battles against Louis, while the duke was busy gaining territory for himself along the Rhine. What finally gave Edward real pause was his reception at Saint-Quentin. The duke of Burgundy had assured him that Saint-Pol, its commander, would open the city's gates to the English as soon as they appeared. Instead, at the first sign of the English, Saint-Pol's artillery opened fire and drove them off.

Within the week Edward opened negotiations with Louis who was most willing to discuss a settlement. Louis had, in fact, let it be known that he saw no good reason why he and Edward should be fighting. On 29 August the two kings met at Picquigny, conversed through the grating in a barrier erected on the bridge across the Somme, and there agreed to terms. Louis promised to give Edward 75,000 crowns to cover his expenses in the war and, in addition, an annual pension of 50,000 crowns for as long as he lived. In order to bind the agreement, Louis' son, the dauphin, was to marry Edward's daughter Elizabeth. Everybody was happy over the terms, that is, all excepting Charles the Rash, of course. Edward got his pension, something he probably had in mind from the beginning; the English lords had what amounted to a glorious, paid vacation, and the English rank and file feasted on the huge amounts of food and spirits that the exultant Louis furnished them. "I did a better piece of work than my father," Louis boasted; "he got the English out of France by long and bloody fighting, while I got rid of them by banquetting them." The Treaty of Picquigny may be viewed, incidentally, as formally terminating the Hundred Years' War.

Two weeks later, in early September (1475), Louis agreed to another armistice with Charles the Rash. The duke wanted to terminate hostilities with Louis in order to be free to concentrate on Lorraine and his eastern ambitions, and Louis was happy to oblige. Not only would this truce leave others to fight the king's battle with the duke, but Louis was confident that, with his financial assistance, they would shortly destroy him. Again Louis was correct. The duke first turned to Lorraine and had no difficulty overrunning the province. Then he marched against the Swiss. They had aided his enemies and they had themselves defeated a Burgundian army the year before. Rather than negotiate a settlement with them, which would not have been difficult despite Louis' money, and which would have left him still in control of a magnificent state, Charles' desire for revenge drove him on. Within the space of twelve months and four engagements, the Swiss had destroyed him.

Charles' campaign started well with the capture early in January 1476 of the Swiss fortress of Grandson. Then to terrorize other Swiss groups into surrendering, the duke had four hundred of the town's defenders hanged and others drowned in the lake. This act of wanton savagery sealed his doom. Now all Switzerland was up in arms. In the mountainous passes to the west of Lake Neuchâtel, the Swiss trapped the duke's army of 15,000 men and soundly trounced it (March 1476). Among his losses Charles counted five hundred pieces of artillery and four hundred tents, not to mention large quantities of silver plate and tapestries which he had taken with him. Shortly after this battle, Louis received two embassies at Lyons where he had gone in order to get news more quickly of what might transpire. He promised the one group, that from Charles the Rash, that he had no intention of breaking his truce. To the other emissaries, the Swiss, who came to implore his military assistance, he gave his best wishes and more money. Then he sat back to wait for more news.

The defeat at Neuchâtel unsettled the already unstable duke. Commines says he "was losing his senses," a judgment historians endorse. He should have halted his war and turned to diplomacy if not withdrawn into Burgundy, for he was practically bankrupt and was finding new loans impossible to negotiate. But his passion to avenge his humiliation at the hands of the Swiss drove him on. He must refurbish his tarnished image, he must prevent any deterioration of his position in Burgundy, and above all, he must punish the Swiss. So without proper preparation he marched a hastily reorganized army against the Swiss fortress of Morat (June 1476). This lay on the road to Berne in the wooded, mountainous terrain the Swiss knew so well but where Charles' army of knights and archers had little room in which to maneuver. During the siege of Morat, Charles lost his last important ally, the king of Naples, who accepted Louis' money and deserted him. Hardly had Charles learned of the king of Naples' defection than he found himself and his army pinned down on all sides by the Swiss. Only the duke and a handful of his men escaped the slaughter.

This disaster at Morat should have sobered the duke into halting his suicidal course for its lesson was manifest. His army had been deficient both in numbers as well as experience. Yet Charles refused to pause long enough to recoup his losses. When he learned that the duke of Lorraine was laying siege to Nancy in order to recover his capital, Charles moved up a hastily recruited army of raw troops and attacked that of the duke which was twice his in size and which included 12,000 Swiss veterans. This time not even Charles escaped the annihilation (5 January 1477). Two days after the battle they found the duke's naked body, his face cloven by a Swiss halberd and gnawed away by wolves.

Louis was beside himself with joy when he learned of the duke's defeat and death at Nancy. He "scarcely knew how to restrain himself." Those dignitaries present at Plessis when the news arrived, he dined and wined, then sat down to plan the harvesting of the rich crop of territories his money, diplomacy, and duplicity had won him. Then something happened. His genius for doing the shrewd thing seems suddenly to have deserted him. As Commines observes, "being free of all fear, he was not granted by God the ability to set about in this affair in the right way." For once Louis miscalculated the complexity of the situation. So long had he looked on Charles the Rash as his *bête noire,* that once the duke was dead, he assumed nothing remained that would prevent his taking over the entire Burgundian domain. The situation actually demanded his greatest ingenuity if he was to garner the lion's share of the spoils. Other kings and other interests were vitally concerned over the disposition of the far-flung possessions which Charles had ruled. The king of Spain had once been Charles' ally. He resented Louis' seizure of Roussillon and he might support any move to block Louis. Edward IV was uneasy over the prospect of Louis' occupying the Low Countries that Charles the Rash had held and thereby cutting off English commerce. Neither did the Flemish cities relish the thought of submitting to Louis' iron rule. The emperor Frederick III and his son Maximilian were also concerned over the Low Countries and Franche-Comté which Charles had held as an imperial fief. Above all there was Mary, Charles' nineteen-year-old daughter, Louis' own godchild, whose good will would have to be won if Louis' ambitions were to be fulfilled.

Instead of moving with his wonted caution, Louis blundered about in a heavy-handed manner reminiscent of the dead duke. He sent troops into Artois and Flanders where they stormed and destroyed several towns, yet failed to pacify the area. Other French troops marched into Burgundy to occupy the capital Dijon and other leading cities, but the governors that Louis appointed ruled with such harshness that much of the duchy rose in revolt. At the same time Louis kept assuring Mary, his dear godchild, that he would do his best to preserve her inheritance, if need be by having her marry his seven-year-old son, the dauphin!

But Mary outwitted her once-so-cunning godfather and in this crisis she revealed a sense of diplomacy her father Charles had lacked. She accepted the suit of Maximilian as the best man to defend her territories and married him in August 1477. War continued for several years in Artois and Flanders where Maximilian aided the local towns and even gained a victory over Louis' army at Guinegate in 1479. Finally late in 1482, by the Treaty of Arras, Louis and Maximilian agreed on a division of Charles' possessions. Picardy, the towns of the Somme, and the duchy of Burgundy were to remain in Louis' possession. He could also hold Artois and Franche-Comté as the dowry of Margaret, daughter of Mary of Burgundy, who was to marry the dauphin. Since this marriage never took place, these two provinces were returned to the empire in 1493, a blow Louis did not experience since he had died in 1483. The real blow that Louis did feel was the loss of Flanders and the Low Countries, the richest portions of the Burgundian legacy. In large measure, this loss was the consequence of his mistakes.

Louis counted other gains and setbacks in his dealings with his vassals and with other countries. Before he died, he acquired by confiscation the estates of Armagnac, Saint-Pol, and Nemours, and by escheat the duchies of Anjou and Bar, the county of Maine, and the county of Provence with its important seaport of Marseilles. He did not annex Savoy, although his sister, its regent, gave him no more concern now that Charles the Rash was dead. He made good his annexation of

Roussillon but he could not prevent the marriage of Ferdinand of Aragon and Isabella of Castile in 1469 and the establishment of a powerful, unified state south of the Pyrenees. After this marriage, there were no longer any muddy waters in that peninsula for him or his successors to fish in. In the case of England Louis faithfully kept sending over annual pension payments. Though Edward squirmed now and then over French activities in Flanders and the vicinity, he liked his ease and his pension too much to interfere. As the caustic Commines observed, it was the "greed for the 50,000 crowns, paid every year into his castle at London, that deadened his [Edward's] heart." Even in Italy where Louis never sent troops or money, he secured a ruling voice in that peninsula's affairs.

At home all feudatories with the exception of the duke of Brittany accepted Louis' rule. The count of Anjou lamented the lost autonomy of the feudal aristocracy. "The king of France," he said, "can do all that he wishes and he has the habit of doing it." Never had there been a French king so powerful as Louis. Together with Henry VII of England (Edward IV's successor) and Ferdinand of Spain, he represented the new breed of kings that was emerging during the closing decades of the Middle Ages. These kings ruled, they no longer reigned. They controlled both aristocracy and Church. They are closer to Louis XIV than to Louis IX. Their peoples looked to them for protection and economic advancement. Louis, and other medieval kings like Louis, rang down the curtain on the Middle Ages.

GOVERNMENT, REFORMS, THE CHURCH

Though Louis was convinced that as the Lord's anointed he could exercise royal authority without formal limitation, he appreciated the wisdom of ruling with at least the seeming knowledge and consent of his people. This helps explain in part the huge correspondence that he conducted with his agents and officials in his desire to keep the people informed of his plans and policies, real or assumed, and, of course, to keep himself informed as to what they thought. In order to ascertain the minds of important people, to influence their opinion, and to create the impression that the public supported his measures, he called assemblies of merchants and notables to discuss matters of common interest. To justify his refusal to turn Normandy over to his brother Charles as he had agreed to do at Conflans, he summoned the estates general at Tours in 1468 when they properly announced that, since he had taken that action without their consent, it was without force. On occasion he would ask towns to send deputies so that he might advise with them over matters of economy, such as the flight of French capital out of the kingdom. One matter he never discussed with any *parlement* or estates general was that of the taille. The estates general had authorized the crown in 1439 to assess and collect this tax for war purposes for as long as the emergency endured. Long before the emergency ever lifted, this tax had become traditional and no one dared remind Louis of its originally temporary character. Provincial estates that retained the right to vote taxes either followed his bidding or offered no protest when he ordered an increase in the rates they had set.

The regular departments of the government, that is, the *conseil,* the *parlement,* and the *chambre des comptes,* continued their operations under the close surveillance of the king. When Louis chose to put a hand in their business they seldom objected. He might even interfere in the judicial prerogatives of *parlement,* withdraw certain matters, mainly political, from its attention, and in certain cases dispense with all forms of judicial procedure as when ordering the imprisonment or execution of men who had betrayed him or appeared about to do so. He was inclined to entrust all suits in which the crown had an interest to the judicial committee of the *conseil.* In general he appointed and dismissed crown officials as he chose, not so frequently, however, as his oppressed subjects would have liked who felt the rapacity of scattered members of the royal bureaucracy. In order to maintain and expedite communications with every quarter of his kingdom, Louis established the *poste* which consisted of relays of four or five horses, stationed at regular intervals on the principal roads of the realm.

Louis also extended his autocratic controls to the towns despite their long history of loyalty to the French crown. Since the thirteenth century, when they were most powerful, their rights had already suffered significant reduction. All Louis did was to complete their subjugation. They still served the crown as allies against the aristocracy. Though the burden of royal fiscal demands had grown heavy, they did not dare challenge the royal authority for two reasons: first, the alternative to royal autocracy was feudal tyranny or anarchy; and second, the rights of self-government the crown had left them were so circumscribed as to make revolt well nigh impossible. Louis appointed mayors when he wished, altered town charters when these provided greater control over financial and judicial matters than he judged prudent, and on occasion replaced town councils with royal commissioners. As a rule Louis preferred oligarchically controlled town governments since he had less difficulty dictating to these. Certain towns did enjoy Louis' favor, namely those on lands of stubborn vassals, for example, to whom he granted charters as the first step toward bringing their lords under his control.

The material key to Louis' success was money, and his ability to raise the enormous sums his wars and diplomacy required, therefore, the secret of his achievement. At the beginning of his reign the average annual revenue from taxation amounted to approximately 1,800,000 livres. By the close of his reign this revenue had risen to 4,800,000, a truly phenomenal increase even when allowing for some inflation. Of a variety of taxes he employed, the taille returned the largest amount. It was the simplest to administer since it could be adjusted to the crown's needs and to the circumstances obtaining in any particular town or province. Those towns which might hesitate to pay the tax could be readily coerced, nor was there great danger of concerted opposition since he could and did exempt individual communities when reason or prudence so recommended. Because much of the countryside had still not recovered from the devastation of the Hundred Years' War, the bulk of the revenues realized from the taille came from the towns. Louis also collected significant amounts from a variety of sales taxes, such as the gabelle (salt tax), which had also started out as emergency measures; from the sale of offices and patents of nobility; from charters to towns; from arbitrary fines levied against Jews; and from forced loans and subsidies.

Because Louis appreciated the critical importance of towns to the growth of royal power, he introduced a number of measures which he hoped would enable them to meet the heavy financial burdens he placed upon them. He favored the concentration of control over individual industries as opposed to broad supervision in the interest of stability if not production. He encouraged the development of the silk industry, the expansion of markets and fairs, he forbade French merchants to attend the fair in Geneva in order to build up the rival fair at Lyons, and just before his death discussed the adoption of uniform weights and measures for the entire kingdom and the suppression of all tolls. To break Venice's monopoly of French trade with the Levant, he fought a privateering war for ten years and concluded it on his terms. He improved harbor facilities at Collioure in Roussillon, while his acquisition of Marseilles set him dreaming of the day a huge French fleet would replace Venice as the principal carrier of Mediterranean trade for the markets of Western Europe. On the Atlantic side of France, because the ports there had been but recently in English hands and the volume of trade far beyond the capacity of French shipping, he negotiated trade agreements with Hanseatic, Spanish, and Portuguese merchants. During intervals of peace, he also encouraged the flow of trade between France and England.

Louis' policy toward the Church was one the papacy generally deprecated although usually half inclined to believe an improvement over that Charles VII, his father, had pursued. As dauphin, Louis had promised the pope that he would abrogate the Pragmatic Sanction of Bourges, which promise led the papacy to expect a significant improvement in French-papal relations upon his accession in 1461. Had Pius II, who was pope at the time, suspected Louis' reason for promising this abrogation, his hopes for the future would have been less sanguine.

The background to the adoption of the Pragmatic Sanction stretches back at least to the period of the Avignonese Residence (1309–77) when the pope had made his home at Avignon in southern France rather than at Rome. During these seventy years, actually since the election of Clement V in 1305, French popes and French cardinals had so dominated the papacy that the French came to consider the institution as almost their own. Then in 1378, scarcely two months after the election of the Italian Urban VI, the French cardinals had renounced their obedience to him on the claim that they had elected him under duress, proceeded to elect another pope (Clement VII), and returned to Avignon. During the period of the schism that followed, that is from 1378 until the election of Martin V by the Council of Constance in 1417, it would have been difficult to distinguish between the policy of the Avignonese papacy on the one hand and that of France on the other, so pervasive was French influence at Avignon. French prelates also dominated this council which gave official endorsement to the views of the conciliarists, that the authority of the general council was superior to that of the pope. During the years following Constance, French bishops had kept conciliar views alive and had headed anti-papal opposition at Basel when a general council convened there in 1431. Under the circumstances, it was to be expected that Charles VII's proclamation of the Pragmatic Sanction at Bourges in 1438 should have carried the approval of the majority of French ecclesiastics.

The Pragmatic Sanction was the most anti-papal pronouncement any Christian king made prior to the era of the Protestant Reformation. It closed off most sources of papal revenue in France, including annates and expectatives, transferred papal authority to the French hierarchy in the appointment to benefices, suppressed appeals to Rome, and prohibited the introduction of papal bulls into France. As a result of this measure, control of the Church in France passed from the papacy to the French episcopacy and aristocracy and to Charles VII. The king would have preferred an arrangement that would have given him sole authority over the external affairs of the Church, but the Hundred Years' War left him no choice. He desperately needed the adherence of the hierarchy and aristocracy and he could assure himself of this by sharing the control of the Church with them. On the other hand he dangled before the eyes of the pope the possibility of abrogating the Pragmatic Sanction in the hope of gaining papal support for his policies outside of France.

When Louis became king in 1461 he had good reason not to delay in abrogating the Sanction as he had promised. As dauphin he had already sensed the fact that the aristocracy and hierarchy derived a good measure of influence and wealth from their control of the Church. By rescinding the decree he would, therefore, be depriving these powerful groups of a source of their strength and at the same time leave himself in a position to deal directly and independently with the pope. Though he confided to the pope that he was abolishing the measure since "it robs you of your authority and is contrary to right and justice," Louis was not one to do favors unless he received at least the equivalent in return. So when papal policy did not fall in line with his in Naples after abrogation of the Sanction, he promptly issued a series of decrees "to defend ourselves against the aggressions of Rome and for the restoration of the ancient Gallican liberties."

Although Louis never revived the Pragmatic Sanction in its entirety, the orders he issued restrictive of papal influence in French affairs restored in effect the situation to what it had been under Charles VII. He would tolerate no meddling in his handling of the clergy, no one could preach without his permission, nor could any bulls be brought into the country that had not received his approval. To the dean and chapter of Angers cathedral he sent a missive warning them to elect his counselor as bishop, for "we will on no account suffer any other to have this bishopric but our own counselor: and if I find any one opposing this, I will have him expelled from the kingdom." An individual here and there might defy him and successfully. When he sent word to Friar Olivier Maillard, a popular preacher, that any more offensive statements might find him in a sack in the river, the courageous priest sent back the reply: "Tell the king I shall arrive in Paradise sooner by water than he will with all his post-horses."

Louis showed little interest in the arts. He left the expensive patronage of writers and artists to his rival Charles the Rash who was willing to finance such luxuries. Still Louis was not lacking a sense of beauty. He showed real taste in directing the work of architects, goldsmiths, and painters who happened to be in his service. The distinguished French artist Fouquet he honored with the title of "king's painter." Louis' letters reveal the sharp, at times witty, more often satirical mind of an educated prince. He showed some favor to universities and their students and he extended his protection to the struggling profession of printers against the hostile guilds of copyists who feared their competition. Louis' principal contribution to the arts was accidental. On his arrival in Tournai in 1461 on his first progress about the country as king, among the prisoners released to honor the occasion was the poet and scoundrel François Villon.

LOUIS' DEATH

Louis scarcely slowed his enormous activities as he grew older, even when his health began to worsen after 1479. He did not travel so much as formerly, though this was due less to physical disability than to his fear of assassins. As age crept upon him, he grew ever more suspicious. Only at Plessis could he feel safe for he had turned his château there into a veritable fortress. Toward the end he acquired a morbid fear of death. His servants had instructions not to mention the "cruel word death" in his presence. Even his confessor was to avoid the term. When he learned that rumor had it he was dying—this was following a severe stroke—he made a great display of his vitality by putting on rich robes, arranging appointments, and even purchasing animals for his zoo. As a last resort, when he was convinced that only heaven could save him, he asked the pope to send him the sainted Francis of Paola. When the holy man arrived at Plessis, Louis met him on his knees and begged him to heal him. Francis gave him little encouragement, told him to think rather of what really mattered, his soul. Though Francis' prayers did not save Louis' life, they may have helped him resign himself to the inevitable. Death came on 31 August 1483. Louis had saved France, but no Frenchman mourned his passing.